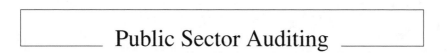

# Public Sector Auditing

# Public Sector Auditing

Is it value for money?

**Sir John Bourn**

John Wiley & Sons, Ltd

### Other Wiley Editorial Offices

John Wiley & Sons Inc., 111 River Street, Hoboken, NJ 07030, USA

Jossey-Bass, 989 Market Street, San Francisco, CA 94103-1741, USA

Wiley-VCH Verlag GmbH, Boschstr. 12, D-69469 Weinheim, Germany

John Wiley & Sons Australia Ltd, 42 McDougall Street, Milton, Queensland 4064, Australia

John Wiley & Sons (Asia) Pte Ltd, 2 Clementi Loop #02-01, Jin Xing Distripark, Singapore 129809

John Wiley & Sons Canada Ltd, 6045 Freemont Blvd, Mississauga, ONT, L5R 4J3, Canada

Wiley also publishes its books in a variety of electronic formats. Some content that appears
in print may not be available in electronic books.

Anniversary Logo Design: Richard J. Pacifico

### Library of Congress Cataloging-in-Publication Data

Bourn, John, Sir, 1934-
    Public sector auditing : is it value for money? / Sir John Bourn.
       p. cm.
    Includes bibliographical references and index.
    ISBN 978-0-470-05722-3 (cloth : alk. paper)
    1. Finance, Public—Auditing.    I. Title.
    HJ9733.B68 2007
    657'.835—dc22

                                            2007035533

A catalogue record for this book is available from the British Library

ISBN 978-0-470-05722-3 (HB)

Typeset in 11/13pt Times by Aptara, New Delhi, India
Printed and bound in Great Britain by TJ International Ltd, Padstow, Cornwall, UK
This book is printed on acid-free paper responsibly manufactured from sustainable forestry
in which at least two trees are planted for each one used for paper production.

# Contents

# Preface

This book is an account of my experience since 1988 as Comptroller and Auditor General of the United Kingdom; as the first Auditor General of Wales from 1998 to 2005; and as the holder of many international audit appointments, including member and chairmanship of the Board of Audit of the United Nations.

I left the British Civil Service to take up the position of Comptroller and Auditor General after some thirty years' civil service experience, where I served in the Air Ministry, Treasury, Civil Service College, Ministry of Defence, and the Northern Ireland Office. During this time, I naturally experienced the work of the National Audit Office.

I had the greatest respect for the role of the office in auditing the financial statements of British central government, and in seeing that money was spent according to the law and Parliamentary expectations. I also saw that the very existence of the office acted as a permanent encouragement to care in the handling of public money.

But I also thought that the National Audit Office had a great opportunity to add to its traditional responsibility for seeing that money was spent legally. It had a new responsibility – given to it by the National Audit Act of 1983 – to encourage the achievement of value for money in government spending programmes by developing performance auditing. We must remember that money may be spent legally, but it still may be wasted, with results that are disappointing and the very reverse of value for money.

This book is an account of how I and my colleagues in the National Audit Office took the programme for value for money auditing forward, and of how, as we did so, and developed new auditing career possibilities and new methodologies, we learned from other audit offices and private sector auditors round the world. The result, I hope, is a primer of how value for money might be usefully and effectively deployed domestically and internationally.

It draws on experiences and reports from a wide range of countries, covering many areas and levels of public administration. It takes account, too, of the changing nature of government in many countries following the collapse of communism; the development of closer links between the public and private sectors in providing government activities and services; the impact of new technologies for communication and handling information; the threat of new forms of criminal behaviours as in money laundering; and the forces of globalisation that have brought countries closer together in many ways, but brought tensions and challenges too.

I therefore hope that this book will show how public sector auditors may make an even greater contribution than now to the effectiveness of democratic governments in the service of all their citizens.

# Acknowledgements

I should like to thank Professor George Jones who suggested that I should produce this book, which draws upon a series of seminars which I gave as a Visiting Professor at the London School of Economics and Political Science. I should also like to thank the Rt Hon Sir Geoffrey Pattie who encouraged me to go ahead with the book, and gave me valuable help and advice.

I should also like to thank my colleagues at the National Audit Office for all their help, advice and suggestions, particularly Michael Whitehouse, who was especially helpful, and also Mark Babington, Tim Banfield, Ed Humpherson, Jeremy Lonsdale, James Robertson and Nick Sloan. Indeed, I owe thanks to everyone in the National Audit Office because this book is very much – though not exclusively – an account of the work that we have done together over the years in the audit of British central government and in our international work.

I should also like to thank the following friends and colleagues who have advised me and suggested most useful ideas, Peter Aliferis, Deputy Executive Director of the Association of Government Accountants of the USA; Pat Barrett, former Auditor General of Australia; Professor Richard Laughlin of Kings College, London; Gilbert Lloyd, Partner at KPMG; Professor Ed Page of the London School of Economics and Political Science and Professor Christopher Pollitt of the Katholieke Universiteit Leuven.

This is a book about public sector auditing; its analysis, ideas and suggestions are designed to be relevant not only to the activities of the United Kingdom government, for which I discharge audit responsibilities as Comptroller and Auditor General, but also to public sector auditing generally in the United Kingdom and internationally.

I have therefore learned a great deal from my colleagues who are public sector auditors in other jurisdictions in the United Kingdom and in other countries; from colleagues with whom I have worked in the International Organisation of Supreme Audit Institutions and the European Organisation of Supreme Organisations; from departments and public bodies for whom I have had audit responsibilities; from colleagues on the Financial Reporting Council; the Accountancy Foundation; and the Council's Public Oversight Board; from members of the United Kingdom Parliament, to whom our Office's reports are presented, especially the three successive Chairs of the Committee of Public Accounts which specialises in our work – the Rt Hon Lord Sheldon, the Rt Hon David Davis MP, and Edward Leigh MP; and the three successive Chairs of the Public Accounts Commission – the Rt Hon Sir Peter Hordern, former member of Parliament for Horsham and Crawley; the Rt Hon Lord Sheldon; and the Rt Hon Alan Williams MP; and from members of the National Assembly for Wales, when I was the first Auditor General for Wales, especially the Audit Committee, and the two Chairs during the currency of my appointment, Janet Davies and the Rt Hon Dafydd Wigley.

I am most grateful to my publisher, Caitlin Cornish for all her help and advice.

Since this book draws so heavily upon the work of the National Audit Office, revenue that accrues to me as the author will all be passed to the National Audit Office.

Finally, while I have had a great deal of help and advice in writing this book, I take full responsibility for its contents.

# 1

# Introduction

Auditing is a necessary but often unpopular activity in modern society. Grudgingly, most of us accept the intellectual case for auditing, though we do not always welcome the auditor's attention to our own affairs. Nevertheless, most of us are re-assured when the 'watchdog barks', in cases where accounts are revealed as defective; fraud is detected; and waste in public programmes is brought out for all to see.

Yet many of us wonder whether the expense of auditing is justified by the results achieved. This is true in both the private and the public sectors. And so far as the public sector is concerned, many of us wonder why the same mistakes seem to be made time and time again – projects delayed; estimates exceeded; public services disappointing.

So the question arises: 'Public Service Auditing – Is it Value for Money?'

And the purpose of this book is to show that it can be value for money. The argument is that:

- Public authorities are fundamentally bureaucracies – hierarchies operating by rules – and hence are more inclined to look inwards to processes and procedures, than outwards to results and outcomes for those whom they have the duty to serve.
- Traditionally, public sector audit, valuable as it could be, through its independence from organisations, and the authority and objectivity this bestows, reinforced the tendency to look inwards by its concentration on seeing that rules and procedures were obeyed and money spent according to them.
- Auditors therefore concentrated on the cataloguing of failure, from which, of course, we may learn what not to do. But valuable as this is, especially in the detection of fraud and waste, an inventory of failures is not a guide to success.
- And the argument of this book is that by analysing and encouraging the successes of public administration, the auditor can act as coach and mentor rather than critic and nark; and his recommendations can

thus help his public sector clients to succeed in the future rather than simply criticising them for failure in the past.

## 1.1   MODERN PUBLIC ADMINISTRATION

As background to the argument, it may be helpful in this introduction to sketch out some of the main features of contemporary public adminis-tration, to set the stage upon which the auditor has to perform, and then to indicate how my argument is developed in the ensuing chapters.

It must be recognised that different states organise their governments and public administrations in different ways. The United Kingdom (UK), China, Portugal, Ireland and Greece are unitary states while others such as Russia, India, the United States of America (USA) and Germany are federal states. Others, notably Denmark, Finland and Sweden, have devolved considerable responsibility for delivery of public services to municipalities. Public services in many European countries have evolved and adapted in response to key historical events such as the need to marshal resources to fight two world wars; and all countries claim to share the moral imperative of tackling poverty and social exclusion and improving general human well being.

Political ideology has shaped public administration in many coun-tries. For several decades after the second world war, many countries throughout the world extended the scope and scale of government activity. Industries were nationalised; national health services inaugu-rated; schemes of social welfare extended. Communist countries sought to bring most economic activities under state control, but many coun-tries which maintained a social market economy, like the UK and France, nevertheless had a substantial state sector, with public en-terprise providing many activities such as electricity, water, gas and railways.

From the 1970s, however, the emphasis changed. In many coun-tries, including former Communist countries, the state was rolled back. Many economic activities were returned to the private sector. In the UK, for example, railways, electricity, water supply, the state airline, and telecommunications were privatised – though where state monopolies were turned into private monopolies or oligopolies, regulators were set up to ensure 'fair play' between shareholders and customers.

More recently, rapid advances in technology have been a major driver of change in public service delivery. What public authorities seek to influence has also changed in many countries. Whereas in the past authorities largely made their own assumptions about services to be provided, they now increasingly seek to influence what might be called 'life style choices' in aspects as diverse as anti social behaviour, diet to prevent or reduce obesity, parenting skills and attitudes towards environmental sustainability.

What has emerged from these influences in many countries is a public sector which no longer has a monopoly on delivery. Increasingly, the private and voluntary sectors play important roles. In other respects, however, public services remain remarkably unchanged. Well defined, often elaborate, processes for decision making remain. Entitlement to most forms of state support, such as welfare benefits, or grants to promote economic development depend on meeting a complex range of rules and regulations. This inherent complexity increases the risk of exclusion, with significant numbers of people intended to benefit not doing so, as well as increasing the potential for administrative inefficiency at significant cost and acting as a disincentive for innovation and entrepreneurship. Many of the inherent tensions which successive governments have grappled with remain such as achieving the optimum balance in driving change by top-down targets or by creating markets and competition, or resolving the tension between central strategies and systems on one hand and delegation of decision-making to the front line on the other.

And herein lies the paradox. In spite of well meaning attempts to reform and improve the public sector, often, as in the UK with significant growth in expenditure on health, education and social welfare, there remains a widespread belief that services are not as good as they ought to, and could, be. In some areas, such as the need to tackle skill gaps and improve productivity, underperformance has consequences for national competitiveness in a global economy. This is, of course, not the complete picture. Most of us would accept that the average standard of living in most countries – though sadly not all – has improved and that as well as economic prosperity, public services such as health and education have contributed to this. Yet there remain significant examples of waste, underperformance, and of citizens, particularly those who are the most vulnerable in society, not receiving the service to which they are entitled to or expect. Much research into why this is the case exists. But reaching consensus around how best to design and deliver public services which meet most people's reasonable expectations and which are affordable and cost effective continues to elude us. And it is here that public audit enters the debate.

## 1.2   THE TRADITIONS OF STATE AUDIT

State audit has existed in some form in nearly all countries – autocracies as well as democracies – for several hundred years. And, indeed, accountability for the use of public funds is a cornerstone of democratic government. The arrangements for public sector audit take different forms throughout the world, though there is scarcely a country which does not have an Auditor General or Court of Audit under one name or another.[1] Within this variety two broad traditions may be distinguished. The first is a common law tradition, as seen in countries of the British Commonwealth, the USA, and some Scandinavian countries, where the main emphasis is upon the auditor general's responsibility to report his findings to the legislature who will then decide what recommendations to make to the government. But the auditor general has no legal powers to punish the transgressions distinguished in his report.

The second tradition is what might be called a Roman law tradition. Here public sector audit is conducted by a court, which can hold hearings, and whose decisions and punishments have legal force. Examples include the Cour des Comptes of France, the Corte de Conti in Italy and the Tribunal de Cuentas in Spain.

In more recent times a number of countries have introduced significant changes to the remit and operation of their state audit offices. A common objective has been to give statutory authority to carry out performance or value for money audits. In Italy for example, major new audit legislation was enacted in 1994 that enhanced the role of the Corte de Conti and facilitated the development of performance audit. In Ireland, the Comptroller and Auditor General (Amendment) Act was passed in 1993, extending the post's remit and placing performance audit on a statutory footing.

In the UK the most significant enhancement of the status of the Comptroller and Auditor General was the National Audit Act 1983. The Act followed increasing parliamentary, academic,[2] and general concern about the influence that the executive, in particular the Treasury, the UK's Ministry of Finance, retained over the resources available to it, as well as the access rights of public audit; together with the oddity that the Comptroller and Auditor General audited the Treasury, while the Treasury audited the Comptroller and Auditor General – a conflict of interest

---

[1] Comptroller and Auditor General (2005) *State Audit in the European Union.*

[2] Normaton, E. L. (1966) *The Accountability and Audit of Government* Manchester University Press.

indeed! Under the terms of the 1983 Act the Comptroller and Audit General formally became an Officer of the House of Commons, emphasising his independence from the executive. And the National Audit Office (NAO) was funded directly by Parliament, not by the executive, as the audit office had previously been. Express powers were given to the post holder to carry out examinations of the economy, efficiency and effectiveness with which central government departments and certain other public bodies had used their resources.[3]

As a result of the Act, and the UK Parliament's support, this value for money work became quickly established. Sixty reports are currently published and presented to Parliament each year. Since the 1983 National Audit Act over one thousand reports covering the full range of government activity have been produced. Assessing value for money requires a rigorous process which commands confidence, particularly of those intended to act in response to findings and recommendations – important if public audit is to have sustainable beneficial impact. **Box 1.1** summarises the generic principles of value for money work and how it is typically conducted. The Appendix to this book provides some account of the wide range of diagnostic and analytical techniques needed. While the Comptroller and Auditor General's remit excludes questioning government policy, the programme of value for money work and other traditional audit activity, particularly the financial audit of the accounts of government departments, provides considerable insight into both success and failure in the implementation and administration of public services and the underlying causes. The NAO value for money studies also increasingly draw on the experience of the private and voluntary sectors and of other countries. This enhances the perspective and insights they can provide and means that the argument and lessons presented in this book have relevance to public auditing generally.

---

**Box 1.1:    What is meant by a value for money examination?**

1. A value for money study, evaluation or critique is about forming an objective assessment about whether a programme, project or activity is designed to, or has achieved, the best use of resources to

---

[3] The audit of local government in England is the responsibility of the Audit Commission. The audit of local authorities in other parts of the UK is the responsibility of the auditor generals of these juristrictions.

optimise costs and benefits (outputs, outcomes, quality of service and increasingly issues of equity).

2. Value for money studies typically follow a structure of diagnosis – what is the issue, e.g. under performance or scope for doing things better to arrive at a hypothesis; the second stage is analysing the underlying data – both quantitative and qualitative to test the hypothesis; the final stage is synthesis, where the data derived from the analysis is triangulated to arrive at well founded conclusions to derive practical recommendations for improvement.

3. As with any major activity it is important that a value for money examination follows principles of good project management. In the UK National Audit Office the approach is:

   • To develop a business case justifying the examination, the issues it will address, the evidence it will collect and how this will be analysed together with a budget and time line for completing the study.

   • Fieldwork stage to complete the analysis, derive conclusions about value for money achieved, and/or potential to do so and formulate recommendations.

   • Give opportunity for departments, agencies or other stakeholders to comment on the findings, interpretation and presentation of evidence and conclusions – but the Auditor General retains ultimate responsibility for his conclusions and right to report to Parliament.

   • Publication

*Source:* UK National Audit Office – *Value for Money Handbook – a guide for building quality into VFM examinations - http://www.nao .org.uk/.*

## 1.3   THE CONTENTS AND ARGUMENT OF THIS BOOK

A wide body of evidence forms the basis of this book and its analysis of why public services are not as good as they might be and, most importantly, how performance could be improved. Regardless of whether it is founded in the Roman or Common Law tradition, public audit has considerable potential to support and encourage continuous improvement for the benefit of citizens both as consumers of services and as taxpayers. To realise this potential does require careful consideration, and the book discusses what is needed if public audit is to be effective and, itself, deliver value for money.

Chapter 2 explores the way in which bureaucratic processes hamper the achievement of the goals of public services. To the extent that bureaucracy represents orderly administration and promotes equity and impartiality it has many achievements. But these have come at a heavy price, and this chapter explores why this is so.

The third chapter deals with the successes and failures of traditional public sector audit. Certainly, the preparation and audit of accounts and other documents gives valuable information about where money has come from and what it has been spent upon. It has been – and still is – a bulwark against fraud and theft. But it does not tell whether value for money spent has been achieved.

Many governments have sought to use such techniques as cost benefit analysis to answer this question. They take us so far, but they rest upon the contested ability to estimate individual and collective preferences in order to calculate the social costs and benefits of government activities over time. The strengths and weaknesses of these approaches and of their audit are also explored in Chapter 3.

Public servants' behaviour is key to better outcomes because they take the critical decisions, subject to their responsibility to politicians, determining the design, delivery and resourcing of public services. Influencing bureaucrats' behaviour, like all human behaviour is inherently complex. The source and quality of information on which policy decisions are made, how performance is measured and acted upon, and the current status of public opinion are just some determinants. The impact of audit, and in particular its potential to be a force for good, should not, however, be understated.

Chapter 4 examines why the recommendations stemming from the audit of cost-benefit and cost-effectiveness approaches are often accepted by governments but frequently fail to change public servants' behaviour. The key to this paradox lies in the public sector audit's traditional focus on failure rather than on the conditions of success. While audit is about exposing under performance and waste, this by itself alone will not encourage learning and an enthusiasm to do better. Basic psychology tells us that people are most likely to learn from success rather than failure. Criticism needs therefore to be constructive and explained and presented in a way that has coherence and meaning to those who need to improve. Doing so requires auditors to have an understanding of human behaviour – a skill not typically associated with the audit profession.

Disenchantment with traditional forms of bureaucracy led to experimentation in other ways of delivering public services. The most prominent of these and the most widely replicated internationally are privatisation and public private partnerships. The next two chapters – 5 and 6 – explore the rationale and implications of these two alternatives to bureaucracy and the impact they are having on accepted notions about the form which public services should take. Public audit in the UK through its traditional role of holding to account for the use of public money has charted the development of these two models of delivery, highlighting what works and, in particular, what is needed for success, as well as highlighting risks that must be managed. Privatisation and public private partnerships have also required public auditors to revisit their methodological approaches to assess value for money and draw on new skills. The implications of this for the public auditor have been far reaching.

Chapter 7 deals with the deleterious consequences of bureaucracies' propensity to spawn more and more rules and regulations. It examines the reasons for this and provides guidance for the auditor's examination of what recommendations can be made to curb and eliminate regulations that generate high transaction costs for their introduction and management; costs that may well outweigh any positive results that they may achieve.

Chapter 8 is concerned with the audit of the quality of public services for the citizen. Regardless of the method of delivery, the ultimate aim of all public services is to meet the reasonable needs of citizens economically and efficiently. In today's society, with its myriad of expectations, bureaucracies with their natural tendency to provide little choice and assume an undifferentiated homogeneous customer base are ill suited to deliver what most people want. The last thirty years has witnessed attempts to both fine tune and radically restructure traditional ways of delivering public services. Increasingly, the private and voluntary sectors are involved in delivery and the internet is transforming public services in ways never thought of before. These major developments have both influenced and are influenced by traditional bureaucratic models of working. This has given rise to tensions that have to be managed, for example, in terms of the balance between central determination of quality standards and discretion to design services that reflect local needs, as well as consequences for value for money. The third component of value for money – effectiveness – is now interpreted more widely to include not only assessing the achievement of desired outputs and outcomes but also evaluating the quality of public services, social inclusion particularly in a multi cultural society; and equity in ensuring access to services. This development is largely influenced by the recognition that value for money must be interpreted as much through the eyes of those who depend on public services as those who design and deliver them. The implications of this for how public audit forms judgements about the quality of public services is the focus of Chapter 8.

The last four chapters consider what might be termed the 'tools' needed to make best use of public money and translate it into high quality services. Chapter 9 explores the meaning and relevance of risk management in the public sector and illustrates that rather than being risk adverse – the widely held perception – bureaucracies are more likely to be risk ignorant with significant consequences. Chapter 10 focuses on the importance of high standards to prevent fraud and impropriety and how in a changing public sector with multiple players this remains critical, if increasingly complex. Chapter 11 considers the application of project and programme management. Chapter 12 deals with the practicalities of measuring performance in a way which promotes rather than inhibits better delivery. Chapter 13 considers how the external auditor should organise his or her affairs if they are to combat bureaucracy effectively.

Finally, Chapter 14 pulls together and rounds off the book's argument and explores the likely implications for external audit as the nature of public service delivery continues to evolve. And the Appendix sets out methodologies used by the UK NAO in undertaking its value for money studies.

# 2
# Why Bureaucracy Will Never Work

Citizens of modern societies look to the state for many of the services that support civilised life such as education, healthcare, defence, law and order, social security and protection in old age. The initiatives and programmes that drive forward such services are often characterised by considerable ambition, and particularly so in recent times. They may be long-term plans aimed at securing major behavioural changes – for example, twenty year initiatives to reduce poverty, programmes to raise levels of literacy, efforts to push employment levels up, or attempts to pull down rates of death due to cancer and stroke. Programmes may require collaboration between many partners, including those outside government in the private and not-for-profit sectors, as well as the creation and maintenance of networks of 'stakeholders' to sustain them.

Many programmes are dependent for their success on major restructurings of organisations, the redeployment or retraining of thousands of staff, or the successful working of new, potentially leading-edge, information technology. Often these projects apply some of the brightest in the public and private sector as well as considerable sums of public resources. All hold out the prospect of significant improvements in delivery performance or longer term outcomes, or else offer increased security and protection against identified risks.

## 2.1 PUBLIC PROGRAMMES ARE OFTEN LATE, COST MORE THAN PLANNED AND DO NOT WORK AS INTENDED

Yet we are often disappointed with the outcomes of these programmes. Despite the effort that goes into planning and implementation, they are often late, cost more than planned, and do not work as intended. Examples of these failures include:

- The costs of public programmes frequently exceed their estimates (**Box 2.1**) and often exceed their benefits. If the measure is cash, costs can exceed revenues, while if the measure is more complex – say the ability of a weapon system to achieve designated speed, accuracy and success rates – the end result is too often disappointing. Moreover, many programmes involving health and education seem to cost more and produce poorer results than originally planned.

---

**Box 2.1:    National Probation Service**[1]

Towards the end of the 1990s, the National Probation Service sought to introduce a new case recording and management system (NPSISS). Implementation was an achievement but the Home Office's poor specification of expected outputs, weaknesses in service monitoring and inadequate control of purchases contributed to the full cost being £118 million, some 70 per cent over forecast. The Home Office programme team suffered from a lack of continuity in leadership and was not fully resourced to deal with the problems; in its first seven years, the programme team had seven different directors. Failure to prioritise necessary preparatory work led to a delay in establishing a new partnership with the contractors to follow on from the end of the previous agreement, leading to the Home Office bearing additional costs. The Department underestimated the technical risks with the project and the development of the system did not keep pace with the developing needs of the probation services.

---

- In many cases, it is found that public sector managers replace public objectives with their own private interests. In some cases, this takes the form of fraud and corruption, but in others it is more subtle. Research programmes designed and funded to investigate one range of phenomena have been turned on their heads by staff who wished to investigate a different range. Astute wording of plans, proposals and progress reports, together with the increasing difficulty outsiders experience in penetrating specialised programmes, have often been adequate defences to enable those concerned to continue doing what most interested them irrespective of their formal remits.
- As a variant of this fault, many public sector programmes have been dominated by producer – rather than consumer – interests, especially if the producers were the effective monopoly suppliers of the goods and services in question, such as in transport, health and education.

---

[1] Comptroller and Auditor General *The Implementation of the National Probation Service Information Systems Strategy* (HC 401, Session 2000–2001).

- Public programmes often produce unintended consequences, or 'externalities' as economists call them. Thus, an arms factory might pollute the land on which it tests its products, inflicting costs on future generations. A nuclear facility might endanger the health of its staff, as well as the well-being of those living nearby. The design of a housing estate might provide a ready haven for vandals and criminals, with its corridors and staircases being ideal for causing trouble and evading arrest. Sometimes these externalities have been beyond contemporary knowledge and have only been revealed with the benefit of hindsight. Often, however, public authorities understood that disregarding externalities offered a 'free good' – the chance to carry out activities at what was, in immediate cost terms, negligible expense.
- On some occasions, participants in the design and delivery of public programmes fail to anticipate potential risks and problems. Even if risks and problems have been anticipated beforehand, partners may not go on to address them early enough and effectively. Often there is simply insufficient agreement between the various players in order to 'carry the day' **(Box 2.2)**.

---

**Box 2.2:    The Paddington Health Campus[2]**

The objective of the Paddington Health Campus scheme in London was to build a high quality teaching and research centre, partially financed by private funds, by merging the activities of the St Mary's teaching hospital, the Brompton and Harefield heart hospitals, and the heart and lung researchers based at Imperial College. The initial cost was £300m in 2000 with completion in 2006. By the time the scheme collapsed in 2006, as a result of insufficient available land, the projected costs stood at £894m. The fatal flaw was that the project was not supported by the staff of the two hospitals; their divergent interests were papered over in an attempt to create agreement where, in reality, little existed. This failure to resolve the divergent interests and create a project that could be delivered successfully highlighted the dangers of not securing agreement among all those whose commitment was vital to secure the success of the scheme – in short, the failure to look outward rather than inward in designing the scheme.

---

[2] Comptroller and Auditor General *The Paddington Health Campus Scheme* (HC 1045, Session 2005–2006).

In recent decades, the perceived seriousness of problems behind failed public programmes has varied between countries. Germany, France and Scandinavian countries were initially less concerned about public programme failure than the US, the UK and Australia. But even so, by the 1970s – and certainly by the 1980s – the cumulative effect of these problems convinced many commentators, politicians and citizens that public sector management had failed to achieve the promise held out for it at the turn of the century. In Communist China, it did not take long for people who had been 'welcomed in 1949 as liberators from Guomindang misrule [to turn into] a new bureaucratic class which monopolised power and privilege and had alienated itself from the masses'.[3] Elsewhere, vast bureaucracies laboured slowly to produce disappointing results; in Communist countries the failure of the public sector in economic management was increasingly evident, the fall of the Berlin Wall in 1990 presaging the rejection of the Communist system across Europe.

In Western Europe, too, nationalised industries were seen as costly and inefficient. Countries like the UK were conscious of a failure to realise all their potential after the Second World War. The immediate post-war period gave rise to great confidence in the country's potential based on the belief that the skills, ingenuity and resources displayed in battle could be transferred to reconstruction. In retrospect, this appears to be what one writer has called 'The Illusion of Limitless Possibility',[4] and subsequent years instead saw a failure by successive governments to secure their objectives of economic growth and steady prices; to harness developments in science and technology in a fully effective way; or to promote rising standards of health, education and welfare quickly enough. By the 1970s the general judgement was one of disappointment in public sector management.

This does not mean that Western societies were failures; in most cases they advanced economically to an outstanding degree. Their populations as a whole were richer (the current generation of pensioners, for example, is on average the most affluent ever[5]), better fed, healthier, lived longer and enjoyed more leisure, had greater opportunities than people elsewhere to travel (with the widespread ownership of cars and more recently, the availability of cheap air flights), and enjoyed the advantages

[3] Short, P. (1999) *Mao: A Life* Hodder and Stoughton.

[4] Barnett, C. (1986) *The Audit of War* Macmillan.

[5] Comptroller and Auditor General *Progress in Tackling Pensioner Poverty: Encouraging Take-up of Entitlements* (HC 1178, Session 2005–2006).

of television and other forms of electronic communication – in particular, the internet and mobile phones in recent years. Whether this has made people happier is another issue – and one which has increasingly become a matter for debate[6] – but a convincing case can be made for progress throughout the Western world which has helped improve the lives of millions of people. As one study puts it, 'whatever faults the United States and the European Union may have – there are many – in recent generations, both have methodically improved daily circumstances for almost everyone.'[7] It seems that the great story of our era is 'average people better off.'

Yet few of these benefits were seen as the result of public sector management, whose outcomes were increasingly seen as disappointing. Pessimism about modern government has existed for a long time. Reforms at the start of the twentieth century stemmed from concerns about poor military performance in the Anglo-Boer War, which suggested the UK was ill-equipped for the modern world. Such pessimism has been voiced by many different perspectives, including both the right and the left of the political spectrum, and both those sympathetic and hostile to public provision. Conservative governments in the early 1970s and in 1980s were concerned with the perceived inefficiency of state provision and brought in businessmen such as Sir Derek Rayner to scrutinise the administration. Conservative thinkers have also railed against the flow of European Union Directives, which they have argued have been interpreted either more zealously than they needed to be, or else more zealously than was the case in other EU countries. Traditionally, socialists have sought to expose the secrecy of bureaucracy or argued that it represented or favoured a particular class position. In the 1970s, Labour ministers such as Tony Benn expressed exasperation at the slow pace of change and the unwillingness of bureaucrats to take risks and innovate.[8]

Such concerns about the ability of bureaucracy[9] to deliver have developed over time, perhaps bolstered by streams of evaluations, reviews, audits and scrutinies, which have created an impression – intentionally

---

[6] Easterbrook, G. (2003) *The Progress Paradox* Random House.

[7] Easterbrook, G. (2003) *The Progress Paradox* Random House.

[8] Benn, T. (1989) *Against the Tide: Diaries 1973–1976* Arrow.

[9] This concern has manifested itself in different ways. In some instances it is concern with the trust worthiness of politicians while some public service professionals such as teachers, doctors and the military continue to command public esteem and respect. Civil servants 'the bureaucrats' come somewhere in between but generally there has been a considerable decline in how they are perceived and they are often portrayed as cushioned against, and uncaring for, the realities of social problems and from commercial life.

or not – that the public sector route was at best inadequate, and at worst incompetent. Looking back, one observer has argued:

> We began by worrying about the capacities of organisations to deliver pro-
> grammes, then signalled an imbalance between the demand for govern-
> ment and its supply, deepening into structural tendencies towards crisis,
> to end up concerned about unprecedented predicaments, the competence
> and integrity of the people in charge, and the institutional arrangements
> of modern parliamentary democracy, bureaucracy and the nation-state.[10]

This disappointment and pessimism is all the more concerning because it has occurred despite a number of factors that should have given the public sector a good chance of success. For example, it is despite the:

- *Quality of staff that the public sector has been able to recruit* – Joining the civil service in the UK has continued to be seen as attractive to many well-educated young people. A recent survey of the most popular destinations for graduates in both the sciences and humanities found that the Foreign & Commonwealth Office, Cabinet Office or Ministry of Defence – or becoming an National Health Service (NHS) manager – remained highly attractive;[11]
- *Amount of goodwill that working within the public sector has gener-ated* – Sennett notes a curious combination of disaffection and com-mitment amongst public service workers in welfare-state, pyramidal bureaucracies.[12] Many of the staff he interviewed in poorly provi-sioned schools or hospitals could have left for better jobs but did not because they felt they were doing something 'useful' and felt they 'made a difference';[13]
- *Scale of resources devoted to government* – Notwithstanding the rhetoric of smaller government and efforts to make savings and effi-ciencies at various times, spending on the public sector has remained at around 40 per cent of Gross Domestic Product (GDP). Enormous sums of money have been devoted to improving health and social pro-vision and maintaining a strong defence capacity, but also to repeat-edly reinventing and reforming the structures of government – what

---

[10] Gray, P. 'Policy Disasters in Europe: an introduction' in Gray, P. (ed) (1998) *Public Policy Disasters in Western Europe* Routledge.

[11] The Guardian, 20 May 2006.

[12] Sennett, R. (2006) *The Culture of the New Capitalism* Yale University Press, 35–36.

[13] Sennett, R. (2006) *The Culture of the New Capitalism* Yale University Press, 35–36.

has been called the 'pandemic of public sector reforms.'[14] The largest specialist consultancies in the world have been employed to complement government provision;

- *Amount of thought devoted to evaluating what works in government programmes stretching back over the last 45 years* – Over recent decades the UK government has commissioned more and more evaluation research work, made it more visible and become more actively engaged with and prepared to support the evaluation communities, including within central departments, the health services, and local authorities. There has – it seems – been no shortage of desire to understand what works.[15]

## 2.2   THE CAUSES OF PUBLIC PROGRAMME FAILURE

What are the reasons for this comparative failure? I will summarise three alternative perspectives. One answer is that public sector management is deemed intrinsically *more difficult* than private sector management for the following reasons:

- the absence of a clear 'bottom line' of profit;
- the need to balance the many interests of different pressure groups and stakeholders;
- the importance of accountability of officials to elected politicians and legislative bodies, with all that this implies in terms of careful record keeping and a culture of conformity and respect;
- the idea that the role of the public domain was 'the organisation of collective purpose, the area in which collective values are pursued';[16]
- the view that public sector management involved an accommodation between three sets of values: Sigma-type values, to keep the organisation lean and purposeful; Theta-type values, to keep it honest and fair; and Lambda-type values, to keep the organisation robust and resilient, capable of effective response to changes and emergencies.[17]

A second argument is that there is simply so *much more government than in the past to go wrong*. The scale of government, the extent of

---

[14] Pollitt, C. and Bouckaert, G. (2000) *Public Management Reform* Oxford University Press.

[15] Gray, A. and Jenkins, B. 'Policy and program evaluation in the United Kingdom: a reflective state?' in Furubo, J. (ed.) (2002) *International Atlas of Evaluation* Transaction.

[16] Stewart, J. and Ranson, S. (1988) 'Management in the public domain' *Public Money and Management* (Spring/Summer), 15.

[17] Hood, C. (1991) 'A Public management for all seasons?' *Public Administration* **69** (Spring).

intervention into every walk of life, the nature of the challenges, the intricacy of networks and policies, and the numerous dependencies on others increases the chance that things will not go to plan or even fail. In the worst cases, such failures can become politically controversial and area often referred to as 'policy fiascos.'[18] Put simply, if there is more government activity, there is more that can go wrong.

A third way of looking at failure is to consider the general *lowering of tolerance of failure* across all parts of society and government caused by heightened expectations of what is possible, especially where Information Technology (IT) is involved. As Bovens puts it 'we became more sensitive to the unintended consequences of government intervention, such as the bureaucratisation of public service delivery, the displacement rather than the resolution of social problems, and the escalating costs of many welfare state provisions.'[19] From this perspective, the increased tailoring of services to the needs of customers – a growing feature of the private sector – is making it ever harder to view public sector developments as successful, since in many cases they fall short of what is seen elsewhere. To the citizen, the question has increasingly become: 'if Amazon.com or Tesco can do it, why can't my local council?.'

## 2.3   BUREAUCRACY'S FUNDAMENTAL FLAW

Yet these perspectives are not the whole answer since, in response to the first argument in particular, all these difficulties could be – and have been – tackled by various strategies of improvement. Strategies have included open book accounting, and consultative machinery designed to achieve compromise and consensus among stakeholders. These tools may have secured short term gains from time to time, but have not delivered permanent improvements.

These explanations do not provide the solution because they do not address the fundamental problem of bureaucracy.[20] Bureaucracy looks inward not outwards, to process rather then outcomes, to hierarchies rather than teams, to rules rather than initiative, and to detachment from, rather than engagement in, human interests **(Box 2.3)**. Morris has talked

---

[18] 't Hart, P. and Bovens, M. (1996) *Understanding Policy Fiascoes* Transaction Publishers, 145–146.

[19] 't Hart, P. and Bovens, M. (1996) *Understanding Policy Fiascoes* Transaction Publishers, 146.

[20] I interpret bureaucracy much more widely than the common perception of 'red tape'. I consider it in the wider sociological context of the impact it has on human behaviour and adverse consequences in terms of mismanagement.

of 'a characteristic mindset among public sector managers; the mindset of administrators rather than of entrepreneurs, leaders or executives.'[21] This mindset, he argues, is as a result of the:

• requirement to be faithful agents of their mandated purposes;
• duty to achieve these purposes as efficiently and effectively as possible;
• assumption of substantial expertise in the field in which they work which allows them to know how to get desired results and assure quality and effectiveness in their operations;
• expectation of administrative competence;
• expectation of being able to prove public resources are not being stolen, wasted or misused.

As a result:

> their orientation is downward, toward the reliable control of organizational operations rather than either outward, toward the achievement of valuable results, or upward, towards renegotiated policy mandates. Instead of viewing their task as initiating or facilitating change, they tend to see it as maintaining a long-term institutional perspective in the face of fickle political whims. Their principal managerial objective is to perfect their organization's operations in traditional roles, not to search for innovations that can change their role or increase their value to the polity.[22]

The consequences are neatly summarised:

> For more than 20 years public services have been seen as insufficiently dynamic: too often they have appeared to be rule bound, unresponsive to changed client and citizen expectations or lifestyles, committed to outdated practices, technologically unadventurous, overly influenced by staff interest and professional concerns, and providing fragmented services that are sometimes costly and largely unaccountable.[23]

---

**Box 2.3:   Introspective Bureaucracies**

The inward looking nature of bureaucracy was exemplified in the following statement about ethical behaviour attributed to Sir Warren

---

[21] Morris, M. (1995) *Creating Public Value* Harvard University Press.

[22] Morris, M. (1995) *Creating Public Value* Harvard University Press. 'Editorial' *Public Money and Management* Vol. 24 Blackwell Publishing, pp. 197–199.

[23] Cornforth, C. and Paton, R. (2004) 'What's different about public and non-profit "turnaround"?' *Public Money and Management* **24**(4) 209–216.

Fisher, Head of the UK Civil Service from 1919 to 1939: 'the civil service has its unwritten code of ethics and conduct for which the most effective sanction lies in the opinion of the Service itself'.[24] There is no acknowledgement here of an ethical responsibility to provide services of quality to the wider community – instead, the first duty is to one's peers, and thence to the public. And successive exemplifications of the code, some in written form, 'still may be inadequate, however, when what civil servants need is guidance on how service-orientated, market-driven public services can treat all citizens equitably and how the paramount interest of the public interest can be maintained'.[25]

## 2.4  LITERARY INSIGHTS

The problem of bureaucracy has been most effectively grasped by writers who were not administrators or economists, but novelists and philosophers who saw that bureaucracy had not guaranteed freedom. Instead, bureaucracy propagated a subtle kind of public control so that citizens of most European, North American and other industrialised societies accepted a degree of authoritarian state control over their lives and fortunes which made a mockery of all the hopes for freedom and self-development proclaimed during the American and French Revolutions of the Eighteenth Century and inherent in all subsequent overturnings of monarchical and aristocratic governments.

The criticism of the modern state as promoting alienation and false consciousness among citizens, reconciling them to the distortions of life in capitalist societies was, of course, one aspect of the philosophy of Karl Marx. But other writers and philosophers also provided acute condemnations which went to the heart of the problems of public sector management. These were often the more effective because as well as reaching more readers they were couched in the symbolic language of the novelist, the analyst of social and political affairs and the philosopher, rather than in the proclamations of the management specialist.

Franz Kafka's posthumously published novels, *The Trial* (1925) and *The Castle* (1926), portray the ordinary person wrestling with the tentacles of modern bureaucracy, accused, for example, of offences

---

[24] Horton, S. (2006) 'The public service ethos in the British Civil Service: an historical institutional analysis' *Public Policy and Administration*, **21**(1), 36.

[25] Horton, S. (2006) 'The public service ethos in the British Civil Service: an historical institutional analysis' *Public Policy and Administration*, **21**(1), 46.

which are never specified and for which he can obtain no explanation. He is always held at bay by a vast and sinister official machine which seems to embody a crazy logic which can never be fully understood, and where all attempts to assert individuality and personal choice are denied by those who, in principle if not in practice, are servants of the public. Kafka, it should be noted, worked all his life as a civil servant dealing with workers' accident insurance.

In his *Animal Farm* (1945) and *1984* (1949), George Orwell too shows how bureaucracy can instigate and support manipulative regimes that deny human freedom in subtle ways, as in propagating a new language, 'Newspeak', whose vocabulary is reduced each year to make questioning thoughts literally unthinkable, and as in his aphorism about totalitarian bureaucracies in *Animal Farm:* 'all animals are equal but some animals are more equal than others'.

More recently, writers of popular culture have cast further light on the power play of bureaucrats. Two of the most popular and, arguably, most timeless television comedies – *Yes Minister* and *Yes, Prime Minister* – depict the traits and machinations of senior bureaucrats in ways which transcend national cultures and allow it to be enjoyed all over the world. Behind the humour, however, there is a sense of futility around the absurd rituals and constraints imposed by bureaucracy. As an official in one story puts it on resigning a post, 'quite honestly, Minister, I want a job where I don't spend endless hours circulating information that isn't relevant about subjects that don't matter to people who aren't interested'. Whilst the civil service recruits and retains very good people, often because of the intrinsic nature of the work, at the same time popular television has managed to capture many of its essential features: the focus on internal gaming, the rules, the insider focus on hierarchy and positioning, and the emphasis on form over substance.

## 2.5   WIDER PROBLEMS WITH BUREAUCRACY

Bureaucracy creates problems in many ways. I would like to suggest six in particular which I will illustrate with examples. Too often, bureaucracies:

- favour the producer and show insufficient concern for the user;
- require the citizen to act and think like a bureaucrat;
- are poor at learning despite gathering enormous amounts of information;
- enmesh themselves in complexity, creating additional problems;

- are poor at examining, assessing and debating their own performance;
- provide little or no incentive to innovate and make better use of resources.

It is an oft-quoted observation that bureaucracy *favours the producer*. Michel Foucault describes how various professions, often seen as bulwarks of the modern state and whose members are often valued public servants, may propagate regimes which define and treat those who are 'ill' or 'mad' or 'criminal'. While such categories are represented as the product of objective research and reason and in the interests of the disadvantaged and the deviant, they may actually operate to maintain the power, influence, income, authority and prestige of the professional groups concerned, and also for the governmental and other organisational structures within which they work. It may seem harsh to think of modern professional people in this way yet experience shows that this possibility should not be ignored – auditors themselves need to guard against it. But, much of the history of the post-war NHS can be seen in terms of a battle between governments and professionals: 'since the 1960s successive governments had seen the professionally based health community as a barrier to service improvement. In addition, professional self-evaluation was often considered weak and inadequate with little emphasis on patients as consumers.'[26]

If bureaucracy has favoured the producers too much, it has also thought too little of those it was intended to serve. Indeed, it often seems it that *it requires citizens to act and think like bureaucrats*. To the sociologist Richard Sennett:

> The welfare state also assumed the form of a bureaucratic pyramid. In social-democratic principle, welfare benefits, like old-age pensions and education, were conceived as universal rights; in practice, even Nordic and British welfare systems obliged their clients to think like bureaucrats in dealing with their own needs. The bureaucratic rules served the bureaucracy first and foremost; elderly, students, the unemployed, and the sick were obliged to behave like officeholders in the Weberian sense rather than as individuals with distinctive life histories. The system focused ever more on institutional self-maintenance and stability rather than effective delivery of care.[27]

---

[26] Gray, A. and Jenkins, B. 'Checking out? Accountability and evaluation in the British regularity state' in Bemelmans-Videc, M-L., Lonsdale, J. and Perrin, B. (eds) (2007) *Making Accountability Work: Dilemmas for Evaluation and for Audit* Transaction Publishers.

[27] Sennett, R. (2006) *The Culture of the New Capitalism* Yale University Press.

The need for citizens to behave like bureaucrats can be seen no better than in the way in which they have been asked to interact with the state **(Box 2.4)**. At times, citizens have been variously required to:

- know which organisation to deal with;
- appreciate the different layers of government and how they fit together;
- understand the language in which the rules are expressed;
- seek out assistance if necessary (having identified where to go and what to ask for);
- find and provide the information they have been asked to provide; and
- if it all goes wrong, negotiate different processes in order to complain.

Government bodies have tended to make a series of assumptions – for example, that the customer could cope with complex information and had conscientiously read all the information provided with an application form. It was no surprise when testing for a recent audit identified that much published benefit literature required a reading age five years above the national average.[28]

There were some encouraging signs: some forms are now shorter; some leaflets are better written and demonstrate a greater regard for 'Plain English' standards; citizens are consulted more often in the design of written material coming out of government; and, call centres are available to assist with applications. But, even now, applicants for many services are expected to negotiate long and complex processes which do not seem designed with them in mind, or suffer at the hands of bodies unable, for example, to pass information within the same organisation. This remains the case, for example, between contact centres dealing with different benefits.

---

**Box 2.4:   Requiring citizens to be bureaucrats**

*Completing forms*[29]

An examination of government forms in 2002 identified a number of features. Central government forms on average required citizens to provide between 40 and 60 pieces of information. Many required

---

[28] Comptroller and Auditor General *Department for Work and Pensions: Using Leaflets to Communicate with the Public about Services and Entitlements* (HC 797, Session 2005–06).

[29] Comptroller and Auditor General *Difficult Forms: How Government Agencies Interact with Citizens* (HC 1145, Session 2002–2003).

people to give over 100 pieces, especially in the welfare and education fields where forms are longest. Until recently, some organisations seemed to have approached the design of forms in a formal and legalistic way, assuming an ideal citizen who conscientiously read all the information given with a form and could cope with very complex information. Our scrutiny identified that questions were often not independently intelligible, often included long preambles and were accompanied by lengthy and complex guidance notes.

*Understanding leaflets*[30]

Results of another study confirmed that information in government leaflets can be unintelligible to intended readers. Applying an internationally recognised readability test, we found that none of the leaflets tested which contained benefit information was likely to be accessible to those with low literacy levels. Eight of the thirteen leaflets tested were most likely to be understood by those with a reading age equivalent to or higher than a 16 year old, or those who have completed at least five years of secondary schooling and reached GCSE level. At this level, it is unlikely that information would be accessible to many of those for whom English is not a first language. The use of some words specific to the Department's business, for example, 'disability', 'incapacity' or 'entitlement', can impact on the assessment of readability.

*Knowing how to complain*[31]

Every year, citizens make more than one million complaints or appeals against perceived poor treatment, mistakes, faults or injustices in dealings with central government. The biggest areas of complaints involve issues around health, social security and taxation. Our examination established that most people have a reasonably clear idea of how they would set about taking action to seek remedy for faults or mistakes, but the main problem is finding whom to talk to in the first place. Government organisations do not have enough information

---

[30] Comptroller and Auditor General *Using Leaflets to Communicate with the Public about Services and Entitlements* (HC 797, Session 2005–2006).

[31] Comptroller and Auditor General *Citizen Redress: What citizens can do if things go wrong with public services* (HC 21, Session 2003–2004).

about the complaints or appeals made to them. Around half cannot effectively answer how many complaints they received last year. And information on appeals needs improving. Too many members of the public see the way government bodies handle complaints and appeals as being complex, slow-moving, expensive and time-consuming.

Another reason why government appears to struggle is because often *bureaucracy is poor at learning lessons or sharing them more widely.* This is ironic since stability and recordkeeping are features of the classic bureaucracy, and also disturbing because, as has been noted elsewhere, 'the most important aspect of policy failure and policy disasters is how mundane they really are'.[32] This point has been particularly obvious in the context of the causes of IT failures. In 2000, the Committee of Public Accounts, concerned at the repeated and frequently high profile problems with the introduction of new IT systems within government, . produced a report looking back on 25 cases it had examined since the early 1990s.[33] The report showed that many of the problems had been repeated over and again, but highlighted that many were about basic management rather than complex technical issues (**Box 2.5**).

---

**Box 2.5:    Key recommendations regarding IT projects**[34]

- Key decisions about IT systems are business decisions, not technical ones.
- The commitment of senior management is essential.
- Identifying end users and their needs is critical to the success of a project.
- Scale and complexity can easily lead to failure – consider breaking a project down into manageable sub-components.
- Management and oversight of a project by skilled and knowledgeable managers is essential.
- Project managers have to be imaginative and skilled in risk control as well as in project management.

---

[32] Bovens M., 't Hart and Peters B. G. (eds) (2001) *Success and Failure in Public Governance: a comparative analysis* Edward Elgar.

[33] Committee of Public Accounts *Improving the Delivery of Government IT Projects* (1st Report, 1999–2000).

[34] Committee of Public Accounts *Improving the delivery of Government IT Projects* (1st Report 1999–2000).

- A high degree of professionalism is required in the definition, negotiation and management of IT contracts.
- Adequate training is essential for both system users and system operators.
- Contingency plans must be in place and they must provide adequate service levels.
- A post-implementation review of the project is essential for both monitoring the success of the project and for learning from it.

Reflecting on the findings, Pollitt commented:

> It is distressing that principles as obvious as [those relating to the importance of senior management commitment, identifying the needs of users, professionalism in negotiating contracts and adequate training for users] have had to be re-stated at all. Yet failures on these points emerge again and again.[35]

It has not just been IT problems, however, and in 2005 the Committee of Public Accounts produced a further – and more widely focused – report which highlighted that right across government, lessons from cases they had examined were not being picked up and implemented more widely, even where they were relevant.[36] The Committee considered a number of aspects of delivery:

- failure to plan carefully prior to implementation;
- the quality of project management;
- complexity and bureaucracy;
- productivity;
- commercial astuteness;
- fraud; and
- implementation of policies and programmes.

In each case, the Committee was able to point to cases where similar mistakes had been made and adequate planning not implemented. Despite the importance of learning from pilot projects, for example, the Department for Education and Skills (DfES) went ahead with the Individual Learning Accounts (ILA) initiatives (**Box 2.6**), even though none of the

---

[35] Pollitt, C. (2003) *The Essential Public Manager* Open University Press, p. 81.

[36] Committee of Public Accounts *Achieving Value for Money in Delivering Public Services* (17th Report 2005–2006).

schemes tested proved workable. A different model was introduced but a rushed implementation resulted in a scheme vulnerable to fraud which cost the taxpayer £67 million. None of the difficulties were a surprise – lessons had simply not been learned.

---

**Box 2.6:    The Individual Learning Accounts**[37]

The innovative Individual Learning Account scheme was aimed at widening participation in learning and helping to overcome financial barriers faced by some people, particularly those with low skills or qualifications. The scheme was implemented too quickly and inadequately planned. The Department for Education and Skills had no detailed business model or quality assurance for courses and there were weaknesses in security arrangements. Concerns that some providers were abusing the system and question marks over the quality of some of the courses led to the scheme being withdrawn in 2001. The Department acted quickly when it found evidence of significant potential fraud and abuse; in particular, that the database holding details of the accounts was being improperly trawled for unused accounts by a few unscrupulous registered learning providers abusing their legitimate access to the system to make claims in respect of these accounts without the knowledge of the account holder. The Department did not at that time know how many accounts were opened. The Department was under pressure to agree the contract quickly. Instead of a risk-sharing partnership, the relationship with the supplier left most of the risks with the Department. The Department excluded the contactor from the Project Board because its presence would be seen as restricting open discussions of policy. This was a major factor in the supplier being treated as a contractor, executing decisions made by the Department, rather than acting as a partner. The Department also decided against introducing a quality assurance system and expected instead that market forces would ensure new providers would replace inefficient ones. This left responsibility for identifying the most appropriate learning to the learners themselves, some of whom were least able to compare and contrast options and determine what learning would suit them best.

This failure to learn sufficiently from past problems is all the more surprising given that government bureaucracies gather enormous amounts of data and yet are unable to answer many, often basic, questions. In 2004, *The Times* reported that the businessman appointed to review the private pensions system had attacked the Government's pension statistics for being 'inadequate'.[38] This came as the Inland Revenue admitted that it had overstated the amount of pensions tax relief it paid by £3 billion a year since 1999. The review had been delayed because of the paucity of government information on pensions and had been made even more difficult by the over-optimism of government mortality predictions. The Office of National Statistics (ONS) (now National Statistics) had recently cut by £12 billion its estimate of how much money Britons put aside in pensions savings in 2002. The faulty figures were behind the exaggeration by the Inland Revenue of the amount of tax relief it gave to people with private pensions. Yet, as an independent review highlighted, the Government and industry collects enormous amounts of pensions data but each was partial in its coverage, none was complete or sufficiently timely for policy purposes, and large and important aspects of pensions such as distribution of pensions contributions by type of contributor were hardly covered at all.[39]

Another sign of a narrow and inward looking focus has been the ability of bureaucracy to *make problems for itself by creating complexity* in rules for which there are few, if any, forces working the other way. Returning to the insights afforded by literature, another novelist, Joseph Heller, in his novel *Catch 22* (1961) described how, as bureaucracy created more rules and regulations, their complexity increased and contradictory rules were created, making co-ordination ever more difficult. The consequence, as Geoff Mulgan has observed recently, is that

> In many countries only one or two people truly understand how the big systems of social security or government finance work, because successive reforms have left behind so many layers of complexity (and it is also sometimes said that anyone who really does understand these systems soon goes mad).[40]

---

[37] Comptroller and Auditor General *Individual Learning Accounts* (HC 1235, Session 2001–2002).

[38] The Times on-line 1 October 2004.

[39] Office of National Statistics (2002) *Review of ONS Pension Contributions Statistics: Report of the Review Panel.*

[40] Mulgan, G. (2006) *Good and Bad Power* Allen Lane, p. 229.

Bureaucracies have often found it hard to avoid greater complexity as **Box 2.7** shows. Almost every imperative pushes in this direction:

- the short-term political desire to resolve specific problems, perhaps quickly, without sufficient consideration for the longer term or wider implications;
- the attempt to keep costs down by making very detailed rules, fine tuned to specific circumstances;
- the (welcome) desire to counter fraudulent claims by gathering detailed evidence of eligibility;
- the personal desire of those involved to create new policy, rather than implement someone else's.

---

**Box 2.7:    Complex systems providing information to doctors**[41]

In the United States, Medicare serves nearly 40 million beneficiaries and is the country's largest health insurer and second largest federal programme. It constitutes a promise to pay for covered medical services provided to the beneficiaries by about one million providers. There are detailed rules governing what should be paid for and under what circumstances. Centers for Medicare & Medicaid Services (CMS) – the federal agency within the Department of Health and Human Services – relies on the assistance of about 50 administration contractors. CMS is charged with communicating information to medical providers including physicians so they can bill properly. The Government Accountability Office undertook an audit which revealed the implications of this complex system. Information given to doctors was often difficult to use, out of date, inaccurate and incomplete. Bulletins were poorly organised and written in dense legal language. Toll-free provider assistance phone lines and web sites were often inadequate. Customer service representatives rarely provided accurate answers to questions, answering only 15 per cent of test calls completely and accurately.

---

Few, if any forces, push in the opposite direction. We can see this in the development of the post-war social security system (**Box 2.8**), where several types of complexity – full scale reform, incremental 'patchwork'

---

[41] Government Accountability Office (2002) *Medicare: Communications With Physicians Can be Improved* (GAO-02-249).

changes, the linkages between benefits and systems, and the complexity associated with delivery mechanisms – combine. As a result, the comprehensive Child Poverty Action Group (CPAG) guide to benefits – used by welfare rights advisers to allow them to assist citizens – has grown four-fold in length in a decade. Recently, there has been greater recognition of the need to tackle the problem of complexity, but such moves are essentially counter-cultural and it remains to be seen how effective they will be.

---

**Box 2.8:    The growing complexity of the benefit system**[42]

Benefit rules are inevitably complex as they strive to meet the needs of people in a wide range of circumstances. The Department has also sought to use benefit regulations to pursue policy objectives, and seek to ensure equity and fairness between individuals in the same or differing situations. It has also tried to provide incentives (for example, to encourage people to work) and rewards (for example, recognising savings) and to meet specific needs by tailoring rules carefully. Detailed rules define clearly who is eligible for benefits, and allow the Department to seek to achieve its aims in a cost-effective manner.

However, the benefit system is in many ways a product of many years of legislative change. Starting in the early Twentieth Century, it has evolved, adjusting to changing economic and social circumstances and political orientations, as well as expanding to meet new needs. Successive governments have advocated simplification, but for a variety of reasons it has rarely occurred. Radical reform is a rare, costly, time-consuming and potentially controversial act. Changes therefore tend to be piecemeal, which inevitably gives rise to adjustments in linked benefits, changes to staff guidance and amendments to customer literature. The interaction between benefits, tax credits and child maintenance adds further complexity. Complexity in the delivery of benefits then arises as a consequence of the complexity of the benefits themselves.

---

[42] Comptroller and Auditor General *Dealing with the Complexity of the Benefits System* (HC 592, Session 2005–2006).

Of course, complexity and rules are not features which by themselves identify an organisation as bureaucratic – they exist to some degree in almost any organisational form. The difference in the public sector is the unrestrained, intentional or not, impact complexity has historically had on the quality of public services.

Even where efforts are made to counter complexity, progress has been limited and can in fact become adjunct to bureaucratic processes. The extent of the problem of complexity has also been recognised in the impact of regulation imposed by government on business. The development of Regulatory Impact Assessments (RIAs) – through which government assesses the impact of proposed regulation on business – has been welcome, but there is much evidence that they are not being used in the right way, their purpose is not always understood and, in many cases, the assessments do not offer a robust challenge to proposals to regulate. The weakest area has been the consideration of the level of compliance with the proposed regulation, where too often departments have assumed that new regulations will be fully complied with. There are also weaknesses in assessments of costs and benefits and in many cases, RIAs are seen as a paper-output rather than being integral to the policy-making process.[43] Ironically, when the Dutch audit office, Algemene Rekenkamer, reported in 2006 on similarly intentioned efforts in The Netherlands to reduce the administrative burden that government imposed, they found efforts were less successful than had been hoped. In part this was because some of the scrapped regulations had not been complied with, others were not as bothersome as had been supposed and, in some cases, companies continued to adhere to defunct rules because it was convenient for them to do so.[44]

Concerns about complexity are not simply of technical interest. The links between complexity and non-take up of benefits have been noted, and other consequences include making it hard for organisations to easily explain rules and responsibilities; making it difficult for staff to handle cases accurately; and creating environments in which errors and fraud can thrive. Mulgan fears that complexity leads to alienation and

---

[43] Comptroller and Auditor General *Evaluation of Regulatory Impact Assessments 2005–06* (HC 1305, Session 2005–2006).

[44] Algemene Rekenkamer *Reducing the Administrative Burden for Businesses* at http://www.rekenkamer.nl (2006).

passivity amongst citizens,[45] a theme taken up by Tony Wright MP, Chair of the Public Administration select committee in the United Kingdom House of Commons, who argued that governance arrangements in modern societies had become so complex that accountability structures had failed to keep pace. He suggested that citizens no longer understood who was responsible for delivering large swathes of public services. This situation, he said, had led to a 'vicious circle' in which the public attached responsibility for almost all matters of public policy to the government and ministers were now scared to let go of responsibility for key services.[46] Wright also questioned whether monitoring arrangements across the public services had developed in a coherent way.

A further problem with bureaucracy has been its *inability to measure and debate its own performance openly.* This is again ironic, since never have so many been involved in assessing and measuring performance within government. One estimate suggests a doubling of scrutinisers in 10 years,[47] and another that the cost of external inspection of UK public services rose steeply from £250 million in 1997–98 to £550 million in 2002–03.[48] There are many aspects to this issue.

A fundamental problem remains in terms of what is to be measured (What exactly is meant by productivity in the public sector? How can it best be measured? What is public service improvement?[49]). The evidence suggests we are some way from being able to answer these questions in a broad based and meaningful way, and the developing debate on 'public value' reminds us of the complexity of measuring exactly what it is that bureaucratic government adds.

There are problems with much of the enormous amounts of data collected by government. The systems validation work carried out by the NAO in recent years has identified that too many of the performance data systems have not developed arrangements to manage all the risks associated with the reliability of the published data. In other words,

---

[45] Mulgan, G. (2006) *Good and Bad Power* Penguin.

[46] Tony Wright Speech to CIPFA Conference, June 2006.

[47] Hood, C. et al. (1999) *Regulation Inside Government: Waste-watchers, quality police and sleaze-busters* University Press Oxford.

[48] Martin, S. (2005) 'Evaluation, inspection and the improvement agenda: contrasting fortunes in an era of evidence-based policy-making' *Evaluation* 11(4) 496–504.

[49] Boyne, G. 'What is public service improvement?' (2003) *Public Administration* 81(2) 211–227.

the information for reporting on performance could be compromised or inaccurate. There also remains the temptation to exaggerate performance or gloss over problems. The British Government's own Annual Report[50] died a death because it was so clearly not a balanced view on achievement.

Finally, *bureaucracy continues to provide very limited incentives to innovate or make savings.*[51] As Schumpeter put it, 'the bureaucratic method of transacting business and the moral atmosphere it spreads... exert a depressing influence on the most active minds'. Strongly hierarchical structures, weak performance reward systems and reluctance to accept new ways of working all contribute to slow progress within bureaucracies towards a more innovative culture. Officials continue to be rewarded for maintaining a stable job brief and avoiding potentially embarrassing and risky initiatives, and limited support exists to encourage suggestions and ideas to percolate upwards. The introduction of outsiders into central government appears to be helping to stimulate change in parts of government thanks to new ideas, sources of inspiration and more ambitious expectations. Yet, the picture arising from our work on innovation in central government is of a strongly hierarchical approach to innovation, with limited involvement of junior staff, long timescales to bring even small innovations 'to market'.[52]

Another aspect of this failure to innovate is the limited incentive for bureaucracies to be commercially astute. Government can often waste public resources because of its commercial inadequacies. The scope for making savings was identified in many audit reports, but a report in 2000 showed that six years after a 1994 Cabinet Office Efficiency Scrutiny had identified £65 million of potential savings, recommendations had not been implemented and nobody knew to what extent savings had been achieved.[53] Another examination found that £150 million in penalties and fines had not been collected and instead had been written off or cancelled because the offender could not be traced or because it was unlikely they would be collected.

---

[50] The Government's Annual Report 1997–98 (Cm 3969) and 1998–99 (Cm 4401).

[51] Schumpeter, J. (1949) *Economic Theory and Entrepreneurial History Change and the Entrepreneur.*

[52] Comptroller and Auditor General *Achieving Innovation in Central Government* (HC 1447, Session 2005–2006).

[53] Efficiency Unit (1994). The Government's use of external consultants, Cabinet Office.

## 2.6   THE FLAWS OF BUREAUCRACY HAVE BEEN REINFORCED BY TRADITIONAL AUDIT

In 1999, the Cabinet Office report on Professional Policy-Making commented that 'we found a widespread view that civil service culture does not welcome new thinking or change'.[54] Traditionally, public sector auditing has reinforced bureaucracy's inherent problems – of caution, adherence to rules, lack of focus on innovation or change. It concentrated on whether the rules were followed, not if outcomes were achieved. Staff regarded the work as 'point hunting', designed to identify individual failures and specific lessons to be learned, with wider lessons considered less important. Few subjects considered arose from any specific analysis of risk or evaluation of departmental systems.[55] To critics of audit such as Behn, auditors focus on 'minor errors' and 'attack the smallest failure to comply with formal rules'.[56]

As a result, for a long time there was concern at what audit was able to contribute to improvements in public services. To some concerned with this, audit looked inadequately resourced and so absorbed in minutiae that it could do little to add value or provide valuable insights. Normanton's concerns of the 1960s about the 'cramping limitations of regularity', primarily concerned with whether money was spent as intended,[57] continued to be repeated more than a decade later in a wide ranging critique of waste in government which argued that:

> Much of the available staff time is absorbed in the purely routine book-keeping duties. . . The amount of staff capacity left for the more constructive forms of criticism, for investigations in depth and the fact-finding which is needed to overcome the neglect of years and the departments' defences is negligible.[58]

Another ten years later, Peter Hennessy's description was hardly flattering as he reflected that:

---

[54] Cabinet Office (2000) *Professional Policy Making For The Twenty First Century.*

[55] Lonsdale, J. (2000) *Advancing Beyond Regularity: developments in value for money methods at the National Audit Office,* Unpublished PhD thesis.

[56] Behn, R. (2001) *Rethinking Democratic Accountability* Brookings.

[57] Normanton, E. (1966) *The Audit and Accountability of Governments* Manchester University Press.

[58] Chapman, L. (1979) *Your Disobedient Servant: The Continuing Story of Whitehall's Overspending* Penguin.

The old Exchequer and Audit tradition of meticulously filleting of the files continues, conducted by a battalion of relentlessly tidy-minded accountants who make a habit of winning the Civil Service bridge competitions when not fashioning ammunition to place in the hands of MPs on the Public Accounts Committee.[59]

Clive Ponting, in his review of Whitehall, lamented that the audit process was 'a contest where from the start the department is on the defensive, determined to justify itself and reject criticism.

The aim of the department is to come out of the process with as little blame as possible'.[60] Such a process went on below the line of sight of those who mattered, as:

A system in which 'little people' in the audit office challenged other 'little people' in government departments for their executive lapses, with Permanent Secretaries in their role as Accounting Officers becoming involved only as spokespersons for their departments when the issues ricocheted up to the Public Accounts Committee.[61]

Despite this – or perhaps because of it – a view of audit took hold and lingered on through the 1990s that audit reinforced some of the worst traits of bureaucracy. As one government minister put it:

There is a perception – opinion varies whether it is a reality – that current scrutiny arrangements inhibit some risk taking in Departments. It is argued that the NAO is critical when departments try to do anything new, which encourages officials to play safe. . . We would be very concerned if enhanced scrutiny simply led to embedding very traditional ways of doing things and closed down innovation and modernisation in government.[62]

We set out in the next chapter how public sector auditing can contribute to value for money in modern government by acknowledging and working to overcome the faults in systems which stem from the bureaucratic approach, whatever surface adjustments may have been made in them.

---

[59] Hennessy, P. (1989) *Whitehall* Fontana Press.

[60] Ponting, C. (1986) *Whitehall: Tragedy and Farce* Sphere Books.

[61] Hood, C. et al. (1999) *Regulation Inside Government: waste-watchers, quality police and sleaze-busters* Oxford University Press.

[62] Hansard, Government Resources and Accounts Bill Standing Committee 18 January 2000.

## 2.7   SUMMARY

Public programmes are often late, cost more than planned and do not work as intended. Examples are legion in costly defence projects, in the spread of hospital acquired infections, and fraud in many social security schemes. Fundamentally the problem has been bureaucracy: hierarchical, rule based organisations, staffed by life time career officials. Bureaucracy was the 'great white hope' of twentieth century organisations – the office equivalent of the industrial division of labour – supposedly offering greater productivity and honesty by officials selected and promoted by objective tests. However, as the twentieth century progressed, it became clear that too often bureaucracy was inward-looking, caught up in its own entrails, enmeshed in red tape, and uncaring for citizens. This was true of bureaucracies in both the 'Capitalist West' and the 'Communist East', but this truth did not go away with the fall of the Berlin Wall and has remained a problem over the following two decades. Traditionally, public sector auditing reinforced bureaucracy by concentrating on checking whether rules were being followed, rather than assessing if outcomes were being achieved.

# 3
# The Failure to Analyse
# Outcomes

The problems of bureaucracy discussed in the previous chapter cannot be overcome through traditional public sector accounting and audit practices alone. Traditional public sector accounting and audit usually has two components:

- the preparation of financial statements relating to a specified period – usually a year – and the audit of those statements to determine whether, in the auditor's opinion, the expenditure has been incurred legally and they give a true and fair view of the transactions recorded; and,
- comments on the regularity and propriety of expenditure which may have been incurred legally but contravened some administrative rule or an ethical or other standard which, while not necessarily anywhere set down, could in the auditor's opinion have usefully been observed.

Both of these components have value but operate in different contexts. A public authority, like a public company, does of course need a system of financial management, accounts preparation and audit that enables it to:

- know what cash, assets and other resources it has at the start and finish of each financial period;
- cost options accurately;
- budget its projects and programmes; and,
- produce annual accounts for external audit.

This system of financial management has been reinforced by recent developments in corporate governance, including:

- analyses of internal controls concerning all activities;
- systems of risk assessment and management;
- internal audit; and,
- audit committees with non-executive directors.

It remains the duty of public sector auditors to attend to all these matters and report upon them publicly as appropriate to the relevant institutions, in the case of the UK, for example, to the UK Parliament; to the devolved administrations; to local authorities; and – through the media – to the public at large.[1] **Box 3.1** summarises the traditional role of the auditor.

---

**Box 3.1:     Traditional role of the public sector auditor**

Most states have some form of public sector auditing with varying degrees of independence. Traditional (Financial) auditing requires the auditor to report annually on the Financial Statements and supporting financial and management controls. The Auditor General usually signs an annual audit opinion stating in his or her opinion and based on his/her work whether the financial statements are true and fair and whether transactions within them have appropriate Parliamentary authority. If a serious misstatement is identified the Auditor General should issue a qualified opinion.

*Source: UK National Audit Office* – http://www.nao.org.uk/.

---

An interesting example of this duty is my disclaimer of the Home Office's accounts for 2005–06 (**Box 3.2**). A disclaimer is a serious matter because it means that an organisation has not been able to produce financial statements capable of being audited. To the outside world it is a strong indicator that financial management is seriously deficient. For a department of state such as the Home Office, then responsible for criminal justice and homeland security, this was a serious situation which could easily undermine key stakeholders' confidence. The media coverage that my disclaimer attracted was important in promoting transparency in the way the department was accounting for public money. The publicity provided further pressure for the department to take the situation seriously, and take appropriate action quickly.

Initiatives to improve the corporate governance of both public and private sector organisations in response to major corporate failures such as ENRON have expanded the role of the auditor in the work he or she is required to do to obtain assurance over organisations' internal controls and financial management. For example, the combined Code on Corporate Governance issued by the UK Financial Reporting Council (the UK's independent regulator for corporate reporting and governance) sets out standards of good practice in internal controls. All companies

---

[1] Pickett, S.K.H. and Pickett, J.M. (2005) *Auditing for Managers: the ultimate risk management tool* John Wiley & Sons, Ltd.

in the UK and listed in the Main Market of the London Stock Exchange have to report in their financial statements how they have applied these standards. Similarly, guidance issued by the Treasury specifies the standards which government departments should follow.[2] I take account of compliance with this in the annual assessment I make of departments' internal controls as part of my financial audit.

---

**Box 3.2:    Disclaiming the Home Office's accounts**

The Home Office is the government department responsible for the police in England and Wales, national security, the justice system and immigration. As external auditor of the Home Office, I am required under Auditing Standards issued by the Auditing Practices Board to obtain evidence to give reasonable assurance that the Department's financial statements are free from material misstatement. In forming my opinion I examine, on a test basis, evidence supporting the disclosures in the financial statements and assess the significant estimates and judgements made in preparing them. I also consider whether the accounting policies are appropriate, consistently applied and adequately disclosed. Under the Government Resources and Accounts Act 2000, I am required to examine and certify all departmental resource accounts. I inform Parliament if a department does not meet the statutory timetable.

I was unable to form an opinion on the Home Office's financial statements for 2004–05 – the accepted term is that I issued a disclaimer. The reasons for this were:

- Problems with a new IT accounting system meant that the Home Office could not produce a cogent set of accounts to the required faster statutory timetables. The audit also revealed significant control weaknesses within the main accounting systems;
- Inability to reconcile cash with the bank position (i.e. match its own records of cash payments and receipts with those shown on its bank statements). Bank reconciliations are one of the most fundamental of all accounting controls as they enable payments, receipts and cash balances to be validated by an external source. They are also a key control for the prevention and detection of fraud; and

---

[2] HM Treasury *Corporate Governance in Central Government Departments: Code of Good Practice* July 2005.

> • Weaknesses in financial management, including poor controls and weaknesses in audit trails and access to key data.
>
> The implications of those weaknesses were that I could not obtain sufficient confidence in the financial systems operated by the Home Office without significant additional work, which was not practical given the statutory requirement for the financial statements to be presented to Parliament by 31 January 2006.
>
> The failure of a major department of state to produce auditable financial statements and my subsequent qualification attracted considerable adverse media coverage and criticism by Members of Parliament.
>
> *Source: C&AG's Report on Home Office Resource Accounts 2004–2005 (HC Session 2005–2006).*

The second component of traditional public sector auditing adds value in clarifying difficulties and enunciating ethical and other standards, as the following examples show. They illustrate the variety of relevant issues, some of which go far back into history. Thus, in 1882 there was a dispute between the Comptroller and Auditor General and the Land Judges' Office as to whether checking the accuracy of the amounts brought to account under the relevant statute was an audit responsibility or a judicial act – an interesting philosophic difference – or example of bureaucratic infighting – resolved finally in the Comptroller and Auditor General's favour.[3] Another example comes from the Anglo-Boer War, where the Army's demand for horses was so great that the globe had to be scoured to find them. The auditors showed initiative in tracking down that an agent in Spain supplying mules was receiving commission from both the British government and from the dealers selling the mules.[4] Also, in that war, the Secretary of State raised the widow's pension of a deceased major to that of a lieutenant colonel, twelve months after his death; a generous act, but one drawn to public attention by the auditor leading to the decision that in order to qualify for a pension of a particular rank the officer concerned must at least have been alive when he was raised to the rank![5]

---

[3] Committee of Public Accounts Fourth Report 1882 (HC 277 1882) Clan III Vote 15.
[4] Committee of Public Accounts Fourth Report 1902 (HC 273 1902) Vote 6.
[5] Committee of Public Accounts Fourth Report 1902 (HC 273 1902) Vote 14.

A more recent example concerns the University of Huddersfield's decision to raise and back date the retiring Vice Chancellor's salary by 50 per cent so that it would carry through to his pension and grant him other financial privileges such as paying his health insurance for life and letting him buy the Vice Chancellor's car at an advantageous price. None of this was illegal; but attention having been drawn to it by a whistleblower, the publicity of a public report by the Comptroller and Auditor General led the University to revise these decisions.[6]

This important aspect of public audit is replicated worldwide as illustrated by an inquiry undertaken in 1999 by the Office of the Auditor General in New Zealand into the chartering of a private aircraft by the Department of Work and Income to enable staff to attend a training course. The Auditor General reported that:

> the expenses incurred in holding the course at the Wairekei Resort Hotel were excessive in comparison to the cost of holding the same course at another more accessible location, when the same organisational objectives could have been achieved. The chartering did not take place simply as a result of self-serving extravagance by staff of the Department. Rather, it appears to have been the final consequence of a series of miscommunications and mistakes. These miscommunications and mistakes, although arguably not enough individually to have caused serious problems, compounded into a significant overall error that has proved costly to the Department (both financially and in terms of its credibility with its stakeholders).[7]

These examples illustrate the beneficial impact which traditional public audit has had in mitigating the potential worse effects of bureaucracies. In the mid nineteenth century the Northcote and Trevelyan Report condemned the nepotism, the incompetence and other defects of the civil service at the time and brought about fundamental change. It is from that period that the UK civil service acquired the principles and standards of propriety, probity and objectivity which are now widely expected of public servants. It is not by chance that the Exchequer and Audit Office, the predecessor of the NAO was established at around the same time. Its remit to scrutinise departments, if not exactly a policing function, provided enough of an incentive to ensure that civil servants took

---

[6] Comptroller and Auditor General *Severance Payments to Senior Staff in the Publicly Funded Education Sector* (HC 2002, Session 1994–1995).

[7] *Events Surrounding the Chartering of Aircraft by The Department of Work and Income* October 1999 – Report by the Controller and Auditor General New Zealand http://www.oag.govt.nz.

seriously their responsibility to exercise propriety in their use of taxpayers' money. This framework of broadly defined principles, transparency and independent scrutiny has served the UK civil service well. It has, however, not always been plain sailing. As governments have reformed the way services are delivered, the model upon which the principles of propriety and responsible public management are based has at times been strained. The most recent example of this is the introduction in the 1980s of a more entrepreneurial culture partly associated with the new public management. As quasi commercial approaches gained prominence, long established systems of control and accountability and, above all, traditional attitudes on the part of those handling public policy were challenged as concentrating on rules rather than outcomes and results. The role of audit was not to question the change in approach but to draw attention to the need to maintain and protect a proper concern for the sensible conduct of public business and care for the honest handling of public money (**Box 3.3**).

---

**Box 3.3:    Maintaining the proper conduct of public business**

In the 1980s and early 1990s there were fundamental changes in the way in which government departments and public bodies such as those in the National Health Service carried out their work. These changes which included the introduction of executive agencies and the growth in numbers of non-departmental public bodies were intended to improve the provision of public services through greater delegation of responsibilities, streamlining, and a more entrepreneurial approach to the work (this reform process has come to be known as the new public management).

At a time of change it is important to ensure that proper standards of control and financial management are maintained. The work of the National Audit Office identified and reported on a number of serious failures in administrative and financial systems which partly reflected a diminution of standards and management control. Examples included the Foreign and Commonwealth Office which introduced a new computerised system which did not work properly which created a climate which was conducive to fraud and theft; the Welsh Development Agency not following the clear legal requirement under which they should have submitted their new redundancy scheme to the Welsh Office for approval before implementing it; and the New

Town Development Corporations which allowed work to the value of £37 million to be undertaken through limited competition and reliance on discreet approaches to selected firms.

As a result of the National Audit Office's work the Committee of Public Accounts issued a report which set out a checklist of points which public bodies need to keep in mind in order to guard against the risk of lapses in the proper conduct of public business – covering the importance of sound financial controls, compliance with rules, the adequate stewardship of public money and achieving value for money.

This example illustrates the important role which external audit has in upholding ethical standards. The reforms associated with the 'new public management' led to much greater private sector involvement in the delivery of public resources. While a more entrepreneurial approach brought benefits it meant that decisions were increasingly made by those who had limited experience of the standards expected in the conduct of public business, or in the interests of achieving rapid change were frustrated by them. These standards are, however, the bedrock of the Civil Service's reputation for integrity. The report by the Committee of Public Accounts was largely instrumental in ensuring that a more business like approach to public sector management was not at the expense of maintaining standards of public probity and efficiency.

*Source: The proper Conduct of Public Business Committee of Public Accounts* – Eighth Report 1993–1994 HC 154.

## 3.1   HOW IS VALUE FOR MONEY TO BE SECURED?

As important as strong financial management is, it will not on its own guarantee value for money. In the absence of a single unifying easily measurable objective such as making a profit, governments struggle as to how best to achieve what is widely accepted to represent value for money.

One solution which has now gained wide acceptance is a much better articulation about what public money is intended to achieve. In this way the justification for expenditure and supporting processes or procedures can be determined and appraised in terms of their likely contribution to desired outcomes. Defining outcomes in a way that secures wide support and is capable of measurement (the risk is that this becomes an end in itself ) to demonstrate achievement is a significant challenge. Outcomes often have a moral imperative and can be diverse, such as reducing child poverty, promoting a healthy life style, and achieving a better balance between housing availability and demand while achieving affordability. The often aspirational nature of these well meaning aims is both a strength and weakness. On the one hand they declare clear strategic direction behind which resources and opinion can be marshalled. But unless they are linked to how they are to be achieved – the means to the end – outcomes quickly lose relevance to those they are intended to inspire. Bureaucracies struggle to develop meaningful outcomes that optimise quality of service with cost effectiveness. The contribution which external audit can make to this and in particular the evaluation of value for money in which some consideration of outcomes achieved is essential, are the central themes of this chapter.

### 3.2    TRADITIONAL OUTPUTS ARE VALUABLE BUT CANNOT DEMONSTRATE VALUE FOR MONEY

As I have said the components of traditional audit are, however, not enough. The audited accounts may show that money has been spent lawfully, and audit reports show that procedures were followed and ethical standards of behaviour observed. Yet, valuable as this information may be, it does not tell us if value for money has been secured. How could value for money be demonstrated?

The answer to this conundrum that has been most influential during the last half century is through the economists' theory of public choice and its applications in cost benefit and cost effectiveness analysis.

### 3.3    PUBLIC CHOICE

The essence of the approach is that:

- every individual both seeks and is the best judge of their own welfare, both material and spiritual;
- the aim of 'social' as distinct from 'individual' action is, or should be, to produce policies whose implementation produces the result that no individual could be more satisfied except at the expense of another. In other words, that no rearrangement of policies and their implementation could result in an increase in welfare;
- while the inevitable limitation of resources means that social action could produce no better result than this, it implies that some individuals

are worse off than they would like to be, since they are conscious of unrealised wishes. And the particular distribution of welfare – its social welfare function – that a society adopts or aims for is the particular responsibility of the government of the day to specify and amend;

- such a specification does not demand that the government should have a policy for everything or entail that the government will necessarily be beneficent rather than tyrannical. Much may – indeed inevitably will – be left to individual action, to the private sector rather than the public sector. And, if there is a predilection among public choice theorists, it is to leave as much initiative as possible to private individuals and the private sector.

The argument here is that politicians and civil servants, like everybody else, may be assumed to be in search of the maximum individual welfare. For many this may include an unselfish concern for the 'public interest'. But for many others the incentive will be to seek to maximise money, power and influence, with potentially disastrous results for the public interest, as attempts are made to boost public expenditure to secure promotion and personal aggrandisement; and to promote policies that serve special rather than general interests; and to implement them in ways that through favouring particular contractors to secure jobs after retirement and other rewards – and through fraud, theft and corruption – provide unjustifiable rewards to public sector workers. Bureaucratic forms of organisation provide fertile soil for personal aggrandisement to flourish, in spite of all the legal, regulatory and conventional safeguards to deter it. It is recognised, of course, that selfishness and corruption may be found in the private sector, and indeed, in all the walks of life and legal safeguards are necessary here as well. But the claim is that the 'invisible hand' of competitive forces channels personal selfishness towards the achievement of public satisfactions. As Mandeville put in *The Fable of the Bees*, 'though every part is full of vice yet the whole a paradise'. And, put shortly, the argument is that the best way of making a fortune is to provide the goods and services that people want to buy – an incentive that is, for the most part, absent from the life of a public service bureaucrat.[8]

---

[8] The line of argument that politicians and public servants tend to put private before public interests is developed in Niskanen Jr, W.A. (1973) *Bureaucracy: Servant or master?* Institute of Economics Affairs London. See also Mueller, D.C. (2003) *Public Choice III*, Chapter 16 Cambridge University Press.

This analysis rests on a whole range of heroic assumptions: that an individual is able to specify his or her own welfare function; that material and spiritual satisfactions can be compared and ranked over time and, within and between individuals; that social institutions such as governments can interpret individual wishes rather than impose their own on others; and that changing tastes and preferences can be accommodated. Within this theoretical framework – anchored in the clouds as it is – the question arises as to how the government is to know which policies can best achieve their social welfare function, dimly articulated as it will be.

One response is to structure public service delivery in its many facets in a way that enables individuals' or organisations' preferences to be exercised. There is a broad spectrum of case examples of where this has happened with varying degrees of success. At the most basic level, in the 1980s in the UK there was a growing willingness to open functions long considered to the preserve of the public sector to market forces. Initially the focus was operational support functions **(Box 3.4)** but by the 1990s following the privatisation of nationalised industries this had been extended to restructure traditional utility monopolies such as gas and electricity to allow individual choice to prevail **(Box 3.5)**. More recently individual choice has been extended to new frontiers particularly in making it possible for patients to choose where they receive healthcare **(Box 3.6)** and for parents to have a say in the school which their children attend. This is further illustrated in a speech by the British Prime Minister in June 2006 on *Public Services for the Twenty-First Century* when he articulated the objective of putting the user of public services first, and to give them both 'choice and voice'. Individual 'choice' is intended to give users greater ability to decide where, when, by whom and how a public service is provided; 'voice' offers opportunities for public service users to express their opinions and have them heard and acted upon.[9] There remain, however, many services where, in spite of the most inventive policy makers, an individual or organisation is unable explicitly to specify their welfare function or preference. In such cases some means of assessing potential benefits and associated costs is needed to make rational choices on the best way to optimise service delivery.

---

[9] Speech by Tony Blair June 2006 – http://www.number10.gov.uk also The UK Government's Approach to Public Service Reform June 2006 – http://www.strategy.gov.uk/publications.

---

**Box 3.4:     Competitive Tendering for Support Services in the National Health Service**

In the 1980s as part of a general drive to improve value for money in the NHS, competitive tendering was introduced for domestic, catering and laundry services. This was a major step change for an organisation which had a strong tradition of relying on in-house resources. These three services cost at the time around £1.2 billion. Of the contracts awarded private sector suppliers won 32 per cent in value in domestic services, 20 per cent in laundry services and 7 per cent in catering. Annual cumulative savings or efficiencies generated by this initiative were estimated at £73 million but as this figure was not fully net of the redundancy costs of staff no longer required the value for money improvements in total cost terms may have been overstated.

*Source: Competitive Tendering in the National Health Service* Report by the Comptroller and Auditor General (HC 319, Session 1986–87).

---

**Box 3.5:     Giving Customers a choice – The Introduction of Competition into the Domestic Gas Market**

In April 1996 people in the UK no longer had to rely on one monopoly supplier for their domestic gas. A major restructuring of the industry initiated by the Government enabled other suppliers to enter the market. As a result customers who had changed supplier up to August 1998 secured a reduction in their bills averaging £78 per year in real terms while those who stayed with the former monopoly supplier British Gas saved on average £48. While, however, 30 per cent of customers found it easy to change supplier 27 per cent said it was difficult. There was lower take up of special services for the elderly and disabled and those using prepayment metres (who tend to be on lower incomes) had benefited least from lower prices. A number of factors suggested that competition alone could not be relied upon to protect customers – rational choice had to be supplemented by some form of regulation to protect all citizens' interests.

*Source: Office of Gas Supply: Giving Customers a choice – the introduction of competition in the domestic gas market*, Report by the Comptroller & Auditor General (HC 403, Session 1998–1999).

---

**Box 3.6:    Patient choice at the Point of GP Referral**

The Department of Health now has a policy that every hospital appointment will be booked for the convenience of the patient making it easier for patients and their General Practitioners (GPs) to chose the hospital and consultant that best meets their need. The aim is to provide patients with the opportunity to chose between 4–5 healthcare providers for elective hospital treatment. This will apply to around 9.4 million patients referred for hospital treatment each year. While the main aim is to improve services for patients it is estimated that greater choice should lead to efficiencies valued at £71 million. A review by the NAO found that the policy's effectiveness could be put at risk by insufficient capacity in terms of GPs' lack of awareness of the policy to offer greater choice. And, of those who did know about it 60 per cent were negative towards it; and the readiness of the IT system – the Choose and Book Service.

*Source: Patient Choice at the Point of GP Referral*, Report by Comptroller and Auditor General (HC 186, Session 2004–2005).

---

### 3.4    COST BENEFIT ANALYSIS AND COST EFFECTIVENESS ANALYSIS

The answer to this problem that emerged in the 1960s and 1970s was to apply some form of cost benefit analysis[10] to policy formulation. Such an approach enables the costs and benefits of each policy option to be expressed in comparable terms – which almost always means monetary terms – over time; these costs and benefits to be discounted to their present values; and the policies with the greatest net present value adopted within the limits of the resources available to and secured by the government. Cost effectiveness analysis[11] is then applied to determine the best way of producing each policy output.

The Treasury's 'Green Book: Appraisal and Evaluation in Central Government' offers guidance on how this might be done. Essentially in an ideal world policy formulation should follow a defined cycle **(Box 3.7)** where its rationale, often reflecting political priorities, is

---

[10] Cost Benefit Analysis initially grew out of welfare economics and the particular study of the economics of public works in the 1930s: it was later adopted and incorporated into public choice theory.

[11] Cost effectiveness analysis assumes a policy outcome is given and seeks to identify the least cost means of achieving the goal (taking into account any ancillary benefits of alternative actions).

clearly articulated; key objectives are defined in terms of desired outputs and ultimately outcomes; a range of options to achieve these is considered and compared both in terms of their costs and benefits (and in particular whether the benefits are likely to accord with the rationale – the underlying political imperative). Finally, perhaps most importantly, implementation is well designed, tested and monitored with overall success evaluated and key lessons learned and acted upon. Within this broad cycle a range of often interrelated issues also needs to be taken into account such as affordability, wider macro economic implications, potential environmental impact, social inclusion and implications in terms of potential regulatory burdens on businesses and citizens. Of course, it is not as simple as that. Policies are rarely developed from a zero base – they evolve and often draw on experience elsewhere. For example, Sure Start, the UK programme to support the development of children during their early years drew extensively on similar policies in the USA.[12] However, assessing costs and forming a reliable estimate of additionality – the increase in benefits directly attributable to the new policy intervention – can be complex. Accurately quantifying future likely value for money with significant accuracy can be difficult, but the structured approach of cost benefit analysis can help identify key risks to value for money which can then be managed.

---

**Box 3.7:    The ROAMEF CYCLE – Rationale, Objectives, Appraisal, Monitoring, Evaluation and Feedback**

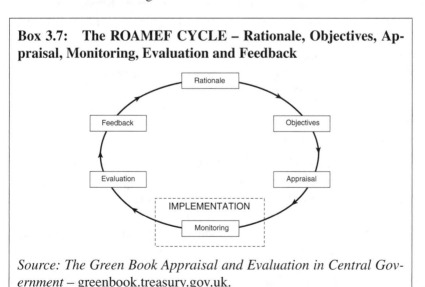

*Source: The Green Book Appraisal and Evaluation in Central Government* – greenbook.treasury.gov.uk.

---

[12] Comptroller and Auditor General *Sure Start Children's Centres* (HC 104, Session 2006–2007).

Option Appraisal is often the most significant part of the analysis. Initially a wide range of options should be identified and reviewed. This helps to set the parameters of an appropriate solution. A shortlist may then be established to keep the process manageable, by applying the techniques summarised below to high level estimates or summary data. The 'do minimum' option should always be carried forward in the shortlist, to act as a check against more interventionist action.

Each option is then appraised by establishing a Base Case. This is the best estimate of its costs and benefits **(Box 3.8)**. These estimates can then be adjusted by considering different scenarios, or the option's sensitivity to changes can be modelled by changing key variables. More fully, the appraisal may develop as follows:

- Identify and value the cost of each option.
- Identify and value the benefits of each option.
- If required, adjust the valued cost and benefits for:
  - distributional impacts (the effects of proposals on different sections of society);
  - relative price movements.
- Adjust for the timing of the incidence of costs and benefits by discounting them, to obtain their present values.
- If necessary, adjust for material differences in tax between options.
- Adjust for risk and optimism to provide the Base Case, and consider the impacts of changes in key variables and different future scenarios on the Base Case.
- Consider unvalued impacts (both costs and benefits), using weighting and scoring techniques if appropriate.

---

**Box 3.8:     Cost Benefit Analysis**

Cost benefit analysis (CBA) is the well established approach in option appraisal. Its first application in the UK government context was as part of an assessment of the construction of the M1 motorway from London to Birmingham in 1960. Since the 1980s CBA has increasingly been applied, both within government departments and independently, to examine aspects of government business wider than investment in, for example, transport, health or construction programmes. In particular, a considerable amount of work has been done on the application of CBA to regulation. The advent of the Private Finance Initiative (PFI) in the UK also provided an impetus for departments to apply CBA techniques to the appraisal and evaluation of PFI and Public Private Partnership deals.

In most CBAs, it is easier to estimate costs than benefits. In dealing with costs, the policy maker is trying to place monetary estimates on what is foregone or the resource cost to the economy as a whole as a result of the action, programme or decision under consideration. In other words, goods or services should be costed at their value in the best alternative use to which they could be put (i.e; *their* opportunity costs). Note that opportunity costs can arise in the absence of case payments, for example if equipment or land, which otherwise could have been used for other purposes, is tied up by a project.

Benefits are sometimes measurable in conventional economic terms. An example is the net revenue of agricultural output resulting from a large scale irrigation project. Difficulties arise when benefits are collective or public in nature, such as impacts on the environment or human health and safety. These are not goods which trade in any market. Nevertheless, strict CBA requires that they should be quantified in monetary terms. Generally the money values which attach to such benefits are either 'revealed' indirectly, by observing how the benefit in question affects the price or quantity of another good, or are elicited by means of questions about preferences addressed to the benefit recipients.

*Source: The Green Book Appraisal and Evaluation in Central Government* – http://www.greenbook.treasury.gov.uk and *Measuring Costs and Benefits – A guide on cost benefit and cost effectiveness analysis* http://www.nao.org.uk

Following option appraisal, decision criteria and judgement should be used to select the best option or options, which should then be refined into a solution. Consultation is important at this stage, regardless of whether it has taken place earlier. Procurement routes should also be considered, including the role of the private sector. Issues that may have a material impact on the successful implementation of proposals must be considered during the appraisal stage, before significant funds are committed. This is to ensure that the outcome envisaged in the appraisal is close to what eventually happens. A good example of the application of cost effectivenss analysis is the Department of Health Meningitis C vaccination programme. Decisions had to be made about the best policy response and the likely impact on quality of life which is notoriously difficult to quantify **(Box 3.9)**.

---

**Box 3.9:    The Department of Health's Meningitis C Vaccination Programme**

1. Meningitis C is a very serious illness that causes an inflammation of the lining of the brain. During the 1990s the number of confirmed cases of the disease began to increase **(Figure 1)** and during 1998 the disease resulted in some 150 deaths mainly amongst children and adolescents. Of those who survived the disease around one in four suffered complications such as amputation, brain damage and deafness.

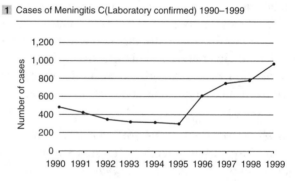

**1** Cases of Meningitis C(Laboratory confirmed) 1990–1999

*Source:* PHLS Meningococcal Reference unit.

2. In response to the impact and growth of Meningitis C the Department of Health (the Department) in July 1999 announced the development of a new safe and effective vaccine and a vaccination programme with the objective of reducing the greatest number of cases and deaths in the shortest possible time. The programme was implemented one year ahead of schedule.

3. The Department administered some 18 million vaccinations between November 1999 and December 2000 and co-ordinated their work with some 29,000 schools, 100 health authorities and around 30,000 General Practitioners. The vaccination programme was the largest since the introduction of the polio vaccine in the 1950s and cost some £300 million including the cost of the vaccine, the cost

of delivering the programme through General Practitioners and nurses, and the costs of an information campaign. It also involved the Department managing a complex pattern of stakeholders.

4. Resources to treat illness and disease are finite and consequently the Department have to set priorities in healthcare to ensure they achieve value for money. The Department examined the costs that would be involved in a vaccination programme with the likely gains in health of:

   • In terms of the additional life years of the people who would no longer be likely to die from the disease;
   • The increased quality of life of those who would not suffer resulting disabilities such as amputation and deafness;
   • The cost in purchasing and delivering the vaccine;
   • The cost savings through reductions in the number of hospital admissions and long term treatment of those who suffered disabilities caused by the disease.

5. The Department identified that it would cost some £1,400 for each year a potential victim remained free from disability as a result of immunisation. The Department compared the cost effectiveness of the vaccination programme with other forms of healthcare intervention that had been assessed using the same criteria and were able to conclude that a vaccination programme delivered good value for money.

*Source: Modern Policy Making: Ensuring Policies Deliver Value for Money.* Report by the Comptroller and Auditor General (HC 289, Session 2001–2002).

Value for money therefore depends not only on policy design, although this is clearly very important, but also on how a policy is implemented – the 'cost effectiveness' dimension referred to above. Since the 1980s in particular, governments have contended with the issue of how best to deliver policies that are cost effective and meet citizens' needs and expectations. This has manifested itself in different models but unifying themes are:

• the separation of policy formulation from implementation (the latter becoming the responsibility of semi autonomous agencies operating at arms length) – the premise being that the skill sets of those involved in policy making is not necessarily the same as that required to secure successful implementation;

- increasing use of markets and competition in the provision of public services (e.g. contracting out and other market type mechanisms); and,
- much more emphasis on performance, outputs, and customer needs.

In New Zealand for example, the State Sector Act 1988 and the Public Finance Act 1989 struck a new framework of relationships between parties involved in public management. With its pronounced emphasis on performance it also rapidly altered the way the public service looked and operated. Ministers became explicitly responsible for achieving key policy outcomes and entered into formal purchase agreements with the chief executives of departments whose responsibility was to deliver a series of outputs at a specified cost. Achievement against these output targets is reported annually together with departments' financial statements and are formally audited by the Office of the Auditor General **(Box 3.10)**. This emphasis on managing for results surfaced in other countries. In the USA for instance the Government Performance and Results (GPRA) Act 1993 requires each Federal agency to develop a strategic plan to lay out its mission, long term goals and objectives and strategies for achieving them.

---

**Box 3.10:    New Zealand experience: A structured approach to achieving value for money: Ministry of Education – Te Tahuhu o te Matauranga**

- The New Zealand public sector reforms of the late 1980s and early 1990s required public bodies to adopt a much more structured framework to achieving desired policy outcomes.
- Parliament votes money for specific outcomes. In 2004–05 the Ministry of Education had 10 classes of outputs ranging from purchasing services to deliver education for children to the administration of education regulations.
- Each output class is supported by a statement of service performance together with dimensions of performance which have to be achieved – covering three aspects the quality, quantity and timeliness of delivery as well as associated costs.

- A statement of key outcome achievements is produced each year for example – 2004/05 the Ministry reported progress in reducing in equalities in education outcomes particularly in terms of improved education achievement by Maori and Pasifa students. This is presented in some detail below:

PARTICIPATION AND FIVE-YEAR COMPLETION RATES FOR MĀORI, PASIFIKA AND ALL FORMAL DOMESTIC STUDENTS 2003

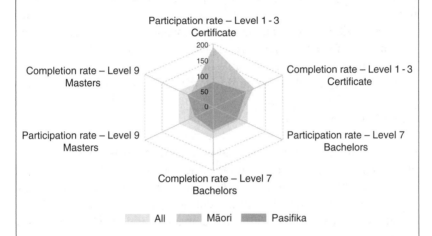

- The external auditors, in this case Ernst and Young acting on behalf of the Controller and Auditor General consider the service performance achievements claimed and for 2004–05 reported that 'the financial statements fairly reflect its service performance achievements measured against the performance targets',

*Commentary: This is a much more structured approach to setting out policy aims and objectives and reporting achievement in a systematic way. It illustrates, however, that reducing required outputs to a concise single definition that is meaningful is often very difficult. And while some attempt is made to report outcome achievement the measures used are essentially intermediate ones - in this case participation rates and are not covered by the Auditor General's audit opinion.*

*Source:* New Zealand Ministry of Education *Annual Report 2005 – http://www.minedu.govnt.nz.*

GPRA defines a performance goal as the target level of performance (either output or outcome) expressed as a tangible, measurable objective, against which achievement is to be compared. If performance goals cannot be expressed in quantitative terms, GPRA allows the Office of Management and Budget (the USA Federal Agency responsible for Finance) to authorise an alternative form of a goal, including a description of a successful and minimally effective programme or other criteria, both stated with enough precision to permit independent assessment of performance.[13]

Since 1998, UK government departments have agreed, alongside the allocation of resources, national targets in the form of Public Service Agreements specifying measurable outcomes that departments strive to achieve. These targets cascade down the delivery chains of organisations involved in public services in the form of more localised targets supported by performance measures.

How is the external auditor to assess the implementation of the planned outputs and outcomes that emerge from cost-benefit and cost-effectiveness analysis – or from the policy decisions of the government that are not based on the use of these techniques but simply represent a response to ideological commitment or immediate pressures. These are often embarked upon with limited analysis or, indeed, scarcely any analysis at all.

The answer that has emerged over the last 20–30 years is, 'By value for money auditing'.

## 3.5    VALUE FOR MONEY AUDITING

What do we mean by value for money audit and what is it seeking to achieve? The widely accepted standard definition is that it is about economy, efficiency and effectiveness. In the UK the 1983 National Audit Act states that the Comptroller and Auditor General may 'carry out examinations into the economy, efficiency and effectiveness with which any (government department or other relevant body) has used its resources in discharging its functions'. The Act does not define these terms but **Box 3.11** illustrates how they have been widely interpreted. They embrace principles of economics in their inherent assumptions about the need to be able to quantify relevant costs and benefits in forming reliable judgements about value for money. It is, however, the effectiveness dimension that is closest to cost benefit and cost effectiveness in its concern

---

[13] Government Accountability Office *GGO-96-66R Performance Reports* (February 1996).

with outcome achievement, and effectiveness can be defined to incorporate a concern for such values as, for example, environmental protection, equity, and other ethical standards.

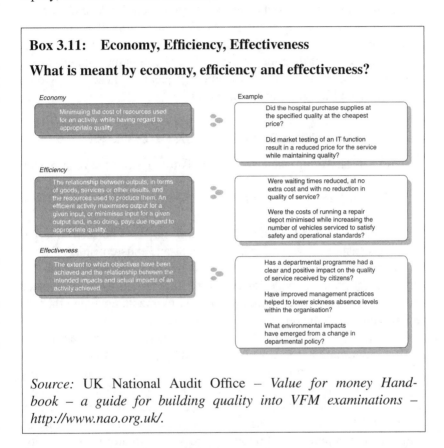

**Box 3.11:   Economy, Efficiency, Effectiveness**

**What is meant by economy, efficiency and effectiveness?**

*Economy*

Minimising the cost of resources used for an activity, while having regard to appropriate quality

*Example*

Did the hospital purchase supplies at the specified quality at the cheapest price?

Did market testing of an IT function result in a reduced price for the service while maintaining quality?

*Efficiency*

The relationship between outputs, in terms of goods, services or other results, and the resources used to produce them. An efficient activity maximises output for a given input, or minimises input for a given output and, in so doing, pays due regard to appropriate quality.

Were waiting times reduced, at no extra cost and with no reduction in quality of service?

Were the costs of running a repair depot minimised while increasing the number of vehicles serviced to satisfy safety and operational standards?

*Effectiveness*

The extent to which objectives have been achieved and the relationship between the intended impacts and actual impacts of an activity achieved.

Has a departmental programme had a clear and positive impact on the quality of service received by citizens?

Have improved management practices helped to lower sickness absence levels within the organisation?

What environmental impacts have emerged from a change in departmental policy?

*Source:* UK National Audit Office – *Value for money Handbook – a guide for building quality into VFM examinations – http://www.nao.org.uk/.*

Value for money, or 'performance audit' as it is known in some countries, owes much to the traditional types of public audit discussed at the beginning of this chapter. This is particularly so in the importance it attaches to reliable and comprehensive evidence which should ideally be capable of standing up to legal challenge, reflecting the legal origins of traditional public audit. This prerequisite is reflected in the principles of standards of practice which most public audit offices follow in carrying out value for money work. For example, the NAO adheres to eight principles which sum up the fundamental qualities and characteristics that should mark our value for money work namely: competence, integrity, rigour, objectivity and independence, accountability, adding value, perseverance, and clear communication. The International Organisation of Supreme

Audit Institutions (INTOSAI) has similarly issued guidelines for undertaking performance and value for money audits which are widely adhered to.[14]

Two defining characteristics have emerged from the development of value for money audit over the last 20–30 years: a much greater focus on outcome achievement and the application of a much wider and sophisticated range of diagnostic and analytical techniques underpinning assessments of value for money, and consequently a need to rely on a much more multidisciplinary skill set.

## 3.6   GREATER FOCUS ON OUTCOMES

One way of analysing value for money is to consider the relationship between inputs, outputs and outcomes (**Box 3.12**). This is usually presented as a linear relationship but often the distinction between output and outcome is imprecise. For example, obtaining a good university degree may be classed as an 'output' but it may also be seen as a reasonable measure of educational attainment and thus considered to be an 'outcome'. What is clear, however, is that the outcomes which citizens expect public services and governments to deliver and influence are now more numerous. Often stimulated by media coverage there is greater interest in the quality of public services.

People are also more concerned about sustainability and the impact on the environment for current and future generation, globalisation and its implications for economic performance and national security, and diversity and the extent to which people are not discriminated against because of their age, gender, disability, sexuality or where they live. In all these areas governments are increasingly active either as regulator, direct deliverer of public services or facilitator in establishing arrangements in which others can deliver services through public funding.

A brief overview of different audit offices' mandates illustrate that public audit is focusing more on outcome achievement. The Netherlands Court of Audit (the Algemene Rekenhamer) in its strategy for 2004–2009[15] highlighted the growing gap between policy formulation and implementation. This is now a important aspect of its work focusing

---

[14] Implementation guidelines for performance auditing: standards and guidelines for performance auditing based on INTOSAI's Auditing Standards and practical experience (http://www .intosai.org).

[15] Algemene Rekenkamer *Performance and operation of Public Administration Strategy 2004–2009* (http://www.rekenkamer.nl).

## Box 3.12:    Relationship between inputs, outputs and outcomes

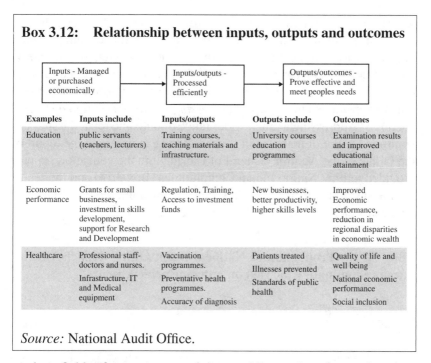

| | | | | |
|---|---|---|---|---|
| Inputs - Managed or purchased economically | → | Inputs/outputs - Processed efficiently | → | Outputs/outcomes - Prove effective and meet peoples needs |

| Examples | Inputs include | Inputs/outputs | Outputs include | Outcomes |
|---|---|---|---|---|
| Education | public servants (teachers, lecturers) | Training courses, teaching materials and infrastructure. | University courses education programmes | Examination results and improved educational attainment |
| Economic performance | Grants for small businesses, investment in skills development, support for Research and Development | Regulation, Training, Access to investment funds | New businesses, better productivity, higher skills levels | Improved Economic performance, reduction in regional disparities in economic wealth |
| Healthcare | Professional staff- doctors and nurses. Infrastructure, IT and Medical equipment | Vaccination programmes. Preventative health programmes. Accuracy of diagnosis | Patients treated Illnesses prevented Standards of public health | Quality of life and well being National economic performance Social inclusion |

*Source:* National Audit Office.

on three fields of government activity – public services (care, education, work and income); security (security in living and working environments, food safety and combating terrorism); and sustainable development (sustainable energy, sustainable use of natural resources and biodiversity). The Brazilian Federal Audit Court has a fourth 'e': to report on equality in the implementation of government programmes. The Office of the Auditor General in Canada was at the forefront of championing environmental reporting to Parliament. These are but just a few examples of how audit mandates are being interpreted in new ways.

In the UK the proportion of NAO reports which consider outcome achievement has continued to increase over the last eight years (**Box 3.13**) and have covered a wide range of issues. An example is the focus on quality of public services such as my report to Parliament on Britain's railway stations which found that passenger satisfaction with railway stations had only marginally improved in recent years and still remained low for many stations and for many of the facilities provided at them.[16] The report *Reducing Brain Damage: faster access to better*

---

[16] Comptroller and Auditor General *Maintaining and Improving Britain's Railway Stations* (HC 132, Session 2005–2006).

*stroke care*[17] highlighted the improvement in outcomes that could be achieved if patients were given rapid access to brain scanning, treated in a specialised stroke unit and given early access to rehabilitation services. Equality of treatment and inclusion is also an important aspect of quality of service and the success of government policies to achieve this were evaluated in my report *Delivering Public Services to a Diverse Society*.[18] Addressing a much wider range of outcome related issues is a common feature of many audit offices. Good examples are the report of the Office of the Auditor General of Canada into the education support provided to First Nation Indian Communities **(Box 3.14)** and the report by the Australian National Audit Office into aviation security following the events of 11 September 2001 **(Box 3.15)**.

---

**Box 3.13:    Proportion of National Audit Office Reports which are predominately focused on outcome achievement**

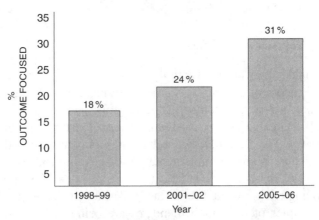

Commentary *The analysis focuses on reports which almost exclusively examine outcome achievement. Other reports cover outcome issues but not exclusively.*

*Source:* UK National Audit Office – websit *http://www.nao.org.uk/*.

---

[17] Comptroller and Auditor General *Reducing Brain Damage: Faster Access to Better Stroke Care* (HC 452, Session 2005–2006).

[18] Comptroller and Auditor General *Delivering Public Services to a Diverse Society* (HC 19, Session 2004–2005).

---

**Box 3.14:    Indian and Northern Affairs Canada – Education programme and Post-Secondary Student Support**

In Canada most First Nations communities are small with fewer than 500 residents. Thus their schools have difficulty providing a range of educational services. Around 40 percent of the Registered Indian population is under the age of 19 compared with 25 percent for the Canadian population. In 2004 the Office of the Auditor General of Canada examined the support provided to First Nation students and reported that:

> A significant education gap exists between First Nations people living on reserves and the Canadian population as a whole and that the time estimated to close this gap has increased slightly from about 27 to 28 years. The number of First Nations people having a post-secondary certificate, diploma, or degree continues to grow. The way [the Department] allocates funds to First Nations does not ensure equitable access to as many student as possible and the Department does not know if the funds allocated have been used for the purpose intended.

*Source:* Office of the Auditor General of Canada/Bureau du verficateur general du Canada *November 2004 Report* http://www.oag-bvg.gc.ca.

---

**Box 3.15:    Aviation Security in Australia**

The Australian Audit Office previously audited aviation security in 1998. Following the events of 11 September 2001 it carried out a further evaluation of the Department of Transport and Regional Development's action to strengthen Australia's aviation security regime. Overall the Audit Office found that the Department had responded well to the events of 11 September. The report concluded, however, that:

> As the body with regulatory responsibilities, the Department could show more pro-active leadership to effectively engage the various organisations and people involved in delivering aviation security, particularly as security relies on everyone playing their part to ensure an effective outcome. The greatest challenge for the Department particularly in light of recent events is to effectively encourage a stronger security culture throughout the industry. The Department can demonstrate

stronger leadership by setting, monitoring and reviewing performance targets for industry, and by using a wider range of management strategies to encourage industry to achieve them. In this context, progress in implementing the recommendations from the 1998 audit has been limited. Instead, the Departments' efforts have been focused on modernising the aviation security regulatory framework.

*Source:* Australian NAO Report No 26 *Aviation Security in Australia 2002–2003* http://www.anao.gov.au.

## 3.7    MORE SOPHISTICATED DIAGNOSTIC AND ANALYTICAL TECHNIQUES

The evaluation of value for money towards much greater focus on the achievement, outputs and outcomes of government programmes has required auditors to draw on a much wider range of techniques. This may include re-performing for evaluative purposes the cost-benefit and cost-effectiveness analyses that governments have used in designing programmes. Where these techniques have not been employed, the auditor may use them himself to evaluate the implementation of the policy options that have been chosen.

This is best illustrated by two examples. In the 1950s a review of defence projects would largely rely on two sources of evidence: file examination and interviews. The auditor would map and describe the events or circumstances leading to a decision or action. Where there was underperformance the aim would be to ascertain the intervention that was largely responsible. In the defence sector a key skill was understanding contract management and this was largely acquired through experience. There was very little reliance on specialist expertise, comparative analysis or qualitative data. A typical evaluation of a defence project today is very different. An appraisal of contract and project management would still be important but in addition the auditor would routinely seek to get the views of those required to use to the equipment to seek assurance over its operational fit for purpose. Specialist technical advice would be sought and a range of data would be triangulated to corroborate conclusions about performance and benefits. A comparison between a review of the procurement of the Swift Aircraft in 1955 and the Bowman Combat Infrastructure Platform in 2006 illustrates the difference in approach very well (**Box 3.16**).

**Box 3.16:    How the evidence base for value for money examinations has developed and expanded**

| Procurement of the Swift Aircraft – 1955 | The Bowman Combat Infrastructure Platform – 2006 |
|---|---|

A contract was placed in 1950 to procure 492 Swift aircraft. The order was subsequently reduced to 170 in 1955 largely because the first 39 aircraft delivered were not up to the standard required for squadron service. The Exchequer and Audit Department (the predecessor to the National Audit Office) investigated why the Ministry of Defence could not seek financial compensation from the supplier for the aircraft not meeting the required specification. The investigation found that:

- The contract specification was too vague and indefinite to support any claims for breach of contract.
- Any claim had been further irreparably damaged by the acceptance by the Ministry both of the proto type and a number of production aircraft.

Bowman is a £2.4 billion programme to transform battlefield communications command and control through the introduction of Bowman digital radios and the advanced Combat Infrastructure Platform (CIP). This study addressed issues around the deliverability of the project and its fit for purpose. The methodology consisted of:

**Setting best practice principles** in programme management: These were used as a baseline against which to evaluate the Bowman project.

**Observation:** Observing the field trials of Bowman CIP equipment and assessing the outcome from Army field trial and operational reports.

**Data analysis.** An evidence database was established which brought together hundreds of documents connected directly or indirectly to the Bowman CIP programme (these included operational field trial reports, through life management plan, concept of use and acceptance and release documents). The database was used to generate specific evaluative questions to programme participants.

**Structured interviews:** Including users of Bowman and contractors and other stakeholders.

The methodology used in this study was fairly limited focusing on:

(i) A review of the contract conditions
(ii) File examination of decisions taken and legal advice sought
(iii) Interviews with key officials

**Photographic and aural evidence:** This was focused on understanding the difficulties of converting land vehicles to Bowman, and on training facilities to understand the computer based initial training on the system.

**Overseas evidence:** Including experience from programmes in Battlefield Digitisation in Canada and the USA.

**Specialist advice:** Systems Consultants Services Ltd, experts in military Command, Control, Communications, Computers and Intelligence systems were employed to conduct an in-depth analysis of the Ministry of Defence's analysis (effectively, why the equipment was needed and what benefits it would bring).

**Triangulation:** Undertook triangulation of all evidence gathered to corroborate emerging findings and conclusions.

*Source: Third Report of the Committee of Public Accounts 1956–1957 HC 243.*

*Source: Delivering Digital Tactical Communications through the Bowman CIP Programme –* Report by the Comptroller and Auditor General HC 1050 Session 2005–2006.

A more recent comparison in the welfare sector of two reports on the Social Fund, which provides loans and grants to people to meet important or emergency expenses they cannot pay out of their regular income **(Box 3.17),** demonstrates how value for money audit continues to develop, drawing on the disciplines of cost benefit and effectiveness analysis, economics, public choice theory and social anthropology. Inevitably, this evolution is requiring reliance on a much wider skill set than traditional audit.

**Box 3.17:    Shifting the focus of VFM audit: The Social Fund**

Around one-fifth of people in the United Kingdom live in low income households and over a quarter of households have no savings. The Social Fund (the Fund) was set up in 1988 and provides loans and grants to those in Great Britain who cannot meet important or emergency expenses out of regular income. It provides a safety net for some of the most vulnerable in society to enable them, for example, to afford household appliances or buy food if they have their benefit money stolen. The NAO has reported twice on the Social Fund – in 1991 and 2005:

| 1991 | 2005 |
|---|---|
| In 1991 the focus was primarily on the economic objectives of the Fund and the efficiency of the processes for distributing the funds. The report commented on the success in containing expenditure. There was interest in targeting on those in greatest need but the report acknowledged that there was limited understanding in this area in the absence of research which the Department of Social Security had only just started to commission. | In 2005 there was greater focus on the whether the Fund was meeting the needs of those facing greatest difficult managing their income. There was more attention paid to the targeting of particular social groups and more attempt to show how a Social Fund loan was the cheapest available to people on low incomes compared to a range of other options. The report also included detailed analysis of geographical variations in outcomes. One major difference in the methodology was use of research by others which helped to broaden the evidence base around the consequences of the use of the Social Fund. |
| *Source: The Social Fund,* Report by Comptroller and Auditor General, HC 190 1990–1991. | *Source: Helping Those in Financial Hardship: The Running of the Social Fund,* Report by Comptroller and Auditor General (HC 179, Session 2004–2005). |

## 3.8   SUMMARY

In summary, what conclusions can we draw from this chapter? In classic systems theory bureaucracies are a complex web of inter relationships both organisational and individual. Traditional public audit seeks to give some transparency to bureaucracies' financial operations and acts to mitigate a natural tendency to pursue individual and organisational self interests at the expense of public welfare. Its support for values such as probity, propriety and good stewardship may help to sustain these civil service cultures which are motivated by a concern for the proper use of public money. This is, however, not enough.

Money may be spent legally, but the outcomes may be disappointing. Governments have often – though by no means always – tried to secure better results by employing cost-benefit and cost-effectiveness techniques. And auditors have sought to appraise the value for money of employing these techniques, as well as evaluating the implementation of policies that are based on ideological commitments or immediate pressures, by examining the economy, efficiency and effectiveness with which policies have been carried out.

Much has been achieved by this approach to value for money auditing. But it is not the final answer, as the next chapter will show.

# 4

# How Effective Audit can be Secured – The Auditor as Coach and Mentor Rather than Critic and Nark

It is often alleged that auditors have little to contribute to organisational improvement and the challenge of finding new ways to deliver public services which meet people's needs at a price as taxpayers they are prepared to pay. A common perception is that auditors are unduly preoccupied with the minutiae of financial analysis and that their innate conservatism steers them to focus on cost reductions and to be risk averse rather than championing new and innovative ways of doing things. As the previous chapter has shown, this need not be the case. Certainly auditors have considerable scope to influence outcomes and behaviours in the way they provide legitimacy to certain actions. The trick is how to marshall such influence in a way that achieves transparency and accountability while also being a force for good. In this chapter I explore ways in which this important goal can be achieved.

In spite of the successes achieved, particularly in its analysis and reporting of outcome achievement, public sector auditing still faces problems. 'Economy', 'efficiency' and 'effectiveness' require fresh definition for every new study. Different meanings are required for studies concerned, say, with the implementation of agricultural policies as compared with defence policies. And who is to define the terms 'economy', 'efficiency' and 'effectiveness': auditor or auditee? Prime facie, it should be the auditee, because the auditee determines the policy outcomes that are desired and has responsibility for seeking to achieve them. But in many cases this is not done, or is done in such general terms that almost whatever happens may be said to be the desired outcome. Examples in **Box 4.1** show how some British Government policies have been open to this criticism. It has, of course, ever been so and some policies by their nature do not lend themselves to much precision in terms of measurable outcomes. A general concept, 'justice' for example, may be

**Box 4.1: Lack of clarity in policy formulation can make meaningful assessments of outcome achievement difficult**

The UK Treasury negotiates three year Public Service Agreements (PSA) with each major department of State. Each PSA sets out the department's high-level aim, priority objectives and key performance targets. These targets are intended to help direct resources to achieve major policy objectives. However, if these targets are inaccurately defined or lack precision or focus, it can be difficult to evaluate achievement and ultimately value for money.

| Sector | Public Sector Agreement Target | Commentary |
|---|---|---|
| Housing | 'Achieve a better balance between housing availability and the demand for housing, including improving affordability, in all English regions while protecting valuable countryside around our towns, cities and in the green belt and the sustainability of towns and cities.' | 1. Lack of clarity as to what is to be achieved including multiple targets that involve trade-offs.<br>2. The target is not directly measurable. |
| Sustainable Development | 'To promote sustainable development across government and in the UK and internationally, as measured by:<br>• the achievement of positive trends in the Government's headline indicators of sustainable development; | 1. The data system underlying the target contains over 60 separate indicators making it very difficult to determine whether the target has been met. |

| | | |
|---|---|---|
| | • *the UK's progress towards delivering the World Summit on Sustainable Development commitments, notably in the areas of sustainable consumption and production, chemicals, biodiversity, oceans, fisheries and agriculture; and*<br>• *progress towards internationally agreed commitments to tackle climate change.'* | 2. Despite being solely owned by the Department for Environment, Food and Rural Affairs, the Department has minimal attributable influence over performance – which in turn weakens accountability arrangements. |
| Sustainable Communities | *'Reduce race inequalities and build community cohesion.'* | 1. The outcomes targeted by the Department lack of clear definitions for 'race inequalities' and 'community cohesion'. |

| | | |
|---|---|---|
| International Development | *'By 2008, deliver improved effectiveness of UK and international support for conflict prevention by addressing long-term structural causes of conflict, managing regional and national tension and violence, and supporting post-conflict reconstruction, where the UK can make a significant contribution, in particular Africa, Asia, Balkans and the Middle East.'* | 1. The target contains multiple performance concepts that are not clearly defined and are difficult to measure.<br><br>2. The Departments have only limited influence over performance against the target.<br><br>3. There are measurement challenges within the target including requiring the Departments to measure effectiveness in addressing the 'long-term structural causes of conflict' within the three year lifespan of the target. |
| Foreign policy | *'To promote sustainable development, underpinned by democracy, good governance and human rights, particularly through effective delivery of programmes in these and related fields.'* | 1. Target is broad and vague<br><br>2. Difficult to assess and attribute underpinning measures to the Foreign and Commonwealth Office action. Many indicators of improvement can arise from multiple actions for example e.g:<br><br>&bull; More countries implementing measures to increase access to information, public participation and access to justice on environmental matters.<br><br>&bull; Improved natural resource management.<br><br>&bull; An increase in the number of countries that have abolished the death penalty. |

*Source: www.hm-treasury.gov.uk/spending_review/spend_sr04/psa/spend_sr04_psaindex.cfm.*

well defined in a general way but be difficult to apply – and may need different approaches in different contexts. And so a multiple range of outcomes may emerge. Time factors also come into play as many years can elapse before discernible outcomes can be evaluated. Programmes intended to promote the well being and development of preschool children such as Sure Start in the UK and Head Start in the USA are good examples. The impact of such investment in terms of educational attainment and social cohesion cannot be fully determined until much later in the life of those intended to benefit. But this should not mean that the auditor abandons the whole enterprise!

In the previous chapter I discussed how value for money audit has its origins firmly in financial audit. This influence has led to a strong bias in favour of quantitative analysis: the prices of goods and services, the sampling of citizens' reactions, and linkages between phenomena derived from regression analysis. All these are valuable yet many aspects of performance require a mix of both quantitative and qualitative assessments, for instance how do we assess the effectiveness of an educational programme? We can certainly see how many students pass examinations but examinations are not the 'be-all and end-all' of education. Schumacher has made the point that focussing exclusively on quantifiable metrics and seeking to measure the immeasurable ultimately result in flawed judgements **(Box 4.2)**.

---

**Box 4.2:    Schumacher's Worries**

As long ago as 1973 E.F. Schumacher said in *Small is Beautiful*:

> To press non-economic values into the framework of the economic calculus, economists use the method of cost/benefit analysis. This is generally thought to be an enlightened and progressive development, as it is at least an attempt to take account of costs and benefits which might otherwise be disregarded altogether. In fact, however, it is a procedure by which the higher is reduced to the level of the lower and the priceless is given a price. It can therefore never serve to clarify the situation and lead to an enlightened decision. All it can do is lead to self-deception or the deception of others; for to undertake a measure the immeasurable is absurd and constitutes but an elaborate method of moving from preconceived notions to foregone conclusions . . . what is worse, and destructive of civilisation, is the pretence that everything has a price or, in other words, that money is the highest of all values.

*Source: Small is Beautiful – 'a study of economies as if people mattered' – first published in 1973 by Blanchard Briggs Ltd.*

---

We do not have to accept this line of argument in full to appreciate the way in which the monetary value of qualitative factors provides an avenue through which concealed value judgements can be smuggled into an analysis to produce results that may be presented as 'objective' but are in fact based on subjective standards. In the last resort, all such valuations are 'subjective' – yet the danger here lies less in the 'subjectivity' rather than in the fact the values may be concealed by the figures. Too often audit reports appear to make sense and are accepted by auditees, but then fail to change behaviour in the promised way. The auditor is found making the same recommendations and getting the same acceptance year after year. Thus audit reports often fail to satisfy those for whom they are designed, such as elected politicians, concerned citizens, suppliers of goods and services, the media, academic audiences, and, above all, the public servants with whom their ultimate relevance for action lies.

An example of this phenomenon is the series of reports which the NAO has published over the last 15 years on the performance of IT enabled change projects **(Box 4.3)**. These explored the reasons for underperformance and, drawing on good practice from across the private and public sectors, as well as internationally, recommended what needed to be done to manage risks better so that a successful outcome was more likely to be achieved. Despite this the UK public sector continues to experience major failures with adverse consequences for public services. For example, the problems encountered in 2005 and 2006 by the Rural Payments Agency which is responsible for processing payments due to farmers in England under the European Union's Single Payment Scheme arose from inadequacies, such as underestimating complexity, not having reliable contingency arrangements, and not ensuring IT and business processes were compatible, even though these were long since identified as key generic risks and warned against.

Of course, there are many factors explaining why IT enabled change encounters problems in both the public and the private sectors.[1] Complexity, technology which is not yet stable and continues to develop, and the scale of change are all contributory factors. The risks associated with each of these and how best to handle them are all well documented, as are the principles of sound programme and project management which need to be adhered to. But for some reason the same mistakes are repeated. The key to the solution is to inspire those who are critical to

---

[1] The Standish Group in the United States report published in 2003 identified that of 13,522 IT projects from both the private and public sectors,only a third were successful.

implementing the desired change to have the confidence to manage risks, to be intelligent clients of industry, and to secure support from all those affected by the change programme, including frontline workers and intended beneficiaries.

## 4.1   HOW CAN PROGRESS BE MADE?

How can auditors stack the odds in their favour so that as well as promoting transparency in the use of public money their reports have a real impact in achieving sustainable improvements in value for money? Our experience suggests there are three ways forward: firstly, using separate methodologies for separate subjects, thus ensuring the best fit between the methodological approach and the subject of evaluation; secondly, focusing on the meanings which participants give to their roles; and, thirdly, for the auditor to act as coach and mentor rather than critic and nark. These are not options. Each approach complements the others and it is the combination of the three that gives the auditor the best chance of making meaningful recommendations. In my discussion of these approaches I use the terms effectiveness audit and evaluation interchangeably as in essence they are broadly the same particularly with what has become knows as 'dialogic evaluation.'[2] Indeed, Richard Laughlin, Jane Broadbent and Jas Gill in their research on evaluating Public Finance Initiative deals highlight the close similarities in approaches adopted by evaluators and value for money auditors.[3]

## 4.2   SEPARATE METHODOLOGIES FOR SEPARATE SUBJECTS

The first way forward is to use separate methodologies for separate subjects. Thus the audit of a programme for training pilots could be derived from an examination of the physical and psychological challenges that pilots must undergo in their professional work. Similarly, the audit of a scheme for the promotion of law and order in a local community will need to be sensitive to the sociology of the area and the thoughts and

---

[2] At the heart of dialogic evaluation is a focus on building and sharing meaning. 'In a post modern world there are multiple legitimate perspectives on human experience and multiple defensible standards for making judgments'. This requires auditors and evaluators to engage in the moral-political complexities, uncertainties and pluralities of modern society – *Evaluation: Special Issue: Dialogue in Evaluation* **7**(2), April 2001.

[3] Laughlin R., Broadbent J., Gill J. (2003) 'Evaluating the private finance initiative in the National Health Service in the UK' *Journal of Accounting, Audit and Accountability* **16**(3).

**Box 4.3: Good practice is accepted but not always implemented**

Over the last 15 years the NAO has published numerous reports, four examples are given below, on the performance of IT enabled change projects and made many recommendations on how good practice should be applied (in spite of this the performance of IT projects remains mixed).

| Report | Background | Findings | Key principle of good practice |
|---|---|---|---|
| Ministry of Defence: Support Information Technology HC 644 1990–91 | In the late 1980s the Ministry of Defence was beginning to invest considerable sums in information technology to support managers and commanders at all levels in their decision making and control roles. | All nine systems had suffered delays from five months to two years, postponing achievement of predicted benefits. Of the four systems subjected to post implementation review, only one had achieved all intended financial and operational benefits. | Clear definitions of user requirements are important before going ahead with projects. Larger complex projects should be broken down into shorter more manageable tranches Post implementation reviews are crucial in ensuring that expected benefits have been achieved and in identifying lessons for the future. |

| | | | |
|---|---|---|---|
| The Immigration and Nationality Directorate Casework Programme HC 277 1998–99 | The Immigration and Nationality Directorate of the Home Office operate immigration controls at ports and process applications from people who have already entered the UK who wish to apply for citizenship, seek asylum, or extend their stay. In April 1996 the Directorate let a contract for a privately financed business change initiative which depended heavily on IT | Considerably delay was experienced in the full implementation of the Casework Programme resulting in backlog of cases – some 76,000 asylum cases and 100,000 nationality cases. | Departments should consider whether programmes of this kind might be too ambitious to be attempted in one go. It is crucial that departments think through the structure of their deals. Departments should always take a close interest in arrangements with sub-contractors, and the firms under which sub-contractors are employed should align the incentives and penalties placed on all service providers to ensure that the project objectives are achieved. |

| New IT Systems for Magistrates' Courts: the LIBRA project, HC 327 2002–03 | This project known as LIBRA was intended to provide a national IT infrastructure and facilitate office automation including standard office software such as e-mail, word processing, spreadsheets and diaries. The original post contract award (July 1998) budget was £146 million but by May 2000 it had risen to £319 million. | The Lord Chancellor's Department procured a contract to provide services to 42 Magistrates, Courts Committees over which it did not have real authority or control, it ran a poor competition, attracting only one bidder, and it failed to take decisive action when the contractor did not deliver what was required. The Department chose to develop IT to support existing processes rather than redesigning business processes in parallel with new IT. This approach contributed to the project's difficulties because the Department was unable to achieve a single view of requirement for the new system across Magistrates, Courts Committees. | IT system changes should be planned to support redesigned business processes. Undertaking one without the other is unlikely to deliver value for money. Standardising IT systems across a number of disparate bodies is only likely to be effective if the appropriate business units work closely together When a department unavoidably finds itself in a single tender situation it should take special care to ensure that value for money is not put at risk. Precautionary measures might for example, include developing a 'should cost' model to assess the reasonableness of a bid. Departments should have up to date contingency plans ready on all major contracts so that there is a fall back position if and when a contract goes wrong. |

| Department for Environment, Food and Rural Affairs, and Rural Payments Agency. The Delays in Administrating the 2005 Single Payment Scheme HC 1631 2005–2006. | Implementation of this scheme had cost £122.3 million by the end of March 2006. The Rural Payments Agency encountered difficulties in processing payments due to farmers under the scheme, totalling around £1,515 million, and failed to meet its own target to pay 96 percent of that sum by the end of March 2006. | The Agency had anticipated that the development of the core IT infrastructure would be complete by December 2004. By this date, however, the Agency had identified 23 changes to the computer systems under development largely to incorporate changes to EU Regulations.<br><br>The Agency implemented key aspects of the IT system without adequate assurance that every component was fully compatible with the rest of the system and supporting business processes.<br><br>Despite limited confidence that the system would be ready on time, development work on the computer system continued and no contingency plan was invoked. | With complex IT projects on which key services depend reliable contingency arrangements need to be in place and tested.<br><br>Close alignment between business and IT development is essential. Structures and governance arrangements for managing complex IT enabled change projects need to be carefully thought through. |

*Source: National Audit Office.*

experiences of those who live there. The key principle underpinning this approach is that those intended to act on the recommendations arising from a value for money report are more likely to do so if they believe in, and see the relevance of, what it is saying. Achieving this requires comprehensive knowledge of the environment and operating framework within which public servants interact on a daily basis. Some understanding of their culture and values is also needed so that recommendations can be framed in a way that reflects their core beliefs. Simply seeking to impose the auditor's perspective even though it may be highly rational and logical is unlikely to be enough. Talmage (**Box 4.4**) illustrates four ways in which an auditor might seek to analyse public programmes, each drawing on different intellectual insights, requiring different audit approaches and leading to different kinds of results:

• the experimentalist approach;
• the eclectic approach;
• the descriptive approach;
• and cost-benefit analysis.

Firstly, the *experimentalist* approach: the auditor acting independently is seeking to establish linkages between cause and effect, for example whether a series of measures is having an impact on reducing school truancy, and to do so in a way which mirrors scientific principles. It is usually not practical for the auditor to establish a 'controlled situation' where the cause and effect hypothesis can be tested to assess its validity.

Much effort is usually needed, however, to establish the external validity of the findings in the real world and this is often done by mapping the range of externalities – in the case of school absence these might be parental attitudes, socio economic factors, curriculum and quality of school buildings – and then seeking to place a value in some way on their relative importance to the outcome. This might be done through observation, and using other well established methods of measurements from other disciplines such as building design quality indicators. An example of an experimentalist approach is a review of the training of fighter aircraft pilots by the Ministry of Defence (**Box 4.5**). There are many factors which are likely to result in a highly effective aircraft pilot. The auditor had to identify and categorise the various variables and seek to explore their relationship with the likely impact on pilot performance and skill level: it was not simply the quality of training. It was not possible to establish a 'control situation' but through a mix

Box 4.4:  Talmage 1982 – Cited in D. Stufflebeam and W. Webster 'An Analysis of Alternative Approaches to Evaluation' 1983 Four methodological Approaches in Programme Evaluation

| | Experimentalists | Eclectics | Describers | Benefit-Cost Analysers |
|---|---|---|---|---|
| Philosophical Base | Positivist | Modified Positivist to pragmatic | Phenomenological | Logical/analytic |
| Disciplinary Base | Psychology | Psychology; sociology; political science | Sociology; anthropology | Economics; accounting |
| Focus of methodology | Identify casual links | Augment search for casual links with process and contextual data | Describe programme holistically and from the perspective of participants | Judge worth of program in terms of cost and benefits |
| Methodology | Experimental and quasi-experimental design | Quasi-experimental designs; case studies; descriptions | Ethnography; case studies; participant observation; triangulation | Benefit-cost analysis |
| Variables | Predetermined as input-output | Predetermined plus emerging | Emerging in course of evaluation | Predetermined |

| | Yes | Where possible | Not necessary | Yes |
|---|---|---|---|---|
| Control of comparison group | | | | |
| Participants' role in carrying out evaluation | None | None to interactive | Varies (may react to field notes) | None |
| Evaluator's Role | Independent of program | Cooperative | Interactive | Independent of program |
| Political pressures (internal-external) | Controlled in design' or ignored | Accommodated | Describe | Ignore |
| Possible scheme that may be evaluated by this methodology | Scheme for pilot training | Scheme for providing grants for agricultural improvements; scheme for encouraging faster access to medical care | Scheme for encouraging participation in programmes of local community improvement | Scheme for constructing roads; bridges; tunnels |

**Box 4.5:   Training new Pilots – A quasi experimentalist review**

Between 1994–95 and 1998–99 the UK Armed Services needed some 250 new pilots each year but some 45 a year (18 percent) fewer than needed entered operational service at the end of training. The NAO study addressed the reasons for this focussing on the major processes and factors influencing pilot training as set out below.

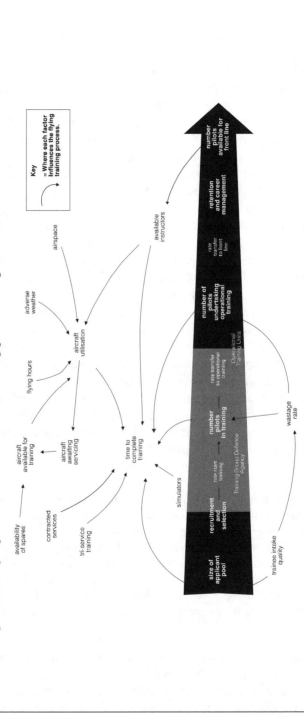

*Source: Training New Pilots* Report by the Comptroller and Auditor General (HC 880, Session 1999–2000).

of quantitative and qualitative data the auditor sought to validate the strength of the relationships.

A variation on experimental design is an *eclectic* approach to evaluation, as also shown in **Box 4.4**, which seeks to augment causal link analysis with much more contextual data and evidence. As compared with an experimentalist approach, an eclectic type study is likely to give greater prominence to viewpoints from a wider source. An example of this type of study is a report published by the NAO in 2005 on how to provide faster access to care for the medical condition known as stroke **(Box 4.6)**. The study drew on multiple perspectives, for example King's College London and the London School of Economics and Political Science carried out an economic 'burden of illness' study to calculate the cost of stroke to the wider economy; patients and their carers were consulted through web forum and focus groups; and a web survey was used to obtain the perspective of hospitals as well as the Royal College of Physicians.

The benefits of a wider evidence basis are the greater authority that the findings and recommendations assume and their acceptability to a larger group of stakeholders. In the case of this report the longer term benefits were more in changing attitudes to a condition which many including the medical profession considered to be essentially an illness of old age. Changing this perception – a quarter of all stroke patients are under 65 years of age – required a much wider focus on stakeholders as well as robust quantitative evidence. The impact of this study is perhaps best illustrated by the support which the recommendations received from the Minister of State responsible for care services who, in speaking to the press, said:

> The National Health Service (NHS) has made tremendous strides in tackling the two biggest killers: cancer and coronary heart disease. We have already made good progress on stroke, as the NAO acknowledges, but we too believe there is more to be done. Over 2,000 people suffer stroke each week – implementing the NAO's recommendations could save as many as an extra ten lives a week. We will take action immediately by spreading examples of best practice and will build a future generation of clinical champions through a programme to expand stroke physician training numbers.

The third approach in **Box 4.4** might be termed as *'describers'*. Here the auditor is primarily looking at value for money from the perspective of beneficiaries of a service or those delivering it. The basis for such an approach is largely anthropological with the focus on human behavioural and motivational issues. An example of this is work the NAO

**Box 4.6:    Reducing Brian Damage: Faster access to better stroke care – a quasi eclectic review**

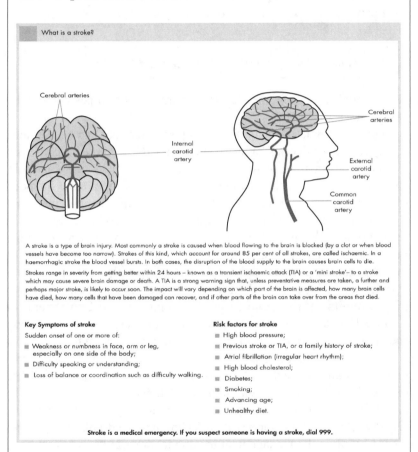

What is a stroke?

Cerebral arteries

Cerebral arteries

Internal carotid artery

External carotid artery

Common carotid artery

A stroke is a type of brain injury. Most commonly a stroke is caused when blood flowing to the brain is blocked (by a clot or when blood vessels have become too narrow). Strokes of this kind, which account for around 85 per cent of all strokes, are called ischaemic. In a haemorrhagic stroke the blood vessel bursts. In both cases, the disruption of the blood supply to the brain causes brain cells to die.

Strokes range in severity from getting better within 24 hours – known as a transient ischaemic attack (TIA) or a 'mini stroke'– to a stroke which may cause severe brain damage or death. A TIA is a strong warning sign that, unless preventative measures are taken, a further and perhaps major stroke, is likely to occur soon. The impact will vary depending on which part of the brain is affected, how many brain cells have died, how many cells that have been damaged can recover, and if other parts of the brain can take over from the areas that died.

**Key Symptoms of stroke**

Sudden onset of one or more of:

- Weakness or numbness in face, arm or leg, especially on one side of the body;
- Difficulty speaking or understanding;
- Loss of balance or coordination such as difficulty walking.

**Risk factors for stroke**

- High blood pressure;
- Previous stroke or TIA, or a family history of stroke;
- Atrial fibrillation (irregular heart rhythm);
- High blood cholesterol;
- Diabetes;
- Smoking;
- Advancing age;
- Unhealthy diet.

**Stroke is a medical emergency. If you suspect someone is having a stroke, dial 999.**

The study addressed what more could be done to improve upon the prevention and treatment of stroke care. Given that it costs about £ 2.8 billion a year in direct care costs.

Key parts of the methodology included:

- a public awareness survey;
- analysis of data on GP practices;
- a review of the 2004 National Sentinel Stroke Audit (the Sentinel Audit) published by the Royal College of Physicians;
- a survey of hospitals to update Sentinel Audit data;

- economic research to model the burden of stroke and the benefits of different interventions and prevention measures;
- case study visits; and
- a patient/carer web forum and focus groups.

*Source:* Department of Health *Reducing Brain Damage: Faster access to better strokecare* (HC 452, Session 2005–2006).

has undertaken on how the British Government promotes community engagement.

Those most in need of support from public services can be alienated if they regard services as having been designed by remote officials with limited understanding or no direct experience of their needs and circumstances. This can have serious consequences. Programmes intended to alleviate social deprivation or tackle long term unemployment can have reduced impact resulting in taxpayers' money being wasted. In recognition of this the UK Government is giving priority to involving intended users in the design of public services. The Home Office, for instance, aims to promote active citizenship so people can tackle the underlying causes of any problems they may face. Police reform is driven by a commitment to citizen focused policing and the Department for Culture, Media and Sport sees culture as having the potential to increase social cohesion provided projects are done with a community, not to a community. In evaluating the success of government initiatives to promote community engagement the NAO draws heavily on qualitative data through interview, group discussion and participation.[4] In a report on the New Deal for Communities, a programme intended to promote economic regeneration, the NAO employed a technique called polarity management to explore the management tension inherent in the programme at a local level and assess how this was typically resolved.[5] The key tensions identified included reconciling full community engagement versus making timely decisions; innovation versus tried and tested methods; being strategic versus the need to invest quickly and demonstrate results; and government versus community control. The message is clear: while overall conclusions and judgements about value for money depend on a

---

[4] Comptroller and Auditor General *English Regions – Getting Citizens Involved: Community Participation in Neighbourhood Renewal* (HC 1070, Session 2003–2004).

[5] Comptroller and Auditor General *English Regions: An early progress report on the New Deal for Communities Programme* (HC 309, Session 2003–2004).

mix of quantitative and qualitative data, recommendations for improvement are more likely to have long lasting impact if they take full account of human behaviour and how the inherent tensions this inevitably gives rise to are managed.

The fourth approach in **Box 4.4** and the most commonly associated with value for money audit is *cost benefit and cost effectiveness* analysis which I discussed in more detail in Chapter 2. The recommendations that can typically arise from this approach not surprisingly tend to be around cost control and increased benefit realisation. One example is a review published by the NAO into the cost benefit and effectiveness of two government schemes to help those on low incomes to purchase a home.[6] The study assessed the implications of adopting different assumptions for the costs and benefits of equity loans and shared ownership, and demonstrated that some £112 million might be released to help an additional 4,130 households. This could be achieved by better targeting and changing the return which social landlords typically received through their use of public money. Another example is a review of the USA Government Accountability Office (GAO) into the cost and loss of benefits from technical problems encountered by polar-orbiting operational environmental satellites (**Box 4.7**). A cost benefit approach is more likely to have greater validity with those who are familiar with the technicalities of quantifying costs and measuring benefits, for example the bureaucrat. The real prize, however, is being able to present such technical information in a way which is easy to assimilate and convincing for the lay reader, and in particular parliamentarians.

Of course these are just four methodological approaches and public services can be judged through a variety of other conceptual models (**Box 4.8**). For example, a new programme such as the UK Government's policy to provide more vocational training for 14–19 year olds is heavily dependent on partnership working. Focusing on the principles which such partnerships need to adhere to for them to be successful may be the best form of evaluative model. A completely different approach but one which might provide more innovative recommendations might be to evaluate the programme in terms of 'metaphors'. That is to consider the best fit in terms of organisational networks, the culture of the diverse bodies involved in the network and the framework provided by the sponsoring department. The metaphor in this case would be the human

---

[6] Comptroller and Auditor General *A Foot on the Ladder: Low Cost Home Ownership Assistance* (HC 1048, Session 2005–2006).

**Box 4.7:     Polar-orbiting Operational Environmental Satellites –
Technical Problems, Cost Increases, and Schedule Delays Trigger
Need for Difficult Trade-Off Decisions
Why GAO Did This Study**

Polar-orbiting environmental satellites provide data and imagery that
are used by weather forecasters, climatologists, and the military to
map and monitor changes in weather, climate, the oceans, and the
environment. The USA's current operational polar-orbiting environmental satellite program is a complex infrastructure that includes
two satellite systems, supporting ground stations, and four central
data processing centres.

In the future, the National Polar-orbiting Operational Environmental Satellite System (NPOESS) is to combine the two current systems
into a single, state-of-the-art environment-monitoring satellite system. This new satellite system is considered critical to the United
States' ability to maintain the continuity of data required for weather
forecasting and global climate monitoring through to the year 2020.

GAO was asked to discuss the NPOESS programme's schedule,
cost, trends, and risks, and to describe plans and implications for
moving the programme forward.

The study reflected aspects of traditional cost benefit analysis
in that it looked at the key options under consideration in August
2005 including removing a key sensor from the first satellite, de-
laying launches of the first two satellites and not launching a pre-
liminary risk-reduction satellite. All of these options impact on the
programme's costs, schedules and the system users who rely on satellite data to develop critical weather products and forecasts, although
the full extent of the impact was not clear to GAO.

*Source:* United States Government Accountability Office – http://
www.gao.gov/cgi-b.

nerve system with a central brain (the department) informed by highly
developed sensory network (the limbs and senses). Applying a biolo-
gist's mindset to the issues might provide completely new insights! The
unifying principle of all these different approaches is, however, that the
relevance of their application is influenced by the circumstances, context or inherent substance of the subject being investigated. By getting
the best fit between methodological approach or conceptual model and

**Box 4.8:** An alternative way of evaluating government programmes

| Analysis by: | Categories | Metaphors | Activities | Principles | Values |
|---|---|---|---|---|---|
| Key charac-teristics | Looking at programmes in terms of the interdependence of: strategy; staff; skills; shared values; structure; style; and overall system.<br><br>The approach has its roots in classic network analysis and is essentially input based. | Analysing organisations as: machines; organisms; brains; cultures; political systems; psychic prisons; flux and transformation; mechanisms; and instruments of domination.<br><br>This approach is largely about the human interaction dimension and how this impacts on the success or failure of organisations. | Analysis based on:<br><br>Issue research; issue filtration; issue definition; forecasting; objectives and priorities; options generation; options analysis; implementation; monitoring and control; evaluation; policy succession and formation.<br><br>This approach is essentially rational and managerialist in focus. | Typical evaluation criteria would be influenced by the principles that governments should:<br><br>– Steer more than they row<br>– empower communities rather than simply deliver services;<br>– encourage competition rather than monopoly;<br>– be driven by their missions, not their rules; | The focus of analysis and evaluation is on the extent to which public management accords with the core values of:<br><br>– lean and purposeful<br>– honest and fair<br>– robust and resilient<br><br>Standards of success should be judged in terms of frugality, rectitude and resilience |

*(Continued)*

Standards by
which failure
should be judged
are waste,
corruption and
catastrophic
failure.

– fund
outcomes
rather than
inputs;
– meet the
needs of the
customer, not
the
bureaucracy;
– concentrate
on earning,
not just
spending;
– invest in
prevention
rather than
cure;
– decentralise
authority; and

| Source | | | | |
|---|---|---|---|---|
| McKinseys 7-S Framework Peters and Waterman In search of Excellence Harper and Row 1982 | Gareth Morgan – Images of Organisation Updated Edition Sage 2006 | Hogwood and Gunn Policy Analysis for Real World Oxford University Press 1984 | – solve problems by leveraging the market place, rather than simply creating public programmes.<br><br>Osborne and Gabler Reinventing Government 1992 | Christopher Hood – A Public Management for all Seasons Journal of Public Administration Volume 69 Spring 1991. |

subject of the study, the chances of producing a more meaningful recommendation which people accept and want to implement are usually increased.

### 4.3 THE MEANINGS WHICH PARTICIPANTS GIVE TO THEIR ROLES

The second way forward is for the auditor to analyse the provision of public programmes through the various meanings that participants give to the activities that they have, or chose to conduct, and the ideas used to express them. Thus it is a mistake to think that everyone has the same view of what an organisation is. A person's understanding depends on factors such as:

- their experience of the organisation, for example as Minister or front door receptionist;
- what their values are, for example as a soldier do they think that chemical weapons are acceptable or morally evil?;
- what their intentions are, for example to get promoted at all costs or to do a good job and go home to the family.

According to this relativist view, there will be no such definite object as 'the organisation' composed of rules, processes, budgets, programmes and audits, but rather a milliard of experiences, values, tensions and other mental phenomena. Proponents of this view will have no easy answers to questions of how to make the organisation 'more efficient', because any policy will mean different things to different people. In addition, with responsibilities passing down the line through systems of delegation and decentralisation, there is also a risk that policies may be turned on their head as people with differing views attempt to guide policies in the direction they see fit. By investigating the variety of meanings held within an organisation it may be possible to understand why policies fail. And this may well help the auditor to make recommendations that have meaning to the various members of the organisation whose work he is examining. The three examples in **Box 4.9**, **4.10 and 4.11** show, respectively how

- the meaning of words may depend upon their social context;
- the concept of 'accountability' – central to so many of the activities of public administration – means different things to different managers;
- social anthropology may show how everyday activities – here handling e-mails – may have a significance for the organisations that is not immediately apparent.

---

**Box 4.9:    The meanings of words, concepts and action must be understood in terms of their context**

*In defining 'discourse analysis', David Marsh and Gerry Stoker assert:*

'The social meaning of words, speeches, actions and institutions are all understood in relation to the overall context of which they form part... For example, the act of marking a cross on a piece of paper and placing it in a box only becomes meaningful within the system of rules, procedures and institutions we call liberal democratic. The significance of voting is thus understood only in relation to the other practices and objects of which it forms a part.'[7]

---

The importance of understanding the meaning which people attach to concepts and required action is particularly critical with major change programmes. This is well illustrated by the British Government's three year efficiency programme, commonly known as the Gershon Programme, introduced in 2004.[8] The aim was to secure £21.5 billion of efficiency gains; reduce the civil service by 80,000 posts and relocate 13,500 to the front line of public services (including reallocating 20,000 public sector posts away from South East England); and embed efficiency in the culture of the public sector. Much effort was spent in defining efficiency and in emphasising that efficiency should not be at the expense of the quality of public services. In spite of this, achieving a shared understanding and commitment to improving efficiency proved to be a significant challenge. Some public sector workers interpreted efficiency and all its connotations as simply cost cutting with, in their view, an inevitable impact on service delivery. As such it was seen as being in direct opposition to the core values which motivated them to work in the public sector. At a more mundane level ambiguity developed in how efficiency was assessed with some improvements being measured net of the investment needed to achieve them and some not taking this cost into account with the result that the efficiency gains were overstated. Different meanings were also placed on the impact of efficiency gains particularly in terms of how those who depend on a service would react:

---

[7] Marsh, D. and Stoker, G. (1995) *Theory and Methods in Political Science* Palgrave Macmillan, p. 119.

[8] Sir Peter Gershon who was commissioned by the British Government in 2003, and reported in 2004, to identify the potential to improve efficiency and establish a culture whereby much greater attention was routinely given to improving efficiency.

for example, the Department for Work and Pensions reported nearly £ 300 million in efficiency gains by paying benefits electronically into their bank accounts. However, not all customers were willing to make the change over and the Department had to reintroduce cheques and the Post Office Card Account as alternative methods of payment. If interpretation of meaning is not considered as a risk which needs to be managed there can be adverse implications. For example the Department of Health secured some £ 1.1 billion in efficiency gains as measured by average length of patient stay in hospital but at the same time there was some evidence that service quality declined as measured by an increase in hospital readmissions.[9]

The meanings attached by those who deliver and benefit from public services need, therefore, to be considered from different perspectives:

- moral – how far they accord with their core beliefs;
- technical – the extent to which there is agreement as to how procedure or process is to be applied and is in accordance with accepted collective wisdom and/or professional norms;
- externalities and the likely implications these might have for meaning – for example the impact of the media or prior experience; and
- the reality or belief test – change may be so far in advance of a person's perception of what is achievable that the meaning they attach to it will be one of extreme scepticism and thus it may fail to achieve support on this account.

Meaning will also differ between cultures and religions. This is becoming increasingly important in a multicultural society. How well the meaning of words and concepts are understood and taken into account is likely to influence the success of a policy and this is also important in how success is evaluated. Ultimately, the impact of the value for money auditor's recommendations in securing acceptance and action will depend on their degree of synergy with accepted meanings.

## 4.4    UNDERSTANDING 'ACCOUNTABILITY'

A second example of how slippery the meaning of concepts can be is illustrated in **Box 4.10** through Janet Newman's analysis of how 'accountability' – surely a bed rock concept of constitutional law and public administration – is defined in various ways and has a multiplicity of meanings.

---

[9] Comptroller and Auditor General *The Efficiency Programme: A Second Review of Progress* (HC156 2006–2007).

**Box 4.10:    Understanding concepts of 'accountability'**

Janet Newman points out that public service managers are accountable in different ways to different authorities. The rules of accountability may conflict, but this is not the only problem and the 'meanings' of accountability may conflict as well:

We need to trace not only multiple actors to whom public managers may be structurally accountable, but also the multiple discourses through which legitimacy is accorded to social action in a dispersed field of power. A quick survey of New Labour policy documents suggests a plurality of constructions of accountability – to customers, consumers, communities, patients, victims (of crime), stakeholders, the business community and so on. At the same time we are witnessing an explosion of academic work producing taxonomies of different forms of accountability; vertical and horizontal; performance, financial and public; collective, corporate, hierarchical and active, individual accountability. I want to highlight the importance – theoretically and empirically – of tracing emerging patterns in the logics of accountability through which actors construct their professional identity and legitimate their actions . . . This means that different kinds of accountability have to be performed by managers. Networks create the space for the active, creative subject able to negotiate their way through dilemmas but also requires them to perform multiple identities in different contexts, at one moment being the agent of government, trying to deliver on its policy pledges; at another, a good public servant being held to account through bureaucratic channels to the relevant minister; at another, a member of a partnership body seeking to cut through bureaucracy in order to make something happen; at another, an organisational leader with accountability to staff and other organisational stakeholders; at another, a responsive change agent, accountable to those whom the organisation is seeking to serve (users, communities, a public at large). The implications are that it may not be possible to find evidence of a coherent ethos of office appropriate to network governance.[10]

The challenge of giving meaning to accountability is well illustrated by the British Government's policy to reduce and prevent childhood obesity with its complex delivery chain of national, regional, local and front line organisations. Child obesity is a complex public health issue that is a growing threat to children's health. It has been estimated that if the

---

[10] Newman, J. (2004) 'Constructing accountability: network government and management agency' *Public Policy and Administration* **19**(4) (Winter) p. 29.

present trend continues, by 2010 the annual cost to the UK economy will be £3.6 billion a year. There is a growing consensus that child obesity needs to be tackled and in recognition of this the British Government in 2004 set a target 'to halt, by 2010, the year-on-year increase in obesity among children under 11 in the context of a broader strategy to tackle obesity in the population as a whole'. The target was owned jointly by three Government Departments with direct impact on children's lives – the Department of Health, the Department for Education and Skills and the Department for Culture, Media and Sport.[11] In many respects the involvement of multiple departments and stakeholders is a strength because it allows a range of approaches to prevention and treatment to be developed: for example encouraging and supporting healthy eating and physical activity, particularly in schools; targeting ante-natal nutrition; media campaigns; and treating those children who have become over weight or obese. A report by the NAO in 2006 highlighted, however, the problems associated with the complex network of organisations – or delivery chain – that has to work together (**Box 4.11**).[12] Roles and responsibilities were particularly unclear at regional level and performance management arrangements differed markedly between the three Departments. For every one regional Government Office for example, there might be three Strategic Health Authorities, six to ten Primary Care Trusts, four county councils, 25 district councils, and four Sports Partnerships, all of which have different responsibilities, organisational arrangements and lines of accountability. This complex network of organisations demonstrates Janet Newman's point very well. While all of the different players accept that child obesity is a growing problem which they have a key role to play in tackling (i.e. they are bound together by a powerful moral justification), the meaning and prominence they give to it in their day to day actions may differ. Getting them all to work together to optimise outcomes can be a challenge. This is because within any complex network of organisations different relationships inevitably develop with both formal and informal accountability arrangements. How funds flow through this network is particularly important. In some instances funding may be disproportionate to its potential impact – advertising to raise public awareness is a good example where relatively small sums

---

[11] Department of Health, *National Standards, Local Action, Health and Social Care Standards and Planning Framework 2005–06–2007–08.*

[12] Comptroller and Auditor General *Tackling Child Obesity – First Steps* (HC 801, Session 2005–2006).

**Box 4.11:    The current delivery chain for tackling child obesity**

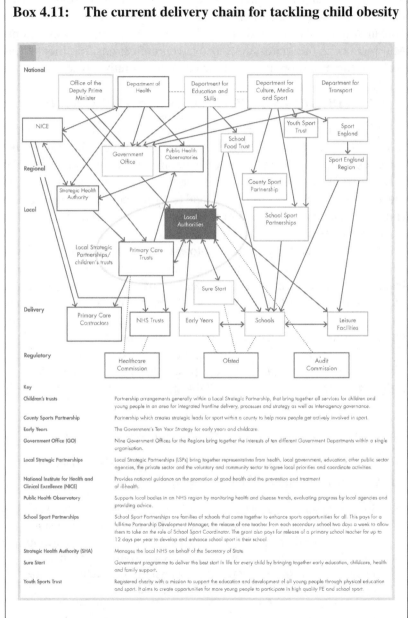

*Source:* Comptroller and Auditor General, *Audit Commission and Healthcare Commission Analysis. Tackling Childhood Obesity First Steps* (HC 801, Session 2005–2006).

of money can have a significant benefit in changing behaviour. So what may be perceived to be a relatively small player in the chain, but be of significant importance, may have limited influence over other organisations. Multiple layers of organisations also have implications for efficiency as each consumes a proportion of funds in administrative overheads.

## 4.5   THE RELEVANCE OF SOCIAL ANTHROPOLOGY

Social anthropology developed as a subject by its proponents who sought to examine societies of which they knew very little – in most cases, societies far removed in terms of economic development and social practice from the societies of Europe and North America from which most social anthropologists come – and to try to understand the meaning and significance of customs and practice that were different from those of other societies.

The application of social anthropology to the management of business and public organisations starts from a similar basis (ie to examine the behaviour of those who work in organisations and to try to understand the meaning and significance that practitioners give to what they may regard as obvious, day to day activities, so that any recommendations that the auditor may make for changes in behaviour may be based upon a good understanding of the values and attitudes of the different groups working in the organisation). This is illustrated by Gillian Tett's example in **Box 4.12** of 'meanings' in the daily life of accountants.

---

**Box 4.12:   The importance of social anthropology**

Gillian Tett shows how 'meanings' in the daily life of accountants may be illustrated by social anthropology.

'So how do you feel about e-mails' asks Simon Roberts, a social anthropologist. 'How has it changed your workload?' This is not what social anthropologist are usually expected to ask: they observe courtship rituals, try to interpret ancient chants, analyse gift-giving or tribal cosmology. Simon Roberts, however, is searching for meanings in the daily life of Peter Quest, a senior auditor, who works for the global accountants PricewaterhouseCoopers (PWC), in a featureless tower block in central London. Quest, who has spent 32 years at the firm, manifests unease. 'I call my e-mails the triffids,' he says, referring to the killer plants in John Wyndham's 1950's novel. 'You can spend all day killing them, then you turn your back for a second and those red things, those triffids, have taken over your screen again! It eats up all your day. When I started my career we used to spend a lot of time talking to clients and colleagues. Now it's harder.'

Robert is patient. 'But I have noticed that people here don't seem to classify e-mails as 'real' work. They sit at their desk doing e-mails and then say, 'Right now let's do some work' – but e-mail is taking up work time. Perhaps that is the problem?"

Quest looks surprised: he hadn't thought about how he thought about e-mails before. Indeed, like any long-time resident in a secure habitat, he hadn't reflected extensively on his daily habits. That is why PWC has taken the unusual – and commendably imaginative – step or bringing in an anthropologist, in an effort to address the issue of workplace culture. 'Everyone at the accountancy firm tends to be the same kind of person,' says Quest. 'This is why it's useful getting an outsider view."

PWC is not alone. Practitioners of social anthropology – the branch of social science dedicated to the study of human culture – have traditionally flocked to exotic spots: examining the sexual mores of Polynesian islander; studying disappearing tribal cultures in the Amazon jungle; wandering with Nuer herders in Sudan. But in the past few years, some have headed off to places such as accountancy firms and technology companies, partly because there are fewer unspoilt 'native' cultures left to study.

But the shift also reflects the growing complexity of public and private sector workplaces and the realisation by companies and governments that they must operate in a global environment. In America, anthropologists have been hired by technology groups including Intel, Microsoft, Apple and Xerox. In the UK, the 'people watchers' can be found not just pacing the corridors of blue chip companies, but also the Ministry of Defence, Immigration Services, National Health Services and Foreign Office, as well as non-government aid agencies.[13]

As social anthropologists – and indeed, others – have shown, it is human behaviour that often has most influence over outcomes. How intended beneficiaries act when faced with a new policy initiative often depends on their emotional or other behavioural response to it. One of the reasons cited why, for example, between 30 and 40 per cent of those eligible for pension credit – the main UK income related state benefit for those of

---

[13] Tett, G. (2005) Office Culture. *Financial Times Magazine* (May 21), p. 22.

pension age – do not claim it is the social stigma they perceive of having to rely on the state for support.[14]

In terms of how organisations operate Anthony Hopwood has concluded that a great deal of accounting has been concerned with the management of vertical relationships.[15] Budgeting, planning and performance evaluation are invariably seen in vertical terms and, when difficulties occur, attempts are often made to reinforce the requirements of command and control that are seen as the necessities of behaviour in vertical relationships. But vertical relationships cannot work by command and control alone. Too often they deny the free passage of all the information necessary for success, confining its flow within the formal constraints of designated report structures. And successful vertical relationships depend upon lateral relationships, with colleagues, suppliers, customers and citizens.

This is often recognised, at least in principle today, by talk of 'empowerment' of subordinates; 'decentralisation', 'delegation', 'local decision making' and 'freedom to innovate'. But providing the framework whereby the behaviour appropriate to such concepts can be understood and encouraged requires the auditor to be sensitive to many of the insights that come from the work of social anthropologists and, indeed, others who have understood the subtleties of human behaviour in co-operative activities.

As an example, in preparing a report[16] on why some schools under perform when measured against the Government's criteria,[17] we employed an educational psychologist to provide advice on the collection and interpretation of evidence. The attributes of a successful school are numerous. Some are relatively easy to measure such as class room size, staffing levels, and technical competency, funding, quality of building and equipment and the curriculum. But other attributes, while equally important, are more difficult to evaluate such as leadership, ethos and

---

[14] Comptroller and Auditor General *Progress in tackling pension poverty: Encouraging take-up of entitlements* (HC 1178, Session 2005–2006).

[15] Hopwood, A.G. (1996) Looking across rather than up and down: on the need to explore the lateral processing of information *Accounting, Organisations and Society* **21**(6) 589–590.

[16] Three broad criteria are used to define a poorly performing school: 'special measures' (failing to provide an acceptable standard of education with leaders who have not demonstrated capacity to make improvements); 'serious weaknesses' (inadequate overall effectiveness or an unacceptable standard of education but with leaders who demonstrated capacity to make improvements); or 'under achieving' (schools that perform significantly less well than others in similar contexts).

[17] Comptroller and Auditor General *Improving Poorly Performing Schools in England* (HC 679, Session 2005–2006).

behaviour management. Where a school is designated as failing, the time it takes to recover will depend on how staff react to what some might perceive as questioning their ability – indeed for some this might impact on their self worth and esteem. None of these are capable of exact measurement but understanding their impact was important in assessing the fitness for purpose of measures to raise educational standards. The advice provided by the educational psychologist helped develop more meaningful recommendations which were more likely to be accepted by the education profession.

The importance of understanding human behaviour in explaining underperformance and in identifying ways in which this can be remedied cannot be understated. Of course, this is not new: the retail sector has for many years known that understanding the customer base, their preferences and motivations are key to the success and longevity of a product or service.

## 4.6   THE AUDITOR AS COACH AND MENTOR

The third way forward, which should certainly take account of the insights of the other two approaches I have outlined, tries to focus on success in a more straightforward way. It is to look at the auditor primarily as a mentor or coach, as one who stands outside the organisation and its staff and whose criticism may be severe, but who is committed to the success of the organisation and to how it can be achieved. There is a considerable body of research on positive psychology, in particular the work of Martin Seligman,[18] which demonstrates that focusing on strengths rather than weaknesses leads to success. Failure may tell you what to avoid but not what to do. Thus, if we are interested in British soccer, we look today at Chelsea, Manchester United and Arsenal and not to teams at the bottom of the second division. In the USA you could do no better than getting coached by the New York Jets if you were considering a career in American Football or the New York Yankees if your preference was baseball. If you are interested in athletics, we look to those who win Olympic Gold medals and not to those who are disqualified or who are eliminated in the heats.

---

[18] Seligman, M.E.P., and Cxikszentmihalyi, M. (2000) 'Positive psychology: an introduction' *American Psychologist* **55**, 5–14, and Seligman M.E.P., Steen, T.A. Park, N, and Peterson C. (2005) 'Positive psychology progress: an empirical validation of interventions' *American Psychologist* **60**, 410–421.

As Comptroller and Auditor General I have promoted this philosophy and it is evident in the outputs which the NAO now produces. For example, in 2004–05 just under half of the 60 value for money reports published contained, or had associated with them in supplementary products, some form of good practice drawn from successes. Identifying successful enterprise whether it be the application of a particular process such as risk management or achievement of a certain type of outcome, for example where a local organisation is providing an exemplary public service, has implications for the auditor's methodological approach. The principles of diagnosing existing levels of performance as a means of analysing in more depth where performance may be suboptimal through for example cause and effect analysis still applies. But the auditor would also focus on where performance exceeded the norm or accepted standard to understand why. In this context techniques such as appreciative inquiry are important because of the emphasis they place on identifying what is working well rather than the opposite – why performance may be lacking. More traditional value for money audit techniques can also be used **(Box 4.13)**.

---

**Box 4.13:    Traditional audit methods can be used to identify successes**

| Technique | Use |
|---|---|
| Benchmarking and comparative analyses | Identifying high performers or lowest cost input/output ratios to understand what contributes to their success |
| Defining excellence | Using expert advice to define excellence and then using this to diagnose and identify exemplars |
| Consultation | Qualitative focus group research derived from users, and managers |
| Expert advice | Recognised leaders in the relevant field are consulted to add strength and authority to what is presented as good practice |

| Meta analysis | Existing research is analysed and evaluated to synthesise and present accepted opinion on good practice |
|---|---|
| User experience | The beneficiaries of a service give their views based on their direct experience as to what success is and whether the case example meets it |

*Source:* National Audit Office.

Of course, as with any approach there are risks and much research and validation is needed to ensure that the exemplar identified demonstrates success which is likely to be sustainable. If success cannot be replicated and sustained, the reputation of the adviser diminishes often to vanishing point – as true of tennis coaches and football managers as auditors. Managing this risk requires considerable rigor in the approach used to identify and validate what is presented as a success. Many terms are deployed by the auditor in promoting successful practice, and it is helpful to distinguish them and make them clear to auditees. Examples are given in **Box 4.14**.

---

**Box 4.14:    Success can cover a broad spectrum**

| Category | – Description |
|---|---|
| Good practice advice | – It refers to a identifiable set of practices (rather than indeterminate advice to be prudent or conclusive in contexts where such terms have no clear meaning). |
| Good practice can be specific | – It can be specific to the working environment in which the agency or department operates for example, the management or defence procurement or the NHS estate. |

| | |
|---|---|
| Good practice can be general | – This may be drawn from one or a select number of organisations' experience which has relevance to other organisations for example, principles of risk management or asset management or community engagement. |
| Exemplars | – These may be one-off examples in a specific field. The example is usually presented as a case example providing a history of key decisions, the context in which they were made, and their impact. This might be a successful construction project which met a range of complex requirements such as being energy efficient, cost-effective to run, sustainable, aesthetically attractive and providing a working environment conducive to efficient working. |
| Gold standard | – Principles of success are derived from a series of examples which are then presented as a model of good practice which should be emulated. An example might be urban regeneration where there are a number of successful programmes, widely accepted as such by professional opinion, for example, Malmo, Barcelona and Boston from which a series of common principles can be drawn together in a standard which commands authority as most likely to achieve a successful outcome if replicated. |
| Integrated models of key success factors | – This is similar to developing a gold or other so described standard. The difference is that the attributes likely to be needed to secure success are analysed |

in much more detail and derived from a much larger sample of examples selected in accordance with predefined criteria. The principles identified are validated by triangulating with a range of other data. An example is identifying the key requirements of delivering successful IT-enabled business change **(Box 4.15).**

There is no doubt that the currency of success is becoming more widely used by audit offices to promote improvements in value for money and other beneficial change. Three examples from the UK, USA and New Zealand illustrate this **(Boxes 4.15–4.17).**

---

**Box 4.15:     Using examples of success to promote good practice – UK experience**

The successful delivery of IT-enabled business change is essential for improving major public services but as shown in Box 2.5 IT projects have too often been associated with high profile failure. This has contributed to undermining the confidence of public sector managers to the extent that the widely held belief is that any IT project is more likely to fail than succeed. It is clearly not in the interests of value for money for such a perception to prevail – the risk is that it becomes a self fulfilling prophecy. Diagnosing why IT projects typically fail to identify lessons which can be applied and so increase the chances of success will not necessarily bring about the required change. This is because the lessons or good practice are associated with failure and experience of human behaviour suggests that the negative connotations reduces the likelihood of them being acted upon. For this reason the NAO analysed some 24 IT projects from both the public and private sectors, within the UK and overseas which were accepted as successful. The projects included for example, the New York City Major's Office Dial 311 programme which provides access to all government information and non-emergency services through a single telephone number in 170 languages, the UK Department of Work and Pensions' initiative to pay benefits directly into recipients' bank accounts, and Transport for London's Oyster electronic ticket payment card. From these examples of success the NAO identified three core principles which contribute to delivering successful IT programmes and projects:

- Ensuring senior level engagement: clear and engaged board leadership, keeping senior decision makers informed of progress and risks and, for example, not creating undue pressure by making premature and unrealistic announcements about delivery dates.
- Acting as an 'intelligent client': understanding the business process the department is aiming to change, having the right programme management skills, training the staff and creating effective and equal relationships with suppliers.
- Realising the benefits: selling the benefits to users, winning wider support for the change, and assessing whether the programme or project has achieved what it set out to do.

*Source: Delivering Successful IT-enabled Business Change* (HC 33, Session 2006–2007).

---

**Box 4.16:    Promoting good practice – USA experience**

The Government Accountability Office (GAO) in USA has a section of its website devoted to promoting good practice. A typical example is a review undertaken into the response to Hurricane Katrina and how best to improve federal contracting practices in disasters recovery operations.

The devastation experienced throughout the Gulf Coast region in the wake of Hurricanes Katrina and Rita has called into question the government's ability to effectively respond to such disasters. The government needs to understand what went right and what went wrong, and to apply these lessons to strengthen its disaster response and recovery operations.

The federal government relies on partnerships across the public and private sectors to achieve critical results in preparing for and responding to natural disasters, with an increasing reliance on contractors to carry out specific aspects of its missions.

GAO identified practices in the public and private sectors that provide insight into how federal agencies can better manage their disaster-related procurements, including:

- Developing knowledge of contractor capabilities and prices by identifying commodities and services and establishing vendor relationships before they are needed.
- Establishing a scalable operations plan to adjust the level of capacity required to effectively respond to needs.
- Formally assigning and communicating disaster-related responsibilities, with joint training for government and contractor personnel; and
- Providing sufficient numbers of field-level contracting staff with the authority needed to meet mission requirements.

*Source:* http://www.gao.gov/cgi-bin/getrpt/GAO-06-714T.

---

**Box 4.17:    Promoting good practice – New Zealand experience**

The Office of the Auditor General in New Zealand is featuring good practice more extensively in its reports. An example is a study published in 2006 into how public entities ensure that resources disbursed to third party organisations in the private and public sectors are used effectively. Drawing on its findings the Office set out principles of good practice based on the examples of both exemplary and less exemplary performance. The principles covered:

- lawfulness;
- accountability;
- openness (transparency)
- value for money (resources are used effectively and efficiently without waste, and in a way that optimises the public benefit);
- fairness;
- integrity.

Each is supported with more detailed guidance, for example the principle concerning value for money discusses in some detail how best to operate in different market conditions. For example in the circumstances of a suboptimal provider market where the guidance recognises that some public entities operate in less than optimal situations, where there is no market of providers or where those that are available do not have quite the capability or capacity that is required. The public entity needs to acknowledge this, and take action to mitigate any risks that might arise. The actions taken, and the reasons for the actions, need to be documented. A public entity should, however, take care that it does not put the continuity of a service unreasonably at risk in its pursuit of the lowest cost. For example, it should not exploit its negotiating position when there is only one potential supplier, or where the third party organisation relies substantially on its public funding. A public entity should take into account the possible effects of its funding decisions on the number of third party organisations available to supply a particular service, and on their ability to deliver it. The public entity needs to fund the organisations at a rate that is fair and reasonable, and sufficient to sustain effective service delivery for the term of the arrangement, and not jeopardise long-term delivery prospects. At the same time, the public entity should avoid accepting a 'low-ball' or 'loss-leading' tender that will not cover the costs, but is submitted to win the tender against a higher cost from an alternative supplier. The other suppliers' cost estimates may perhaps be more realistically based on effective service delivery.

*Source: Principles to Underpin Management by Public Entities of Funding to Non-government Organisations June 2000 http://www. org.govt.nz.*

We should also not assume that what constitutes success and good practice should be the judgement of the auditor alone. Indeed, there is a great deal to be learnt from participatory evaluation, the concept that those influenced by a programme, actively involved in delivering it or who are beneficiaries will have unique perspectives on what works well and what does not.[19] The auditor needs, therefore, to consult widely to validate what is initially perceived to be a success or good practice.

## 4.7     CONCLUSION

The prime benefit of the value for money auditing lies in its ability through convincing analysis and meaningful recommendations to

---

[19] The starting point for this type of evaluation is to capture and understand the perceptions of those groups involved with and affected by the programme examined.

promote sustainable improvements in value for money. Analysing programmes in terms of 'economy', 'efficiency' and 'effectiveness' has some advantages but difficulties too: 'economy', 'efficiency' and 'effectiveness' need defining afresh for each subject to reflect the difference in context, policy and circumstances. Audit reports often appear to make sense and are accepted by the auditee, yet fail to change behaviour. Progress can be made by recognising, first, that the auditor can choose from a wide variety of approaches, and does not have to be confined to narrow definitions of economy, efficiency and effectiveness; secondly that he must also be sensitive to the different meanings that members of the same organisation give to the words, concepts and activities that are used and employed in the discharge of public programmes; and third, that he should see his role as that of a coach and mentor and not simply as critic and nark.

Public sector auditing – indeed auditing as a whole – may have taken the wrong road in becoming primarily associated with a concern for failure. Public sector auditing should look for the conditions of success, explain them, and thus help public authorities succeed in meeting the needs of the country's citizens. It is not to be expected that complete success, even if we could describe it, could always be attained. And it must be recognised that social change will bring new challenges. So improvements are always provisional and audit is an iterative process over time. Nevertheless, through the debate and dialogue that is implicit in this approach, there is the prospect that public sector audit can indeed be 'value for money'. The following chapters will illustrate this approach in the battle to overcome the defects of bureaucracy in public programmes.

## 4.8   SUMMARY

Value for money auditing in terms of analysing economy, efficiency and effectiveness has some advantages but difficulties too:

- Economy, efficiency and effectiveness need defining afresh for each subject – agricultural programmes are very different from defence programme for example.
- Audit reports often appear to make sense, are accepted by the auditee, yet fail to change behaviour. The same reports are made year after year.

Progress can be made by recognising that the auditor:

- can choose from a wide variety of approaches, and does not have to be confined to narrow definitions of economy, efficiency and effectiveness;
- must be sensitive to the different meanings that members of the same organisation give to the words, concepts and activities that are used and employed in the discharge of public programmes;
- should appreciate that human beings learn more from success than failure, and see the auditor's role as more of a coach and mentor than a negative critic and nark.

# 5
# Privatisation – The Alternative to Bureaucracy?

The second half of the twentieth century saw increased levels of disenchantment with bureaucracy. Many of the countries which had enthusiastically endorsed increased state control after the Second World War came to see it as failing to meet the expectations which had accompanied the arrival of communist regimes in many countries, and the nationalisation of many industries and activities in countries which maintained a market economy. Many such regimes that relied to a large degree on the state, perhaps inevitably, did not produce benefits in living standards and personal freedom in line with their promises.[1]

The final quarter of the twentieth century was marked by two developments that would have wide-ranging and long-lasting ramifications for the perceived role of the state. While the fall of the Berlin Wall in 1989, subsequent pro-market reforms in Central and Eastern Europe, and the break up of the Soviet Union marked the final demise of communism, in the West attention was shifting to new ways of providing public services. In the UK, Mrs Thatcher had been elected as Prime Minister in 1979 after the so called 'winter of discontent'. The breakdown of many public services at this time – including the failure in certain highly publicised cases to bury the dead – seemed to sound the death knell of the post-second world war approach to public services provision which assumed that if the state had won the war, it could guarantee a prosperous peace. With the difficulties encountered by nationalised industries and public services in the west and the fall of communism in the east, in the last two decades of the twentieth century the ball was more situated in the court of private enterprise than in that of state control.

---

[1] There were, of course, some exceptions. Public opinion in some countries remained loyal to features of the post-war welfare state. Politicians wishing to cut costs and entitlement or to privatise important elements of the welfare state met stiff resistance in Europe and the USA for some areas as they did in the UK.

Private enterprise was increasingly seen as the vehicle most capable of answering the ills of the public services. The governing idea was that private enterprise could only flourish by providing the goods and services that people wanted to buy, and that the incentives that encourage businesses to operate successfully are simply absent in the public services, enmeshed as they are in bureaucratic rules and regulations and where success is not always measured by the satisfaction of customers but by the ability to negotiate the back stairs of bureaucracy and attach yourself to rising stars. Like all simple prescriptions for social and economic change this was a vast over-simplification. Examples abounded of public servants who went the last mile for those to whom they had responsibilities and of business corporations, protected by monopoly power, where the evils and diseconomies of bureaucracy were of a Kafkaesque scale.

But the mood of the times was for privatisation and, subsequently, for bringing private money and incentives into the provision of public services. Attention was drawn, for example, to the thinking of Friedrick von Hayek, notably in his popular treatment of the issues in the *Road to Serfdom* where he pointed to the impossibility of the bureaucrat ever having enough information with which to run an economy, and to the proposition that the powers required by the planner would lead to total-itarianism.[2] By 2006, all but one of the major British industries owned by the state in 1980 had been privatised (**Box 5.1**).

---

**Box 5.1:  Major Nationalised Industries in The United Kingdom**

| 1980 | 2006 |
|------|------|
| Airports | Airports |
| Buses | Buses |
| Coal | Coal |
| Electricity | Electricity |
| Gas | Gas |

---

[2] Von Hayek, F. (1994) *The Road to Serfdom* University of Chicago Press.

| National Airlines | ~~National Airlines~~ |
| Royal Mail | Royal Mail |
| Railways | ~~Railways~~ |
| Ship building | ~~Ship building~~ |
| Telecommunications | ~~Telecommunications~~ |
| Water | ~~Water~~ |

*Source:* National Audit Office.

The auditor is therefore faced with evaluating the implementation of this changed approach to the provision of public services. This chapter categorises the various types of public service provision available and deals with the audit of privatisations. The next chapter deals with the audit of the private finance initiative and public private partnerships.

## 5.1   PRIVATE AND PUBLIC SECTOR APPROACHES COMPARED

In carrying forward the programme of more fundamentally involving the private sector in the provision of public services, a number of approaches can be distinguished and compared with traditional ways of conducting government business.

'Privatisation' is where a public service and the assets supporting it are sold either by converting the organisation into a limited liability company and selling its shares, or by selling it as a going concern to another company, or by selling it to the staff currently providing the service. If a marketable output was possible but monopoly elements would prevail, then a regulated private sector solution would be right. That became the path for the energy and water utilities, for example.

In the Private Finance Initiative (PFI), instead of the public service providing assets and running a service (e.g. building and maintaining roads), the private sector builds and maintains the asset and sells the services it provides to the public sector (e.g. the public sector might pay a rent for the public use of the road or the public users of the roads might pay a toll). This arrangement may cover part of the total service, as with the National Health Service (NHS) in the UK where the recent new hospital building programme has very largely been procured under PFI but the clinical personnel work in the public sector. Alternatively, both the facilities and operational activity can be provided by the private sector, as in the case for some British prisons.

In a Public Private Partnership (PPP), a public authority contributes part of the initial finance for a programme and may have greater involvement in the management decisions on how the services are delivered than would be the case with a PFI project. The arrangement may take the form of a substantial government shareholding in a company and the appointment of some its directors.

Public authorities have always contracted out or outsourced some of their activities. In past centuries mercenary armies and tax farming were examples of contracting out public activities. In more modern times, it was the practice of the US and British government to contract out the construction of some part of their naval ship building, and private companies have often been used to supply such goods and services as stationery, printing, office furniture, and catering. But in recent years, there has been in some countries, notably the UK, a programme to outsource the provision of many more good and services, such as information and technology services in the NHS and the tax collecting departments; the facilities management of many buildings; and legal and internal audit services.

If there were good reasons to retain public sector involvement, for instance if the market would not provide a public service, then an arms length agency or non-departmental public body could be considered. Examples in the UK are the Health and Safety Executive and the Competition Commission. These organisations are part of the executive branch of government, with their chairs, board members, directors and chief executives appointed by ministers, and financed by money voted by Parliament and, in some cases, charges. But they do, within the limits of the discretion allowed to them, have a degree of freedom in the work they do and how they discharge it.

The traditional bureaucratic way of providing public services was by government departments headed by ministers and employing directly paid civil servants or other public servants to deliver 'in-house'. Examples in most countries include the Ministries of Finance and Defence, and the Army, Navy and Air Force.

The relationship between these approaches is shown in **Box 5.2**:

**Box 5.2:    The models of private sector involvement in the provision of public sector**

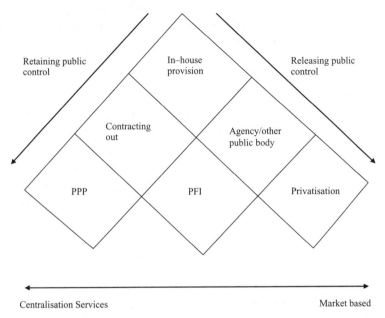

Retaining public control

In–house provision

Releasing public control

Contracting out

Agency/other public body

PPP

PFI

Privatisation

Centralisation Services

Market based

*Source:* National Audit Office.

**Box 5.3:    Some of the important trade offs in public-private provision of services to which the auditor needs to align in her analyses of this area of government work**

| | Potential benefits | Potential disadvantages |
|---|---|---|
| **Privatisation** | Benefits of competition | Creation of monopoly/ oligopoly Problems of regulation Social consequences for the government |

| | | |
|---|---|---|
| | Raising revenue | Undervaluing assets, windfall gains for private sector and former public sector managers |
| | Product and process innovation | Monopoly/oligopoly which does not respond to customer needs |
| **PFI/PPP** | Delivery more likely to be to time and cost | Higher financing costs and possibilities for windfall gains for private sector |
| | Price certainty | Overcharging and private sector re-financing gains |
| | Transfer of risks | Inappropriate risks transferred, at high cost |
| | Assets maintained | Lock-in to long contracts |
| | Life time costings | Lock-in to payments when times are tight |
| | Funds available | Inappropriate balance sheet treatment |
| | Innovative solutions | Risk averse financing institutions. High overhead costs including advisors' fees |
| **Conventional public sector procurement** | Financing at sovereign risk rates | Business case that under-estimate costs |
| | Greater flexibility to change services | Badly maintained assets |
| | Public sector not for profit ethos | Focus on inputs and not outcomes |

*Source:* National Audit Office.

## 5.2  GETTING THE BEST FROM PRIVATISATION

General experience from both a UK and international perspective yields the following guidance that may usefully inform the auditor's work.

## 5.3   THE PRIVATISATION PROCESS – THE GENERAL ISSUES

Audit experience suggests that the three essential characteristics of a successful privatisation in terms of fairness between the public and private sectors are:

* **Title** – it must be clear who owns the assets being privatised. Although this may sound obvious, it is not always clear. The British Government sold an agricultural research station to Unilever only to learn that, as a charitable organisation, the proceeds of the sale had to go to the governing body of the facility rather than to the Treasury.[3] And, in Central and Eastern Europe and parts of the former Soviet Union, confusion about title enabled a fair number of people to lay claim to ownership on the flimsiest basis.

* **Valuation** – it is important to value what is being privatised. Valuation is not an exact science, and different approaches exist – historic cost less depreciation, disposal value, replacement value, present value of discounted estimates of future returns. The important point is to have some benchmark against which likely receipts can be judged. Again, in former communist countries the absence of functioning markets made valuation in some cases almost impossible. And this again enabled some bidders to obtain valuable assets, including oil and gas reserves, at very low prices.

* **Competition** – successful privatisation demands competitive pressure to the maximum extent and to the last feasible moment before the sale. Governments sometimes abridge this process, and they often want the fact of a sale more than the size of the proceeds. Ideas for nominating 'preferred bidders' simplify the sale process, but can pave the way to lower sale prices as the preferred bidder can have the whip hand over the seller.

All these points need to be borne in the mind when choosing and evaluating privatisation methods. There are three main options:

* **Flotations** – converting a public authority into a limited liability company and selling the shares on the stock exchange. This has many attractions, for example it is simple in principle because it only requires a valuation to determine the sale price, and opens the door to

---

[3] *New Scientist* (1989) '*Treasury must wait 21 years for key to door of plant research institute*' Issue 1691, 18 November.

competition. Floatations are facilitated by the existence of a developed stock market, although before floating a public entity a decision has to be made on whether to sell all the shares at once, which may flood the market, or to keep some back in the hope of doing better by selling them in tranches.

- **Trade sales or auctions** – the assets of a public authority can be put up for auction to the highest bidder. For this to work well it is necessary to have a comprehensive valuation and full and open competition. In these cases, a good price can be secured that represents value to both the buyer and seller. The temptation for governments is to try to offload the asset so as to claim a 'successful privatisation' through a restricted competition or none at all. And there are examples of 'under the counter' trade sales to 'cronies'.

- **Management buyouts** – here the privatisation is accomplished by selling the public authority to its management and staff. In many ways this seems ideal – those who know the authority's activity continue to run it. The management will often have to borrow the money to make their offer, and the problem is that they are the people who really know the business of the organisation and will be naturally keen to get it at the best price they can. How data can be assembled to give the selling government – and any other bidders – accurate information is a big challenge. An example of the difficulties is the privatisation of bus companies in the UK.

Privatisations are difficult in all countries. This has especially been true in former communist countries where:

- title to land and property was often insecure, as noted above;
- valuation was difficult in the absence of market prices, again as noted;
- there were few domestic buyers with cash, so often sales were facilitated by distributing vouchers to citizens so that they could 'purchase' shares in privatised entitles. Often those who received the vouchers were willing to sell them for ready cash, with the result that those who bought up the vouchers were able to secure virtually monopoly control of privatised entitles;
- the managers of privatised entitles tended to lack the skills to perform effectively in the market economies, and they were often required to operate companies whose assets were old and inappropriate;
- under communism they had assured markets, but when it went their markets largely disappeared and their products were not easily saleable on the international markets. This was a particular problem for

countries like the Baltic States which had previously been part of the Soviet Union.

In short, in countries like the UK privatisation took place within a functioning market economy, but in communist states privatisation was one of the principal means of creating a market economy and such significant realignments brought their own problems. For example, Báger points to a number of differences of both scale and kind in the Hungarian experience:[4]

- the scale of what has to be achieved to create a market economy;
- the likelihood of both over and under regulation in different industries;
- the wider and deeper social and economic impacts;
- uncertainty about the balance to be struck between the size of the remaining state and market sectors;
- the scale of privatisation which, if conducted with speed and with the introduction of foreign capital, may undermine national strategic development aims; and
- the existence of a real conflict between getting results and the need to de-monopolise the new industries in the market sector.

Voszka points to a different phenomenon, namely the extreme concentration of power (**Box 5.4**), something shared by the Russian Federation with the creation of the small group of oligarchs.[5]
Considering the progress of privatisation in Russia more generally, the Audit Chamber of the Russian Federation came to the following unfavourable conclusions about privatisation:[6]

- A broad class of effective owners was not formed;
- Economic restructuring did not lead to the desired increase in industrial efficiency;
- The investment attracted during the course of privatisation proved inadequate for the development of the economy; and
- International competitiveness was not maintained in a number of sectors.

---

[4] Báger, G. (2004) *Conclusions of the Study of Privatisation in Hungary* Hungarian State Audit Office. Research and Development Institute, Budapest.

[5] Voszka, E. (1999) 'Privatization in Hungary: results and open issues' *Economic Reform Today,* Issue No. 2.

[6] State Research Institute of Systems Analysis, Audit Chamber of the Russian Federation (2005) *State Property Privatisation in the Russian Federation 1993–2003*, Moscow.

**Box 5.4:     Concentration of ownership in Hungary among the top 100 companies in 1997**

| Number of owners | Number of firms | % of registered firms (N=86) | Number of firms with one majority owner[1] | % of firms with one majority owner (N=86) |
|---|---|---|---|---|
| One | 49 | 57.0 | 49 | 57.0 |
| Two | 1 | 1.2 | 1 | 1.2 |
| Three | 0 | 0.0 | 0 | 0.0 |
| Maximum 3 | 50 | 58.1 | 50 | 58.1 |
| More than 3 | 36 | 41.9 | 16 | 18.6 |
| **Total** | **86** | **100.0** | **66** | **76.7** |

Source: Voszka (1999).                    [1]with more than 50 % of shares

It remains to be seen whether privatisation in former command and control economies will bring about the desired transformation, or more precisely: if one has faith in the market system how long will 'transformation' take?

## 5.4     GETTING THE BEST FROM PRIVATISATION

**Box 5.5** sets out a high level view of what makes for successful privatisations: it is drawn mainly from the experience of UK audit work and is based on the assumption that there has been separate consideration about the identification of candidates for privatisation. This is something that national authorities have to decide for themselves, though the considerations set out above in **Box 5.3** with regard to potential advantages and disadvantages are relevant.

The more detailed issues that follow comprise an overall question resolved by four key drivers. This 4-Pillars approach is also developed in the next chapter for PPP/PFI, first in relation to getting a good deal from the private sector and then making sure that the deal operates well over the term of the contract.

The conceptual approach comprises a series of questions that can be answered either 'yes' or 'no'. In practice, the answers of course inevitably lie somewhere between these poles, but forcing a binary choice makes the issues clearer than formulations that are expressed, for instance, in terms of 'to what extent . . . ', that permit almost any answer.

**Box 5.5:     The 4-Pillars (in bold) underpinning the successful privatisation of state assets**

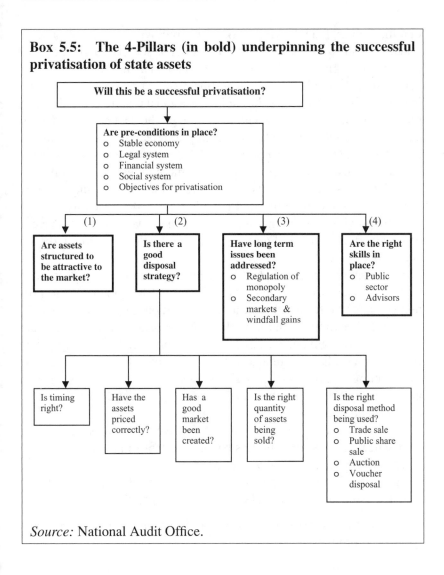

*Source:* National Audit Office.

## 5.5   THE IMPORTANCE OF HAVING THE RIGHT PRE-CONDITIONS IN PLACE TO MAXIMISE THE SUCCESS OF PRIVATISATION

Pre-conditions for privatisation are those concerned with the establishment of effective democratic and free market mechanisms. In the former communist countries, these sorts of pre-conditions did not exist at first but have come to be seen as essential for making the transition and included the establishment of sound macroeconomic conditions in the face of initial substantial falls in GDP, rising unemployment and disruption of trade, even allowing for the possibility of optimistic measurement under the previous regimes.[7] With a shortage of capital in the emerging former communist economies, foreign investment was a principal source of the investment needed to renew the capital base and it required confidence in the stability of the economy with respect to public debt and the inflation and exchange rates, as well as the ability to repatriate profits. This led to systems of US dollar denominated debt instruments and the tying of exchange rates to more stable currencies, more or less successfully.

Wider issues are the probity of the bureaucracy, and policies towards corruption and the importance of good law and order generally, Becker (1968)[8] providing a seminal analysis. Crime is very likely to have a deterrent effect on flows of foreign investment and job creation (Krkoska and Robeck, 2006).[9]

There remains an important role for institutions such as the European Bank for Reconstruction and Development (EBRD) including to promote structural reform, competition, privatisation and entrepreneurship. Support linked to such conditions through co-financing can also promote strong corporate governance, including environmental sensitivity.[10] The Bank's own evaluation indicates that not all its projects were successful, pointing to the problems of risk in newly emerging economies and issues such as changing shareholding and the impact on the operation of funded entities.[11]

Based on its experience the World Bank has drawn out a number of practical lessons for countries trying to establish the economic preconditions for successful privatisation:[12]

Early attention must be paid to the need for a regulatory regime where divested assets involve natural monopoly or oligopoly:

- Transparency is a key to increasing public accountability and discouraging corruption;

---

[7] International Monetary Fund (2000), *Transition Economies: An IMF Perspective on Progress and Prospect,* Issues Brief, 2000/08.

[8] Becker G. (1968) Crime and punishment: 'an economic approach' *The Journal of Political Economy* **76**, 169–217.

[9] Krkoska L and Robeck K. (2006) *The Impact of Crime on the Enterprise Sector: Transition versus non-transition countries* European Bank for Reconstruction and Development July.

[10] EBRD (2005) *Annual Report 2005: Annual Review and Financial Report,* EBRD.

[11] EBRD (2005) op cit., Section 7.

[12] World Bank (2004) *Economies in Transition: an Operations Evaluation Department evaluation of World Bank Assistance,* Washington.

- There is a need for a systematic, rather than an ad hoc approach to public sector management reform, based on a comprehensive long-term institutional development and reform strategy;
- Measures are needed at an early stage to enforce prudential regulations, including limits on loan concentration and related party lending, with outside lending conditioned on such measures;
- State ownership needs to be strengthened through stronger governance, tighter budget constraints, divestiture of sectors, and restrictions on the scope of banking licenses;
- High priority must be afforded to training bank supervisors, lawyers and judges, accountants, auditors and other skilled professionals. In addition, bank supervision needs to be improved, and international accounting standards need to be enforced – not just adopted – as preconditions for external, and;
- The overall focus should be on implementation just as much as on the passage of laws.

While stressing that there is no absolute answer, the OECD has similarly produced a set of common features of successful privatisations (OECD 2003):

- Strong political commitment to privatisation at the highest level in order to overcome bureaucratic inertia and to resolve inter-institution rivalries in order to move the process forward;
- Clearly identified and prioritised objectives in order to provide the policy with focus and a sense of trade-offs that may be required;
- A transparent process to enhance the integrity of the privatisation process, gain credibility with potential investors and political support from the public;
- An effective communication campaign directed at the stakeholders in particular, to explain the policy objectives of privatisation and the means by which they are to be achieved in order to respond to public concerns and to gain support for the policy;
- Allocation of adequate resources (which includes human and financial resources), in order to meet the demands of the policy for the skills and resources that are required to accomplish the many tasks involved in privatisation.

Alongside such actions, it is equally important, as noted above, that legal systems exist that guarantee secure title to assets, with civil justice systems that provided effective recourse if needed, for instance in the event of default or bankruptcy. Beyond this, privatisation and transition to a market economy can lead to social problems. Former public sector industries, across the world and in all continents, may not be able to compete with imports and efficiency will tend to increase in any case, resulting in job losses if not rising unemployment.[13] Social adjustment programmes therefore have as an important a role as economic reform.

It is also important to note that privatisation needs to be underpinned by clear objectives, such as achieving efficiency gains and encouraging share ownership across society. Without clear objectives, it is unlikely that the state will maximise the benefits and minimise the risks of the privatisation. These objectives are also useful for the auditor, as they provide an analytical framework. NAO reports on privatisation adopted this method. Practical audit experience provides a number of lessons for achieving favourable outcomes from privatisation, and I turn to each of the sub-issues in **Box 4.5** in turn, viz:

- structuring the assets;
- disposing of the assets;
- addressing longer term issues;
- having the right skills.

### 5.5.1   Structuring Assets to Maximise the Success of Privatisation

A significant issue in planning for the divestment of public assets is the treatment of loss making entities. The market is unlikely to want to take over activity that is unlikely to be profitable in the long term. But if state assets are loss making as they tend to be, there is a difficult question to resolve which is whether such losses reflect inefficiencies that the market can address or whether they are intrinsic to the service being provided. This is likely to be especially true where provision of service continues that is justified on social grounds.

This much is obvious, but in practice such issues provide fertile ground for bureaucratic manipulation. On 25 September 1996 the Department of Trade and Industry sold all its 80 million shares in AEA Technology by flotation for £228 million. AEA Technology comprised the former commercial activities of the United Kingdom Atomic Energy Authority,

---

[13] Haltiwanger, J. Singh, M. (1999) 'Cross-country evidence on public sector retrenchment' *The World Bank Economic Review* **13**(1) 23–66.

(UKAEA), the public sector body that conducted nuclear research and development.

Restructuring AEA Technology, and separating it from UKAEA before the sale, cost £121million. The sponsoring Department of Trade and Industry considered that these costs were not sale costs. The department said that substantial restructuring was necessary to ensure AEA Technology's commercial viability, while the restructuring and separation of AEA Technology would also have been necessary to promote competition for nuclear decommissioning work and drive down decommissioning costs even if AEA Technology had remained in the public sector. It must remain a matter of speculation, however, when the restructuring would have taken place, what form it would have taken and how much this would have cost if the business had remained in public ownership.

Against this background I concluded that it was reasonable to regard at least part of these costs as expenditure related to the sale. But even though the report was generous in not pressing the point as much as it could have done – these things are indeed uncertain – the department held to the opposite view over the £121 million. It admitted that this was substantial in relation to the proceeds of the sale at £278 million, but 'modest' in relation to the liabilities of the organisation at £7 billion, presented by the department on an undiscounted basis.[14] The Committee of Public Accounts agreed with my report, saying 'it is unacceptable for departments to seek to inflate net sale proceeds by ignoring expenditure related to the sale'.[15]

More conventional as a sweetener is the write-off of debts. Before privatisation, Railtrack Group plc, the company responsible for fixed rail infrastructure such as track, signalling and stations, owed the Government almost £1.5 billion. The Government cancelled this old debt and created a new one, but of only £586 million, writing off £869 million. The Department of Transport also reduced the level of new debt in Railtrack by £225 million below what would otherwise have been feasible, in order to provide capacity for borrowing to fund Thameslink, a major rail investment.

It was expected that this reduction in debt would be offset by an increase in the equity proceeds by reducing the dividend yield which

---

[14] HM Treasury (1998) *Treasury Minute on the Sixtieth Report from the Committee of Public Accounts*, CM 4069.

[15] PAC (1998) *The Sale of AEA Technology*, Sixtieth Report, Session 1997–98, Conclusion xv.

investors required. There was little evidence to suggest that such a measure was necessary, partly as the debt reduction represented only part of the cost of Thameslink. Six major institutional investors whom we consulted told us that the Thameslink project did not have a significant influence on their valuations. The decision may have cost the taxpayer £125 million in lower proceeds.[16]

The conclusion is that meeting the policy objective to privatise may well be, perhaps not surprisingly, in contradiction with obtaining the best value for the taxpayer. This may or may not be a bad thing in that governments elected on a market liberalising ticket have objectives other than maximum sales proceeds, for instance creating more competitive markets in the long term or widening share ownership and developing a 'stakeholder' democracy. It makes it clear, however, that there may be hidden costs.

### 5.5.2   Having a Good Disposal Strategy

There are five key components to this:

#### 5.5.2.1   Protecting the Taxpayer by Putting in Place a Good Strategy for Privatisation

Timing is usually important in achieving the best sales proceeds from privatisation. The flotation of Railtrack features again. I concluded that the timing of the sale probably had an adverse impact on the value achieved, since it was carried out at a time when the market was only beginning to understand the new commercial and regulatory structures within the rail industry. The market was not in a position to make a fully formed judgement. A delay to the sale of Railtrack, even only by a few months, would have been helpful to institutional investors and analysts, as it would have enabled them to gain a better appreciation of Railtrack's business within the privatised rail industry. Investors would also have had more time to understand the regulatory regime and Railtrack's commercial relationships with its principal customers (the train operating companies) and suppliers (the infrastructure maintenance and track renewal companies).[17]

Another sale organised by the Department of Transport concerned three rolling stock leasing companies – Angel Train Contracts Limited,

---

[16] Comptroller and Auditor General *The Flotation of Railtrack* (HC 25, Session 1998–1999).
[17] Comptroller and Auditor General *The Flotation of Railtrack* (HC 25, Session 1998–1999).

Eversholt Leasing Limited and Porterbrook Leasing Company Limited – to three separate purchasers. The sale was completed in January and February 1996 and it raised some £1.8 billion in total. I found that by February 1997, these purchasers had sold the businesses on at a substantial profit:[18]

- Angel was sold in December 1997 to the Royal Bank of Scotland Group in a transaction valuing the business at some £1.1 billion, 58 per cent more than the £696 million received by the Department.
- Porterbrook was sold to Stagecoach Holdings in August 1996 for £826 million, 56 per cent more than the £528 million received by the Department.
- In February 1997 the Forward Trust Group, part of HSBC Holdings plc, bought Eversholt for £726 million, 40 per cent more than the £518 million received by the Department.

Why did this happen? In essence, the sale took place too soon. The over-riding objective of the then Government was to secure the sale of the companies as soon as practicable. The Government saw major advantages in the early sale of these very large businesses, so they could take place ahead of the privatisation of Railtrack and the train operating companies, including early receipt of substantial proceeds and added impetus to rail privatisation. The chosen timing of the sale had an adverse impact on proceeds because of uncertainty over the financial prospects for the companies. The prospective customers of the rolling stock companies, the train operators, had little or no relevant track record in the to-be-privatised industry; and bidders were not in any case certain that the overall rail privatisation programme would be completed because there was stated political opposition to it.

### 5.5.2.2 Pricing Assets Correctly

The pricing of assets is a difficult exercise, especially if there is no basis of commercial operation to act as a guide. In the case of the sale of another set of railway assets, the British Rail Maintenance Depots, I reported that the Department did not carry out any valuations at all. Their argument was that there were no comparable companies in the market on which financial information was available, so that a benchmark valuation

---

[18] Comptroller and Auditor General *Privatisation of the Rolling Stock Leasing Companies* (HC 576, Session 1997–1998).

would not have been helpful to the sales process and would have been poor value for money. The private sector took a somewhat different view and carried out valuations on the basis of analyses of the projected cash flows of the businesses. The lack of valuations by the public sector was strange, as I found that British Rail's advisers had done similar calculations early in the process but they had not featured later on.[19]

### 5.5.2.3   Establishing a Good Market

Establishing a good market with competitive bidding for state assets is of course essential to achieve a good price. To a degree this comes back to structuring the assets in the best way to attract interest, but practical considerations can intervene. In the sale of railway depots, I found that there was little effective competition between bidders.[20] This was partly because of British Rail's desire to sell the depots to a number of parties, to avoid selling some combinations of depots and not to close one particular depot.

There were also concerns on the part of some potential bidders about the success of the wider rail privatisation programme, which curtailed interest. In the end, two bidders negotiated significant reductions to their bids, suggesting that price tension was not strong, despite the efforts of the vendor to avoid letting the purchasers know that they were effectively (although not formally) preferred bidders.

This is not the only case. When it came to selling the Royal Dockyards at Devonport and Rosyth the Ministry of Defence was unable to generate much competition.[21] The Ministry had to compare the sale arrangements with a theoretical case of what might have happened if they had continued with the Government Owned Contractor Operated arrangements at the dockyards. The consideration obtained in the end represented a significant discount on the Ministry's own valuations of the businesses – a discount of 56 per cent at Devonport and 36 per cent for Rosyth. At Rosyth, the new owners also took the benefit of a £ 6.5 million abatement of consideration to reflect their redundancy liabilities, and a deferred payment of the purchase price of £ 6 million. Furthermore, to

---

[19] Comptroller and Auditor General *British Rail Maintenance Limited: Sale of Maintenance Depots* (HC 583, Session 1995–1996) and PAC, (1997), *British Rail Maintenance Limited: The Sale of Maintenance Depots*, HC 168, Twenty-second Report, Session 1996–1997.

[20] Comptroller and Auditor General *British Rail Maintenance Limited: Sale of Maintenance Depots* (HC 583, Session 1995–1996).

[21] Comptroller and Auditor General *Sales of the Royal Dockyards* (HC 748, Session 1997–1998).

enable the new owners of the Devonport dockyard to finance their capital expenditure programme, the Ministry agreed to the purchaser taking the assets into their balance sheet at a value some £ 33 million higher than the consideration received. The effect was to increase the depreciation and profit elements in the cost of future refitting of navy ships.

The need for good provision of information is another key factor. As the twenty first century approached, the Government resolved upon a scheme to build a Millennium Exhibition. This was to be of a scale and stature comparable with the Great Exhibition of 1851, which had been housed in Paxton's Crystal Palace, and with the centennial anniversary Festival of Britain in 1951, which aimed to raise the nation's spirits after the austerity and sufferings of the War. The resulting Millennium Dome was a triumph of engineering as one of the largest, if not the largest, single roofed structures in the world and it opened on time as the clock struck at midnight for 1 January 2000.

Unfortunately the Dome was a financial failure. Visitor numbers failed to meet expectations. Naturally, the senior managers were replaced and more grants were made. By August 2000, however, the external accountants judged that the project was insolvent. I will not go into the reasons for the difficulties which I uncovered, which can be found elsewhere (**Box 5.6**).[22] The point at hand is that the Dome is situated in one of the main growth areas proposed for economic regeneration and development in the South East of England. Public investment in remediation, servicing and landscaping works and in transport links had opened up the site for intensive and profitable redevelopment. After various false starts, a deal with a developer was concluded in May 2002. It turned out that there had been confusion among potential bidders about how much land was on offer.[23] Information emerged to each consortium in a piecemeal and unstructured manner which did little to further the sale objectives.

### 5.5.2.4  Selling the Right Quantity of Assets

It may not be clear in the early days of a privatisation programme what the risks and rewards are likely to be. The political imperative, as well as the economic imperative in transition economies, is likely to be to

---

[22] Comptroller and Auditor General *The Millennium Dome* (HC 936, Session 1999–2000).

[23] Comptroller and Auditor General *Regeneration of the Millennium Dome and Associated Land* (HC 178, Session 2004–2005).

make progress in a way that is hard for another political party to reverse at a later date.

---

**Box 5.6:     The Millennium Dome**

The Millennium Dome is a unique project. It was conceived as a Millennium Exhibition of a scale and stature comparable with that of the Great Exhibition of 1851 and the Festival of Britain of 1951. The project was to provide the centrepiece for the nation's Millennium celebrations by opening on New Year's Eve and running through the year 2000.

The project was to be funded from the National Lottery, visitors and commercial sponsors. It was intended that the Dome should be a lasting millennium legacy and to secure this a competition was launched to find a buyer who would run the Dome as a viable commercial entity after 2000.

The initial competition to find a future use for the Millennium Dome began in March 1999, but failed to find a buyer about to complete the deal on acceptable terms. The main reasons behind the lack of success of this original competition were the complex nature of the competition process and the difficulty the Government faced in deriving sufficient confidence about the deliverability of innovative proposals from bidders.

In March 2001 a second sale process was initiated. It followed a different approach in adopting limited competition, against a background of little market enthusiasm for a rerun of open competition, widespread doubts about the risks and costs of participation, and little specific interest in the Dome. The scale of the final deal expanded to include over 100 acres more land than had been explicitly offered.

In 2004 a deal was concluded with Meridian Delta Ltd and the Aschutz Entertainment Group (Anschutz) for the redevelopment over 20 years of the whole northern Greenwich Peninsula, including reuse of the Dome. The deal is complex. It preserves the Dome in place until

2018, housing a large indoor arena and leisure complex, and provides for a major office development and some 10,000 new homes on the adjacent land.

*Source:* Comptroller and Auditor General *The Millennium Dome* (HC 936, Session 1999–2000), Comptroller and Auditor General *Regeneration of the Millennium Dome and Associated Land* (HC 178, Session 2004–2005).

This was shown in 1977 with an Initial Public Offering (IPO) for the oil company British Petroleum. Even at this initial stage in UK privatisation the Department of Trade and Industry wanted to guard against the possibility that large profits would be made at the taxpayer's expense, a situation that might have occurred if the offering was underpriced and the shares rose substantially in value in the long term, beyond any reasonable premium needed to create interest during the sale itself.[24] As a result, only 51 per cent of the shares were offered up for sale.

It was therefore surprising that, as late as December 1990, the twelve regional electricity companies in England and Wales were sold in their entirety. Among the reasons for complete disposal was a statement of intent by the main Opposition Political party to repurchase sufficient shares to give more then 51 per cent state control of the companies to the State. This was thought by the Government to be likely to reduce investor confidence particularly in a partial sale.[25]

The sale of National Power and PowerGen, which at the time generated most of the electricity produced in England and Wales, took a different course in 1991. The successful sale of the regional electricity companies among other factors indicated that it was possible to give more attention to getting the offer price of shares right. Approximately 60 per cent of the shares were sold at the initial offering, with the rest sold at a later date.[26]

The sale of the water authorities in 1992, however, was not phased. The Committee of Public Accounts said 'as our predecessors stated in 1987–88, there can be considerable benefits in a phased sale. Although

---

[24] Comptroller and Auditor General *Sale of Shareholding in British Telecommunications plc* (HC 495, Session1984–1985).

[25] Comptroller and Auditor General *The Sale of the Twelve Regional Electricity Companies* (HC 10, Session 1992–1993).

[26] Comptroller and Auditor General *The Sale of National Power and PowerGen* (HC 46, Session 1992–1993).

the Department took account of our predecessors' views in reaching their decision, we regret that a phased sale was not undertaken'.[27]

To return to the 1996 flotation of Railtrack Group plc, all the shares were sold *en bloc*, rather than in a phased sale, because a phased sale would have resulted in fewer proceeds initially, not just because of the reduced number of shares on offer, but also because the initial share price would most likely have been lower. But overall, when illustrative calculations based on a number of assumptions were carried out, I judged that overall sales proceeds might have been increased by at least £ 600 million if the Government had been able to effect a phased sale and had retained 20 per cent of the shares, and by £ 1.5 billion had they retained 40 per cent.[28]

### 5.5.2.5   The Right Disposal Method

As noted above there are several ways to divest state assets and there is no simple answer to what is most appropriate. In Britain all the methods described have been used, including trade sales and sales to the public, which have involved incentives to hold shares and payment by instalments. Another variant still is the 'bought deal', which involves the sale of shares at a given price to an intermediary, who sells on to investors taking the risk or benefits of a subsequent change in price. The Treasury developed a process by which the intermediaries bid for the shares in a competitive auction without the sale becoming public knowledge, avoiding the risk of a fall in prices if the trading market at large had known about and anticipated an increased supply of shares.

In other countries sales may have different priority objectives. For example, privatisation may have the distribution of ownership of assets as a main, rather than subsidiary, objective. The voucher schemes used in the early 1990s in transition economies are a case in point as a relevant method of disposal to a large number of citizens, where shares were in effect given to the population, or could be bought for small sums.

The auction is another disposal method which has been used in Britain. An interesting example I looked at was the successful sale of part of the UK's gold reserves. In May 1999 the Government announced that it would sell around 415 tonnes of UK gold reserves over the medium

---

[27] PAC (1992) *Sale of the Water Authorities in England and Wales*, HC 140, Seventh Report, Session 1992–1993.

[28] Comptroller and Auditor General *The Flotation of Railtrack* (HC 25, Session 1998–1999) paragraph 21.

term to restructure the UK's reserve holdings to achieve a better balance in the portfolio by increasing the proportion held in currency.[29] Prices achieved were competitive and in line with the gold market price at the time, despite the size of the sales.

### 5.5.3   Addressing Longer Term Issues

Two additional issues promote debate. Should the government hold a 'golden share' or a substantial shareholding in privatised companies to prevent them coming under the control of owners regarded as politically undesirable? In Russia, the government has moved to prevent the control of privatised gas and oil companies coming under foreign ownership. This is, of course, a political question, not for the auditor, though restrictions on ownership make the shares of any company less attractive in the market. And second, how should privatised industries be regulated? If privatisation puts an organisation into a freely competitive market, no special regulation may be necessary. But if, as is usually the case, privatised companies are monopolies or oligopolies then regulatory agencies are often established to provide a fair balance between consumers and shareholders.

The need for regulation stems in part from the natural monopoly nature of privatised 'pipes and wires' industries such as, gas and electricity. Even here though, the separation out of the common carrier assets, such as the national electricity grid, which are the fundamental 'natural' part of utility 'monopoly', provides a basis for allowing effective competition between different producers. Economies of scale, which might drive concentration in industries up, need not be a restraining factor on new entrants. The 1983 Energy Act for instance established the right of any producer, even one with just a domestic wind generator on the roof, to have their electricity bought by the then pre-privatised monolithic Central Electricity Generating Board and the local Area Electricity Boards, at economically sound prices related to marginal costs, through the principle of 'avoidable costs'.

In Britain at least, the process of privatisation led to the sequential establishment of regulatory bodies where the method of regulation commonly adopted by the regulators was the RPI-X pricing formula, where RPI stands for the retail price index and X stands for efficiency gains

---

[29] Comptroller and Auditor General *The Sale of Part of the UK Gold Reserves* (HC 86, Session 2000–2001).

to be made and which offset increases to potential price movements of the product due to general inflation. A major issue here is asymmetry of information. The industry knows far better than anyone else what its true cost structure is. And there is always a danger of the regulator being 'captured' by those he or she is established to regulate, if only because close dealings with regulatees may secure sympathetic consideration from the regulators.

### 5.5.4 Having the Right Skills

It is clear from the above that the role of advisors can be all important in privatisation. Their advice is often essential in determining the right price for assets, the best sale approach and method of disposal. Advisors are not, however, infallible and they certainly add to sale costs. In the sale of the Royal Dockyards described above the sales costs were some 40 percent greater than the department originally estimated and a cost of £ 15.7 million represented over a quarter of the amount the department actually received on completion.[30] Advisors' costs in the sale of the government and parliamentary printer, the Stationery Office, when added to the sale costs of £ 3.1 million, were equivalent to 44 per cent of the sale proceeds of £ 12 million.[31]

The cost of advisors may be small numerically in the context of a disposal programme involving a significant part of the economy, but there are clear economies of scale. In contrast to the Stationery Office case, the Railtrack flotation raising £ 1.9 billion involved advisors' costs of £ 11 million within overall costs of £ 39 million:[32]

- Overall costs can be controlled through the use of pre-determined ceilings and monitoring. Departmental teams can bring in staff who have worked on other sales as a source of expertise. And advice can be commissioned through a competition;
- Conflicts of interest which advisers may have must be identified and avoided. Different parts of large advisory firms may be able potentially to gain from knowledge elsewhere in the organisation. Commissions which depend on achieved sales volumes and in particular achieving a

---

[30] Comptroller and Auditor General *Sales of the Royal Dockyards* (HC 748 Session 1997–1998).

[31] Comptroller and Auditor General *The Sale of the Stationery Office* (HC 522, Session 1997–1998).

[32] Comptroller and Auditor General *Department of the Environment, Transport and Regions: The Flotation of Railtrack* (HC25 1998–99).

sale of all shares on offer could in principle lead to advice that would depress the offer price. A safeguard is the reputational advantage that an advisor may wish to preserve more than make short term financial gain but this may not always be the case;

- Last but not least, it is clear that advisors are only one component in achieving value for money, not in the sense that they represent, normally at least, a small proportion of sales revenues, but in the sense that the adoption of even the soundest advice is dependent on it being *useful* in meeting the privatisation objectives.

**What have been the results of privatisation:**

- Has the consumer gained through putting state entitles into the private sector?
- Have real prices fallen?
- Has quality improved?

The answer is mixed. A study by David Parker[33] showed that:

- In most of the UK public utilities prices have fallen (e.g. average telecommunications charges fell by 48 per cent between 1984 and 1989). It is debatable as to whether this would have occurred without privatisation and the innovation this brought;
- Quality of services has improved in most privatised industries, often as the result of regulator's pressure;
- The rates of return on capital employed has tended to increase (e.g. for water, rate of return on capital employed increased from 9.8 per cent at privatisation to 11.1 per cent by 1996/97). Shareholders, directors and staff have also gained, though most privatised industries employ many less people than under state ownership; and,
- There is also the point that improvements were often the result of technical advances, though the changes of ownership may have encouraged their adoption.

## 5.6   CONCLUSION

Has privatisation worked? There is no one answer. But three views may be distinguished which may assist the auditor. There is something, but not everything to be said for them all. The first is from Michael Jack,

---

[33] Parker, D. (2004) *The UK's Privatisation Experiment: The passage of time permits a sober assessment,* CESIFO Working Paper, February, No. 1126.

Chief Secretary of the Treasury in the British Government in 1996. He spoke when early experience reflected the advantages gained from the substantial change that privatisation entailed (**Box 5.7**).

---

**Box 5.7:**

'Before privatisation, nationalised industries operated in a regime that was against the interests of the public, in whose name they were ostensibly run. Their prices were set at the whim of Whitehall as their management were shielded from the commercial realities of competition and the profit motive. They had no incentive to improve service to their customers, and their investment needs often went unfulfilled as commercially sensible investment was routinely squeezed out in the face of more pressing public spending needs.

The resulting inefficiencies were paid for by the customer through higher prices and poor service, by the taxpayer through subsidy, and by the economy generally through underinvestment. As my hon. Friend rightly said, privatisation has dealt with those issues. In contrast, the transfer to the private sector, where there is the discipline of the market or, where necessary, of independent regulation, has transformed the performance of our once nationalised companies.' (Jack 1996)

*Source:* Jack, Michael (1996) *Adjournment Debate, House of Commons*, 15 May, Hansard Columns 904, 905.

---

Secondly, there is the study by David Parker, already noted above. Writing in 2004, eight years after Michael Jack, he gave a generally though not completely supportive view. In essence, he argued that the ownership change implied by privatisation has not been enough to secure improvements in price and service quality. Where they have been secured it has been due to competition and/or for effective regulation, aided by technological advance.

Thirdly, Anthony Hilton writing in the *Evening Standard* in 2006 takes account of privatisation experience spanning almost a quarter of a century, and a British experience where privatised companies can be bought and sold internationally, just like other companies.[34] His argument that

---

[34] Hilton, A. (2006) 'Depressing truth behind rush for Thames Water' *Evening Standard* 7 August, p. 25.

short term gains from privatisation have been gathered in perhaps implies that, in the long run, privatisation marks less of a sea change than its protagonists claim **(Box 5.8)**.

---

**Box 5.8:**

It would be hard to find a greater example of the gulf between the City and the country than in the attitudes to Thames Water. German utility RWE has decided to sell the business it paid £ 7 billion for in 2000 and financial buyers are popping up from all over the world to line put in their bids.

Because it is such a lot of money, the bidders are working in teams – there are consortia with backers in Canada, the US, Australia, the Middle East, Hong Kong, and continental Europe. Indeed, the list of buyers underlines two interesting facts about the modern world – we really do have an international capital market, and with interest rates and returns on conventional assets at historic lows, investors running pools of capital will consider any proposition that appears to offer a secure investment and good rate of return.

Thames is clearly well thought-of in this section of the investment community. Contrast this within what the customers think of it. Though it would for many years have been considered a quite impossible challenge, utilities in general and Thames Water in particular have successfully displaced the banks as the businesses most despised by their customers.

You don't have to look far to see why. First, the business is a monopoly and, in common with other privatised utilities, society relies on a regulator to protect the public interest. But the regulator's tools are limited and in the end come down to capping the return companies can make on their assets as a way of imposing the discipline that if they want to make more they have to cut costs and get more efficient.

Unfortunately, the good intentions of the regulator often bring perverse results. Caps on investment returns have given companies insufficient incentive to modernise while the constant pressure to cut costs, though it removed a lot of fat in the early years, has also destroyed any reputation the companies might have had for customer service. So the perception of Thames Water customers is that they pay more and more for what so often appears to be a deteriorating service.

---

One can see why. The company has applied for a drought order which gives it the right to cut supplies to customers. It has failed to hit its targets for cutting leaks and been ordered by the regulator to up its efforts by spending an extra £ 150 million. It has a further £ 140 million to pay in fines for failing to meet the required standards of customer service. And the Environmental Agency labels it as one of the country's worst polluters.

With this legacy, one might have expected buyers to steer clear of the business, in part because other costly horrors might be lurking there, but also because we are told these days that companies value their reputations and will go to great lengths to avoid damaging them.

The truth, however, is that private companies by and large care a lot less about risk to their reputation than quoted companies do – witness the behaviour of some of the private equity houses and hedge funds. Equally to the point, reputational risk really only bites when the company's customers have a choice. These businesses are monopolies where the customer cannot switch to another supplier and they can behave accordingly.

From the customer's perspective, the line-up of potential buyers for Thames Water is therefore infinitely depressing because they are all financially driven, tempted by the security of the guaranteed returns rather than the challenge to improve customer service and deliver better value.

This is the crux of the matter, the reason why many of these privatisations are beginning to have outlived their usefulness. Monopolies need a regulator and a regulator, however diligent, is no substitute for consumer choice. But it is the customers, not the owners of the business, who suffer as a consequence.

*Source:* Hilton, A. (2006) 'Depressing truth behind rush for Thames Water' Evening Standard 7 August, p. 25.

This chapter has set out the range of considerations that an auditor could usefully bear in mind when required to audit a privatisation process and its subsequent regulation. These considerations derive from a real understanding of the issues that arise, and more details of this approach are given in the guidelines produced by the Working Group under United Kingdom chairmanship on the Audit of Privatisation of the International Organisation of Supreme Audit Institutions – the international body of presidents of courts of audit and auditors general of the member countries of the United Nations.[35] **Box 5.8** illustrates some of the key areas or questions the auditor might focus on to promote the best value for money solution in any consideration of whether privatisation is likely to represent the best option to achieve long term sustainable value for money.

---

**Box 5.9:    Arriving at the best value for money option: Key issues which the auditor can helpfully focus on**

The auditor has an important function to protect the taxpayer and hold the public sector to account in any decision to privatise but in drawing on accumulated knowledge and experience should suggest questions in a way which can help arrive at the best long term value for money solution. Areas of interest are likely to be:

- whether privatisation is an appropriate action, in terms of whether market based provision of public services provides an acceptable trade-off between greater market discipline based efficiency and any social, equity, distributional or other government policy objectives;
- whether alternatives to privatisation offer greater benefits;
- that disposal of state assets is handled in the most effective way, in particular whether clear and appropriate objectives are set for the privatisation and whether it will be organised in a way likely to produce the greatest benefit for the taxpayer in terms of the price achieved;
- the extent to which the privatised sectors are subject to competition or effective regulation, to protect the citizen from the abuse of monopoly power;
- ensuring that lessons from past privatisations are identified, promoted as good practice and applied for future disposals.

*Source:* National Audit Office.

---

[35] INTOSAI Working Group on the Audit of Privatisations (1998) *Guidelines on the Best Practice for the Audit of Economic Regulation.*

INTOSAI Working Group on the Audit of Privatisation (2001) *Guidelines on the Best Practice for the Audit of Economic Regulation.*

## 5.7  SUMMARY

Privatisation has been the great attempt of the last quarter of the twentieth century to break free from defects in bureaucracy. It was facilitated world wide by the collapse of communism and rising interest in public choice theories and market solutions.

However, problems can occur where privatisation neglects:

- Securing title to property being privatised – a problem in many ex-communist countries;
- Valuation – not a science but certainly an art that can be well or badly conducted;
- Competitive pressure – vital if the best outcome is to be secured.

The auditor of the privatisation process and its subsequent regulation[36] needs to attend to these problems and advise on them, paying special attention to the methods used, including: sales of shares; trade sales and auctions; sales to management and staff, and; above all, drawing conclusions on performance so far and making recommendations for the future.

Finally, on the question of whether privatisation so far has been a success in terms of lower prices and better quality of goods and services, the evidence suggests that this often is the case but that the change of ownership in privatisation by itself is often less significant than the competitive pressure and technical change that the privatisation facilitates. And where privatisation still leaves elements of monopoly or oligopoly, regulatory activity can balance the interest of shareholders, management and consumers, but does not always do so.

---

[36] The auditor's role does end once the former state owned industry is privatised. In the UK for example, the Comptroller and Auditor General is now the auditor of the statutory bodies established to regulate the privatised industries. As such the Comptroller and Auditor General is able to report to Parliament on a range of performance issues for example, on the extent to which the interests of those who rely on the industry are protected.

# 6
# Public Private Partnerships – Another Option

In the introductory section of the previous chapter, which set out at **Box 5.2** the various models of private sector involvement in the provision of services, a distinction was drawn between Private Finance Initiative (PFI) schemes, where the state bought a service rather than created an asset and Public Private Partnerships (PPP), where the public authorities contributes part of the initial finance of a project and may be involved in the delivery of the service.

Taking PFI schemes first, **Box 6.1** compares responsibilities between PFI and conventional procurement and **Box 6.2** compares the payment profiles over time between the two approaches.

**Box 6.1: Comparison of responsibilities under PFI and conventional procurements**

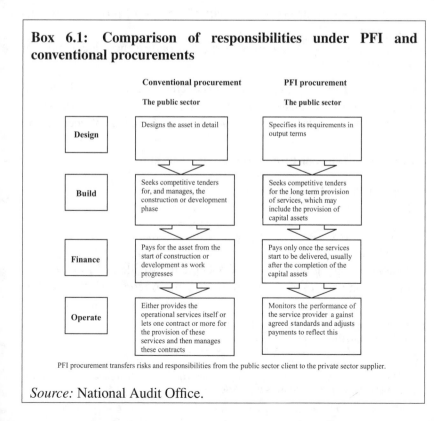

|  | Conventional procurement<br>The public sector | PFI procurement<br>The public sector |
|---|---|---|
| **Design** | Designs the asset in detail | Specifies its requirements in output terms |
| **Build** | Seeks competitive tenders for, and manages, the construction or development phase | Seeks competitive tenders for the long term provision of services, which may include the provision of capital assets |
| **Finance** | Pays for the asset from the start of construction or development as work progresses | Pays only once the services start to be delivered, usually after the completion of the capital assets |
| **Operate** | Either provides the operational services itself or lets one contract or more for the provision of these services and then manages these contracts | Monitors the performance of the service provider against agreed standards and adjusts payments to reflect this |

PFI procurement transfers risks and responsibilities from the public sector client to the private sector supplier.

*Source:* National Audit Office.

**Box 6.2:     Payments under PFI and traditional procurement**

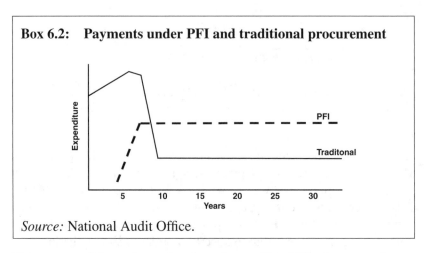

*Source:* National Audit Office.

These are useful starting points in understanding PFI schemes and part-nerships, since while the latter kind of arrangement will not have the simplicities of orthodox PFI schemes, the essential points of difference from conventional procurement remain:

- private money contributes all or part of the cost of providing the ser-vice; and
- private sector expertise contributes all or part of the management of the service.

The variety of PFI and partnership arrangements is legion and **Box 6.3** sets out some of the most important, with international examples drawn from the reports made to the INTOSAI Working Group mentioned above.

**Box 6.3:     Types of Public Private Partnership[1]**

| Type of Public Private Partnership | Example |
| --- | --- |
| *Joint ventures.* The private and public sectors set up a jointly owned company to complete a project which brings benefits to both parties. | In the UK the Radiocommunication Agency has entered into a partnership with CMG plc to provide IT infrastructure and to market the Agency's skills in radio wave management to potential wireless customers. |

---

[1] INTOSAI Working Group on the Audit of Privatisation (2004), *Guidelines on Best Practice for the Audit of Risk in Public/Private Partnership.*

*Franchises.* The private sector is permitted to provide and charge the public for services which would normally be provided by the state, in return for a fee.

In Argentina, the right to provide utilities to the public was granted to private licence holders in 1989. The licence holders operate under the regulation of Public Utility Control Bodies.

*Concessions.* Similar to franchise agreements except that the private sector will usually provide finance to build the necessary infrastructure, such as a bridge or road.

In Hungry, an international consortium constructed, developed and financed the toll road M1/M15, which connects Vienna and Budapest.

*Privately financed investment projects.* A private company obtains the funds to design, construct/refurbish and operate/maintain a public asset such as a hospital. Once the asset is operating a regular fee is paid by the public sector for a set period (usually 20–35 years). At the end of this period, the asset reverts to public ownership.

In the UK, O2, a private company has signed a framework agreement to provide a new radio service to all of the police forces in England Scotland and Wales. O2 will finance, design and build the fixed assets required to transmit radio signals. They will then operate the system for 19 years.

*Retaining minority shares in privatised companies.* The state retains an agreed percentage of the shares, in order to keep some control over the provision of services to the public.

In Hungary, the Herend China Manufacture Company was privatised through a management buy-out, with the state retaining a 25 per cent shareholding.

| | |
|---|---|
| *Market Testing.* Private companies are invited to tender for a contract to provide public services, in competition with the existing public sector provider. | In the UK, competitions have been held to manage five prisons. Bids were judged on the basis of cost, security and the quality of regimes provided for prisoners. Of these, two are now managed by private companies. The other three competitions were won by public sector teams. The management contracts will be re-let after 10 years. |
| *Use of private sector methods in public bodies,* such as performance measurements, incentive schemes for staff and rationalisation of resources. | In Denmark, the bus division of the state railway (a public corporation) was split from the rest of the company, in order to ensure that the company competed on equal terms with private transport companies, thus improving the quality of service offered to the public. |

*Source: Guidelines on Best Practice for the Audit of Risk in Public/Private Partnership* INTOSAI 2004.

## 6.1   GETTING THE BEST FROM PFI/PPP DEALS

The assessment of value for money obtained from PPP/PFI is complicated by the fact that contractual provision spans decades – typically three in the UK. It requires an audit approach that is *cumulative*, which asks how good a deal the taxpayer has obtained so far. An encouraging answer does not mean that that is the conclusion to be drawn over the whole life of the project.

In terms of project life cycle, the first high level cut comes once a deal has been agreed and the contract signed. Beyond that, the project is into its delivery phase and then operation. Unlike the assessment of the deal, the evaluation of operational value for money requires a longitudinal methodology (which has implications for the cost of the audit). The possibility arises that bad deals may work well and good deals may work badly, though the latter is perhaps not as likely as the former.

As with privatisation, the broad principles that have emerged from our audit work can be set out in terms of two more sets of 4-pillars. **Box 6.4** sets out the main issues for considering whether the process up to financial close was good value for money for the taxpayer, which is

## Box 6.4:    The 4-Pillars, in bold, for determining if a PPP/PFI deal is a good one

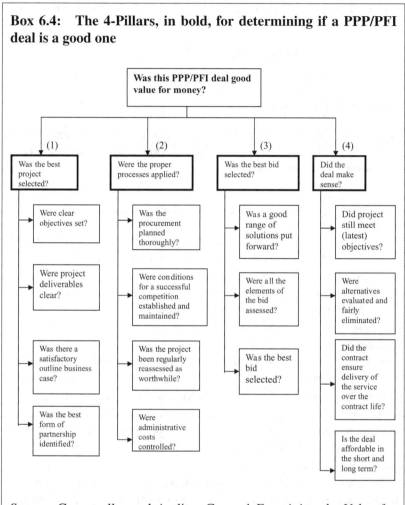

*Source:* Comptroller and Auditor General *Examining the Value for Money of Deals under the Private Finance Initiative* (HC 739, Session 1998–1999).

taken from a report we produced based on experience from the start of the PFI programme up to the late 1990s.[2] The passage of time indicates that the fundamentals still hold true, though at the time, we described the report as 'interim'. This was on the basis that experience would grow,

---

[2] Comptroller and Auditor General *Examining the Value for Money of Deals under the Private Finance Initiative* (HC 739, Session 1998–1999) based on Appendix 1.

as indeed it has. I return to this question below. The fundamental audit questions are:

- was the best project selected?
- were the proper processes applied?
- was the best bid selected? and
- did the deal make sense?

Beyond this the ultimate question is whether the PFI route delivers long term better value for money compared to more conventional ways of delivering public services.

## 6.2   SELECTING THE BEST PROJECT

Selection of the best project, and in particular the associated sub-issue about the right form of partnership, involves strategic thinking that makes no assumption in the first instance about whether the PPP/PFI route is desirable or the best. The thought process here depends on the stand-point, and the highest vantage point corresponds to thinking about public spending as a whole, rather than about whatever individual service might be considered for PPP/PFI or not.

**Box 6.5** illustrates the possibilities that are resolved by different decision making processes. Working downwards, decisions about resource allocation across government are for the Finance Ministry in the United Kingdom and are subject to Comprehensive Spending Reviews, which result in fixed three-year Departmental Expenditure Limits. Public Service Agreements (PSA), define the key improvements that the public can expect from these resources.

Decisions about allocation of resources within an individual public authority depend on investment appraisal in its widest sense. A number of Departments have used the ROAMEF approach, described in chapter 3, which seeks to justify each policy choice in terms of a Rationale, Objectives, Cost-benefit Appraisal, Monitoring, Evaluation requirements, as well as Feedback.[3] The last means applying the lessons of monitoring and evaluation to policy design and improvement and is very important.

---

[3] HM Treasury (2003), *The Green Book: appraisal and evaluation in central government*, The Stationery Office, London.

**Box 6.5: Schematic 'yes-no' choices in public procurement which may or may not lead to PPP/PFI solution**

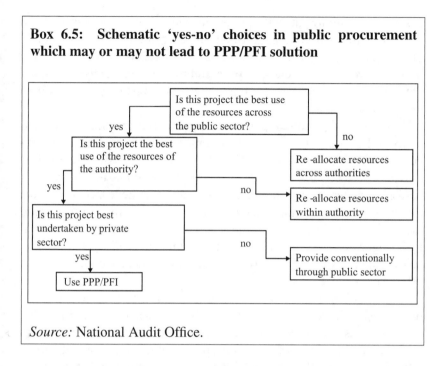

*Source:* National Audit Office.

One level down, a project that has been justified in general terms can then be considered against the different delivery options. The objective is to discover how the different options compare with each other, through the process of the *public sector comparator* calculation. It compares the costs of different options of procurement over their full lifetime, for example over a 30 year contract, to find a net present value. This might be in the form of a set of costs of different ways of providing the same mix of outputs of a given standard. Alternatively, it would be possible to conduct the comparator test along the lines of a more sophisticated cost benefit exercise, in which both benefits and costs are allowed to vary to some extent.[4] The Public Sector Comparator is an area in which the National Audit Office has been as central as it has been critical.

The Ministry of Defence (MOD) requires secure, modern and efficient working accommodation in central London, close to Downing Street, from which to direct Britain's defence operations. Looking at its needs it decided to redevelop its Main Building. The PFI deal was going to

---

[4] See for example: Grout, P. A. (2005) 'Value for money measurement in public-private partnerships', *European Investment Bank Papers.* **10**(2) 32–57.

cost £746.1 million at 2000 prices discounted at 6 per cent over 30 years. Calculations were made about the cost of a conventional public procurement. The answer came out at £746.2 million. What can be made of this microscopic difference? We recommended that decisions should not be based on transparently thin wafers, and meaning 'thin' as both small and tendentious.[5]

A further and important point is that public sector comparators generally did not take into account the improvements in traditional procurement which were being achieved as a result of lessons learned on previous projects. Instead, judgements were needed as to whether past performance would continue unchanged in the future, especially where that past performance had been particularly poor.[6] The Treasury heard these points and in 2003 the system was changed to ensure an economically rigorous appraisal of a project's outline business case prior to its procurement, to allow an alternative route to be chosen at this stage if it offers better value for money.[7]

One question begs to be asked: how was it that the early answers tended to be biased towards a PPP solution? In fact, the main driver that had led to answers pointing to a PFI solution in particular, especially in health and education, was that conventional financing required capital allocations and in the United Kingdom, as perhaps in other countries too, these were not easily to be had from the UK Finance Ministry, the Treasury. On the other hand, if PFI projects could be put on the private sector balance sheet, and not that of the public sector, then the Treasury's financing and borrowing capacity would not be strained. The bureaucratic system duly responded and most projects were arranged so as to be off-balance sheet.

Public sector comparators showed what they had to show; and some PPP assets appeared on neither the private nor public balance sheets!

Turning again to obtaining good value at the strategic thinking stage, the clarity of objectives is an obvious but problematic issue, and doubly so if combined with a lack of competition. There is a very good example. The Government decided in the early 1990s to develop a national standard IT strategy for Magistrates' Courts, contracting for this through a PFI project known as Libra, at a planned cost of some £180 million over

---

[5] Comptroller and Auditor General *Redevelopment of MOD Main Building* (HC 748, Session 2001–2002).

[6] PAC (2000) *The PFI Contract for the New Dartford and Gravesham Hospital*, HC 131, Twelfth Report, Session 1999–00, conclusion x, The Stationery Office, London.

[7] HM Treasury (2003) *PFI: Meeting the Investment Challenge*, Section 7, London.

$10\frac{1}{2}$ years. Based on our investigations, as described in Box 4.3, it was judged by Parliament to be one of the worst PFI deals.[8] The competition for the work attracted only one bidder, and there was a lack of decisive action when the contractor did not deliver what was required. For its part, the contractor had not understood the requirements, had taken on excessive risk and had under priced its bid.[9]

## 6.3   APPLYING THE PROPER PROCESSES TO PPP/PFI

As for privatisation, establishing a competitive market of bidders for PFI/PPP projects is a fundamental requirement for getting good value. A number of lessons have emerged from examinations of PPP/PFI deals, which indicate where processes should be established or existing ones strengthened to achieve good value for money from PPP:

- If there is limited interest on the part of the market, the project may not be formulated well enough.
- Competitive tension among a number of bidders needs to be maintained for as long as possible and the period between selection of preferred bidder and award of contract should be kept to a minimum. The contracting process has typically comprised taking forward discussions with bidders until one, the single 'preferred bidder', is chosen. After this point, competitive tension is lost and exclusive negotiations with the single remaining bidder about outstanding issues are likely to be poor value for money. In countries within the European Union, the new Competitive Dialogue procedure introduced from 31 January 2006, stemming from the EU Procurement Directive 2004/18/EC and applying to complex deals, limits post-preferred bidder discussion to fine tuning and clarificatory issues.[10] Whether this will be enough to cope with the problems remains to be seen. For example, the competition for the Dartford and Gravesham Hospital in the south of England ended up with one bidder, although this consortium was not told of the withdrawal of the other original bidder. Most of the contract terms were negotiated with the single bidder and the cost rose by

---

[8] PAC (2003) Summary and Conclusions, *New IT System for Magistrates' Courts: The Libra Project*, HC 434, Forty-fourth Report, Session 2002–2003, The Stationery Office, London.

[9] Comptroller and Auditor General *New IT systems for Magistrates' Courts: the Libra project*, (HC 327, Session 2002–2003).

[10] Office of Government Commerce (2006) *Regulatory Impact Assessment—Public Contracts Regulations 2006.*

33 per cent in real terms over the indicative bid submitted, though partly as a result of changes made by the public sector client.[11] The increase was finally mitigated to a 17 per cent increase but the lessons of limited competition are clear.

- Public sector delay adds to cost pressure. An example is the 35 years PFI contract for the new West Middlesex Hospital, with an estimated net present value of around £125 million. In this deal the preferred bidder agreed to hold its price for seven months but it took the Hospital 11 months to close the deal. Deal creep occurred and the price increased by approaching 10 per cent after the commitment period had ended.[12] In its defence, the sponsoring Department of Health pointed out that part of the delay was caused by additional negotiations, arising from the introduction of a new standard form contract. The purpose of the standardisation was to make the PFI contacting process more efficient.

- Thinking is needed against the contingency that deals, especially complex ones, may go wrong. The National Physical Laboratory (NPL) is one of the world's leading laboratories working on the measurement of physical properties such as time, length and mass. New facilities, including over 400 laboratories, were to be built and managed under a 25-year PFI contract planned to cost approximately £96 million. The contractors had problems meeting the stringent specifications for temperature and noise levels within the laboratories, causing postponement of completion from 2001 to an expected finish in 2007.[13] The contract was the first to be terminated on the grounds of serious deficiencies in contractor performance. Before signing the contract, the public sector should make an assessment (a) to see whether more needs to be done to reduce risks and (b) to confirm that the contract provides adequate incentives for all parties to avoid problems, or cure them if they occur.

- Designs should as far as possible be frozen and all costs included. The British Broadcasting Corporation (BBC) White City 2 property development in West London comprises three new buildings which were built next to an existing BBC building known as White City 1.

---

[11] Comptroller and Auditor General *The PFI Contract for the New Dartford & Gravesham Hospital* (HC 423, Session 1998–1999).

[12] Comptroller and Auditor General *The PFI Contract for the Redevelopment of West Middlesex University Hospital* (HC 49 Session, 2002–2003).

[13] Comptroller and Auditor General *The Termination of the PFI Contract for the National Physical Laboratory* (HC 1044, Session 2005–2006).

After signing the contract, the BBC made 300 variations to the scheme, and costs rose by over £ 60 million within a contract costing £ 210m, an increase of 29 per cent.[14] The BBC said that the £ 60 million was not part of the construction project and was known about at the time of the original investment case.[15] It was not, however, included in the full project cost at the time of its appraisal.

* Contracting costs need to be kept under review. Small deals – under £ 20 million in the UK – do not always on their own justify the overhead costs of the contracting process and the associated advisors, though such deals may be bundled up into a bigger portfolio and be taken forward in this way.

## 6.4   SELECTING THE BEST BID

The evaluation work carried out on PPP/PFI points to thinking of the procurement process as a linked and interdependent series of activities, building up progressively to a good conclusion if done well. For instance, the best bid is only as good as the best of the bids submitted, and this reinforces the importance of getting well designed projects and good competition as discussed in the previous sections. Even then, the process is not without its pitfalls.

The Inland Revenue and Customs and Excise entered into a £ 1.5 billion Strategic Transfer of the Estate to the Private Sector (STEPS) PFI deal to transfer ownership and management of the Departments' estates to the consortium, saving an estimated £ 300 million over 20 years. The deal was very competitive at some £ 500 million cheaper than the other bids and some £ 300 million lower than the best alternative to a PFI deal. This indicates the need for a 'Plan B' in such circumstances, against the possibility that very low costs deals may turn out in the longer term to have been underpriced.

The deal was, however, above all an irony of a rare magnitude for the revenue departments. The departments knew that the contractor was owned by shareholders based outside the UK, but they did not clarify the company's tax plans, or find out that it intended to hold the properties offshore until late in the procurement process.[16] The fully legal gains to

---

[14] PAC (2006) *The BBC's White City 2 development*, HC 652, Twenty–fourth Report of Session 2005–2006, The Stationery Office, London.

[15] PAC (2006) *The BBC's White City 2 Development*, HC 652, Twenty–fourth Report of Session 2005–2006, The Stationery Office, London.

[16] Comptroller and Auditor General (2004) *PFI: The STEPS Deal* (HC 530, Session 2003–2004).

the contractor from tax avoidance may or may not have fed through in the form of a lower price for the deal.

A key issue in selecting the best bid is the incentivisation within the deal for the contractor to perform well. Leaving the details of this until after the contract is signed, as has happened in some cases, is unlikely to produce the best result, but beyond this, developing a well functioning performance management system within PPP/PFI deals has proved hard. PPP/PFI contracts are based on payments for outputs and their delivery has to be judged against a range of suitable criteria contained in the contract. An acceptable level of performance merits the full contractual payment. It should be noted in this context that perfection is too expensive a commodity. A slight relaxation often tends to have little practical impact but produces a more affordable solution. A performance level of 95 per cent against the criterion is set typically as the goal, shown as the dashed line in **Box 6.6**.

**Box 6.6** shows two schedules of deduction for under-performance. Schedule A declines steeply as performance falls and results in a small deduction from the full payment, D1, as shown on the horizontal axis according to where schedule A crosses the actual level of performance. Schedule B declines less quickly and produces a much higher deduction, D2, for the same degree of failing.

---

**Box 6.6:    Incentivisation in performance PPP/PFI management systems**

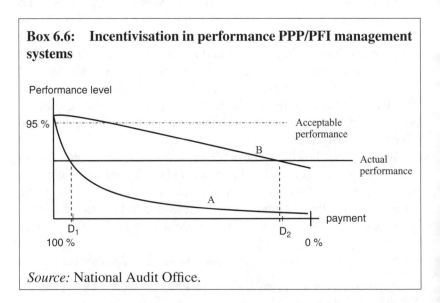

*Source:* National Audit Office.

---

Designing the 'right' schedule is essential if a balance is to be struck between an incentive that stimulates good performance and a deduction that reduces interest in signing the contract. Some issues have emerged from experience:

- Events will inevitably occur that are not covered in the contract. At one PFI hospital there was uncertainty as to who was responsible for de-icing the car park when there was an exceptionally heavy snowfall. In this case, a common sense approach by all parties prevailed.
- There is a balance to be struck between a pragmatic approach and contract resolution procedures, which can be time consuming.
- There is also a balance to be found between ensuring the performance management system provides relevant information without it becoming unmanageable.
- Systems work better if subjectivity in measurement criteria is minimised.
- There will be relationship issues in applying a rigorous management system which co-operation, and a shared view of business objectives between the public and private sectors, can overcome.

A different but critical issue in selecting a bid is the pricing of risk. The public sector needs to understand fully the economics of PFI bids and that PPP/PFI is not an opportunity to shift all risks to the private sector, which would be very expensive and poor value for money. The principle is that risks must be borne by the party best able to carry them. Private contractors for example have no control over the number of inmates there will be in a PFI prison, or over the flow of traffic down a PFI road not subject to a toll. Forced to take such demand risks, contractors will price cautiously, that is to say, price high. In such situations, risks are normally best carried by the public sector.

Some other risks not evidently transferable in the early days may, however, become more predictable with experience, and the scope for transfer may increase over time. The risk of delay from discovering archaeological remains when buildings are erected has increasingly moved to the private sector, on the basis that it always tends to occur, at least in London.

The range of risks that must be considered is substantial:

- design and construction – the project coming in over time and over budget;
- commissioning and operating costs – the project does not work as required and costs more to operate than planned;
- demand risk – the services produced are not required to the degree provided. For example, advances in medical science lead to shorter hospital stays; and so to the need for fewer facilities;

- residual value – a risk to whoever owns the assets at the end of the contract period;
- technological and obsolescence risk – important in the IT field where technical advance can soon make today's solutions relatively unattractive;
- regulatory risk – new laws and taxes may bite on the project;
- project financing risk – can the private sector raise its capital, and if so by equity or banks? Is there scope for refinancing at lower interest rates if the project is successful?
- contractor default – if the contractor fails, does the public sector have a 'Plan B' and can it secure any compensation?;
- political risk – a change of government or a re-alignment of policy means that the project is cancelled.

Views have to be taken by all relevant parties on where the responsibility for these risks should lie. In the last resort, of course, they lie with the government which has to maintain the public services provided by PFI/PPP contracts. The Channel Tunnel Rail Link connecting London and the continent via the Channel Tunnel is a £5.8 billion project which started as a PFI. The passenger projections proved to be too optimistic and the market would not invest in the private consortium. The consortium did not have the financial strength or equity capital to sustain that risk if things went wrong and as risks materialised, the Government eventually underwrote all of the debt, though no actual additional financial support has been given to date.[17]

It is worth concluding this section with a reflection on losing bids and the information they may contain. Rejected bids may contain signs of possible weaknesses in the tender specification which reflect on what is contained in the successful contractor's bid. The Criminal Records Bureau was established as a Public Private Partnership between the Passport and Records Agency and a contractor, and the Bureau has the objective of widening access to criminal records so that employers can make better informed recruitment decisions. Losing bidders for the Bureau's contract had questioned both the realism of the timetable, and the assumption that 85 per cent of disclosure applications would be made by phone. The Agency took action to obtain independent assurance on

---

[17] Comptroller and Auditor General *Progress on the Channel Tunnel Rail Link* (HC 77, Session 2005–2006).

the successful candidate's bid, but did not adequately heed the warning signs within other contractors' bids.[18]

## 6.5   CHECKING THE DEAL MAKES SENSE

The fourth pillar in **Box 6.8** is the deceptively simple requirement that a deal still makes sense as financial close approaches. This amounts to checking that all that has gone before still fits business objectives. A whole series of small and subtle alterations during the specification, tendering and preferred bidder phases can lead to a project that has deviated from the original vision. Good practice indicates that senior management needs to re-think and make checks on issues such as the following:

- Does the contract reflect the deal that has been negotiated?
- Is the deal still affordable?
- Is the bid too cheap? There were many factors in the near collapse of Jarvis, a PFI contractor in the field of schools and railways among others, but underpricing to get business was one.
- Are handover/termination arrangements clearly specified?
- Are there appropriate sanctions/bonuses within the payment regime to incentivise the contractors?
- Are the performance measures in line with business requirements?
- Are there appropriate provisions for dealing with changing requirements?
- Are there mechanisms to review value for money during the life of the deal?

The last two requirements arise because of the length of PPP/PFI deals. It is inevitable over, say, a 30 year PFI contract that service changes will be required, while new contractors might appear that could offer better value than an incumbent. There need to be adequate procedures for resolving any disputes over pricing and any other aspects of proposed changes. The facility to benchmark costs at regular intervals in the life of PPP/PFI contracts is now standard, but it is too soon to know how well this will work and what lessons there will be.

---

[18] Comptroller and Auditor General *Criminal Records Bureau Delivering Safer Recruitment?* (HC 266 Session 2003–2004).

## 6.6   DELIVERING LONG TERM VALUE FOR MONEY

Over 700 PPP and PFI deals have been signed in Britain, of which over 500 are now operational. Getting the best value in the long operational phase of PPP/PFI projects will contribute substantially to getting value for money from the whole deal, from start to finish. It is also the part of the PPP/PFI process about which we know the least, as despite the increasing number of operational schemes, the length of time for which they have been operating is short in relation to the overall contract lengths. Some basic principles can be set out, however, as in **Box 6.7**, again using a 4-Pillars approach.

---

**Box 6.7: The 4-Pillars of good value for money in the operational phase of PPP/PFI projects**

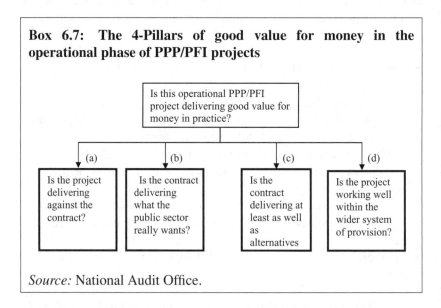

*Source:* National Audit Office.

---

### 6.6.1   (a) And (b) Delivery and Getting What Is Really Wanted

A consideration of operational performance against the contract immediately highlights the interdependencies across time. Without good and well functioning performance management systems put in place during the contract negotiations, the public sector will never know if contract deliverables are being achieved. Some underlying principles for this are set out above. In addition, as above again, effective change management processes are needed if a contract is delivering as specified but it turns out in the short term that something else was in fact wanted, or if needs change anyway in the longer term.

What does experience indicate is achieved from the deals? In practice, PPP/PFI facilities, such as those in the health sector, are newer and better, such as under the 'LIFT' programme to replace old premises and consulting rooms of doctors with modern buildings. Most of the developments to date have been well received by local stakeholders, although some proposals have provoked local opposition; for example because rents may be higher than for former premises. They will make a wider range of services available in a primary care setting, such as minor surgery and scanning. In particular, there will be better management of chronic diseases which account for 80 per cent of GP consultations.[19] Similar procurement models are already being used in other sectors, notably in secondary education.

In the case of PFI prisons, performance was mixed. At the time of our study in 2003 we said the following is a summary that can be generalised to other sectors, as I do below for hospitals:

> The experience of the prison sector shows that the use of the PFI is neither a guarantee of success nor the cause of inevitable failure. Like other methods of providing public services, there are successes and failures and they cannot be ascribed to a single factor. PFI has brought some results which are encouraging and some which are disappointing. But what is clear is that competition has helped to drive up standards and improve efficiency across the prison system as a whole.[20]

Above all, for success in PPP/PFI, trust must be created and remain on both sides. This has sometimes been difficult to achieve for reasons of cultural differences. Many public servants have looked at the private sector as a set of clever and unscrupulous people only interested in money; many private sector people have looked on public servants as pedantic bureaucrats who do not live in the real world. If these attitudes exist, real co-operative working cannot be achieved. In the early days of PFI/PPP, the public sector often thought that the best way to handle the private sector was through tight contracts that put all the risk on the contractor; and to penalise them – through the courts if necessary – if they did not perform. The private sector sought to lay off for this

---

[19] Comptroller and Auditor General *Department of Health Innovation in the NHS: Local Improvement Finance Trusts*, (HC 28, Session 2005–2006).

[20] Bourn, J (2003) *Press Notice: The Operational Performance of PFI Prisons*, HC 700, Session 2002–2003.

approach by arguing about the contract and charging the highest price they could to guard against the risks. It is essential to get beyond this approach if PFI and PPP are to work successfully.

Obtaining what is wanted from the letter of a contract in terms of the deliverables is only a partial measure of success, even if those deliverables are exactly what users and commissioners wanted. Brand new public service delivery assets are almost by definition bound to be superior to what went before. The underlying question is whether the PPP/PFI delivers something better than could have been obtained through a different procurement route. I have already mentioned the benchmarking we carried out for prisons. **Box 6.8** provides a further comparison in this sector, for the issue of respect shown to the prisoners by staff. It shows that PFI produced a statistically significant improvement in all categories, comparing public and PFI prisons.

---

**Box 6.8:    Prisoners' views on the respect shown towards them by staff**

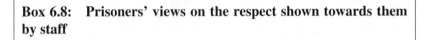

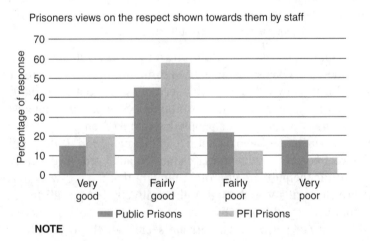

**NOTE**

Figures calculated as a % of Survey size: Public 1073 PFI 761
Analysis: Significantly different. tested as the 596 level.
Using the two-sample Wlicoxon rent sum test.

*Source:* Comptroller and Auditor General *The Operational Performance of PFI Prisons* (HC 700, Session 2003–2003).

---

## 6.6.2    (c) Delivering as least as well as alternatives

**Box 6.9** shows a comparison of the major eight 'first wave' PFI hospitals in England with the same number of conventionally funded and similar hospitals in England. The comparison was not a straightforward one to make because all sizeable hospital construction investment in recent years has been exclusively carried out through PFI. It was a

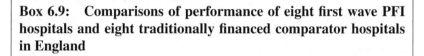

**Box 6.9:   Comparisons of performance of eight first wave PFI hospitals and eight traditionally financed comparator hospitals in England**

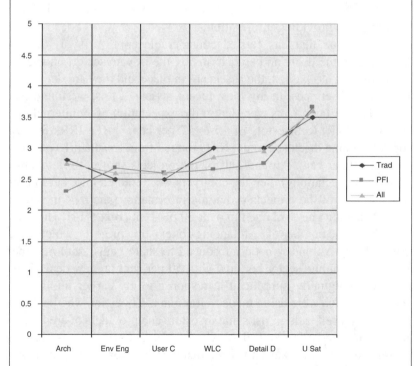

Criteria used: Architecture; Environmental engineering; User comfort; Minimisation of whole life costs; detailed design; User satisfaction

*Source: Building Research Establishment Survey of Hospitals* 2005 conducted for NAO.

case of standardising for characteristics such as case mix, location and broad class of activity of hospitals, for example, whether they were teaching institutions. The comparisons were based on six criteria, which in turn were supported by a range of sub-criteria, in order to reduce subjectivity as far as possible, for example on questions like quality of design. Scores run from zero to 5, and as can be seen, and bearing in mind the uncertainties of the methodology, there is little to choose between the results of either procurement route.

A related but different question is whether there is evidence on whether the PPP/PFI decision really did result in the best deal in the long term. Some evidence comes from the returns that have accrued to investing private sector shareholders, though in most cases we do not have the evidence on outturns. In some, however, the financial structure has been re-financed and this has been done in agreement with the public body concerned so providing information.

A PFI issue that has caused considerable controversy is the re-financing of the deals on better terms by the private sector, once construction risk has passed, the assets are in place and they are delivering the required services. In my most recent review of this, we found that most early PFI contracts were let on the expectation of an internal rate of return (IRR) to investors of 15 to 17 per cent.[21] The IRRs following refinancing disclosed to the NAO ranged from less than 10 per cent to over 70 per cent. Around half of the projects showed little change from the expectations when the contracts were entered into, but in four deals (a fifth of the projects providing information) the IRR including the refinancing gain had risen to over 50 per cent **(Box 6.10)**. This Box also shows the number of re-financings of existing projects, which were covered by a voluntary code introduced to share gains, with a 30 per cent for the public sector but now with 50 per cent on new deals. This code was originally introduced in response to my earlier findings on the gains which were being made.[22] It remains a question whether large IRRs rightly reflect high risks that investors and providers of credit may have seen in early days of PFI, or whether, the deals were over-priced to begin with. It seems likely, however, that the scope for large re-financing gains has passed as the PPP/PFI market has matured.

---

[21] Comptroller and Auditor General *A Framework for evaluating the implementation of Private Finance Initiative projects*: Volumes 1 and 2.

[22] HM Treasury (2002) Refinancing of early PFI transactions Code of Conduct.

**Box 6.10:     The IRR of PFI projects post refinancing**

| Post refinancing Internal Rate of Return (%) | Number of Code refinancings[a] | Number of other refinancings | Total |
|---|---|---|---|
| 70+ | 2 | – | 2 |
| 60–70 | 1 | – | 1 |
| 50–60 | 1 | – | 1 |
| 40–50 | – | 1 | 1 |
| 30–40 | – | 1 | 1 |
| 20–30 | – | 1 | 1 |
| 10–20 | 3 | 7 | 10 |
| 0–10 | – | 3 | 3 |
| | | | |
| Total | 7 | 13 | 20 |
| | | | |
| No response/Returned incomplete information | 8 | 8 | 16 |
| | | | |
| Total PFI projects surveyed* | 15 | 21 | 36 |

A full analysis by project is set out in Appendix 9. We set out below the three projects with the highest investors IRR and the three with the lowest investors IRR following refinancing based on the information which project teams provided to us.

**The three projects with the highest investor IRRs following refinancing were:**

| Project | Total refinancing gain | Pre refinancing internal rate of return to investors | Post refinancing internal rate of return to investors | Main initial investors |
|---|---|---|---|---|
| Debden Park School | £1 million | 16% | 71% | Jarvis PLC, Barclays Capital |
| Bromley Hospital | £45 million | 27% | 71% | Innisfree, Barclays, Taylor Woodraw Construction |
| Norfolk & Norwich Hospital | £116 million | 16% | 60% | Innisfree, Barclays, Private Equity, 3i PLC & Serco Group |

[a] Number of refinancings where there were contractual provisions for sharing gains but gains were shared in accordance with a code. Following reports by the NAO and Committee of Public Accounts, the OGC launched a Code, with the support of the CBI, which expects the private sector to voluntarily share 30 per cent of refinancing gains with the public sector.

*Source:* Comptroller and Auditor General, Update on PFI Debt Refinancing and the PFI equity market, (HC 1040, Session 2005–2006).

The lessons that have emerged are:

- Making sure that deals are done well in the first instance to minimise windfall gains for the private sector later on.
- The importance of putting mechanisms into contracts to enable sharing of gains.
- The need for the public sector to make very careful assessments of the risks involved, especially if private sector debt levels are increased or the term of the contract is extended.
- The need for tough but realistic negotiations to get the best deal for the public sector from the re-financing.

The high returns generated by re-financing finally reached a point where the Committee of Public Accounts described them as the 'unacceptable face of capitalism'.[23] This has led to reduced interest in refinancing as such, but in its place there has been a growth in the development of the 'secondary market', in which the private consortium that developed the project sells its shares on. Buyers such as life assurance and pension companies find PFI shares attractive, as these companies have policy premia to invest and streams of liabilities that correspond well to the cash flow that PFI projects generate over a number of decades.

There is currently a small number of PFI investment funds quoted on the London Stock Exchange and more are being formed. The visibility of the price of quoted shares imposes a discipline on the investment funds to ensure that the PFI projects perform well and indeed exerts pressure to generate increased returns. Pension funds and similar investors operate under rules that permit greater investment in quoted than unquoted companies, so find the investment in the quoted PFI investment funds attractive for this reason as well.

As a result, the secondary demand to invest in PFI has been strong and the value of these funds has risen. Whereas secondary investors have previously been buying shares based on the value implied by discounting the vendor investor's expected cash flows from the project at around seven to eight per cent, shares were now being bought after applying a discount rate as low as five per cent, which gives a higher valuation.

The rise in the value of PFI assets in this way again raises the question of whether the public sector paid too much when it entered into the deals in the first place. The counter-argument is that the gain in value comes from the quality of the secondary PFI fund managers. But even if true, with experience building up on this, the public sector should now be expecting to build such efficiency gains over the life of PFI projects into the initial deal price.

### 6.6.3     (d) Making Deals Work Well Within a System

A point that is often not considered as much as it should be is how well PPP/PFI procurements fit within a system of provision (though this is a consideration that applies equally to all methods of procurement). A road is part of road network, and schools and health care facilities are parts of

---

[23] Committee of Public Accounts (2006) *The Refinancing of the Norfolk and Norwich PFI Hospital*, (35th Report, Session 2005–2006).

local education and health economies respectively. Business cases may or may not reflect this and this can lead to operational difficulties. The West Middlesex PFI hospital could only pay its way by taking money away from other parts of the health system.[24] As funding in total is limited within a sector, decisions on PFI deals cannot be taken in isolation.

## 6.7   GOOD PRACTICE FOR THE FUTURE

Thinking moves on all the time and no less so than in the field of getting good value for money and assessing whether that goal has been achieved. As knowledge builds up, the power of the analytical microscope increases. There is not space here to expand on the most detailed approach that auditors can use and it is in any case freely available.[25] Projects are considered in six life cycle stages and against six cross cutting themes, which can be presented in the form of a matrix, each cell of which is populated by a high level audit indicator. Intended primarily for post hoc evaluation, such indicators are also helpful to those engaged in taking public private partnerships forward. **Box 6.11** sets out the high level audit criteria.[26]

A big challenge for the future will be whether PPP/PFI deals have the flexibility to respond to the need for change. What we know now is that it is possible to build flexibility into contracts and maximise the chances that what is delivered will satisfy users' public sector requirements in the long term. The following are important ingredients:

- Consultation with all stakeholders;
- The use of physical life sized mock-ups, for example of hospital ward layout;
- Computer animations of designs;
- Computer modelling of user flows through buildings;
- Modular designs that can be re-configured easily, for example by removing partition rooms to create larger rooms or vice versa;
- Provision of reasonable spare footprint to accommodate a likely expansion;

---

[24] PAC (2003) *The PFI Contract for the Redevelopment of West Middlesex University Hospital*, HC 155, Nineteenth Report, Session 2002–03, The Stationery Office, London.
[25] Comptroller and Auditor General *A Framework for Evaluating the Implementation of Private Finance Initiative Projects*: Volumes 1 and 2.
[26] Comptroller and Auditor General *A Framework for Evaluating the Implementation of Private Finance Initiative Projects*: Volume 2.

**Box 6.11:    Evaluation Framework for the implementation of PFI projects**

| | Strategic analysis | Tendering | Contract completion | Pre-Operational Implementation | Early operational | Mature operational |
|---|---|---|---|---|---|---|
| Fit with business requirements | Good Outline Business Case with clear deliverables | Relevant output, payment and measurement specifications | Relevant contract and project strategy | Delivery of asset to specification | Contract being met | Service provision is meeting business requirements |
| PFI is appropriate delivery mechanism | Clear case for PFI | Baseline of current performance and get innovation in bids | Review that PFI is right | Continue baselining | Consider termination if poor construction outturn | Assessment of whether PFI deal is delivering |
| Stakeholder support | Identify and consult with key stakeholders | Key stakeholder support | Stakeholder support maintained | Stakeholders informed of progress | Review of stakeholder satisfaction | Continued review of stakeholder satisfaction |

**Box 6.11:   (Continued)**

| Quality of project management | Design of Project Management | Effective project management structures | Getting the best deal | Planning for operational phase | Right skills and relationships for contract management | Maintaining right skills and relationships |
|---|---|---|---|---|---|---|
| Balance of cost, quality and finance | Groundwork for optimal outcome | Good quality bids received | Good balance between price and quality | Changes made are VFM | Deal remains affordable | Maximising quality and affordability |
| Quality of risk management | Identification of project risks | Right risk management procedures | Appropriate risk transfer agreed | Risk mitigation procedures working | Risk Transfer sticks | Risk management procedures updated |

*Source*: National Audit Office.

- Designing with an eye to multiple usages types, so that buildings can be sold on or be re-used by other parts of the public sector.
- In looking at getting what is really wanted, the role of the contract is only a start. Experience indicates that as important is the professional relationship that builds up between the public sector locally and the PPP/PFI provider. My work indicates that a successful relationship is best achieved when:[27]
  - Authorities and contractors balance both contractual and relationship issues to approach projects in a spirit of partnership and with a common vision of how they will work together to achieve a mutually successful outcome to the project.
  - Authorities regularly reassess their relationships with contractors and the value for money their projects are delivering, to identify ways in which relationships can be improved.
  - Staff on both sides have the skills critical to good contract management. Early attention to staffing, training and contract management issues helps develop successful relationships.

## 6.8    QUESTIONS FOR THE FUTURE

Summing up, the evaluation of the overall PFI/PPP programme for the auditor's guidance requires a consideration of at least the following issues.

*Can the extra borrowing costs of PFI and PPP finance really be offset by greater efficiency?* The record shows that this is in principle possible; the expertise of the private sector, aided by the pressure on them from their banks and other lenders, can produce programmes that have cost and quality advantages over past public sector programmes. But this does not invariably happen and case by case analysis is required to set up and evaluate performance.

*Is it right to contract out 'core services'?* This is ultimately a political question. So far we have seen, for example, prisons and hospital services contracted out – core services of the modern state indeed. But so far at least, while the private sector supplies and maintains much military equipment, it does not supply front line troops or police.

---

[27] Comptroller and Auditor General *Managing the Rrelationship to Secure a successful Partnership in PFI Projects* (HC 375, Session 2001–2002).

*Are staff at a disadvantage if they are transferred to a private sector firm as part of a PFI project?* There is no clear answer. In some cases they may have better pay and conditions. Protection exists in the UK through the TUPE scheme to protect wages and pensions at the levels staff enjoyed before their transfer. In the long run, of course, all staff, public and private sector, are at the mercy of changing priorities and the risk of redundancy.

*PFI partners may obtain so much detailed knowledge of a scheme that it is in effect impossible to replace them.* Yet the Inland Revenue and Customs department did replace their IT partner – EDS – by holding a competition at the conclusion of the contract period that was won by Capgemini.

*Are 20 and 30 year contracts too long?* It is necessary to have break points, and to provide opportunities for revising the project and its financing in the light of technical change, efficiency improvements and changing government requirements. This may alter the distribution of the risks between the partners.

*Are re-financing and the PFI secondary market just devices to generate excessive profits?* The NAO's work has shown that re-financing – which is only possible if a project is successful – did generate unreasonable profits in some early projects. It is necessary to share gains from re-financing; and to consider whether gains from selling on PFI/PPP contracts to other companies should also be shared. It may be necessary, also, to consider if sales are acceptable if the new owner appears to be more interested in selling on the contract again than in the service provided.

*Is it right to pay bid costs?* Often, bidding for PFI/PPP projects is expensive and time consuming. As a general rule of public finance, bidders should finance their own bids. But the British Government have helped some bidders in cases of great complexity, such as the competition for the contract previously held by EDS for the Revenue and Customs, because of the desire to encourage competition and support a market. Again there is no clear rule on this, but these are the relevant considerations. Also important is for the public sector to speed up the time it can take to consider PFI/PPP bids. Lengthy timescales raise the cost of bidding because staff and other assets must often be held in baulk for the public authority's decision.

Finally, it is clear that PFI and PPP is not a magic key that transforms public services. The quality of PFI based services varies and may be as good as the best but also as bad as the worst. **Box 6.12** is a newspaper

report of what seemed to one user to be a disappointing outcome, typical
or not.

---

**Box 6.12:    Ex-Head of PFI School attacks 'money-wasting'**

The former head teacher of one of the first secondary schools to
be built by a private company attacked the Government yesterday
for using 'ineffective, bureaucratic and money wasting' firms to run
classrooms.

Monica Cross, 56, who in April quit as the head of Highlands
School in Enfield, north London, accused Equion, the company that
maintains the £24 million school, of using cheap building materials, overcharging for work and failing to provide essential services
for pupils. In a stinging rebuke of Labour's flagship private finance
initiative (PFI) scheme, she claimed that parts of the building were
already desperately in need of repair, only six years after Tony Blair
opened the 1,450-pupil school.

PFI was originally a conservative idea, but was expanded by Labour
after it came to power in 1997.

It involves private firms financing the construction of public buildings such as hospitals and schools and under contracts, often lasting
up to 30 years. They are paid fees by the Government.

Mrs Cross, who resigned to become the head of a new academy
school in south London, said that PFI had 'crippled' the school.

'It was naïve to think that a commercial company would have
a social conscience. It's a huge waste of public money,' she said.
'Simple requests to replace a door handle took months to approve
due to labyrinthine bureaucratic processes.'

'We couldn't use the food technology room for the first year because the facilities were non-existent. There was a shortage of computers and they weren't powerful enough.'

She added: 'We could afford only the bare essentials for our pupils
because so much of our budget was going on the PFI scheme.'

Giving an example of money wasting, Mrs Cross claimed that she
was quoted £18,000 by a local builder for work on the staff kitchen
and meeting room, but after Equion added its fees and mark-up, the
costs rose to £37,000.

An Equion spokesman said: 'Equion was awarded the contract following a competitive tender process involving a number of bidders

and was selected on the basis that we met the London Borough of Enfield's requirements and that the solution we put forward was deemed to be affordable and represented good value for money.'

A report by the Commission for Architecture and the Built Environment last month found that half the secondary schools built in the past five years were poorly constructed, badly designed and failed to provide inspiring places for children to learn.

It found that schools built under the PFI scheme rated worse than others, with all but one of the worst 10 being privately financed.

*Source:* Daily Telegraph – 18 August 2006.

But as the NAO's work has shown, there are many examples of success which our work has supported through pursing lines of enquiry (**Box 6.13**) which, while robust and penetrating, sought to elicit what worked well. Broadly speaking, they tend to be in the simplest areas, where one private sector partner provides one service to a public sector partner as, for example, the provision of helicopter training and the provision of commercial vehicle fleets to the armed services. Private sector consortia providing complex and changing services, especially IT have more often run into trouble, though even here the work of the NAO has shown how success may be pursued through re-competition, though the Treasury has now ruled that PFI is not an appropriate way to procure IT services.

---

**Box 6.13:    Lines of enquiry to identify whether private capital is likely to be the best option for delivering a public services**

The auditor acts in an independent capacity in a policy area where the financial private sector has an incentive to promote the use of private capital in providing public services for profit and where the public sector may lack experience of the advantages and disadvantages of using PFI and obtaining the best deals. The auditor has a key role in considering:

- whether the involvement of the private sector will help achieve public sector service delivery objectives;
- whether PFI is the best value for money procurement route for public services, compared with public sector provision, contracting out or other partnership arrangements, and whether the PFI

procurement choice is biased by factors such as claiming that such investment is not on the public sector balance sheet;
- that PFI deals are carried out in a way that gets the best deal for the taxpayer, through greatest competition among bidders and with appropriate transfer or risks so that the party best able to bear them assumes them;
- that operational performance of PFI projects matches expectations and that the opportunities to re-finance deals in their early days are capped or subject to gain sharing arrangements with the public sector;
- whether post project evaluations take place, are of sufficient rigour, and that good practice is identified and acted upon;
- identifying and spreading best practice of good PFI procurement practice. The National Audit Office's evaluation framework provides a good guide for auditors on these issues.

*Source:* National Audit Office.

Finally, to be good value for money, PFI has to offer advantages that offset the higher cost of borrowing which the private sector faces compared to that of the government. This issue could be tackled by the government raising money at its rates to loan to the private sector, but subject to the private sector partner obtaining a strong guarantee for the repayment of the loan. This allows the borrowing cost to be the closest possible to the rate for government securities. The approach is currently being used experimentally in the United Kingdom in the Treasury Credit Guarantee Scheme. Two hospital projects are being financed in this way. Of course, if this approach is to be justified, all the relevant considerations set out in this chapter on how to secure successful PFI and PPP projects must all be secured.

### 6.9   SUMMARY

Public Private Partnerships come in many forms:

- Joint ventures;
- Franchises;
- Concessions;
- Privately financed investment projects;
- Retaining minority shares in privatised companies;

- Market Testing against bids from a public sector provider;
- Use of private sector methods in public bodies.

*But they all have the characteristics of bringing private sector money and/or private sector skills into the provision of public services.*

In evaluating the value for money of such schemes the auditor should have regard to:

- the business case for the project – financial and qualitative;
- tendering arrangements to secure competition;
- contract completion and review that the best deal been secured, with stakeholder support, price and quality combined, and appropriate risk transfer agreed;
- pre-operational implementation;
- early operational implementation, with the right skills and relationships for contract management;
- mature operational implementation, with the right adjustments to adapt to changing technology, requirements and financing.

And the auditor should be able to advise as required on:

- whether the extra borrowing costs of partnerships are justified by superior performance over conventional procurement;
- delays in managing the bid process, and the justification for paying bidding costs;
- the protection of and arrangements for staff transferred from public to private sector;
- arrangements for dispute resolution and the payment of compensation;
- the scope for a new competition or other measures when the old contract is complete, and the associated implementations of these arrangements;
- contract break points and their management;
- the value for money of refinancing arrangements;
- the balance of risk between the parties at the outset and as the contract continues;
- above all, the securing of trust between the parties and working to shared business objectives.

# 7
# Regulations – Bureaucracy's Tentacles

As Chapters 5 and 6 on privatisation and PFI/PPP showed, over the last 40 years the locus of many economic activities has shifted from public to private. Whereas in the past huge swathes of industrial activity were undertaken by publicly-owned entities, today the preferred model for industries such as telecoms, water, post, as well as heavy industry such as steel and shipbuilding is one of private capital, private ownership and private enterprise. In short, we have seen a change from public monopoly to regulated private monopoly – with a parallel increase in the importance of regulators as economic actors. At the same time, there has been a considerable growth in government regulation over a whole range of activities and businesses.[1] This chapter considers the causes and consequences of regulatory growth and how this impinges upon the work of the auditor.

## 7.1 BUREAUCRACIES CAUSE REGULATIONS TO GROW – FOR COMMENDABLE AND LESS COMMENDABLE REASONS

Bureaucracies thrive on rules and regulations. Norman Augustine illustrated this in his book 'Augustine's Laws',[2] which correlated the growth of US procurement regulations with the growth rate of weeds. It showed that, as with weeds, regulations start innocently but their tentacles, branches and leaves spread rapidly – and they are just as hard to remove once they put down roots as weeds. This analogy applies not just to procurement regulations but to the whole array of regulations created by governments to control, sanction and limit the behaviour of individuals in organisations and societies. Like US procurement laws, all these rules

---

[1] Greater regulation may also be explained by wider societal changes in attitudes and greater cultural diversity. More information about the potential impact of failures in health and safety are driving the state increasingly to regulate to contain such risks.

[2] Augustine, N. (1997) *Augustine's Laws*, 6th edn, Viking, Virginia.

and regulations grow unchecked like weeds. **Box 7.1** illustrates Augustine's argument, and **Box 7.2** is another example of complex regulation.

---

**Box 7.1:    Growth of a Regulation**

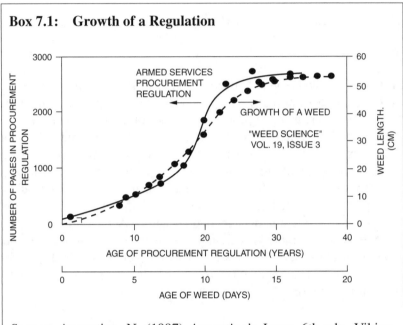

*Source:* Augustine, N. (1997) *Augustine's Laws*, 6th edn, Viking, Virginia.

---

Why do regulations grow in bureaucratic states? The main driver has been risk. Regulation is a product of the way in which society perceives and responds to risk. Earlier chapters have brought out the importance of risk management to the way contemporary government manages its own operations and Chapter 9 provides further analyses. Regulation extends this principle of organisational management to society as a whole: when risks – to individuals and consumers – arise in society, regulation is put forward as the obvious government response.

Four risks in particular have underpinned the growth in regulation:

- the risk of market abuse by dominant companies. As countries have privatised formerly state-owned enterprises, they have often tended to transfer public monopolies to the private sector. Realising that private sector monopolies may have a greater incentive to charge excessive prices, countries have sought to create independent regulators to constrain this form of abuse. In the UK, for example, the privatisation of water companies as a series of regional monopolies was accompanied by the creation of Ofwat[3] as water regulator, with responsibility for controlling the price and quality of service offered by private sector water companies. Similar regulators exist for postal services (the Postal Services Commission or Postcomm); energy (the Office of Gas and Electricity Markets, or Ofgem); and telecommunications (the Office of Communications, known as Ofcom). All of these regulators began their life as the Government's response to the risk of market abuse by newly privatised industries[4] – and have extended their organisational life long beyond the original vision, so that even as competition extends its reach in all those formerly monopoly industries, the regulators continue to exist, and indeed thrive. As a result of the importance of these regulators, and the apparent mystery of their continued life, auditing the work of such regulators has been the subject of discussion in, and guidelines from, the International Organisation of Supreme Audit Institutions (INTOSAI) Working Group on the Audit of Privatisation.[5]

- the risk of wider market failure. As noted in Section 2.1, economists and policy makers recognise that, while markets may be efficient in the technical sense of matching resources to demand, they may ignore or even create wider external problems (known as 'externalities'). Such externalities arise typically in the environmental sector, where an efficient market may nevertheless degrade some element of the environment, such as air quality, water habitats or, according to an ever-growing anxiety across most advanced democracies, the very nature of the climate itself. Market failures are also perceived in the employment market, where an efficient market may not appear to protect workers against some risks, such as discrimination on the basis of ethnicity or gender. The typical policy response to market failures such as these is to create regulations and regulators designed to prevent and prohibit the market failure. However, the regulations once introduced are rarely retested against their originating rationale, or indeed

---

[3] Ofwat's full name is the Office of Water Services. It is responsible for ensuring that licensed water companies fulfil their duties and meet the needs of consumers of water. It sets both prices and quality of service targets for licensed water companies.

[4] Or newly-commercialised – the postal regulator focuses on Royal Mail, which remains a publicly-owned entity, but one whose commercial orientation has increased in recent years.

[5] The full title of these Guidelines is Guidelines on Best Practice for the Audit of Economic Regulation. They can be found at http://www.nao.org.uk/intosai/wgap/ecregguidelines.htm.

whether the market failures they were originally sought to address are still problematic. So rules mount up without any systematic challenge.

• the risk of uncompetitive behaviour. Even competitive markets can from time to time suffer a tendency to relapse into anticompetitive arrangements. This is partly a reflection of Adam Smith's view that members of a trade rarely meet other than to fix prices;[6] and partly because a rampant desire for market share and even monopoly reflects the Schumpeterian impulse towards creative destruction within markets. The lure of anti-competitive behaviour can often manifest itself as the creation of cartels or other restrictions that harm consumers because they deny them the benefits of a choice between competing suppliers. In the UK, for example a recent case identified price-fixing between manufacturers and retailers of the replica England football shirt. The manufacturers refused to supply the shirt unless retailers promised to sell it for no less than £40. This price-fixing agreement came to the attention of the UK's competition regulator, the Office of Fair Trading (OFT). After the OFT's intervention to break the price fixing agreement, prices of England shirts fell by around 35 per cent.[7]

• the risk of closed markets: markets thrive on clear, open, transparent rules. As a result, governments can create and amend regulations out of a desire to enhance the operation of markets. This desire to harmonise national legislations into a single, common set of rules has been the main driver of European legislation. Yet this commendable desire to create an open market has led to a vast efflorescence of ever-more detailed rules. According to the British Chambers of Commerce, the European Union makes some 3,400 regulations and directives per annum. They must each be transposed into domestic regulations – which typically adds a further layer of rules and complexity. The UK, for example, adds $2\frac{1}{3}$ times as many words as the originating EU directive. An EU directive on labelling air conditioners contained 2,409 words, but the UK version contained 7,504 words (though this may be a curiously British phenomenon, since the French version contained only 1,061 words).[8]

---

[6] 'People of the same trade seldom meet together, even for merriment and diversion, but the conversation ends in a conspiracy against the public, or in some contrivance to raise prices'. *The Wealth of Nations*, Book I, Chapter X.

[7] This case, and the Office of Fair Trading's work enforcing the Competition Act more generally, has been covered more extensively by the National Audit Office, *Enforcing Competition in Markets*, HC 593, 2005–2006.

[8] Amber, T., Chitterder, F., and Obodovski, M. (2004) *How much Regulation is Gold Plate?* British Chamber of Commerce, London.

In addition, regulations are claimed to resolve a series of problems faced by bureaucracy. They may offer efficiency – removing the need and cost of judgement; a greater level of safety, for example by specifying health and safety conditions; fairness, in that similar cases can be dealt with similarly; and offer an apparently cost-free tool for seeking to change the behaviour of individuals and organisations. On this last point, Karen Yeung has set this out clearly in her analysis of the regulation of competition in different economies. She defines regulation as 'the sustained and focused attempt by the state to alter behaviour thought to be of value to the community'.[9] It is therefore as much about desired states of mind and behaviour as it is about formal rules – and, according to the pioneering work of Braithwaite and Ayres, there is a spectrum of tools available to Governments to produce the required behavioural change, ranging from formal rules through to advocacy, persuasion and naming and shaming. For Braithwaite and Ayres, the task of Government is to choose when to deploy different tools: when to proscribe; when to persuade; and when to punish.[10] But regardless of the tool of regulation, the centrality of the behavioural outcome is clear: there is a behaviour, or the perceived risk of a behaviour, that Government wishes to modify or constrain. And formal regulation through statutory rules is typically seen the quickest, easiest and most publicly visible tool for delivering the change. Hence regulation's attractiveness.

As a result of this attractiveness, regulations are often a response to a crisis or problem hitherto unknown or unobserved by society. For example, in the Northwest of England, a small cockle-picking industry has developed; cockles being a form of shellfish. Because of the labour-intensive nature of the task, and the relatively high costs of labour, the workers who undertook this task were organised by a series of labour-agencies known as 'gang masters'. These 'gang masters' often employed immigrant workers illegally, since they were willing to bear the unpleasant working conditions and low wages. On 5 February 2004, 23 Chinese workers died when they were caught by rising tides in the Morecombe Bay area. The ensuing public outcry led to the creation of a new set of regulations, and a new regulatory agency, the Gangmaster Licensing Authority. It is now illegal to operate as a 'gang master' without a licence, and a whole new regulatory apparatus now exists to monitor and control the activities of a 'gang master' – even though the use of illegal

[9] Yeung, K. (2005) *Securing Compliance*. Hart Publishing.
[10] Braithwaite, J. and Ayres, I. (1992) *Responsive Regulation: Transcending the Deregulation Debate*. Oxford University Press, New York.

workers was against the law under even existing regulations; existing regulations, moreover, that were seen as appropriate and proportionate to most known problems.[11]

## 7.2   THE COSTS OF THESE REGULATIONS ARE HIDDEN, AND QUITE PERNICIOUS

Some regulations are no doubt justified. They have a long pedigree in political economies, as a recent review for the Treasury demonstrated:

> Business regulation is a long-established function of government. In about 350 BCE, Aristotle described a set of regulators in ancient Athens: 'Formerly there were ten Corn Commissioners, five for Piraeus, and five for the city; but now there are twenty for the city and fifteen for Piraeus. Their duties are to see that the unprepared corn in the market is offered for sale at reasonable prices, and that the bakers sell their loaves at a price proportionate to that of wheat, and that the loaves are of the proper weight; for the law requires the Commissioners to fix the standard weight'. In the UK, the earliest identifiable inspectorate was established under the Health and Morals of Apprentices Act in 1804. The Health and Safety Executive can trace its origins back to 1833, and the regulation of trade, markets and hallmarks stretches even farther back, into the earliest years of the English state.[12]

Yet the public sector auditor may well have to ask whether the cumulative effect of these regulations is value for money. Regulation's very benefit – a clear, consistent response to risks for the protection of society – may produce rigidity. Is it reasonable to cope with *apparently* similar situations by removing discretion and judgement? It seems unlikely that inflexibility is an appropriate answer in complex, postmodern societies, where relevant information for judgements is much more easily and cheaply available. Regulations also generate a voracious demand for extra staff within regulatory institutions, and within the organisations that are subject to regulation. This is because, despite their apparent clarity and simplicity, regulations rarely close down debate. Instead, they lead to 'guidance' to interpret them, and more regulations to deal with special cases.

---

[11] The Better Regulation Commission – *Whose Risk is it Anyway?*, October 2006, p. 12

[12] HM Treasury (2005) *The Hampton Review of Inspection and Enforcement*, para. 1.5. Philip Hampton was the Chairman of J. Sainsbury plc, a major UK grocery supplier.

In a sense, then, there is an echo here of the old military preoccupation with ensuring an acceptable minimum standard of performance by enforcing procedures which unavoidably suppress the maximum level. A. Gordon's 'The Rules of the Game'[13] examines the deleterious consequences of this approach. Gordon brings out the view that British naval administration in the nineteenth century developed increasingly centralised procedures and co-ordination in all operations, including major engagements with an enemy fleet. He demonstrates how this military approach had unhappy consequences for the Royal Navy, culminating in the failure – at least compared with past glories such as the Battle of Trafalgar – at the Battle of Jutland in 1916. Gordon's picture is of a military institution so beset by rules for every situation that the scope for discretion by individual commanders was considerably eroded. In the face of the chaos and unpredictability of a major sea battle – what is often called the fog of war – the Royal Navy was diminished by this lack of initiative, and unable to take the opportunity to win the battle decisively even though its actions ensured that the German fleet remained in home ports for the rest of the war. The rules – and the cast of mind they encouraged – may have helped to avoid defeat; but they may well have denied the achievement of victory.

Regulations also impose costs on society. The extent to which this is true is only recently becoming apparent. In 1997, the OECD asserted that:

> Today, regulatory costs are the least controlled and least accountable amongst government costs. Many governments have no idea how much of their national wealth they are spending through regulation.

The UK's Better Regulation Task Force addressed the cost of regulation as follows:

> Regulation, as well as providing us with necessary protection and safeguarding our rights, also represents a significant cost for the economy. This cost is borne by government, regulators and those being regulated, including businesses, public sector organisations, the voluntary sector and ultimately tax-paying citizens.... Information from the United States and the Netherlands suggests that the total cost of regulation is 10% - 12% of GDP. It is unlikely to be much different in the UK, so regulation here is probably costing us around £ 100 billion per year. This is more than the

---

[13] Gordon, A. (1996) *The Rules of the Game*. John Murray.

combined annual yield from VAT and fuel duty and not much less than
the projected 2005/6 income tax yield.[14]

Several governments have now implemented projects to measure and
reduce the administrative cost of regulation. Typically, these projects require Government departments to 'map' the legislation they are responsible for and identify and quantify the administrative burdens involved
in complying with those regulations.

The Dutch Government has been one of the leading proponents of
reducing the administrative burdens of regulation on business. Over the
last three years it has developed a methodology, the Standard Cost Model
(SCM), for defining and quantifying these burdens, and has set a target
of 25 percent for reductions in these costs. This model has attracted
considerable interest in other countries, with Denmark using a similar approach and Sweden and Norway applying elements to their own
situation. The UK Government's Administrative Burdens work is based
on the Standard Cost Model, first proposed by the Dutch, hence the
colloquialism 'The Dutch Model'. The Dutch model states: 'Administrative burdens are the cost to the businesses of complying with the
information obligations resulting from Government-imposed legislation
and regulations'.

The Standard Cost Model is designed to enable a consistent calculation across all parts of government. This should: allow the comparison of the administrative burden of individual laws; provide a baseline
valuation of across all of government; allow the costing of alternatives
to existing laws; and enable the measurement of changes in administrative burdens over time. The model outlines 17 different types of action
involved in fulfilling an information obligation, for example: receiving
data; gathering information; filling out a form; copying the form, and
so on. It then calculates the amount of time an organisation spends in
completing an action, and the value of the time used. Adding up the
number of times a firm performs each action will give an indication
of the burden imposed on that organisation. And from here the total
administrative burden can be calculated from the number of businesses
performing an action.

As noted above in the discussion of the development of naval administration there is an even more pernicious cost, arising from the way in
which a growing corpus of regulation erodes personal responsibility and

---

[14] Better Regulation Task Force 2005. *Less is More.*

risk-taking. While each individual regulatory response may be justified in the light of some defined risk, the cumulative effect can be pernicious. This is because an overly protective regime, which seeks to minimise and remove any residual risk to consumers, employees and citizens, can reduce the incentive on individuals to manage their own interests. In devising regulations, therefore, there should be a proper consideration of where the risks lie; and of how to balance the need for protection against the need to foster a society where people accept and share responsibility for managing life's risks. As the Better Regulation Commission concluded:

> [this report] focuses on a growing disquiet about the management of risk in society and what is seen by many as a rising tide of regulation, exacerbated by periodic inappropriate responses to 'risks of the day' ... There is a sense that the current public debate about risk places an over reliance on Government to manage all risks, at the cost of eroded personal responsibility[15].

## 7.3   THE AUDITOR CAN HELP TO SOME EXTENT...

It is not for the auditor to abolish regulations. Regulations are typically determined at the political level, as an expression of the political will of the day, and it goes beyond the remit of auditors to question the merits of policy objectives.

But auditors cannot ignore the costs – direct, indirect; economic or psychological – imposed by regulation. An example is given at **Box 7.2**. The auditor can help in the drive to make regulation more proportionate, targeted and flexible because so many of the problems with which the auditor has to deal stem from overly prescriptive or overly ambitious regulation. Poorly implemented systems; significant costs to taxpayers, businesses and consumers; collapses in the legitimacy of the regulatory institution or government responsible for them; all these problems arise from flaws in the design and implementation of regulation.

---

**Box 7.2:   Regulation ... and Flags**

Speaking at the Lord Mayor's Banquet for Bankers and Merchants of the City of London on 21 June 2006 Mr Mervyn King, the Governor

---

[15] Better Regulation Commission, *op.cit.*

of the Bank of England illustrated aspects of the modern approach often seen to regulation, when he said 'A key ingredient of the city's success has been, as the Lord Mayor remarked, a stable set of rules within which to play up and play the game. Simple, clear rules of the games are essential for a market economy to function. But excessive regulation makes life difficult for all of us. In March of this year I received a letter from a certain government department which read as follows:

'Dear Mr. King; I am writing to inform you about how the changes to Crown immunity . . . in relation to planning legislation, will affect flying national flags. . . . Flags are defined as advertisements under the Town and Country Planning (Control of Advertisements) Regulation 1992. Under these regulations you are allowed to fly the national flag of any country . . . from a single vertical flagpole without requiring the prior express consent of the local planning authority. The European Union flag is not classified as a national Flag under the current regulations . . . the Office of the Deputy Prime Minister is proposing to change the Regulations'. Until then, however, consent is required. The letter continued: 'I have been advised that consent usually takes six to eight weeks to obtain and costs £75. You need to send the completed advertisement consent form plus a fee with a covering letter explaining when and where you wish to fly the flag providing details of the size of the flag and photos of the flagpole in relation to the building.'

As with all other elements of the auditor's task, here the auditor begins by understanding the business of regulation, and why it is generally easier to create regulations – in response to some newly perceived risk – than it is to remove them. There are two main causes of this inertia:

- Vested interests: there is a complex and equivocal relationship between business/government and regulation. There are many who benefit from regulatory regimes. For example, in the UK, the Financial Services Authority (FSA) has been criticised for several years for imposing too-stringent requirements on investment banks operating in the City of London. When the FSA recently announced its plan to remove training requirements, however, most banks complained that they in fact valued these requirements since the common basis they provided made it easier to recruit staff with well-understood credentials. The very regulations that were complained of, often bitterly, were supported as a source of market advantage as soon as they were threatened with removal. It is therefore necessary for the auditor to understand, engage with and where appropriate challenge vested interests that see regulation as a source of commercial advantage.

• The ratchet affect of zero tolerance: as we saw earlier, a large proportion of regulation derives from an urge to reduce risks to zero. As a result, the desire for a proportionate and risk based approach to regulation runs up against the public demand for zero tolerance of harms and risk. To take another UK-based example: in the early 1990s, a series of attacks on children by so-called 'dangerous dogs' – dogs specially bred to accentuate their physical strength and aggressive instincts – led to the passage of the Dangerous Dogs Act. This Act is now seen as a byword for inappropriate, poorly targeted regulation – yet it has not been repealed. As a result, there is a clear ratchet effect as the forces impelling the growth of regulation overpower the quieter voices calling for its removal.

The auditor can also deploy an overarching framework to target the worst regulations. One common framework is the Better Regulation Task Force's five principles of good regulation:

• Transparency: this principle requires clarity, not complexity, in regulation, so that people understand the problem being regulated, and how the regulation solves the problem.
• Accountability: regulation should be accountable to those who are affected by it – i.e. regulation is not an end in itself and those regulated should have opportunity where appropriate to have a say in the regulatory framework and its ongoing development.
• Proportionality: regulation should only intervene when necessary. Remedies should be appropriate to the risk posed, and costs identified and minimised.
• Consistency: regulation should not treat one case differently from any other without good reason.
• Targeting: regulation should only target the relevant important factors.

Armed with this understanding of the difficulties of reducing regulation, and a set of principles, the auditor can help political authorities target the most costly and ill-thought through regulations.

   The auditor can also support the use of tools within government which promise to control the flow of new regulations, and cut back the stock of existing regulation. In the UK, as noted in Section 2.5, the principal tool for restricting the flow of new regulation is the Regulatory

Impact Assessment. Regulatory Impact Assessments have been used since 1998 and are required for any form of regulation, including formal legislation, codes of practice or information campaigns, which impact on business, the public sector and voluntary organisations. They allow policy makers to analyse the likely impacts – economic, social and environmental – of a policy change and the options for implementing it. The UK Government considers Regulatory Impact Assessments to be a key tool in delivering better regulation and supporting its aim of regulating only when necessary. And their use has spread rapidly across the OECD, with most countries now espousing some form of impact assessment, and the European Commission committing, through its 2002 Action Plan on Better Regulation, to the implementation of a programme of impact assessment for all new policies.

But in spite of their promise, Regulatory Impact Assessments are not always properly used. Too often they are seen as a paper-output – an add on at the end – rather than being integral to the process of policy-making. And there is little evidence of these assessments leading on occasion to the decision not to have a new regulation at all.[16]

Finally, as well as seeking to restrict the flow of new regulations, the auditor can also sometimes applaud when existing regulations are broken. In 2002, the NAO praised the innovative acquisition of the Heart Hospital[17] by University College London Hospitals. By acting quickly, and circumventing standard bureaucratic procedures for capital investment, University College London Hospitals acquired the Heart Hospital for £ 27.5 million, some £ 8.5 million less than the valuation provided by an independent valuer, and £ 17.5 million less than the cost of building an equivalent facility. As a result of this innovative rule-breaking, patient services improved, with waiting times falling from 12 months to six months for key heart procedures.

---

[16] The NAO has published three annual evaluations of the quality of Regulatory Impact Assessments, in 2004, 2005 and 2006, as follows: Evaluation of Regulatory Impact Assessments Compendium Report 2004–2005 (HC 341 2004–2005); Evaluation of Regulatory Impact Assessments Compendium Report 2003–2004 (HC 358 2003–2004); and the National Audit Office, Evaluation of Regulatory Impact Assessments, 2005–2006 (HC 1305 2005–2006). These reports show that there is no evidence that RIAs are used to challenge systematically the need for new regulations.

[17] It had been owned and operated as a cardiac facility by the NHS until 1991 when the property was sold. Between 1996 and 1998 the hospital owners, Parkway Holdings Limited invested approximately £ 45 million in acquiring the hospital, refurbishing it, and in purchasing new medical equipment. Despite this investment, the Heart Hospital was operating at only one third capacity, leading to financial loses and Parkway's decision to sell the hospital. National Audit Office, Innovation in the National Health Service – The acquisition of the Heart Hospital (HC157, 2002 – 2003).

**Box 7.3** illustrates the kind of questions the auditor can raise when investigating how well existing regulations are working, and whether new ones would be justified.

---

**Box 7.3:     How well are regulations working?**

Questions for the Auditor to ask about

- Existing regulations
- Proposals for new regulations

Focussed on the problem?

Proportional to the risk?

User friendly?

Fairly administered?

Coverage of the relevant population?

Sanctions appropriate?

Social benefits of compliance to exceed social costs of compliance?

Open to review and evaluation?

Finally

- Should a new regulation be introduced?
- Should an existing regulation be abolished?
- Are there better ways of achieving the objective than regulation?

---

## 7.4   ...BUT SOCIETY'S ADDICTION TO RULES AND REGULATIONS MAKE IT HARD TO DO

Nevertheless, the auditor's assistance to those parts of government keen to cut regulation can sometimes feel forlorn. We have to remember that although people deplore regulations, they often want to hang on to them for 'comfort'. This was described beautifully by the Chair of the UK's Better Regulation Commission, Rick Haythornthwaite, when he compared society's guilty attachment to regulation to an adult's continuing love for a teddy bear that he or she knows is a vestige of childhood.[18] We do not want to admit our love for regulation, Mr Haythornthwaite argues, and we must first recognise it before we can start to wean ourselves off it.

---

[18] Rick Haythornthwaite (2006) 'Britain's secret shame: we just love red tape', Financial Times, 9 February.

Furthermore, even if we manage to get rid of regulations, we need a more sophisticated and self confident form of public administration that stands up for its judgements rather than using the crutches of rules. It requires civil servants to assess the case for new rules on the basis of the costs they impose. They must also consider whether the rules address a risk that government has any business at all in seeking to manage. And they must be bold in proposing to cut back the voracious growth of regulatory weeds, willing to pull up regulations by the roots in the face of vested interests and a political conversation more interested in new problems and new solutions than removing defunct or outdated existing regulations.

In short, public administration must be sophisticated, and rigorously independent. This chapter has shown how the auditor can contribute to this end, by drawing attention to some of the strangleholds exerted by the regulation tentacles of bureaucracy. And **Box 7.4** sums up the argument from a different angle in terms of 'why Rules are not the Answer' as

---

## Box 7.4:   WHY RULES ARE NOT THE ANSWER

One interesting feature of our investigations was to collect the arguments for and against rules-based standards. We found that some reasons could be used to argue the case either way. It became apparent at an early stage of our investigations that rejecting rules-based standards was the starting point for some commentators. Finding an alternative approach in principles was, for some, the second stage. We wanted to be sure that in advocating principles-based standards we were not merely joining an 'anti-rules' campaign. However, we did not find any sustainable argument supporting rules-based standards. In this section we present the conflicting views that we discovered, followed by our evaluation.

**FOR RULES:** *Rules-based standards are what the participants (preparers, auditors and regulators) want. Rules-based standards provide detailed guidance and clarification and precise answers to questions.*

**AGAINST RULES:** *Rules-based standards reduce or eliminate the exercise of professional judgement and lead to de-skilling of the profession.*

We believe that participants, particularly in the US, have initially been conditioned to rules through the process of education and training and have then continued to look for the rule as the starting point in answering a problem. When exposure drafts are issued there are requests to standard setters for more explanation or more detailed information. We note that in the UK the experience of FRS 5 *Reporting the substance of transactions* has shown that judgement-based accounting can operate successfully to report

economic reality in a situation where previously there had been over-reliance on rules governing legal form.

Those applying the rule may feel that they have a precise answer but there is no guarantee that precision means fair presentation. Comfort is drawn from mechanistic application of the detail rather than standing back to make a professional judgement on the overall picture.

**FOR RULES:** *Rules-based standards are authoritative and enforceable.*

**AGAINST RULES:** *Rules-based standards do not prevent dishonest practice.*

Authority and enforcement are qualities of regulators, not of the words in the rules. A regulator can be equally, or more, challenging of judgement in requiring justification. Regulators must have the capacity to understand and question the judgement on the basis of stated principles, rather than seeking refuge in rules designed to ease operation of the regulatory process. However, we believe that neither rules-based standards nor principles-based standards can prevent dishonest practice.

**FOR RULES:** *Rules-based standards provide greater comparability.*

**AGAINST RULES:** *Rules-based standards do not guarantee comparability.*

Comparability has come to mean 'all the same'. However, we believe financial statements should be capable of comparison when the economic reality of similar transactions and events are understood in a similar way by the users of those financial statements. The disclosure by the preparer of judgements made is key to that understanding.

> **FOR RULES:** *The complexity of rules-based standards is only a consequence of the complexity of the underlying business.*

> **AGAINST RULES:** *Rules-based standards cause complexity and delay in keeping abreast of change.*

We take the view that reacting to complexity by creating rules is an example of chasing a problem after it has occurred. We expect that a well-defined set of principles will provide the framework for dealing with complexity as it arises, retaining a strong focus on representing the economic reality.

> **FOR RULES:** *Rules-based standards offer equal access to emerging opinions.*

> **AGAINST RULES:** *Rules-based standards can never be comprehensive.*

We do not expect a system of principles-based standards to remain static. Discussion of the principles will bring out emerging opinions and we would expect the participants (auditors, preparers, users and regulators) to engage proactively in the debate. The mechanisms for sharing those opinions are not determined by the nature of the accounting standards.

> **FOR RULES:** *Rules-based standards deter creative accounting.*

> **AGAINST RULES:** *Rules-based standards foster creative accounting by diverting judgement from economic reality to the detail of application.*

We feel that there are sufficient recent examples of creative accounting under rules-based regimes to make it unnecessary to quote specific cases. Interviewees said to us that rules create a road-map for avoidance and divert attention from the need for fair presentation or a true and fair view.

> **FOR RULES:** *Rules-based standards set out greater detail, which is especially important where translation is needed.*

> **AGAINST RULES:** *Greater detail in rules requires to be translated, with correspondingly greater difficulties.*

We recognise that there is a need for considerable technical guidance in countries where principles-based standards are a new idea and there has been a custom of relying on statutory regulation and strong governmental guidance. However, we do not believe that accounting standards themselves have an educative role. We expect that professional bodies and professional accountancy firms in those countries that have developed principles-based approaches to accounting will be willing to provide support and guidance in the transition. We also recognise that accounting standards written in English may contain wording that does not translate well but we see this as an issue for a terminology discussion rather than a factor requiring rules-based standards.

*Source:* From *Principles not rules: A Question of Judgement*, Edinburgh Institute of Chartered Accountants of Scotland 2006 PP. 8–9.

seen by a review by professional accountants of whether accounting standards should be based on rules or general principles.

## 7.5 SUMMARY

Bureaucracies thrive on rules and regulations. Why is this so? They seem to be the way to get:

- Efficiency – removing the need and cost of judgement;
- Safety – specifying health and safety conditions;
- Fairness – similar cases dealt with similarly;

- A response to a crisis or scandal – a rule that will make a similar event impossible or most unlikely.

In short, regulations are a nineteenth century tool for dealing with a twenty first century problem.

It is not for the auditor to abolish regulations. But he can certainly appraise them by following five principles

- Transparency: this principle requires clarity, not complexity, in regulation, so that people understand the problem being regulated, and how the regulation solves the problem.
- Accountability: regulation should be accountable to those who are affected by it – i.e. regulation is not an end in itself and those regulated should have opportunity where appropriate to have a say in the regulatory framework and its ongoing development.
- Proportionality: regulation should only intervene when necessary. Remedies should be appropriate to the risk posed, and costs identified and minimised.
- Consistency: regulation should not treat one case differently from any other without good reason.
- Targeting: regulation should only target the relevant important factors, factors,

And by asking questions about existing regulations and proposals for new regulations. Are they

- Focussed on the problem?
- Proportional to the risk?
- User friendly?
- Fairly administered?
- Coverage of the relevant population?
- Sanctions appropriate?
- Social benefits of compliance to exceed social costs of compliance?
- Open to review and evaluation?

Finally

- Should a new regulation be introduced?
- Should an existing regulation be abolished?
- Are there better ways of achieving the objective than regulation?

And, if we reduce the burden of regulations, this will require a more sophisticated form of public administration that makes good judgements and stands up for them rather than using the crutches of rules.

# 8
# Meeting Citizens' Needs – Quality of Public Services

Since the creation of political organisations, governments have sought to satisfy enough of their citizens' needs for order, property rights and sustenance to maintain the ruler's position, wealth and powers as emperors, kings and democratically elected leaders. Initially this was done by protecting the realm from invasion and revolt by rewarding vassals who would fight for them; by providing at least some elements of law and order, and subsequently sometimes assisting the very poorest to survive poverty and worklessness (in part, to prevent them undermining the semblance of peace that then existed) and, from the nineteenth century onwards, seeking to intervene to address forms of gross inequality and exploitation. The nature of citizens' needs and the way in which the governments have sought to address them has changed substantially over time. The development of a welfare state, an increasingly consumerist society, and now the arrival of the 'information age' have altered and, without doubt, raised citizens' expectations of public services. Indeed, at times it seems that the public sector is destined to be continually playing 'catch up' with the private sector as the latter raises citizens' expectations of customer service and the public sector seeks to manage the 'expectation gap' thereby created.

The trend over the last two decades towards what has been dubbed 'new public management' has seen a number of changes in the delivery of public services. There has been a greater focus on meeting the end needs of the user, with less concern about the means or processes for getting there. The problem is compounded by the appearance of what has been termed the 'sceptical citizen-consumer',[1] and the increasing willingness of individuals to complain – with a growing recourse to the law – not just about their bin collection service or holes in the road but also about their General Practitioner or surgeon. And the media is more willing to platform these personal grievances than was the case in previous generations.

---

[1] Newman, J. (2001) *Modernising Governance*, Sage.

Against this background, millions of public servants continue to provide a huge variety of services to citizens. Many are excellent, even if others have been poorly designed and executed. This chapter examines the influences on the quality of public services, arguing that too often bureaucracy puts citizens' needs towards the 'bottom of the pack' because it has traditionally been inward looking and has sought to deal with the outside world with a system of rules which it often does not fully comprehend itself.

Another key point is that no government is entirely free as to the scope and nature of the services it provides. Firstly, every administration inherits the legacy of past developments which means that service provision is always created piecemeal. What we have today is an amalgamation of services created over time. Secondly, much available public expenditure is already committed; for example, pensions and benefits must be paid to those eligible. Thirdly, as generations of politicians have found to their cost, attempts to make major changes to key services – the NHS in the UK is a classic example – are fraught with difficulty, and commitments to specific groups or to particular ways of delivering services are major constraints on radical reform. Finally, expectations are high and at times, unrealistic. As Mulgan[2] has put it 'The ideal service for most people is closer to the ones that are available to the wealthy, whether in private hospitals, or from tailors, lawyers and financial planners. These services are human, immediate, personalised and rich in communication, anticipating need rather than just meeting it and going the extra step'. Governments are thus always at risk of disappointing those they seek to help since such standards can seldom be afforded.

Despite the apparent desire to improve public services, one constant theme has been that governments have often failed to help themselves in the ways they have gone about implementation; in particular, successive governments have:

- contributed to some confusion as to whether citizens are customers, consumers or clients of public services which in some cases has raised expectations which are difficult to meet (**Box 8.1**);
- created complex, unresponsive systems and processes which have made services difficult to access;

---

[2] Mulgan, G. (2006) *Good and Bad Power* Allen Lane.

- failed to deliver services in efficient or effective ways, apparently not learning from past experience;
- been slow to acknowledge and respond to the growing diversity of UK society and failed to develop sufficient understanding of customer needs nor paid sufficient heed to their views and concerns, especially after poor service has been provided;
- been poor at communicating what is available and capturing the information needed from citizens to provide high quality services;
- failed to create incentives for staff to strive to enhance customer service or develop innovative approaches; and
- not developed adequate means of providing redress.

Caught up in the difficulties of administering a complex and comprehensive social service programme, providers and legislators have often failed to see public services from a citizen's perspective. The next section of this chapter examines some of the barriers to high quality services which we have seen from our audit work. The subsequent section deals with improving the quality of public services; the penultimate section deals with the audit implications of these developments; and this is followed by a concluding section and summary.

---

**Box 8.1:   It's all in the definition. Are citizens, consumers, customers or clients of public services?**

(i) *Consumers* is the overall term for all individuals who consume goods and services from various providers, public and private. Within that broad category individuals can have many relationships with producers/providers.

(ii) *Customers* are in a relationship where individuals have a choice between suppliers, and are willing to pay to obtain their choice of goods and services. There have to be multiple suppliers offering interchangeable outputs, and suppliers can discriminate between potential customers, targeting some through marketing and excluding others.

(iii) *Clients* are in a relationship where a professional expert judges that the consumer has a certain need, thus controlling access to the service, while the client has a shared desire for the outcome they both seek. Both can be seen as co-owning or co-producing the output.

(iv) *Citizens* are in relationship between the individual and state institutions, for which the individual provides taxes, for which individuals vote, and to which they express their views about the rules that govern everyone. These rules express a collective view about how society, the national and local communities, should develop, propounding what is in the public interest overall. They also seek to reconcile different notions of what is in the public interest concerning social justice and equity, and balance between resources and desired policies, and between priorities.

*Source:* Professor George Jones OBE in correspondence with the author.

## 8.1  BARRIERS TO HIGH QUALITY SERVICES

The main barriers relevant to the auditors' work include:

- overly complex and unresponsive services;
- failures in delivery and in learning lessons;
- slow response to increasing social diversity and identifying customer needs;
- poor communications;
- few incentives to innovate; and
- weakness in complaints and redress arrangements.

### 8.1.1  Overly Complex and Unresponsive Services

Public services have grown up piecemeal, built on election promises and in response to developments in society and the economy, such as the growth in the number of women in the workplace or improvements in life expectancy. The benefits system reflects such changes and might be compared to the accretion of different layers of rock over time. This leads to several different types of complexity. **Box 8.2** summarises different aspects of complexity in the benefits system including internal complexity, complexity arising from its interface with other systems (tax credits) and the complexity arising from repeated changes and refinements.[3] All contribute to making the delivery of

---

[3] Comptroller and Auditor General *Dealing with the complexity of the benefits system* (HC 592, Session 2005–2006).

many aspects of the service difficult. Within the system, provision for disabled people is a particularly good example of support which has grown up since 1945 in piecemeal fashion, with the result that there are now overlapping programmes and schemes,[4] which can cause confusion amongst potential users and their advisers. The tax credits system is another area where the complexity can lead to unresponsive services. The department recalculates the value of awards annually; in 2004–05 it identified one-third of 2003–04 awards had been overpaid, mainly because family income had increased by more than declared at the time of the original declaration. The annual basis of the award means that recipients need to be able to anticipate and plan for the consequences of changes in their income, which is clearly a problem for many families.[5]

Complexity also leads to poor communication between and within agencies, creating inefficiency in many programmes. For example, within the Department for Work and Pensions, the ability of agency contact centres to share customer information has been limited by IT arrangements and at times customers have to provide the same personal information more than once.[6] Incompatible administrative systems have been a major problem affecting joint working between the NHS and social services, as have a lack of common geographical boundaries. Both have contributed to poorer quality services for vulnerable patients.[7] Frequently, government has expected users to understand the different elements of government, with those most in need often interacting with the largest number of agencies.

Citizens can be foiled at the very beginning of their interaction with the government. Filling in forms is one of the most common ways that citizens interact with central departments, executive agencies and other public sector bodies but many have been badly designed, are hard to understand and difficult to complete and make onerous requests in terms of supporting documentation. Rather than giving 'quick start'

---

[4] Comptroller and Auditor General *Gaining and retaining a job: the Department for Work and Pensions' support for disabled people* (HC 455, Session 2005–2006).

[5] Comptroller and Auditor General *Inland Revenue Standard Report 2004–2005*.

[6] Comptroller and Auditor General *Developing effective services through contact centres* (HC 941, Session 2005–2006).

[7] Comptroller and Auditor General *Ensuring the effective discharge of older patients from NHS Acute Hospitals* (HC 392, Session 2002–2003).

**Box 8.2: Summary of different types of interaction in the benefits system**

| Type of interaction | Relation with complexity | Examples |
|---|---|---|
| **Design changes** – substantial developments in the benefits system which may occur to meet changing socio-economic circumstances or to pursue particular policy objectives. | • Can either increase or decrease complexity.<br>• May include the explicit goal of simplification of the benefits system. | • Introduction of Jobseeker's Allowance in 1996<br>• Introduction of Pension Credit in 2003<br>• The piloting of Local Housing Allowances as a simplification of Housing Benefit. |
| **Patchwork changes** – more minor changes occur when there is a need for regulations to be adapted to changing circumstances or priorities. | • Can increase complexity through the introduction of a wider range of responses to different circumstances, even when the intention is otherwise. | • Separate Housing Benefit rules for under-25s<br>• New regulations for Disability Living Allowance to deal with complexity arising from judicial decisions. |
| **Horizontal links or interfaces** – exist between benefits and/or between different agencies administering benefits or other forms of support such as tax credits. | • Horizontal interfaces give rise to complexity when different benefits addressing the same client group are administered in different ways, either by the same or different agencies. | • Different paydays for different benefits<br>• Changes of circumstances needing to be reported at different times for benefits and tax credits, reflecting the different periods for which payment is assessed<br>• Housing Benefit and tax credits treating income and capital differently |

**Box 8.2:** *(Continued)*

**Vertical interfaces** – exist between different layers of the Department and its agencies. Vertical interfaces can involve creating greater detail to tailor general rules to the more specific needs of lower levels in the organisation.

- Gives rise to complexity when there is a perception that higher level rules are not adequate for customer service.
- When different subordinate units implement the same higher unit guidance differently, complexity is created.

- Day-to-day benefit administration governed by voluminous guidance interpreting legislation and regulations e.g. 48 chapters in the Decision-Makers' Guide
- Housing Benefit administered to widely varying standards by local authorities with decisions reflecting local circumstances

**Delivery interactions** – exist between the Department and the individual customer, and include filling out forms, reporting requirements, interviews, and the transfer of money. The Department has the responsibility for delivery.

- Complexity through delivery occurs because of the way front–line services are provided – for example, multiple points of contact, detailed forms – which can place a burden on benefit recipients.

- Many customers consider claim forms hard to complete
- Customers may be unclear what changes of circumstances they need to report and to whom

advice, many forms are accompanied by long guidance pamphlets.[8] **Box 8.3** shows some examples of difficult features found on many of the forms.

Completing a form is often only the first step in a long process to receive a public service. At times, citizens have needed to visit multiple local offices to complete one transaction, something that is especially difficult for those with mobility problems like the elderly or disabled. Even for those with access to good transportation, shuttling around to different agencies, departments and offices requires time and energy.[9] Undoubtedly, there is a need for eligibility checks and, as in the case of the benefits system, some complexity in the system is intentional to ensure that those receiving the services are those for which the service was originally intended. However, these requirements should not turn away or dissuade those who are legitimately eligible for services and entitlements. Ultimately, service providers must balance the possibility of over-burdening users with rules and demands for information with the need to safeguard public money. This is perhaps one of the great tasks for modern governments.

### 8.1.2  The failure to deliver efficiently and effectively and to learn lessons

One of the major themes in the delivery of public services is the failure of government to learn, or learn sufficiently, lessons from its experiences of delivering services. This was highlighted in a recent report of the Committee of Public Accounts[10] which noted that 'whilst those organisations examined in our hearings act on our recommendations, there is less evidence of lessons being taken forward more widely across Whitehall.'

Given that they are the basis for so many of our public services, IT projects are a particularly worrying – and expensive – case in point. As noted in Chapter Four, in 2006, problems were experienced in the administration of the Single Payment Scheme in England – a scheme for paying a total of £1.5 billion to 116,000 farmers, many of whom were dependent on the payments. During the year, the scheme went badly

---

[8] Comptroller and Auditor General *Difficult Forms: How Government Departments Interact with Citizens* (HC 255, Session 2003–2004).

[9] Disability Alliance (2004) *Race Equality in the Benefits System* Disability Alliance.

[10] Committee of Public Accounts *Achieving value for money in the delivery of public services* (17th Report 2005–2006).

**Box 8.3:   Checklist of Difficult Features on Government Forms**

The NAO study on how users interact with government led to the development of a checklist of features that most often cause customers to have problems with filling in government forms. It allows service providers to make a systematic and comprehensive evaluation of their forms and gives them the tools to consider the overall level of difficulty of each form. Below are some basic features with examples of elements that customers may find difficult.

| | |
|---|---|
| Fundamentals | • The form is multi-purpose, designed for several types of customers. Customers must read questions in detail to work out if they apply to them or not. |
| Legibility and spacing | • The font sizes used are small or vary in size, with type sizes and styles used inconsistently.<br>• It is not clear which spaces to use for some answers. |
| Language | • The form or accompanying guidance uses complex language (e.g. many multi-syllable words, long sentences, or sentences with many qualifying clauses.)<br>• The form includes unfamiliar concepts or ideas rarely used in ordinary life.<br>• Acronyms are used for key concepts. |
| Sequencing | • Customers are given complex routing instructions (e.g. fill in some questions, then skip others, then fill in some more questions). |

**Box 8.3:** *(Continued)*

| | |
|---|---|
| Identification or Documentation | • The form requires an unfamiliar or esoteric ID number (one that customers do not use regularly but have to look up on another document). |
| Threats and Confidentiality | • The form threatens legal or financial penalties for false or inaccurate entries. |
| | • The form provides no clear assurances to safeguard confidentiality (e.g. there is no statement of privacy policy or no assurance that use of the form will comply with the Data Protection Act). |
| Guidance Provided | • There is no 'quick start' section at the beginning of the guidance, designed to help people start filling in the form with minimum fuss. |
| | • The guidance leaflet or booklet is lengthy or difficult to follow, with no attempts to make it easier to read. |
| Phone and Web Facilities | • No help is available over the phone or on the web on how to complete the form. |
| | • Phone help or advice is available, but the phone helpline number is buried in the guidance, and not on the form itself. |
| | • The form cannot be completed and submitted online, over the Web. |
| Return Features | • The form has no return envelope or address label, so customers must write out the return address themselves. |

*Source:* Improving and Reviewing Government Forms: a practical guide: The National Audit Office.

wrong, with payments delayed, costs escalating, causing considerable distress to farmers and to the Chief Executive being removed.[11] Yet, our analysis of the case showed how many of the contributory factors had been seen many times before in IT projects, as **Box 8.4** shows.

---

**Box 8.4:     Failure to learn: The Rural Payments Agency**

Difficulties encountered by a government agency in making payments under the EU's Single Payment Scheme have caused distress to a significant minority of farmers, cost farmers money in additional interest and bank charges, and undermined the farming industry's confidence in the agency, according to a report published today. The risks and complexities involved in delivery had not been fully appreciated and as a consequence the Rural Payments Agency underestimated the amount of work involved.

The Single Payment Scheme is worth £1,515 million to 116,000 farmers in England. Defra and the Agency notified farmers that they aimed to start payments in February and make 96 per cent of payments by the end of March. The Agency encountered difficulties and by 31 March had paid £225 million (15 per cent) to 31,000 farmers (27 per cent). The Agency had processed 95 per cent of payments by the end of June, but in the interim the Chief Executive had been removed from his post.

The cost of implementing the scheme was budgeted at £76 million but, by March 2006, had reached £122 million, with further cost increases likely. Defra and the Agency had expected to reduce the Agency's staff by 1,800 and make efficiency savings of £164 million by 2008–09, but difficulties in processing claims led to the recruitment of additional agency staff and there appears to be little prospect that much of the savings will now be realised in this timeframe.

The problems which the RPA experienced had been seen many times before. For example:

* The timetable to introduce the scheme was tight, and became tighter following changes to the original specification of the IT system to incorporate changes to EU Regulations, legal clarification of the

---

[11] Comptroller and Auditor General *Department for Environment, Food and Rural Affairs, and Rural Payments Agency: the delays in administering the 2005 Single Payment Scheme in England* (HC 1631, Session 2005–2006) and Tracey Payne, a member of the NAO's staff in 'Trouble at mill' *Whitehall and Westminster Review* (21 November 2006).

Regulations, Ministerial decisions and operational changes such as the design of the application form.

• Difficulties within the Agency's control contributed to delays in making payments. Each element of the IT system was tested, but the system was never tested as a whole before the scheme was introduced, and problems arose once it went live.

• The Agency did not adequately pilot land registration and under-estimated the amount of work involved in mapping the land. The Agency also underestimated the amount of work involved in processing each claim and had to rely on often inexperienced temporary and agency staff to clear the backlog.

• Problems with the Single Payment Scheme were not picked up early enough, both by the Agency and Defra, for corrective action to be taken.

• Contingency plans were mothballed because continued work on them would have spread more thinly the limited staff with the necessary understanding of the scheme and technical skills, and because the Agency believed there was a better chance of making payments on time with the main system. Progress reports from the former Chief Executive of the Agency were unduly optimistic but, in the absence of adequate management information systems, robust and objective data showing the progress that had been made was not available.

• The Agency did not pilot the application process adequately. As a result, it underestimated the amount of work involved in processing claims, particularly relating to mapping the parcels of land being claimed for. The Agency had 2.1 million maps to deal with instead of the 1.7 million it had expected.

• One dairy farmer in the South West told the NAO that four versions of the maps of his land went back and forth, and even then, the final version on the Rural Land Register was not accurate. The result was a substantial backlog of claims. The agency had expected to receive 200 maps a week, but got around 1,200. by September 2005, there were 31,000 forms in its in-tray.

• The agency also tried to save time and so meet the tight timetable by stripping out elements of the IT system, including the part which would have given them information on the progress of each claim. In consequence, the agency found it difficult to determine how much work remained outstanding on claims, and how long it would take to complete them.

- Over-optimistic reports from the Agency's then chief executive, partly due to the inadequate management information, meant there was no objective measure of progress. Throughout the project, consideration was given to fallback options, but actually implementing these contingency plans was rejected at several stages. It was not until April 2006 that the contingency to make partial payments was finally invoked.
- The immediate victims of the delays were farmers. In the NAO survey, 20 per cent of farmers said they had suffered stress and anxiety as a result. The NAO estimates that the delays cost farmers between £ 18m and £ 22.5m in interest and bank fees on additional loans and bank fees.
- This apparent inability to help was widespread. When the NAO rang the call centre, the recorded message said: 'There is nothing that the call-centre staff can tell you about your payment'.

*Source:* Comptroller and Auditor General Department for Environment, Food and Rural Affairs, and Rural Payments Agency *The delays in administering the 2005 Single Payment Scheme in England* (HC 1631, Session 2005–06) and Tracey Payne, a member of the NAO's staff in 'Trouble at mill' *Whitehall and Westminster Review* (21 November 2006.)

### 8.1.3  Responding Slowly to Increasing Diversity and to Identifying Customer Needs

The bureaucratic approach may well have had some advantages – citizens in different parts of the country received similar services. But this also assumed that citizens had broadly similar needs or could respond in similar ways. There has been only recent recognition of the special needs of some generally under-served population groups including ethnic minorities, the old, poor and disabled. The Disability Discrimination Act 1995 and more recently, age discrimination legislation, have been enacted to provide protection to certain citizens.

Generally though, public bodies have been slow to gain an adequate understanding of the needs of those who use their services. Understanding the need to provide services tailored to different needs and circumstances is in its infancy. As a result, those from ethnic minorities can receive a reduced service; for example, people from ethnic minorities of pension age are more likely not to be taking up their entitlement to Pension Credit. People with mental health difficulties face greater than average difficulties in dealing with government; for example, in attending medical examinations.[12] There is also considerable variation in the quality of information departments have on their key users and client groups.[13] Many departments do not know the frequency and ways in which citizens access particular government services.

A distinction should perhaps also be made between what might be called 'old' and 'new' public services. With the former it was not uncommon for librarians, for example, to be willing and able to help you locate a book or even decide what to read. Similarly, social workers looking after the elderly were likely to be the same person each week rather than a new person from an agency each day which is now more typical.

New technology offers risks and opportunities. As more services are provided via the internet, there is an opportunity to expand services to deal with a wider range of needs. However, it may exclude those who do not have regular access to a computer or an internet connection.[14] Efforts have been made to make internet services available to everyone, but a shift toward service online can disproportionately and negatively affect the old and less educated, who are not technically literate, and those of lower incomes, who may not have the funds to buy their own equipment. This point has been picked up by immigrant advocacy groups in the current debate in the USA[15] about new federal immigration measures. Proposals for online filing of applications has been described as a 'digital barrier' likely to sharply reduce the ability of some legal immigrants to become US citizens.

### 8.1.4   Poor at Communicating Basic Service Information

Providing relevant, understandable information regarding the services available has been another important quality of service issue for a number of organisations. Printed leaflets or booklets still play an important

---

[12] Comptroller and Auditor General *Progress in Tackling Pensioner Poverty: encouraging take up of entitlements* (HC 1178 Session 2006); *Progress in Improving the Medical Assessment of Incapacity and Disability Benefits* (2003) (HC 1171, Session 2002–2003).

[13] Comptroller and Auditor General *Delivering Public Services to a Diverse Society* (HC 19-I 2004–2005).

[14] Comptroller and Auditor General *Progress in Making E-services Accessible to All: encouraging use by older people* (HC 428, Session 2002–2003).

[15] Los Angeles Times, 29 October 2006.

role in advertising services but they can be difficult to obtain, read and understand. Our review of leaflets found that some key ones for people seeking work or enquiring about certain benefits were not widely available. Furthermore, the average reading level of most guidance leaflets or booklets was above the average reading level of the general population,[16] a point also highlighted in a recent US Government Accountability Office analysis of the language used by credit card companies in the USA to explain terms and conditions.[17] Even if the leaflets were made widely available to the public, they are of little help if the average reader cannot glean important information from them. A good leaflet includes language that is complete, accurate and easy to understand, a simple design or layout and sources for more information (such as helpline numbers) prominently displayed.

The 'traditional' form of guidance – face-to-face meetings – is becoming increasingly rare (except where the state is keen to see particular groups such as job-seekers who are required to attend interviews), or at least is swiftly conducted to ensure targets are met (appointments with General Practitioners, for example, are usually booked for less than 10 minutes). Because many services are now provided by the telephone or internet, citizens do not know where to go to speak to someone in person. Some organisations – such as those providing for pensioners – no longer have a presence on the high street and opening hours may be reduced as resources are diverted to newer forms of communication.[18]

An increasingly common method of communicating with citizens is by telephone. Improved technology at lower costs has made innovations like call centres common place, but accessibility has been a problem. In general, call centres have achieved high levels of customer satisfaction, but there are still disturbing cases where they have been unable to cope with demand. In 2004–05, for example, Department for Work and Pensions call centres failed to answer 21 million calls. Even when people can get through there are still frustrations; our examination of the Inland Revenue in 2004–05 reported that telephone helpline staff for tax self

---

[16] Comptroller and Auditor General *Using Leaflets to Communicate with the Public about Services and Entitlements* (HC 797, Session 2005–2006).

[17] GAO *Credit Card: Increased Complexity in Rates and Fees Heightens Need for More Effective Disclosures to Consumers* (GAO-06-929, published September 2006).

[18] Comptroller and Auditor General *Using Call Centres to Deliver Public Services* (HC 134, Session 2002–2003); Comptroller and Auditor General *Citizens' Redress: What citizens can do if things go wrong with public services* (HC 21, Session 2004–2005).

assessment often lacked the knowledge to answer questions consistently and accurately, highlighting the need for better training.

### 8.1.5    Created Few Incentives to Innovate

One of the features of private sector firms is the importance of innovation. The alternative for a company is likely to be death and failure. Such a dramatic demise is not a certainty in the public sector as we have seen with several poorly performing organisations. The Public Trust Office provided a very poor service to some of the most vulnerable in society for many years before finally being abolished after several independent scrutinies.

The place of innovation in improving public sector service delivery has been little studied until recently.[19] From NAO research we know that within the civil service, many employees' suggestion schemes are not working well or are not highly valued by managers. Indeed, they were mentioned as a factor in only one innovation nominated for our study. Innovation seems mainly to come from the top down[20] and so often seems out of touch with conditions on the ground.

In contrast to the weak drivers of innovation, the barriers to change in public services are strong and well established. Three groups of causes have been identified. The first is that difficulties with working with other parties with different interests were important, followed by a generalised reluctance to embrace new ways of working or to experiment. And a third aspect was fragmentation within an organisation throwing up difficulties in getting agreement around objectives.[21]

### 8.1.6    Weakness in Complaints and Redress Arrangements

It is inevitable that even in the best run programmes, mistakes and misunderstandings will occur. Mistakes occur in both the public and private sectors. With the latter there are numerous examples of bad customer service in day to day to life – in the servicing of cars, with banks, and commercially funded travel. In the private sector there is, however,

---

[19] Comptroller and Auditor General *Achieving Innovation in Central Government Organisations* (HC 1447, Session 2005–2006).

[20] Comptroller and Auditor General *Achieving Innovation in Central Government Organisations* (HC 1447, Session 2005–2006).

[21] Comptroller and Auditor General *Achieving Innovation in Central Government Organisations* (HC 1447, Session 2005–2006).

often a much greater customer service ethos and recognition that brand strength will be quickly lost if customers are generally dissatisfied. In the public sector when something goes wrong, citizens are often left wondering how to secure redress. Any complaint or redress system must balance citizens' demands for quick, inexpensive easy resolution with the need for rigour, fairness and finality. Despite recent attempts at reform, the current arrangements are complex with few citizens able to take full advantage and receive redress for unfair treatment or inadequate service. Indeed, as illustrated by **Box 8.5**, seeking redress requires a lot of persistence by the complainant or appellant to secure a useful outcome.

My 2004 study of citizens redress and a related white paper by the Department for Constitutional Affairs found that most citizens have only a very vague idea of the correct procedure for bringing forth resolution to disputes with public services. In general, citizens regard redress arrangements in government services as time-consuming, complex to access or understand, slow moving, expensive, and weakly directed to meeting their needs or expectations.[22]

---

**Box 8.5:    British Citizens' Redress**

Below is a diagram of the possible interaction of the complaint and appeal processes. Many citizens do not realise the bifurcation of the system into two related, but separate processes.

- complaints are expressions of dissatisfaction with any aspect of department or agency conduct but are almost universally seen more narrowly by departments and agencies, as being concerned with defective processes or poor handling of an individual's case. Hence organisations often regard complaints as raising issues of administrative blame. They are indicators of things having gone wrong in some way, perhaps through delays in handling a matter, neglect or other failures to conduct business properly.

- appeals are expressions of dissatisfaction with substantive decisions made by the department or agency. Appeals are not generally treated by departments and agencies as raising matters of administrative fault. For instance, an appeal may be the consequence of citizens not supplying correct information or making a mistake in their initial application.

---

[22] Comptroller and Auditor General *Citizen's Redress*, 13.

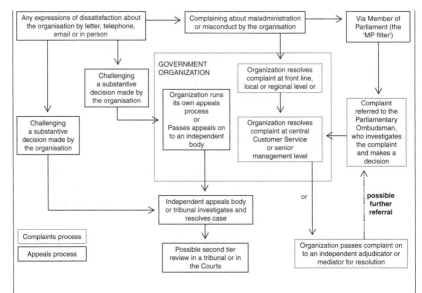

*Source: Citizen's redress: what citizens can do if things go wrong with public services* (HC 21, Session 2004–2005).

In 2004, the British system dealt with over 1.3 million complaints, appeals or tribunals, costing £510 million.[23] Of course, the number of unsatisfied citizens is probably understated as many who receive poor service or unfair treatment either do not know how or are unwilling to put in the time, money and effort to make a formal protest. Citizens cite many different reasons for avoiding seeking redress including: the difficulty of finding whom to talk to in the first place, an inability to get through by phone, the difficulties of writing in, and the impersonality of large government organisations.

There are variations in the ways that similar cases are treated by different bodies. There are often long procedural trails, involving an escalation into more involved and expensive processes, with no reliable means to assess how efficiently and effectively the different systems operate. A citizen could have a fairly easy and pleasant experience resolving one complaint, but end up frustrated by attempts to reconcile a similar complaint with a different agency. Efforts should be made to introduce more

---

[23] Comptroller and Auditor General *Citizens' Redress*, 9.

consistency into the redress process so that citizens know what to expect and how to proceed with common problems.

The incentive to seek redress is decreased even further if citizens do not believe that their concerns will be promptly addressed and ameliorated. Many expect to find much better treatment in the private sector. Around three quarters expect businesses to be quicker in responding to complaints and to give them more individual attention. Much of the complexity in the redress system is justified by the aim of fairness yet it appears that government could take some useful hints from private organisations in the area of complaints.

## 8.2 IMPROVING THE QUALITY OF PUBLIC SERVICES

Thus far, we have examined the obstacles to providing public services that better meet citizens' needs. We have highlighted experiences and frustrations shared by many at some point during their interaction with public services. I have argued that aspects of the bureaucratic approach – overly complex and unresponsive arrangements, a failure to learn from past mistakes, a lack of awareness of the varied needs of citizens, limited incentives in the system to improve performance and poor feedback mechanisms through redress systems – have led to some poor quality services.

Much of this will not come as surprise. For more than twenty years now British governments have put improving the quality of public services at the forefront of political debate, trying to tackle exactly these kind of problems. The goal of better services has been the justification for widespread privatisation of public services in the 1980s, for a whole raft of initiatives, Charters, Charter Marks, hot-lines, league tables, efficiency reviews, capability reviews to name just a few. An especially interesting initiative was the idea of promulgating 'charters' which set out the standards of service that citizens should expect when dealing with public authorities. The first in the UK, the Citizen's Charter, introduced by the Prime Minister, John Major, in 1991 covered such matters as standards of service, time taken to secure a reply, and procedures for making complaints, though they did not confer legal rights to the standards they enunciated.

Possibilities of concern to the auditor include:

- relevance of charters to citizens as consumers;
- understanding and listening to consumers;

- listening to and learning from staff;
- allowing informed choice; and
- seeking accountability and transparency about performance.

### 8.2.1   Relevance of Charters to Citizens as Consumers

The Charter movement took off in a surprising way. It met the mood of the moment in that there was clear synergy with the emphasis being given to acknowledge excellence by other semi independent organisations representing citizens' interest such as the National Consumer Council and its counterparts in Scotland and Wales.[24] By 1997, there were 40 main charters and 10,000 charters that were not centrally controlled. Details are in **Box 8.6**:

---

**Box 8.6:   National Charters in the UK in 1997**

*United Kingdom*
Taxpayer's Charter (Inland Revenue)
Taxpayer's Charter (HM Customs and Excise)
Traveller's Charter (HM Customs and Excise)

*Great Britain*
Benefits Agency Customer Charter
Child Support Agency Charter
Contributor's Charter
Employer's Charter
Jobseeker's Charter
Redundancy Payments Service Charter

*England and Wales*
Charters for Court Users
Victim's Charter

*England Only*
Charter for Further Education
Charter for Higher Education
Council Tenant's Charter
London Bus Passenger's Charter
London Underground's Customer Charter

---

[24] The National Consumer Council's role is to promote the interests of consumers through research, supporting consumers representatives and working with decision-makers to campaign for change. Eighty per cent of its funding is from government.

Parent's Charter
Patient's Charter
Road User's Charter

*Scotland Only*
Further and Higher Education Charter in Scotland
Justice Charter for Scotland
Parent's Charter in Scotland
Patients Charter
Tenant's Charter for Scotland

*Wales only*
Charter for Further Education
Charter for Higher Education
Charter for Council Tenants in Wales
Charter for Parent in Wales
Charter for Patients in Wales

*Northern Ireland only*
A Charter for Patients and Clients
Bus Passenger's Charter
Charter for Further Education in Northern Ireland
Child Support Agency (NI) Charter
Courts' Charter for Northern Ireland
Northern Ireland Housing Executive Tenant's Charter
Northern Ireland Railway Passenger's Charter
Parent's Charter
Royal Ulster Constabulary Charter
Social Security Agency Customer Charter
Training and Employment Agency Customer's Charter.

*Source: Hansard, House of Commons, Written Answers*, 25
November 1997, cols. 471–472.

'The initial enthusiasm for charters in the UK in the 1990s was re-
markable. By March 1994 there were officially 38 different individual
government charter documents in the UK (Deakin, 1994, p.50). By
1997 there were 40 main charters and over 10,000 local charters that
were not centrally controlled (Hansard, 1997). The enthusiastic but
ad hoc nature of the spread of charters in the UK is confirmed by
the fact that some of the new charters were established in some parts
of the UK but not in others. It has been estimated that the number
of national charters in the UK grew to 200 (Milakovich, 2003). In

1998 the Labour Government replaced the Citizen's Charter with a 'Service First' programme that attempted to address a number of important criticisms. By 2002 Service First had incorporated citizen's charters covering a wide range of public services. Nevertheless, that too has lost its momentum and the Service First programme has now been completed though some information is kept in the archive area of the Cabinet Office (2004b) website. It is therefore not surprising that, for example, Drewry (2002, p. 12) concluded that the original Citizen's Charter had 'perished, or at least atrophied'. Certainly in the UK charters have been increasingly displaced as a factor in maintaining standards of public administration by a continuing flow of new initiatives such as the application of specific targets'.

'Nick Montagu, the Chairman of the Board of Inland Revenue, wrote in the following report (Inland Revenue, 1999, p. 6) that 'the Taxpayer's Charter – which we shared with Customs and Excise and which has served us well – no longer covers everything we do'. Instead he announced the introduction of 'Our Service Commitment to You'. Although it had a resemblance to the Taxpayer's Charter it replaced, the new document seemed to lack at least some of the precision, focus and impact of its predecessor. Although new and separate 'Customer Charter' for taxpayers and national insurance contributors were agreed with Ministers at the same time as the new Service Commitment, in subsequent annual reports from 2000 to the most recent in 2003 references to charters have all but disappeared and have been replaced with references to a scheme that awards a 'Charter Mark' to public services that meet certain criteria.'

*Source:* S. James, K. Murphy and M. Reinhart (2005) 'The Citizen's Charter: How Such Initiatives Might be more Effective' *Public Policy and Administration* **20** (2) Summer, 4–6.

But the Charter movement atrophied. Ideas from charters were embodied in new and different documents, but often lost their sharpness, and gradually charters came to have little or no place in British public administration. Why was this? The answer seems to be that the charters were introduced with minimum discussion with the public servants who would have to implement them or with the various groups whose affairs were purported to be covered by them. Nobody felt that they were part of real life, with a meaning in the everyday world of officials and citizens – 'one of the criticisms was a lack of ownership by civil servants who sometimes regarded it as nothing more than yet another initiative'.[25]

In contrast, the Australian Taxpayer's Charters has met with more success. It was developed over two years, in consultation with staff, the general public, tax advisers, and the business community. It was launched in 1987, it was revised in the light of experience in 2003; surveys show it is seen as generally helpful by taxpayers and one tax official was quoted as saying 'I don't think about the Charter much, its just the way we do things round here'.[26]

But beyond charters and other devices, the model that has been held out in many countries, especially perhaps in the United Kingdom, as offering a superior way of meeting the needs of citizens is the model of the retail market; the system which supplies food, clothes, holiday, furniture - all the myriad requirements of daily living. The organisations that supply these goods and services come in all shapes and sizes. But they are subject to the spurs of competition; changing tastes; special needs of particular groups of consumers; new entrants with new products; and they prosper or fail by their ability to provide the goods and services that people want and have the money to pay for, and not by adhering to internal bureaucratic rules – though some firms that were once successful have succumbed to the rigidities of bureaucracy and have consequently failed.

Of course, supporters of this approach acknowledge that the retail market sometimes cheats and fails its customers, and in the short term may exploit market imperfections, such as monopoly and oligopoly. And very few indeed believe that all public services can be provided on the retail model; courts of law and judges seem to most of us to be in a different world from Sainsbury's, Tesco's, Marks and Spencer's and such firms.

Nevertheless, there are lessons to be learned and scope for improvement in public services by considering what the retail sector's concerns with outcomes has to offer. And the auditor may well be able to advise on the way that public bodies need to:

* show greater understanding of the customer by listening to them more;
* be proactive rather than responsive, anticipating needs rather than playing catch up;

---

[25] S. James, K. Murphy and M. Reinhart (2005) 'The Citizen's Charter: How Such Initiatives Might be More Effective' *Public Policy and Administration* **20**(2) Summer 10.

[26] Op cit. pp. 8–15.

- treat innovation as a routine part of service delivery;
- listen to front line staff, who often know better than their seniors what customers want and need;
- make effective use of new technology;
- help citizens to make informed choices about things that matter to them;
- build services around known needs; and,
- ensure there is accountability and transparency about performance.

To support such developments, audit arrangements need to support a customer focus through what it looks at and how it conducts its work.

**Understanding and listening to customers**: The increasingly diverse make-up of our society means that up-to-date information about users is even more important for service providers, and even more difficult to keep up to date. The public sector has only relatively recently started to employ the same type of customer consultation techniques that have become common place in the private sector including focus groups, customer surveys and creating opportunities for feedback directly after the service is performed. Such feedback allows companies to refine or indeed radically alter their products where they identify that they are starting to lose popularity and market share. Tesco's offers an interesting example of this in **Box 8.7**. At various times in recent years it has seen the need to reinvent itself as customers lost interest in many of its products. Only by listening to its customers has the company been able to meet changing expectations.

---

**Box 8.7:    Tesco's Club Card**

Humby, Hay and Harrison were given a simple brief by Tim Mason, Tesco's marketing director at the time. 'Convince the board that Clubcard adds value to the business,' he said. They had to win over Lord MacLaurin, Tesco's Chairman and the man who had scrapped Green Shield stamps, the old loyalty scheme, when he wrestled power from founder Jack Cohen in the 1970's.

The trials ran throughout 1994. 'We had a lot of data about how people shop,' explains Humby. 'You know, 'Did you buy cheese? Did you buy milk?' But we were finding things that really woke up lots of people.

'Clubcard has brought about a step-change in the size of the company,' he says. 'We started off being able to understand the departments that people shopped in and the frequency at which they shopped, and we worked with those two variables.'

'We are actually analysing what you do in a grocery store. The success of Dunnhumby's approach lay in not just saying 'you are Oxbridge-educated, and born in the north, therefore you behave in these ways', but instead saying who you are is driven by what you buy – so we group people by products – and by how you behave. So we will look at people who shop in an Extra once a month, or a Tesco Express five times a week. It is an extremely good, thoughtful tool for analysing food shopping'.

By knowing these customers, Tesco can guess what they might like. Mason says that Clubcard data informed a series of strategic decisions, such as the move into smaller store formats and the launch of the internet shopping site. It also shaped the development and sale of Tesco mobile phones, pet insurance and Finest food range.

Humby gives another example of Clubcard's many uses (he clearly loves it too, as he grins from ear to ear while describing it). 'One of the biggest successes in terms of analysis was watching how people shopped in the wine section. We could see that people were trading up to stuff Tesco didn't stock. At Christmas, people wanted to buy 'posh' wine; those who usually bought a cheap wine went from spending £2.99 a bottle to £5.99 a bottle – but where were the people who should have been trading up from £5.99 to £7.99? They were in Oddbins (the specialist wine retailer) – because Tesco didn't have a full enough range.'

*Source:* Dunnhumby in Financial Times Magazine, pp. 18–22 for 11 November 2006.

In a broadly similar kind of way, the Ufi (a company established by the Department for Education and Skills to develop people's skills and work with employers to increase employees's capabilities now provides 500,000 learners with the opportunity to develop their skills) and the Learndirect initiative[27] is a good example of a public service that has been developed in the light of a well informed understanding of public needs.

---

[27] Comptroller and Auditor General *Extending Access to Learning through Technology: Ufi and the learndirect service* (HC 460, Session 2005–2006).

The Department for Education and Skills wanted Ufi to be innovative and adopt approaches that marked it out from existing providers. Ufi applied consumer marketing techniques to develop a good understanding of what people wanted and needed, and to help direct its marketing activity. It commissioned extensive research on adult learners, which looked at barriers to learning, learners' characteristics and what motivates them to learn. The focus was also on what persuades people with literacy and numeracy needs to take up courses to help improve their skills. Thus, Ufi used the results of its extensive research to help establish and continuously develop the main services for learners and businesses.[28] Such work helped develop a differentiated approach to learning such as depicted below in **Box 8.8**.

**Box 8.8:    First time online**

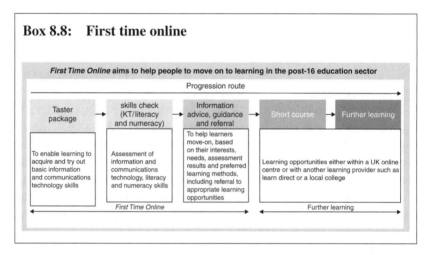

By separating citizens into different user groups and differentiating between their needs, agencies and departments can better identify who they are trying to serve and who is actually using their services. A good example of this is the work undertaken in the development of The Pension Service – an agency of the Department for Work and Pensions. Created in 2002 the organisation was developed in the light of research carried out to understand the different groups of pensioners. Rather than assume that they were a homogenous group (impossible given we are talking about 11 million people), the research identified that many were 'Independent' – fit and active and thus able to access services with little

---

[28] Comptroller and Auditor General *Extending Access to Learning through Technology: Ufi and the learndirect service* (HC 460, Session 2005–2006).

assistance. A further group required some assistance in accessing services due to health or disability issues, but had enough money or family support to maintain their independence. And the final group – termed 'Fully Assisted' needed greater assistance because either they lived alone with a disability and on a low income or because they were in care. In the light of such understanding, The Pension Service was able to develop a differentiated service, tailored to the needs of these different groups. In particular, a local service is available for the most needy, but for the majority, a telephone based service has become the core delivery mechanism, responding to evidence that pensioners disliked visiting social security offices.[29] By gaining such an understanding of their clients The Pension Service has come to be seen as an innovative and responsive service provider.

Looking to the future, however, there is scope for even greater responsiveness. One growing aspect of private sector service is the ability of customers to find out what others who have used a service thought about the experience. Should you want to know about a particular hotel you can find many sites which include previous users' views. To date, few if any public services provide this information, but the development of websites such as www.patientopinion.org, established by a Sheffield GP and described as a 'social enterprise', suggests there is demand. Anyone wanting to know what previous patients have thought of their local hospital can consult this site, which states that it is 'all about enabling patients to share their experiences of health care'. It promises to be updated every day with stories and comments from patients with the aim of helping the NHS.

**Being proactive rather than reactive:** High quality services anticipate the needs of their customers. A feature of Amazon and other on-line companies is their ability to link known preferences to other possible interests. Thus, a purchaser of a CD by a particular artist will be told that 'people who bought this CD also bought. . . '. Linking makes good commercial sense but it also has a read across to the public sector and can already be seen in some areas. For example:

- EAGA – the Energy Action Grants Agency Limited,[30] a charity providing the government's energy efficiency scheme, Warm Front – has

---

[29] Comptroller and Auditor General *Tackling Pensioner Poverty: encouraging take-up of entitlements* (HC 37, Session 2002–2003).

[30] http://www.eaga.com.

taken to undertaking benefit health checks when their applicants apply for a grant to have insulation and heating improvements undertaken.

* Pensioners receiving the Guarantee element of Pension Credit are now automatically 'passported' by the Department for Work and Pensions to 100 per cent Housing and Council Tax Benefit, paid by local authorities. And since 2005, those who apply for Pension Credit are able to claim these benefits during the same phone call.[31]

Such approaches are taking a round view of customer needs and taking advantage of one contact in order to alert people to other opportunities. Only through doing this will public services provide a responsive service which no longer requires the citizen to know where to go or to provide the same information more than once.

**Listening to and learning from staff**: Private sector firms know that if they do not develop and adapt they will die. Innovation is essential. Our evidence suggests that many public bodies are low level innovators, with innovation seen as a 'bolt on' and requiring some external trigger – either political or ministerial pressures or efficiency drives – to stimulate action. Earlier we saw there are many barriers to innovation including a reluctance to embrace new ways of working and fragmentation within government. There are also insufficient incentives to encourage thinking inside the bureaucracy and a sense that, in general, it is wiser for an ambitious official to manage the current portfolio, rather than seek to extend or enlarge it in new and potentially risky ways. This is precisely symptomatic of bureaucratic thinking; the rewards of success will be less than the penalties of failure; and the scales will be weighted in favour of assessing change as potentially likely to fail. But when change is stimulated by external or political pressure, it is often embraced without enough thought, analysis and piloting as examples in this book show.

In contrast, many retail firms place a lot of emphasis on continuous innovation as a way of driving its business forward. Suggestions for change from staff at all levels are encouraged and actively processed to consider their merit. Linked to this, many retail organisations appreciate that it is staff who work in local offices and call centres who are often those who know the customer best. They know that operational staff have key knowledge which can help save money or improve customer

---

[31] Comptroller and Auditor General *Progress in Tackling Pensioner Poverty: encouraging take-up of entitlements* (HC 1178, Session 2005–2006).

service. Many give a high priority to their staff suggestion and feedback schemes, which are well communicated to their staff and backed by clear processes for handling suggestions and rewarding employees. Only by doing this will public services capture the wealth of knowledge and understanding of their staff that will underpin high quality services.

**Making good use of the possibilities of new technology to re-engineer services**: Many public services have made huge improvements and innovation in providing public services through IT. It is no exaggeration to say that to remain competitive all modern societies need to embrace the opportunities of new technology. In the private sector, the potential of IT is being realised – on-line shopping, for example, has grown every Christmas in recent years and is expected to reach £ 39 billion by 2010 in the UK;[32] on-banking has meant queuing in the branch is a thing of the past for many millions of people. IT provides new opportunities for marketing and for selling. The website e-bay brings together buyers and sellers in the simplest – but at the same time, most sophisticated – of auction arrangements.

The successful introduction of IT systems is a crucial element in major Government programmes to deliver better services to the public – whether through providing new services, making existing services more efficient and responsive to citizens' needs, or by improving organisational performance. The Government's Transformational Government strategy, published in 2005, recognised the need to design all public services around the needs of different groups of citizens rather than to suit producers. To achieve success, public bodies need to actively market their services just as if they were commercial organisations. We have seen this with the Department of Trade and Industry's campaign when it introduced Consumer Direct, but also Transport for London had a targeted campaign of posters, press advertising and emails to customers to sell the Oyster card. And they need to go beyond immediate users to influence wider stakeholders such as trade unions, lobby groups and consumer bodies. Introducing a major IT system successfully needs to be planned just like a commercial advertising campaign.

Looking abroad, Canada's Government On-Line (GOL) initiative has also accomplished its mission objectives of providing users with more accessible government, delivering more responsive services and offering

---

[32] http://www.e-consultancy.com/news-blog/361569/uk-online-spending-to-double-by-2010.html.

electronic transaction that are protected and secure (**Box 8.9**). The initiative complies with two overarching principles:

- **client-centricity,** organising electronic service delivery according to clients' needs and priorities. When citizens, businesses and international clients are looking for a service, they do not have to know which department or agency is mandated to deliver it; and
- using a **whole-of-government approach,** where services must be integrated as opposed to simply being grouped together in order to satisfy the expressed needs of clients, regardless of organisational boundaries and jurisdictions.

---

**Box 8.9:    Making good use of new technology: The Government On-line Initiative in Canada**

GOL has achieved impressive results in e-government services. Below are a few of the many successes.

- **The Canada Customs and Revenue Agency** (CCRA) website (www.ccra-adrc.gc.ca) has identified businesses as a key user group and targeted services to assist them in meeting their fiscal obligations and receiving their entitlements. It has improved the organization of information on the website and offers more channels for filing returns and paying taxes. 'NETFILE,' an Internet-based filing service, allows certain business customers to file their returns for Goods and Services Tax/Harmonized Sales Tax directly over the Internet. This service complements the electronic banking section which includes a direct deposit payment option and links to the websites of participating financial institutions that allow payment electronically.
- **Canada Post Corporation** (CPC) (www.canadapost.ca) provides a wide range of business and citizen services positioning itself as a trusted partner for both private enterprise and other government agencies. A service called 'Manage My Account' allows businesses or anyone with a customer number to manage their postal accounts online. This service makes it simple for users to view their up-to-date account activities online, accessible 24 hours a day. It also offers a range of 'Election Solutions,' services that manage the secure flow of information required to manage an election.
- **The Canada benefits site** (www.canadabenefits.gc.ca) offers a 'whole of government' approach to benefit provision. Information provided is both national and regional across a range of departments

---

and agencies. Users can access the information by personalizing the benefits finder to their own needs, searching for general information by life stage or role or by an A–Z index of benefits. The site provides details of each benefit and how to go about getting these benefits in each given situation with links to more detailed information offered by the authority responsible. A variety of transactions can be completed online.

*Source:* Accenture (2003) 'eGovernment Leadership: Engaging the Customer Study' and Canada Government On-line website (http://www.gol-ged.gc.ca.)

**Allowing informed choice**: There has been a lot of talk in recent years of citizens being able to choose the service they receive or the timing and location of where they receive it. This has particularly been the case in politically sensitive areas such as health and education. However, a market based system can only function under certain conditions: the most important of which are competition (the existence of options) and the availability of information (for example, guidance on which option to choose). Proper choice also assumes that customers have the opportunity to leave and take up genuine alternatives.

To date, there has been limited progress in creating genuine choice in public services. It is clear that not everyone is equipped to make their choice heard and individual choices may conflict with the choices available to others. There is a considerable way to go in many areas of public provision to ensure users have sufficient relevant information to inform their choices. And users want independent information they can trust, which has been lacking in many cases. Capacity of provision is also a key limiting factor, although we have seen some innovative methods of offering choice within existing capacity constraints. For example, choice based letting schemes allow more choice of accommodation to tenants within existing social housing constraints.[33]

There are other examples of the emergence of the means for more informed choice. A major concern that governments in many countries have is that many people are making little or no provision for their retirement and that they risk ending their days in poverty. But there is considerable research evidence that suggests that people have little or no idea how to make choices about their financial future. One of the

---

[33] Comptroller and Auditor General (2004) *Choice Memorandum presented to the Select Committee on Public Administration.*

problems is that it is very difficult for people to know what they will receive when they retire. In response to this, the Department for Work and Pensions has introduced a pensions forecasting facility **(Box 8.10)** to allow citizens to make better informed decisions.

---

**Box 8.10:    Department for Work and Pensions**

Citizens can use the internet to access Department for Work and Pension and HM Revenue and Customs computer systems to get an online state pension forecast in real time. Citizens can access this through the Pension Service (PS) website, and the Government Gateway, receiving predictions based on data from NIRS2, and calculations made by Department for Work and Pensions software.

*Origins and development* The main triggers for the innovation are cited as responding to new government initiatives and Ministerial priorities. This corresponds to the Informed Choice agenda, e-government strategy, joining up government aims, and various different initiatives from Ministerial level.

*Staff and budget* Around thirty staff are involved in the innovation: ten within the PS (including one senior manager) plus about twenty staff in partner organisations and two staff contracted to the PS. The total cost is £ 18.2 million. This includes running and operating costs for five years. Some unforeseen costs included passing on costs to other areas of the organisation, and an increase in technical support.

*High impact areas* The e-service has achieved a high impact on improving service delivery to customers and has been a way of offering extended services to end users. The innovation has been nominated for the Government Computing BT awards and the e-Europe award for e-government.

*Key impact statistic (projected or achieved)* Up until 31 March 2006, 120,000 have registered and over 130,000 forecasts have been delivered. A forecast calculation can now be delivered in 30–45 seconds rather than the 40 days wait using the paper-based post method. Although there has been no marketing, use of the service continues to exceed predictions.

*Source: Comptroller and Auditor General Achieving Innovation in Central Government Organisations (HC 1447 Session 2005–06).*

**Building services around known needs**: As governments listen more to citizens and come to understand their needs, they must design their services accordingly.

The Oyster card is a form of electronic ticketing used on Transport for London and National Rail Services within the Greater London area of the UK. The card was first issued to the public in 2003. By March 2007 over 10 million Oyster cards had been issued and more than 80 per cent of all journey on services run by Transport for London used the Oyster card.

The Oyster card shows what can be achieved when a public service is developed in the same way. The focus of the development for a transport 'smartcard' to improve the transport system in London was around the key performance indicators of customer satisfaction, especially journey time and time spent queuing for tickets – two areas of dissatisfaction with past service provision. There was also the aspiration of allowing a seamless service between different modes of travel. The business case, taking account only of revenue saving, was not strong enough, but when social and passenger benefits were added it was a compelling case. Introduced in 2003, the project has been a great success because it was designed around customer needs – material improvement in terms of ease of ticket purchase, reduced queuing times and boarding time on buses, and improved availability of vending outlets.[34]

Two recent developments in the health service also show how building services around known needs can work. NHS Walk-In Centres were designed to provide people with quick and convenient access to a range of medical services, and the NHS Direct initiative has been fitted in successfully to existing provision, particularly as a gateway to out-of-hours healthcare (**Box 8.11**).

Private firms try to remove impediments to efficiency and are constantly refining their practices to eliminate activity that does not add value. There is no doubt that providing many public services is difficult, especially as demands and complexity increase but too often government appears not to be doing enough to assist itself to the same degree.

Capturing personal information about people is a good example of this. A common complaint from citizens is that they are often asked for the same information more than once. This is irritating and a sign of poor service but also increases the chance that incorrect information or

---

[34] Comptroller and Auditor General *Achieving Innovation in Central Government Organisations: Detailed research findings* (HC 1447-II, Session 2005–2006) pp. 47–49.

**Box 8.11:    NHS Direct as a gateway to out-of hours healthcare**

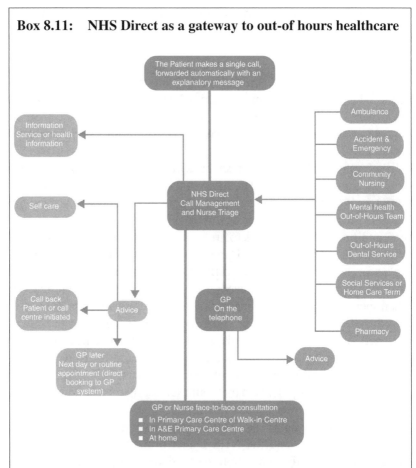

*Source: Independent review of GP out-of-hours services in England (2000). Raising standards for patients new partnerships in out-of-hours care.*

contradictory information will enter the system, creating problems later which in turn will create delays. In line with private sector examples, developments in the use of pre-populated forms is helping governments to help themselves and at the same time enhance services. Some overseas authorities pre-populate tax returns with data already held on individuals. This can yield improvements in timeliness of filing and reduce the opportunity for non-compliance, although it does depend on the quality of information held by the tax authority. Australian taxpayers, for example, when filing electronically for the second time are presented with an electronic form with previous personal details they provided, which they can edit.[35]

**Seeking accountability and transparency about performance:** Private firms often have clear and publicly available information which alerts observers to their success or lack of it, including sales figures, profitability, turnover and share value. In all the suggestions for reform and change in the public sector, we should not lose sight of the continued need for politicians and public managers to remain accountable to citizens. In part, introducing market-like forces into the public service model has been designed to make public managers more accountable to their citizens and their performance easier to understand.

Whether this really works now is debatable. Information is not always available, and where it is, is not always meaningful or easily understood. Systems supporting published information may be weak.[36] Making summary information attractive enough for the layman is a challenge. In the USA, the development of the Program Assessment Rating Tool (PART) and www.expectmore.gov website is designed to increase the amount of information available about the performance of government in delivering services. PART is a standard questionnaire which asks

> approximately 25 important, yet common sense, questions about a program's performance and management. For each question, there is a short answer and a detailed explanation with supporting evidence. The answers determine a program's overall rating. Once each assessment is completed, we develop a program improvement plan so we can follow up and improve the program's performance.[37]

This has been developed by the Office of Management and Budget, and has been designed 'so the public can see how effectively tax dollars are being spent'.

The approach is a serious attempt to make government performance information easily digestible to the lay reader, with an easy to use website allowing the reader to drill down. The home page simply distinguishes between those 'Programs that are performing' and 'Programs categorised as not performing'. These all contribute to increased

---

[35] Comptroller and Auditor General *Filing of Income Tax Self Assessment Returns* (HC 74, Session 2005–2006).

[36] Comptroller and Auditor General *Public Service Agreements*.

[37] http://www.whitehouse.gov/omb/expectmore/about.html.

transparency around the delivery of public programmes, shedding some light on the complexity of government activity and offering a chance for citizens to see for themselves what is and is not working. The initiative has not been without its critics. One non-profit organisation monitoring PART has commented

> It is hard to determine whether the PART is measuring programs accurately, consistently and in a value-neutral way. Even if it achieves these, there has been little attention paid to the question of whether the PART is measuring the right kind of outcomes.[38]

Despite these potential limitations, nevertheless the move to provide easily accessible information on public programmes in a form that citizens can understand is a highly welcome one.

## 8.3   THE IMPLICATIONS FOR AUDIT

The shift towards a customer focus provides considerable scope to make better use of the audit function. Traditionally as we have seen in Chapter 2, audit has been associated with cost cutting, rules and process. It has been depicted as dry, inhuman and interested in criticising those who are trying to serve the public. Yet this image can be far from true. For many years, audit has taken a wider focus with regard to services to the citizen than just looking at their efficiency or the costs from the point of view of the taxpayer, important as they are. As far back as the late 1980s the NAO has produced reports with a strong quality of service flavour, for example, NHS outpatient services looking at how long patients had to wait for an appointment.[39]

**Box 8.12** summarises the various approaches for taking a user perspective. One angle has been to look at citizens as service users, often using surveys of user experiences. Thus, auditors seek to gather evidence on what citizens think of the service they receive. Focus groups, market research evidence and contact with representative bodies all provide the basis for considering whether users are happy with services.

---

[38] OMB Watch *The OMB Watcher* February 2005 in Radin, B. (2006) *Challenging the Performance Movement: Accountability, Complexity and Democratic Values*, Georgetown University Press, Washington.

[39] Pollitt, C. et al. (1999) *Performance or Compliance? Performance Audit and Public Management in Five Countries* Oxford University Press, p. 99.

Audits have also looked at citizens as consumers. Much of the NAO's work on the privatised utilities, for example, has drawn attention to weaknesses in the way in which customers are treated and has generated advice and guidance on how to secure an improved service. Other studies have focused on people with particular needs (e.g. disabled workers) or certain client groups (e.g. pensioners, self assessment taxpayers) examining how successfully provision has been tailored to their requirements. And attention has also been on the capacity of public services to deliver effectively – for example, whether they are sufficiently 'joined-up', or whether staff have the information, skills and training to provide an appropriate service.

---

**Box 8.12:   Types of VFM study taking a user focus**

| Category | Examples of NAO reports |
| --- | --- |
| **Citizens as service users** | • **Tackling cancer: Improving the patient journey (HC 288 2004–2005)** – examined patients' experiences' of cancer services, based on a national survey. The NAO survey found that patients were generally more positive about their experience than in 2000, although it identified that some patients – notably in London and those with prostate cancer – were less positive. The report also identified aspects of the experience that were still not good including the communication of information and symptom relief. |
| **Citizens as consumers** | • **Ofgem Social Action Plan and Household Energy Efficiency** (HC 878 2004–2005) – examined efforts made by Ofgem to help vulnerable consumers, such as the elderly and those on benefits. The report found that many consumers could save money by switching from pre-payment meters to monthly direct debit. But most people on pre-payment meters didn't realise they were paying 'over the odds'. |

- **Helping consumers benefit from competition in the telecommunications market** (HC 768 2003–2004) – examined steps taken by Oftel to improve consumer awareness in the fixed line telecommuncations market to help consumers take advantage of the choices available. The report found that consumers are benefiting from Oftel's work to improve competition by investigating and addressing anti-competitive behaviour but Oftel could focus more sharply its efforts to raise consumer awareness so that more consumers can realise savings.

**Citizens with special needs**

- **Gaining and retaining a job: the Department for Work and Pensions' Support for Disabled People** (HC 455 Session 2005–2006) – examined support for disabled people to help them find and retain a job. It found that the array of programmes were quite confusing and although many benefited from involvement, the quality of training was not always high quality and there was less attention paid to helping those who developed disabilities whilst in work.

**Client groups**

- **Tackling the barriers to the employment of older workers** (HC 1026 2003–04) – examined the services available to help people over 50 find work including examining the barriers to employment. This highlighted the barriers to older people working including lack of skills and age discrimination. It looked at the assistance available to them and how successful it was proving.

- **Developing effective policies for older people (HC 518 2002–2003)** – an overview of the development of policies for older people, including how government consults with this group and understand their needs. This report looked at the efforts across government to consult with older people in developing services, to research and understands their needs and design services in the light of this understanding.

**Services for customers**

- **The Provision of Out-of-Hours care in England (HC 1041 2005–2006)** – examined arrangements for out of hours primary medical care and the effect changes to arrangements had on patient care. The report found that the service was beginning to reach a satisfactory standard but no providers are meeting all the requirements and few are reaching the requirements for speed of response.

- **Filing of Income Tax self-assessment Returns (HC 74 2005–2006)** – examined efforts to ease the burden on taxpayers and improvements in processing. The report found that the Department had arranged for around one million taxpayers with very simple financial affairs not to have to file Self Assessment returns. The Department has also moved around a further 1.5 million taxpayers on to a short tax return to make it quicker and easier for people with simple tax affairs to complete. These measures should reduce compliance costs for taxpayers and the Department, but there is also scope to improve communications with taxpayers to help them submit prompt and accurate returns.

*Source:* National Audit Office – http://www.nao.org.uk/.

An important aspect of taking a customer focus is the way in which the audit work is undertaken and presented, as much as the content.

Bureaucracy is characterised by the use of language and practices which exclude. The aim of audit should be to shed light on how well government serves the citizen, to use the language of the layman where possible, to involve users in studies and, where possible, to seek to reach excluded groups and give voice to them. Much has been achieved but it is clear that the challenge for auditors in the coming years will be to engage more directly with citizens themselves (rather than only using representative bodies consisting of professionals, however well meaning they may be) to gather their views. There must be greater effort made to involve citizens in designing the approaches used so that studies do not inadvertently or otherwise only reflect the views of those who are, essentially, professional observers of government.

## 8.4   CONCLUSIONS

For more than 20 years now, successive governments have argued that a major – perhaps the major – task for the public sector is to improve the standard of public services. Numerous initiatives have been tried. This chapter has argued that whilst governments face constraints in what they can provide for citizens, nevertheless, they have not helped themselves by generally taking a bureaucratic approach to delivery. This has not given sufficient attention to the needs of users. Cumulatively, services are better in many ways – many services are faster, more accessible, there is more information available about them. But there is still some way to go to reduce bureaucracy, understand users better and stimulate a culture of continuous innovation. These changes will not happen over night, but to make substantial progress governments must pay greater heed to the lessons of the retail sector.

## 8.5   SUMMARY

The concentration of bureaucracies on looking inwards to their processes and rules has hindered the provision of high quality services to the citizen. Auditors need to be alive to:

- the creation of complex, unresponsive systems and processes which make services difficult for the citizen to access;
- failure to learn from past experiences of difficulties;
- the slowness to respond to the growing diversity of United Kingdom society and its implications for changing service needs;

- poor communication of what services are available and capturing the information needed from citizens to provide high quality services.
- failure to provide incentives and encouragement to staff to enhance services to users or develop innovative processes;
- inadequate arrangements for the redress of grievances and complaints.

The auditor can encourage public authorities to improve public services by:

- the encouragement and training of staff to look outwards to outcomes and not to concentrate upon looking inwards to rules and processes;
- showing greater understanding of users by listening to them more – getting individual views through market research as well as securing the views of stakeholders and pressure groups;
- treating innovation as routine;
- listening to frontline staff, who often know better than their seniors what citizens and customers need;
- making effective use of technology.

Many of these insights come from the retail market, where firms can only prosper by supplying what their customers want. And while not all retailing works well for the customers, and governments operate in a political rather than a business environment, there are useful lessons to be taken from successful retail experience which the auditor can use in his recommendations to auditees.

# 9

## Risk Averse or Risk Ignorant?

Governments have always recognised that success involves the assessment and management of risks. Throughout history the major risks have been revolution and invasion; and the desire of emperors, kings and other rulers to maintain their position has been the continuing preoccupation of those who have 'climbed to the top of the greasy pole'.

In recent years sophisticated tools have been developed and applied to these security risks, for example: scenario planning; horizon-scanning; simulation based on extensive data sets to predict potential adverse outcomes; and attempts to convert uncertainty – where possible outcomes cannot be gauged and ranked – into risk, where probability assessments can be calculated.

Traditionally, however, the assessment and management of risk has not been central to the design of many other government programmes such as social welfare initiatives, adjustments to taxation, and programmes for the reform of the machinery of government. A key component of risk is, of course, uncertainty – and it will always be impossible to predict every eventuality which might come out of the blue. Risk management is therefore about an organisation's resilience to uncertainty and its ability to respond to the unpredictable. In the public sector, however, too often, once decisions were made and funding and staff earmarked, the assumption has been that it would all just happen. Sadly, however, this has not always been the case and the failure to address risks has jeopardised the success of many government projects. Public servants are often said to be risk averse, so risk averse, if truth be told, that in the past they often did not know what risks they were taking. Indeed, it could be said that some public servants have been 'risk ignorant' rather than 'risk averse'.

When a new policy is considered, the three questions that are most usually asked are:

- Can we get the money?
- How can we present the new policy?
- How can we deal with criticism from Parliament, political opponents and the media?

But questions about the risks that will have to be assessed and managed if the policy is to be successfully implemented are rarely considered at this stage, and it would be pertinent to ask: what is the reason behind this 'risk ignorance'?

## 9.1   RISK IGNORANCE AND BUREAUCRACY

As the arguments in this book have shown, the main answer lies in the inward preoccupation of bureaucracy. In a traditional bureaucracy, greater attention is paid to specifying arrangements connected with current bureaucratic conventions and processes than to engaging with the external environment, save, as noted above, for presentational considerations. This is a problem throughout the public sector.

Governments attempt to deal with two broad categories of risk: risk to the public and the wider UK interest, and risks in delivering its own business. In discharging these responsibilities, governments have three overlapping responsibilities (**Box 9.1**):[1]

- **Regulatory**: where individuals or businesses impose risks, government's role is mainly as a regulator, setting the rules of the game. For example, the Food Standards Agency is an independent government department set up by an act of Parliament in 2000 to protect the public's health and consumer interests in relation to food.
- **Stewardship**: where risks cannot be attributed to any specific individual or body, governments may take on a stewardship role to provide protection or mitigate the consequences. For example, around five million people in two million properties live in flood risk areas in England and Wales. The Environment Agency has responsibilities for reducing the likelihood of flooding from rivers and sea.
- **Management**: in relation to their own business including the provision of services to citizens, governments are responsible for the identification and management of risk. Examples range from the provision of health care and support for the elderly to the building and management of prisons. The shift to delivering services in partnership with the private and voluntary sectors through a range of contractual relationships has led to the emergence of new risks and increased the complexity of service delivery.

---

[1] Prime Minister's Strategy Unit (2002) *Risk: improving government's capability to handle risk and uncertainty* (November).

**Box 9.1:   Government roles**

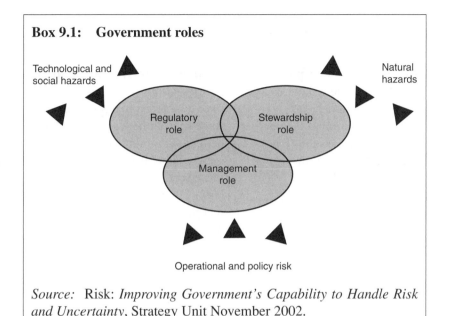

Source: Risk: *Improving Government's Capability to Handle Risk and Uncertainty*, Strategy Unit November 2002.

For a policy to be successful the risks associated with implementing it need to be carefully identified and managed. As policy-making often has to respond to a range of factors the risks of intended benefits or value for money not being achieved are increased. A number of historical examples illustrate this complexity and some of the associated risks **(Box 9.2)**. Inherent in many of these examples is the long standing contradiction in how the public sector in the UK is often perceived. As noted above, public services are frequently characterised in the public's mind as hidebound by bureaucracy and meaningless processes and this has contributed, particularly in the private sector, to the view that departments are risk averse and lack entrepreneurship and a quest for innovation. Along a similar theme civil servants are regarded as conforming to the model of incrementalists (i.e. small steps into the unknown are preferable to giant leaps). As the examples show the reality is often very different with departments taking considerable risks with little awareness of them or their possible consequences; reinforcing Lindblom's thesis that radical decision making is almost inevitably less successful.[2] As noted above this 'risk ignorance' has been a significant factor in explaining policy failure or underperformance.

---

[2] Lindblom, C. (1959) 'Science of Muddling Through' *Public Administration* Vol 19.

**Box 9.2:    There are often many different factors and risks that can influence whether a policy will be successful or not**

• **Consideration of policy options.** Where there is an apparent widespread consensus around the need for a policy, assumptions within the policy may go unchallenged and its development may only consider a limited range of options so 'what if' scenarios or innovative opportunities to deliver the policy more creatively may be overlooked. For example, the consensus about the need for high rise buildings to meet mass housing needs in the late 1950s may have resulted in other practical cost effective options not being given serious enough consideration.[3]

• **Having reliable assumptions on which to base policies.** Where confidence in the evidence on which policies are based is apparently strong, over confidence may lead to incorrect assumptions. For example, the assumption that Bovine Spongiform

• **Need for extensive consultation.** Many sections of society may have an interest in a policy and some may be better organised and better at communicating their views. There is always a risk that those sections of society that are less well organised become marginalised. As a result a policy may be less effective as it reflects only the interests of well organised stakeholders. For example, when competition was introduced into the domestic gas and electricity industries the economic regulator, the Office of Gas and Electricity Markets, had to strike a balance between the commercial interests of powerful energy companies and protecting elderly and low income customers.

• **Responding rapidly to external events**: Where policy is developed in response to external events of factors the need to respond rapidly may mean that policy is formed without a full assessment of all relevant information or recognition of the increased risks which designing and implementing apolicy rapidly

---

[3] Dunleavy, P. (1981) *The Politics of Mass Housing in Britain, 1945–1975: a study of corporate power and professional influence in the welfare state* Oxford University Press.

Encephalopathy could not cross the species barrier to other animals.[4]

brings. For example, the Dangerous Dogs Act 1991 was introduced in response to the public's concern at the increase in incidents of dogs attacking in public but the measures brought into force – muzzling all dogs of certain breeds that were considered dangerous – proved difficult to implement.[5]

- **Taking account of the likely reaction of those intended to benefit from the policy.** Where policy is developed mainly as a result of internal review it may be based primarily around departmental or institutional interests and so fail to take sufficient account of those who are intended to benefit. For example, the introduction of the Community Charge (poll tax) in 1989 significantly underestimated the public's reaction to it.[6]

- **Policies may develop incrementally.** Where policy evolves incrementally it may be continually adapted within a long established and accepted framework when a more fundamental review may be needed. For example, between 1948 and 1976 there was general consensus among economists that following Keynesian principles was the best way of managing the economy. Economic policies were therefore developed and adapted within this framework and it was not until 1976 that a fundamental shift in policy occurred to respond to changed economic circumstances.[7]

*Source: Modern Policy-Making Ensuring Policies Deliver Value for Money.* Report by the Comptroller and Auditor General (HC 289, Session 2001–2002).

[4] Greer, A. (1994) 'Policy co-ordination and the British Administrative System: evidence from the BSE Inquiry' *Parliamentary Affairs* **52**(4) 589–615.

[5] Hood, C. Baldwin, R. and Rothstein, H. (2000) *Assessing the Dangerous Dogs Act: When Does Regulatory Law Fail?* P.L. Summer, Sweet and Maxwell.

[6] Butler, P.D., Adonis, A. and Travers, T. (1994) *The Politics of the Poll Tax* Oxford University Press.

[7] Ling, T. (1997) *The British State Since 1945* Cambridge Polity Press.

Areas of risk ignorance of special concern to the auditor are:

- the application of technology;
- human behaviour;
- asymmetry of information;
- agency interdependence;
- media impact; and
- the 'Risk Management of Everything'.

## 9.2    THE APPLICATION OF TECHNOLOGY

In many areas of public activity there has been the assumption that the application of technology will produce rapid and cost effective benefits. This belief has often been held by men and women at the top of organisations who know little about modern technology and have an unwarranted respect for what they hope and believe it can easily achieve. It is clear that in seeking to use technology to improve service delivery departments have often underestimated both complexity and the challenges of such business change. This is well illustrated by the attempts in 1996 of the Benefits Agency in partnership with the Post Office and a private sector supplier to pay benefits through an electronic payment card at Post Offices. Because of significant delays, by May 1999 the concept was outdated. The Benefits Agency had, inter alia, failed to grasp the speed with which technology was advancing **(Box 9.3)**.

---

**Box 9.3:    Benefits Payment Card**

In 1996 the Benefits Agency and Post Office Counters Ltd jointly awarded a Private Finance Initiative contract to Pathway, a subsidiary of the ICL computer services group. The Benefits Payment Card project was intended to replace by 1999 existing paper methods of paying social security benefits with a magnetic stripe payment card, and to automate the national network of post offices through which most benefits are paid. The project was vast and complex and estimated to cost £ 1 billion in payments to Pathway. By October 1996 the contracting parties had successfully implemented a limited version of the system. But designing and developing a fully functional system proved much more complex and took much longer than expected. The programme at the time the contract was signed assumed that it would take ten months to start a live trial of the full system. In fact, although practical trials had started this stage had not been reached at the time the contract was terminated nearly three years later.

Source: The Cancellation of the Benefits Payment Card Project. Report by the Comptroller and Auditor General (HC 857, Session 1999–2000).

Other examples show a failure to appreciate that technical skills are not enough for risk management to be effective. Non-technical skills such as cognitive ability, situation awareness and the perception of a wide range of information, often presented piecemeal or disjoined, together with quick assimilation of its meaning, leadership and team work all underpinned by communication skills are essential (**Box 9.4**).[8]

---

**Box 9.4:   Challenger incident (1985)**

A space shuttle and seven astronauts were lost when an O-ring on one of the rocket boosters was faulty, allowing flames to ignite an external fuel tack. The Challenger incident was an example of an organisational-technical failure-technical in that the 'O' rings did not do their job, and organisational in that the incubation period of the technical failure was characterised by poor communication, inadequate information handling, faulty technical decision-making, and failure to comply with regulations instituted to assure safety. In addition, the regulatory system failed to identify and address the risks associated with programme management and design problems.

Source: Columbia Accident Investigation Board (2003) Space Shuttle Columbia and Her Crew. Houston NASA.

---

## 9.3   HUMAN BEHAVIOUR

Risk ignorance has often been manifest in a lack of understanding or misjudgement of human behaviour and how it is likely to respond to a new policy. Two examples demonstrate this clearly. In 2003 the then

---

[8] Flin, R. and Crichton, M. *Risk Based Decision–Making: Mitigating Threat-Maximising Opportunity* in Comptroller and Auditor General *Managing Risks to Improve Public Services* (HC 1078, Session 2003–2004).

Inland Revenue introduced Child Tax Credit and Working Tax Credits (the New Tax Credits) which were intended to be simpler for people to understand and to administer.[9] In practice, many people found the scheme difficult to understand and many complained about the frustration and misery it caused to claimants who were often some of the most vulnerable people in society. In addition, administration of the scheme was complex. As a result of the complexity, significant numbers of poor people received overpayments which if they had to repay each week was likely to leave them destitute. Some of those who realised they were being overpaid tried to repay the money but Inland Revenue declined the offer and told them that they would need to repay in the following year, increasing the level of distress. To compound the problem the Department preferred not to launch a campaign to draw attention to compensation available for claimants who suffered as a result of the system problems **(Box 9.5)**. The importance of understanding human behaviour and key factors likely to influence this is further illustrated by the Child Support Reforms introduced in 2003. These seriously underestimated the challenge of working through often complicated emotional, financial and legal issues to bring about financial stability for children and parents **(Box 9.6)**. The message is clear – risk ignorance can arise where departments underestimate how people are likely to respond to a new policy, particularly where because of inherent complexity or technical difficulties the new programme underperforms or is delayed.

---

**Box 9.5:    Tax credits**

The Government replaced the Working Families and Disabled Person's Tax Credits with Child Tax Credit and Working Tax Credits (the New Tax Credits) in April 2003. Some 5.7 million families received Tax Credits in 2003–04 at a cost of £ 16 billion. In April 2004,[10] the Committee reported on the severe problems following the introduction of the New Tax Credits, which meant that several hundred thousand claimants were not paid on time.

---

[9] Now HM Customs and Revenue.
[10] 14th Report from the Committee of Public Accounts *Inland Revenue: Tax Credits* (HC 89, Session 2003–2004).

The Government intended the New Tax Credits to provide a system that was simple for people to understand and to administer. In practice many people have found the scheme difficult to understand. Many have complained to the Inland Revenue about the system and the frustration and misery it has caused to claimants. The administration of the schemes has also proved complex and HM Revenue and Customs has not met its targets for the accuracy of processing and calculating awards.

Many people received overpayments of Tax Credits in 2003–04, some caused by software errors and Departmental mistakes. But the design of the system also results in other claimants being routinely overpaid Tax Credits, which the Department seeks to recover in future years. The overpayments and subsequent recovery make it difficult for claimants to plan their finances.

The Department's estimates of fraud and error, published in 2003, indicated that overpayments were between 10 and 14 per cent by value.[11]

*Source:* Inland Revenue: *Tax Credits and Deleted Tax cases*, fifth report of Committee of Public Accounts – Session 2005–2006.

---

**Box 9.6:   Child Support Reforms**

The Child Support Agency was established in 1993 to ensure that parents meet their financial responsibilities towards their children when parents live apart. But many fathers proved impossible to find or mothers refused to identify them. On average cases were taking 34 weeks to clear and it cost the Agency 70 pence to collect £1 in maintenance from parents and one-in-three non-resident parents did not pay any maintenance which the Agency had assessed as due. There were well publicised problems with the delivery of a new IT system but from the outset the policy was inherently complex. The Department made false assumptions about how people would behave at emotionally difficult times in their lives; for

---

[11] Comptroller and Auditor General, *Standard Report on the Accounts of the Inland Revenue 2003–2004* (HC 1082, Session 2003–2004), paras 2.24–2.26.

example after the birth of a child to a single mother or during divorce proceedings.

*Source: Child Support Agency – Implementation of the Child Support Reforms.* Report by the Comptroller and Auditor General (HC 1174, Session 2005–2006).

## 9.4   ASYMMETRY OF INFORMATION

Asymmetry of information or knowledge can contribute to risk ignorance particularly in contractual relationships where a supplier is better
informed than a department. The example of guided weapons contracts
placed by the Ministry of Aviation with Ferranti Ltd in the early 1960s
illustrates this well. The company was able to make profits in excess of
70 per cent because it had a great deal of information over and above
that available to the Ministry's technical cost officers at the time the
contract was signed. The Committee of Public Accounts concluded that
the Ministry had negotiated in ignorance of the facts with a contractor
who knew the facts and had taken advantage of their ignorance.[12]

More commercially astute contract strategies and open book accounting as part of greater partnership working can help shift the balance more in the department's favour. The importance of achieving
symmetry in information remains, however, relevant today and even
more so in the delivery of front line services. Increasingly, expenditure committed by departments to improve healthcare, education and
criminal justice passes through three or four administrative tiers before it reaches those intended to benefit. As brought out on page 94,
the target to reduce childhood obesity for example, involves four levels of separate organisations – national, regional, local and frontline in
a complex chain of delivery relationships.[13] Each organisation in the
chain will have different information or experience. While all may be
publicly committed to the shared mission of tackling childhood obesity because it is clearly to the common good, the priority they give
to it will be influenced by their other organisational objectives. The
extent to which there are imbalances in knowledge or information about
local circumstances, skill levels, attitude of teachers or health workers

---

[12] Second Report of the Committee of Public Accounts (1963–1964).
[13] Comptroller and Auditor General *Tackling Child Obesity – First steps* (HC 801, Session 2005–2006).

or supplier performance will increase the degree of risk ignorance and ultimately the risk of the policy failing.

The increasing involvement of the private sector in the construction of public infrastructure and the delivery of services through public private partnerships requires careful consideration as to the degree of risk it is cost effective to transfer. As noted on page 152, in the early days of Private Finance Initiative deals, departments demonstrated some naivety in their assumptions about the cost implications for taxpayers of transferring certain risks to the private sector. For example, with the first four contracts to design, build, finance and operate roads in the mid 1990s the Department of Transport wanted operators to take a share of the traffic risk to help create a road industry which would be sensitive to road usage.[14] To achieve this, operators were paid each year primarily according to the use made of the road and as such their income varied as traffic volume varied. The operators did not have the ability to manage or control this risk and as a consequence negotiated increased in the costs which transferred to the department under the contract. This was reflected in the reduction in the estimated quantifiable savings from £ 168 million to £ 100 million arising from the four contracts. It is a mistake, therefore, to transfer risks without considering who, in the end, is likely to bear their costs.

The assumption that a contract, albeit awarded through full competition, will deliver a satisfactory sustainable outcome can be seriously misplaced. Some risks will always remain with the client department. For example, the original contract for Inland Revenue's national insurance computer system (NIRS2) proved insufficiently flexible to accommodate legislative changes introduced in 1998 just three years after the original contract was awarded. The department underestimated the likelihood of future legislative change. The necessity to award a contract extension increased costs by more than £ 70 million. The clear message is that public authorities must consider carefully whether contracts should include specific mechanisms to deal with major enhancements of this nature including expecting bidders to propose separate pricing structures for such enhancements.[15]

---

[14] Comptroller and Auditor General *Department of the Environment, Transport and the Regions: The Private Finance Initiative: the first four design, build and operate roads contracts* (HC 476, Session 1997–1998).

[15] Comptroller and Auditor General *NIRS2: Contract extension* (HC 335, Session 2001–2002).

## 9.5   AGENCY INTERDEPENDENCE

A final example of risk ignorance is where the component parts of a major change programme or policy enhancement are reasonably managed on an individual basis but the inter-dependency between them is ignored or underestimated. This is illustrated by the Passport Agency's inability to handle the demand for passports in the summer of 1999 when the backlog reached some 565,000 applications. A number of significant changes were introduced all at the same time: a new computerised passport processing system was introduced to support the greater use of technology; existing manual systems were re-engineered; two new private sector partners were appointed to assist in processing passports; and a major policy change was introduced requiring children under 16 to have their own passport and no longer be covered by their parents, thus increasing demand. Problems in rolling out the new computer system in the peak summer period increased the time it took to process new applications and a 'run on the bank' syndrome developed as people believed they would be unable to renew their passports in time for their annual holidays.

The situation could have been avoided if the Passport Agency had seen the interdependency between the various changes underway and had put adequate contingency arrangements in place. Analysis of lessons learned from this example illustrate the lack of risk awareness which prevailed at the time **(Box 9.7)**. In short, running simultaneous changes increases risks exponentially rather than additionally.

---

**Box 9.7:   United Kingdom Passport Agency: The Passport delays of the Summer of 1999 – Ten Key Lessons**

1. Public bodies offering a demand-led public service should be aware of capacity constraints, and have contingency plans in place to cope with any likely surge in demand, taking full account of reasonable public expectations of service standards, the likely cost and the level of risk.
2. Public bodies providing demand-led services should ensure that their forecasting techniques, though necessarily imprecise, are nonetheless sufficiently robust to enable them to manage their

business efficiently, for example to enable them to plan their capacity needs.

3. The business case drawn up to justify any new computer system should test the likely financial cost of different options on a sufficiently wide range of volumes, and allow an informed judgement, taking account of the impact of any likely changes in policy.

4. Public bodies should undertake a formal risk analysis before introducing new computer systems and have realistic plans to maintain services to the public if things go wrong.

5. Project managers should plan for adequate testing of the new system before committing to live operation, in particular for staff to learn and work the system.

6. Pilot tests of any new system which is critical to business performance should be on a limited scale so that any shortcomings do not have a major impact on service delivery. Where pilots need to be on a large scale to test operations at high volumes, the risks should be identified and addressed in contingency plans.

7. Organisations should pay special attention to the interaction between the new system and those expected to use it, and take into account users' views on the practicability and usability of the new system.

8. Agencies should make a realistic assessment of whether they have the capacity to deal with potential problems and be prepared to seek early assistance from their parent departments and elsewhere if necessary.

9. When service delivery is threatened, public bodies should have the capability to keep the public well informed, so as to avoid unnecessary anxiety and relieve pressure on services.

10. Public bodies should have adequate systems for recording performance, and ensure that they are in a position to claim any compensation due from contractors for failure to meet agreed performance standards, subject to appropriate risk-sharing within the partnership.

*Source:* The United Kingdom Passport Agency: The Passport Delays of Summer 1999, Report by the Comptroller and Auditor General (HC 812, Session 1998–1999).

## 9.6   THE IMPACT OF THE MEDIA

In a society of almost instant communications public servants need to be adept at managing the consequences of media attention. On the one hand they need to avoid accusations of distorting the presentation of key information – a phenomenon now widely known as 'spin doctoring'. Yet they cannot be immune to the consequences of media attention. This is well illustrated by the implementation of the Child Support reforms in the UK **(Box 9.6)**. The success of the reforms depended greatly on public confidence that where a non resident parent was capable financially of contributing to the upbringing of their children but would not do so, the Child Support Agency would enforce compliance, legally if necessary. The Agency's poor track record in enforcing compliance was heavily reported in the media with the consequence that anyone considering not paying any child maintenance knew they had a good chance of not being detected or avoiding serious punishment. By reducing public confidence this made the situation worse with one in three non-resident parents failing to pay any of the money they owe with amounts owing reaching some £ 3.5 billion.

## 9.7   'THE RISK MANAGEMENT OF EVERYTHING'

The preceding examples show that successful risk analysis and management requires that it should be an activity that is central to organisational behaviour and second nature in decision making. This does not mean that 'risk management' should be turned into another bureaucratic process through which people go as a 'box ticking exercise' that allows them to escape responsibility for their actions by claiming to have followed all the 'proper procedures'. Michael Power has warned of this in 'The Risk Management of Everything'[16] as shown in **Box 9.8**.

---

**Box 9.8:   The Risk Management of Everything**

'Individuals, organisation and societies have no choice but to organise in the face of uncertainty, to act 'as if' they know the risks they face. Since any form of organisation is also a form of closure, of restriction and limitation, then it is a source of risk itself. The management

---

[16] Power, M. (2004) *The Risk Management of Everything* Demos.

of uncertainty is inherently paradoxical, an effort to know the unknowable. It has been said that the present age is more aware of what it does not know, but the rise of a broad risk management mandate since the mid-1990s suggest also a continuing ambition to control and managerialise the future. This ambition is reflected in the heightened accent on internal control systems in organisations, in the creation of new risk categories and definitions to focus managerial effort, in the creation of new agent and risk responsibility structures, and in the development of new procedures and routines which seek to align risk with a moral discourse of good governance. The reach of this ambition seems to be the risk management of everything.

Risk management as a concept, though unclear, has re-entered organisational life as a demand for decisions in areas where some pretence of knowledge is a necessary defence against anxiety. The appearance of manageability is created by a material abundance of standards, textbooks and technical manuals, but the rewriting of organisational process in the name of risk is no mere technical development. It also implicates a new moral economy of organisational life at all levels: the state, public regulators, professional associations and private corporations.

In many cases, there are benefits from these developments. Not least, a better sense of risk in private and public sector organisations may enhance the quality of decisions. However, as this essay has argued, there is also a dark side to this trend, namely the emergence of secondary or reputation risk management at all levels of society.

The ubiquitous risk management blueprint is the result of a variety of factors: a response to specific scandals, opportunism by occupational communities for professional development, new modes of regulatory action and the mutation of earlier concerns with accountability. But a deeper cause is to be found at the cultural level in the rise of a distinctive individualism in which risk management services a need for protection from blame.

According to the anthropologist Mary Douglas, we choose what to fear in order to support our way of life. At present it would seem that a dominant object of fear is loss of reputation. Beneath the surface of the risk management of everything, and its claims as a value enhancing practice, lurks a deep fear of the possible negative consequences of being responsible and answerable'.

Indeed, as Chapter seven has shown, bureaucratic organisations are by their nature especially vulnerable to the temptation to try to deal with the outside world by transmuting their engagement with it into sets of rules and procedures. Instead:

> an intelligent risk management would not allow control systems, and their advocates, to swamp managerial attention and independent critical imagination ... Risk management would be characterised more by learning and experiment rather than by rule based processes... however an intelligent risk management will not throw the baby out with the bath water... To the extent that process represents the codification of accumulated wisdom, it should be sustained subject to the possibility of construct challenge[17]

In short, the aim must be to 'live the risks', and for their analysis and management to be central to – but not the whole of – the work of the public organisation. How can this be done? As the next section of this chapter shows, effective risk management requires:

- top level commitment;
- synergy through the delivery chain;
- understanding and managing common risks;
- reliable, timely and up-to-date information; and,
- scrutiny and challenge.

## 9.8   THE REQUIREMENTS FOR EFFECTIVE RISK MANAGEMENT – GENERAL

The effectiveness of risk management therefore depends on the way in which risk processes and capabilities are developed. There is a danger that in bureaucratic organisations existing informal risk management develop in a way that gives undue prominence to process. The aim should be risk management which is intelligent, explicit and systematic (**Box 9.9**). Achieving this requires as a minimum: time and top level commitment; risk responsibility and accountability to be clearly articulated and backed up by scrutiny and robust challenge; judgements about risk to be based on reliable, timely and up to date information; synergy in the way risk is handled throughout the delivery chain including contingency planning; and finally, for public authorities to have a common and consistent understanding of the common risks which they share and work to manage them.

---

[17] Power, M. (2004) *The Risk Management of Everything* Demos.

**Box 9.9:    The effectiveness of risk management depends on the way in which risk processes and capabilities are developed and applied**

*Source: Managing Risks to Improve Public Services* – Report by the Comptroller and Auditor General HC 1078 Session 2003–2004.

## 9.9    EFFECTIVE RISK MANAGEMENT – TOP LEVEL COMMITMENT

Motivation and ownership are important in influencing whether risk management is taken seriously. Employees need to believe that risk management will make a tangible difference to what matters to them. There are several ways of achieving this – for example, at its most basic by linking successful risk management to financial reward either profit or salary. But close alignment with personal standing or value beliefs is arguably more important and most likely to achieve sustainable cultural change. And in the public sector the drive to make a difference to people's quality of life can be a key motivator or ethic demonstrating the link between risk management and the achievement of key objectives. In health and safety, managing risk is firmly established because not to do so could threaten human well being. Similarly, in professions such as nursing, demonstrating the contribution risk management can make, for example to prevent hospital acquired infection or to help speed patient recovery, can be effective in achieving a culture that 'lives the risks'. An equally powerful incentive is the belief that not paying attention to risks could result in feelings of guilt through failure or association with it, or result in personal disadvantage through, for example, having to discharge significant effort in remedying costly or time consuming failures.

What might be referred to as the 'psychology of risk management' therefore requires careful thought. Ultimately, getting this right depends on clearly visible leadership which consistently signals support for risk management. This can be done by drawing a direct link between the structures and processes senior management have put in place and the better achievement of organisational objectives and targets. Changing behaviours so that key staff understand how to identify and respond to risk is, therefore, a major task which inevitably takes time, particularly in large organisations. A sustained effort is needed by the boards of public authorities to make sure that the benefits of good risk management are clearly communicated to staff and that they have the information, training and support to make it work. These include the potential benefits to be secured from innovative or novel approaches to developing and delivering services through well managed risk taking.

Linking risk reporting to key objectives (**Boxes 9.10 and 9.11**) can help ensure that risks are correctly prioritised for executive board attention rather than risk management being a 'bolt on' activity or control mechanism with no clear link to performance. Risk registers, for example, should be a means to better performance rather then ends in

| Box 9.10: Reuters – Risk management needs to be designed to be more than a compliance tool | Box 9.11: GlaxoSmithKline – How Audit Committees can strengthen risk management through challenge and scrutiny |
|---|---|
| **REUTERS** Reuters operates in the highly competitive business of news provision and financial information, where good risk management is key to maintaining its competitive edge. Risk analysis and identification are an integral part of objective setting for business units. Focusing on those risks that impact on major objectives helps Reuters to move away from simple catalogues of potential risks to identifying those that need active senior management input if the business is to succeed. |  In the pharmaceutical industry, errors can cost human life. GlaxoSmithKline seeks to strengthen its management of risks which might result in such errors through a series of committees and audit functions that oversee key requirements such as regulatory compliance, research and development and clinical practice. The Audit Committee consisting entirely of non-executive directors meets with the compliance and audit functions to provide constructive challenge to their identification and handling of risk. |

*Source: Managing Risk to Improve Public Services.* Report by the Comptroller and Auditor General (HC 1078- 1, Session 2003–2004).

themselves. If risk registers are maintained separately from management reporting they are not likely to meet their intended purpose. Instead they are likely to become no more than a vehicle where every possible risk is filed however small and then forgotten, rather than an effective management tool for purposeful action.

In this connection it is helpful to distinguish between:

- risks which an organisation can do very little about, except to try to make sure that staff, records and assets survive as far as possible for what opportunities may be available through insurance and in other ways. Examples might be an aircraft crashing on a headquarters building or terrorist attack;

- risk to the successful implementation of major programmes, such as failure to secure sufficient trained staff and difficulties in communicating with citizens affected by programmes;
- risks which can be laid off through existing – but very important – 'low level' procedures as, for example procedures to safeguard the handling of money against fraud and theft and against the award of contracts to suppliers who have no real likelihood of being able to meet the obligations that they assume.

A test or barometer of the effectiveness of leadership in establishing staffs' ownership of risk management is the extent to which they feel confident that they can report problems, failures and threats without fear of unjustified censure or penalty. While it is important that each top risk is 'owned' by an executive director or a senior member of staff who has overall responsibility for managing it, a mature risk culture recognises that when risks are taken they will not always succeed. And it is important to create incentives and encouragement for all staff to acknowledge and learn from difficulties rather than to conceal them, and to report and manage threats to delivery sooner rather than later. This can help organisations manage problems before they spiral out of control.

### 9.10   EFFECTIVE RISK MANAGEMENT – SYNERGY THROUGH THE DELIVERY CHAIN

Delivery of modern and efficient public services increasingly requires reliance upon a range of partners, often in complex delivery chains and networks of organisations including local authorities, and other public bodies[18] sponsored by departments but operating at arm's length, private sector suppliers and voluntary organisations. Inevitably, this creates new and increased risks and departments need to apply the same principles of accountability, challenge and openness that they apply to their internal risk management so that responsibility for managing risk is clear throughout the delivery network. Outsourcing through contractors offers new, often innovative ways to deliver services but, in turn, can result in

---

[18] Sponsored Bodies play a significant role in the United Kingdom in the delivery of objectives for departments, and can account for a substantial proportion of overall expenditure. Individual Sponsored Bodies vary widely in staffing, structure and expenditure levels. Some cover national issues from a single location, while others have large national networks or operate within a region. Sponsored Bodies include groups of similar Bodies such as the Regional Development Agencies, individually large Agencies such as the Highways Agency, and specialised bodies such as English Nature.

complexities and interdependencies that create a new set of risks; the more complex the delivery network, the more those risks compound. Whatever arrangements are in place, failure to understand and exchange practice on risk management can leave all those in the delivery network exposed. The importance of a common understanding of risks and how best to manage them, for example through a joint risk register or sharing of risk registers, is particularly important for authorities which are ultimately accountable for delivery of services and use of public money but have little direct control over delivery mechanisms. This can often be the case, for example, in the education sector and in instances where local authorities deliver services directly funded by departments.

Establishing formal partnership or contractual arrangements can assign responsibility for risks but these should not be so detailed that they become too bureaucratic and allow little discretion to adapt services to reflect local needs and circumstances. Where much smaller organisations such as those from the voluntary sector are involved models of corporate governance expected of much larger organisations may not be practical. Departments need to work here with smaller organisations to develop arrangements and processes that are more commensurate with their size and the risks they are likely to encounter.

Sponsorship brings its own risks, not least the potential for inefficient structure and processes to develop ad hoc over time. Risk can seldom be wholly confined to one particular 'box', or in this case the sponsored body. Even where risk has been wholly delegated to a sponsored body it has not been transferred and therefore the group as a whole remains accountable.

Events or circumstances will always arise at some point which are beyond an organisation's direct control; for instance postal strikes, power failures, weather disruptions as well as more dramatic events such as terrorist attacks. The potential impact of such eventualities can be exponentially greater where a service is delivered through a complex web of delivery relationships. Organisations must expect and plan for disruptions to public service delivery that are beyond their control and have in place reliable contingency arrangements. The Prescription Pricing Authority, for example, identified the risk of a postal strike as the key and overwhelming threat to its main objective – to process prescription payment claims from pharmacists and dispensing doctors quickly and accurately. Senior level risk workshops analysed how to address the risk in the short term and, in the longer term, the need to reduce dependency on a single means to receive claims for payment. This combined with

the potential to make use of new technology resulted in planned changes
to the Prescription Pricing Authority's system to enable pharmacists and
doctors to lodge claims for payment electronically (**Box 9.12**).

---

**Box 9.12:    Prescription Pricing Authority – preventing external
circumstances affecting service delivery**

 Pharmacists and dispensing doctors send pre-
scriptions following dispensing to the Prescrip-
tion Pricing Authority (PPA) monthly, which calculates and authorises payments accordingly. A postal dispute could
cause financial hardship, particularly to small pharmacy businesses,
whose cash flow may be dependent on payments from the PPA. To
address this risk, in the short term, the PPA secured a contract with an
alternative provider of collection and delivery services to help ensure
that dispensers would receive prompt payments in the event of postal
disruption. The PPA also recognised that in the longer term the risk
of reliance on postal services was too high and introduced changes in
its working methods through e-prescribing, now included as part of
the NHS National Programme for IT. One of the many benefits from
the change of working methods should be to enable pharmacists and
dispensing doctors to lodge records of prescriptions dispensed more
quickly and efficiently, while reducing dependency on postal services.

*Source: Managing Risk to Improve Public Services* – Report by the
Comptroller and Auditor General (HC 1078, Session 2003–2004).

---

## 9.11   EFFECTIVE RISK MANAGEMENT –
## UNDERSTANDING AND MANAGING COMMON RISKS
## TOGETHER

Risks (and opportunities) do not conveniently arrange themselves around
organisational boundaries, and public authorities, private firms and voluntary organisations need effective mechanisms to work together, to
share knowledge, information and understanding about risks, and how
to address them. Not to do so can have significant implications for public
services and also for value for money. Examples include public authorities' commercial dealings with suppliers to manage common risks and

to maximise their collective buying power. Communication is another risk where, if not well managed, authorities can convey conflicting or ambiguous messages which can undermine public confidence and trust. The need to engage effectively on issues of major public concern is also important. This is well illustrated by the efforts made by the Department for Environment, Food and Rural Affairs to engage with the public over genetically modified organisms **(Box 9.13).**

---

**Box 9.13: Department for Environment, Food and Rural Affairs – Facilitating a public debate**

European Union member states were expected to have to make decisions in 2003 on the growing of Genetically modified (GM) crops. In preparation, the Department for Environment, Food and Rural Affairs, together with the Department of Trade and Industry, the Office of Science and Technology and the devolved administrations in Scotland, Wales and Northern Ireland, were responsible for supporting *GM Nation?*, a public debate on the issues surrounding GM technology. The GM debate comprised nine foundation workshops to establish an understanding of current attitudes, a package of stimulus material, a booklet, CD and video and the *GM Nation?* Events which ran for six weeks from June 3 to July 18, 2003. Key channels of communications were the open public meetings, opportunities for stakeholders to voice their concerns, and an independent website that allowed a free and ongoing debate (www.gmnation.org).

There was widespread public interest in the debate, with hundreds of public meetings and 37,000 feedback forms returned. The GM debate together with a parallel review of the economics of GM crops, the science underpinning GM technology and the results of a four year programme of farm-scale evaluations GM crops informed government policy-making. In March 2004, the Secretary of State published a GM Policy statement setting out the conditions under which GM crops would be permitted for cultivation.

*Source: Managing Risk to Improve Public Services* – Report by the Comptroller and Auditor General (HC 1078, Session 2003–2004).

Other areas where departments need to work together and share information to tackle risks include shortfalls in aspects of performance such as implementation of major IT projects, and also how ideas and good practice in innovation are secured so that they can be learned from and acted on elsewhere. Departments can best do this by developing networks to help foster understanding of the risks that they face and by ensuring that their identification and assessment of risks focuses very clearly on the interconnections and dependencies with other departments. They need then to engage in regular dialogue about how their respective risk management strategies support one another.

## 9.12   EFFECTIVE RISK MANAGEMENT – RELIABLE, TIMELY AND UP TO DATE INFORMATION

Bureaucracies collect a lot of information. But most of it has traditionally been about internal processes rather than external events and the value and attitudes of those who will be affected by the implementation of its policies. Again, information about the values and attitudes of their staff, which is relevant to the implementation of their programmes is often not collected and analysed.

Public authorities frequently fail to learn from experience. Records may be kept – often described as the 'collective memory' – but if they are to be seen as relevant to events in a changing world it is not enough to leave them in files in the basement. They need to be examined reasonably often and their relevance to current events built into policy planning and implementation. Without this, the 'collective memory' will die, especially as staff turnover removes from the scene people with practical experience of the issue concerned.

Exercises and rehearsals can help to reinforce 'collective memory'. Fire drills are a common experience, and those who have been caught in a fire know the advantages of the simulated experience that fire drills can give. The military clearly appreciate the value of practical exercises, and prepare thoroughly for different types of warfare. But bureaucratic organisations often neglect the scope for exercises that take advantage of the collective memory and focus it upon current concerns.

A special feature of societal risk assessment is its schizophrenic quality. There are many events which cause an immediate outcry that it must 'never happen again'. They include terrorist attacks; aircraft and train crashes with great loss of life; floods; and crimes seen as especially repellent. And where events cannot be eliminated, most clearly in the case of natural disasters such as volcanic eruptions, earthquakes and hurricanes, the call is for measures to be permanently in place that can swiftly alleviate the distress.

Often the immediate response is to institute measures of such a comprehensive nature that their expense and interference with ordinary life is so great that they suffer a progressive simplification and even abandonment. This means that the risks may, as it were, reappear; and, while it is generally appreciated that this is so, they continue to be run until the next major tragedy occurs. So people return to live on volcanic slopes; governments fail to erect flood defences; and hospitals again neglect the hygiene procedures that they re-introduced after the last onset of hospital acquired infection.

As **Box 9.14** shows, the US Government Accountability Office warned many times of the dangers to New Orleans that Hurricane Katrina visited upon the city in 2005. Yet this analysis was disregarded and no adequate action was taken to protect the city.

---

**Box 9.14:     Responding to natural disasters: Hurricane Katrina**

GAO's past work has noted a host of needed improvements in a variety of government programs related to Hurricane Katrina and other natural disasters. For example, GAO found that there has been a number of challenges in preparing health care providers for catastrophic events. In addition, GAO's work on energy issues has noted the interconnectedness of petroleum markets and revealed the vulnerability of these markets to disruptions, natural or otherwise. GAO's environmental work has indicated that the loss of wetlands has increased the severity of damage from hurricanes, and that cleanup of contaminated sites takes a tremendous amount of coordination and funding. Finally, GAO's work on telecommunications issues has found that interoperable emergency communications are challenged by insufficient collaboration among federal, state, and local governments. In these areas, among others, GAO has made a number of recommendations which are still open.

*Source:* GAO-05-1053T *Hurricane Katrina: Providing Oversight of the Nation's Preparedness, Response, and Recovery Activities* (2005).

Departments need information on costs, the preferences and needs of key beneficiaries of public services and data on a wide range of aspects of performance such as waiting times, productivity and quality of service. Equally importantly, they require data on likely future developments such as climatic changes or shifts in population and estimated economic performance. Advances in information technology – in particular the development of global and international networks – and market research means that departments can often be deluged with data. They need to form careful judgements about the level of information needed to manage risks effectively. Too little information and decisions can be flawed; too much and there can be information overload, paralysing decision-making as every piece of data is analysed for its implications.

## 9.13    EFFECTIVE RISK MANAGEMENT – SCRUTINY AND CHALLENGE

The performance of public authorities is open to constant challenge from a range of organisations and individuals including legislative assemblies, regional and locally elected councils, pressure groups, whistleblowers, and critics using Freedom of Information to obtain data.

Information about the performance of public authorities can be valuable to the public entities under examination. All too often, however, performance data is seen as negative criticism which must be fended off by 'positive' public relations campaigns. In this way some useful 'wheat' is thrown out with the 'chaff', and public authorities often fail to learn from outside criticism.

Bureaucracies find it hard to scrutinise and challenge their performance on the basis of outside assessments, though they are often quite good at scrutinising the extent to which internal processes are followed. The GAO showed in its analysis of the response to Hurricane Katrina how the obsession with internal bureaucratic processed delayed responses that public authorities could have made to this emergency.[19]

Yet a proper balance can be maintained between responding to outside events and orderly administration. The British Army showed how

---

[19] GAD–05–1053 – *Hurricane Katrina: Providing Oversight of the Nation's Preparedness, Response and Recovery Activities.*

this could be done in military operations in Kosovo, where proper financial controls were maintained while military operations were conducted.[20]

A valuable development is to introduce audit committees into public organisations. Audit Committees are a key element of a robust constructive challenge process and are now having a more prominent role in departments. Their effectiveness is enhanced by having non-executives in their membership and they can provide overall assurance on the way in which departments manage their risks. For example, in British government, such assurance also underpins the Accounting Officer's[21] annual Statement on Internal Control.

## 9.14   CONCLUSION

Greater awareness of uncertainty, recognition that plans rarely proceed exactly as intended and better understanding of human behaviour and motivation – all of which are what risk management is about – can equip organisations to be better placed to succeed. But for risk management to work it needs to be linked to key operations – in fact, integrated fully into organisational life. For risk management to have a chance of being sustainable there needs to be continuing reinforcing actions that help to maintain considerations about risk at the centre of decision making. External challenge provided by non-executive membership of management of boards and audit committees can be effective in providing this. External audit through the perspective it can provide on risk and the internal control environment is also important.

Ultimately, however, it is leadership and the importance it attaches to risk management which will have most influence in establishing an organisational culture that truly 'lives the risks'. In successful organisations chief executives and their boards seek regular assurance that risk management is taken seriously and applied effectively. The NAO has developed a simple tool which allows organisations and their boards to assess the fitness for purpose of their approach to risk management **(Box 9.15)**.

---

[20] Report by the Comptroller and Auditor General *Kosovo: The Financial Management of Military Operations* (HC 530, Session 1999–2000).

[21] The Accounting Officer is the equivalent of the chief executive or chief operating officer. They are accountable for ensuring resources provided by Parliament achieve value for money.

**Box 9.15:    Assessing the 'fit for purpose' of an organisation's risk management**

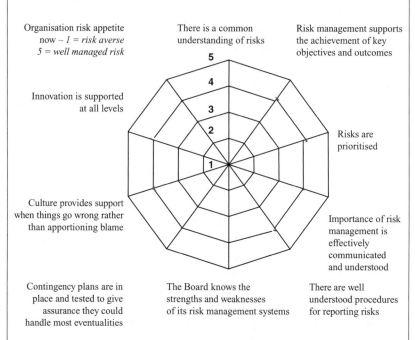

Organisation risk appetite
now – *1 = risk averse*
*5 = well managed risk*

There is a common
understanding of risks

Risk management supports
the achievement of key
objectives and outcomes

Innovation is supported
at all levels

Risks are
prioritised

Culture provides support
when things go wrong rather
than apportioning blame

Importance of risk
management is
effectively
communicated
and understood

Contingency plans are in
place and tested to give
assurance they could
handle most eventualities

The Board knows the
strengths and weaknesses
of its risk management systems

There are well
understood procedures
for reporting risks

The simple web analysis enables a Management Board to assess how well its organisation is equipped to handle risk and realise the benefits. The closer the organisation is to the outer boundary the more likely it is to meet the attributes of reliable risk management.

*Source: Report by the Comptroller and Auditor General* (HC 1078–11, Session 2003–2004).

## 9.15    SUMMARY

Government departments always recognised that many activities involved assessing and managing risks:

- war and peace;
- diplomatic recognition and withdrawal; and
- economic 'boom' and 'slump'.

Risk has always been seen as endemic in these activities. But traditionally risk – its assessment and management – has not usually been seen as part of other programmes:

- programmes of social welfare and benefits;
- programmes of taxation adjustment and reform;
- programmes for the reform of the machinery of government.

Once the decision has been taken to embark on a programme, and money and staff had been earmarked, the presumption of many in public organisations was that everything would then fall into place. Sadly this has not always been the case. The public sector is often said to be risk averse, so risk averse that it often does not know what risks it is taking. Consequently, the public sector has been described as 'risk ignorant' rather than 'risk averse'.

Public sector audit can combat bureaucratic tendencies to look inward to processes instead of outwards to outcomes, by drawing out:

- practical examples of good risk assessment and management;
- the importance of:
  - time and commitment of top level people;
  - clarity about how much risk can be managed at each level in an organisation;
  - clarity about distribution of risk in collaborative enterprises: PFI projects, outsourcing joined-up government, collaboration between central and local government and voluntary organisations;
  - reliable and up to date information;
  - scrutiny and challenge.

Assuming that risk has been well thought through, playing the 'blame game' is not the right prescription for when things go wrong. Rather, the causes of failure need to be analysed and precautions instituted to confront them successfully in the future.

The ability to negotiate risks successfully can be enhanced by specific arrangements for scrutiny and challenge. Organisations can, for example, listen to outside critics rather than 'write them off', and take account of useful private sector developments. Following the Enron and WorldCom scandals, the revised Combined Code in the UK has underlined the importance in the private sector of internal controls, including audit committees populated by both executive and non-executive directors. To support departmental audit committees, the NAO has:

- prepared a self-assessment tool to assist audit committees in their review of departments' approach to risk management;
- issued guidance on the effective corporate governance of departments' sponsored bodies; and,
- helped to develop and promote the non-executive network so that non-executive audit committee members can share their experiences.

Risk assessment and management is not something to be put in a risk register for perfunctory examination. Effective risk assessment and management must look to outcomes not simply processes. To do this you need relevant objectives and targets, and to achieve them you need to assess and manage risks. Above all, we all have to 'live the risks'.

# 10

# Vulnerability to Fraud, Theft and Corruption

Bureaucratic systems are designed to bring order into the conduct of public administration. But the trust that is placed in bureaucratic rules and procedures also provides opportunities for fraud, theft and corruption. For the potential fraudster knows that apparent compliance with bureaucratic requirements – whether it be the provision of utility bills, a passport or a signature – will often be sufficient to obtain the benefits he or she is after irrespective of the fraudster's actual circumstances. In short, bureaucracies create links between personal information and actual personal identity that can be easy to exploit.

In a wider context, every single technique of administrative improvement – the typewriter, telephone, personal computer, fax machine, systems of electronic payment, and methods of money transfer – carries with it opportunities for dishonesty, from the 'hand in the till' of yesterday's office boy to the ingenuity of today's money launderer. These developments provide scope for the three kinds of dishonesty which the auditor is often required to examine and report upon,[1] even though his role is not that of police detective or prosecutor – viz fraud, theft and corruption.

## 10.1  VARIETIES OF FRAUD, THEFT AND CORRUPTION

Fraud, theft and corruption can be found at multiple levels, including:

- where there is an underpaid civil service, usually in the context of a society plagued by poverty and inequality, which exacts money for every minor public service rendered (such as licences and passports);

---

[1] The auditor is required to consider whether or not fraud prevents a risk of material misstatement to a set of financial statements, and in so doing to maintain an attitude of professional scepticism which identifying and assessing these risks. (International Standard on Auditing 240, The Auditor's responsibility to consider fraud in an audit of financial statements).

- where the structure of a political authority is one where leaders are expected to enrich themselves, and their supporters and their families as the only way to get rich and keep power. This mentality assumes that to make one's way in the world, it is necessary to attach oneself to a patron or a 'rising star' to exchange favours with, and eventually supplant;
- where bribes, kickbacks and presents oil the wheels of commercial and contractual transactions, for example, bribes to get contracts, or payments being received after contracts are awarded. These may be small scale, or massive, as some examples of bribery to secure large arms and construction contracts show;
- where an economy is dominated by an illegal activity, such as the drugs trade, and the administration, politicians, army and police are paid to allow it to continue in a kind of symbiotic relationship. For example, in the USA prohibition provided opportunities for boot-legging and gangsterism and corruption was rife.

And while there will be societies where some or all these levels of dishonesty can be found, we consider ourselves to be comparatively fortunate in the UK to be free of the levels of endemic corruption that have been identified and reported in many countries. We are helped by long term economic prosperity. It is easier to uphold ethical values when you have a good standard of living and where fraud is socially unacceptable. In this sense strong social norms constitute incentives as much as fines and formal prosecutions. Many observers have commented on the problems of corruption in less developed countries where public servants are poorly paid and supplement their incomes through fraudulent activity, or where senior positions have to be 'bought' and therefore used to generate huge returns for the incumbent or to reward political supporters.

The travel writer Peter Biddlecombe made light of this in his travels through Africa,[2] stating that if trying to find the head of the Customs Office one should look for the largest and best appointed house adjoining the airport. Paul Volcker's report into the Oil-for-Food programme[3] in Iraq likewise found the need for those in power to have access to huge

---

[2] Biddlecombe, P. (2002) *French Lessons in Africa, Travels with my Briefcase through French Africa* Abacus.

[3] Volcker, P.A. Goldstone, R. and Peith, M. (2005) *Report on the Manipulation of the Oil for Food Programme.*

quantities of funds, obtained through kickbacks and contract skimming to maintain political support. A subsequent investigation by the US GAO found that of 759 contracts examined there was an average overpricing (to allow for skimming) of 21 per cent.[4]

However, it is not just in the less developed world that systematic corruption can be found. Paul Heywood commented[5] on scandals such as the P2 Masonic Scandal in Italy which brought about the collapse of Banco Ambrosiano and revealed the involvement of more than 900 high-ranking members of Italian society in what a Parliamentary Commission described as a 'secret criminal organisation'.[6] Although no evidence was found of individual crimes, the commission's review suggested systematic organised criminal activity.

In the United States, recent high-profile examples of large scale fraud or corruption include the examples of Enron and WorldCom, where corporate results were manipulated to overstate the profitability of businesses and to hide massive liabilities. These have shown that fraud and corruption is not something that is restricted to the developing world.

In the UK there have been high profile corporate failures as a result of fraudulent or illicit activity such as Maxwell,[7] Polly Peck[8] and Barings[9] and we continue to lose nearly £1 billion a year as a result of benefit fraud, and recent attempts of organised criminal gangs to subvert tax credits as a means of gaining funds for illegal purposes has shown there to be a very real risk of fraud and abuse within the benefits system.[10] Each year, HM Revenue and Customs has recently been losing more

[4] General Accounting Office (2005). *Observations on the Oil for Food Programme.*

[5] Heywood, P. (1997) *Political Corruption.* Political Studies Number 3.

[6] Anselmi, T. (1982) *Commission Report.* Italian Chamber of Deputies.

[7] Robert Maxwell illegally siphoned £480 million from his company pension schemes and used the proceeds to prop up the share prices of his companies which he had pledged as security for bank loans (Bower, T. (1992) *Maxwell* Viking).

[8] Asil Nadir, Chief Executive of Polly Peck International was charged with 18 counts of false accounting for moving millions of pounds from company bank accounts to support quoted share prices which were used as security for lines of credit supplied by banks, and concealing almost £1 billion of debt.

[9] Nick Leeson, a Barings derivatives trader, based on the Singapore Monetary Exchange brought about the bank's collapse by incurring losses of £827 million on unauthorised speculative trades which he concealed in a hidden account.

[10] Comptroller and Auditor General *Department for Work and Pensions Resource Account* (HC 447, Session 2005–2006).

than £12 billion as a result of fraud and error within the VAT system and over £2.5 billion a year as a result of the smuggling of tobacco to avoid the payment of UK duty.[11] An investigation by Revenue and Customs also suggested £2.8 billion of fraud and error on self assessment returns completed by taxpayers.

Therefore, although we in the UK consider ourselves to be comparatively free from the risks of fraud and corruption, somewhere in our society a number of people are doing very well on it. Whilst groups such as Transparency International generally support the view that fraud is not a great problem for the UK, it is important for auditors to identify who or what is responsible for those risks which are resulting in the loss of such significant amounts of public money and to work to counter them. The work of the Fraud Advisory Panel,[12] for instance, warns of a growing risk of fraud with identity theft being a particular area of concern. Indeed it was the theft of payroll data from the Department of Work and Pensions that resulted in an unprecedented attack on the on-line registration system for tax credits, leading to its suspension.

## 10.2  WHAT ARE FRAUD, CORRUPTION AND THEFT?

Defining fraud and corruption is not the simple task that it might initially appear. Until the passing of the Fraud Act 2006, there was no clear legal definition in the UK for fraud. Likewise, corruption is similarly hard to define, and there are differences between the legal definitions that apply and those that might be applied socially, culturally or politically.

## 10.3  DEFINITION OF TERMS

The terms have variable meanings and legal definitions in different societies and over time, but in assessing fraud, corruption and theft, I suggest

---

[11] HM Revenue and Customs *Annual Report and Autumn Performance Report 2004–2005* (CM 6691, 2005–2006).

[12] The Fraud Advisory Panel is a registered charity comprising of volunteers drawn from the public and private sectors. Its role is to raise awareness of the immense social and economic damage that is caused by fraud and to help the public and private sectors, and the public at large, to fight back. The Panel was founded, in 1998, by the Institute of Chartered Accountants in England & Wales (ICAEW).

the following 'core' definitions:

- **Fraud** – the intentional distortion of financial statements or other records by persons internal or external to the authority which is carried out to conceal the misappropriation of assets or otherwise for gain;
- **Theft** – dishonest appropriation of property with the intent of depriving the owner of it permanently; and
- **Corruption** – the offering, giving, soliciting or acceptance of an inducement or reward which may influence the action of any person to behave dishonestly.

The external auditor's role in detecting fraud is defined in International Standard on Auditing 240[13] – The Auditor's Responsibility to Consider Fraud in an Audit of Financial Statement. This distinguishes management's responsibility to take all reasonable action to prevent fraud from the auditor's responsibility to carry out work as part of his audit of financial statements to obtain information that can be used to identify the risk of material misstatement due to fraud.

The lack of a clear legal definition of fraud in the UK prior to recent legislation created what could be seen as a 'purposeful ambiguity'. The *Ghosh*[14] test of dishonesty (1982), defined below, required the jury to address two questions:

- Was the defendant's act dishonest by the standards of reasonable and honest people?
- Did the defendant realise that his act would be regarded as dishonest by reasonable an honest people?

This test for 'dishonesty' is subjective and has spill-over complications for the prosecution of fraud, corruption and even theft. Conduct will not be considered dishonest (and therefore not fraud) if the defendant can prove that he had a reasonable belief of legal right.

---

[13] International Auditing Standards are issued by the International Auditing and Assurance Standards Board (IAASB) – http://www.ifac.org//AASB/.

[14] Court of Appeal, Criminal Division. *R v Ghosh* [1982] QB 1053, Lords Land, Lloyd and Eastham.

Compare this to the much more rigorous test of fraud in place within the American legal system, which may facilitate the easier prosecution of fraud:

- **A false statement of material fact** – Not all false statements are fraudulent. To be fraudulent, a false statement must relate to a material fact. It should also substantially affect a person's decision to enter into a contract or pursue a certain course of action. A false statement of fact that does not bear on the disputed transaction will not be considered fraudulent;
- **Knowledge on the part of the defendant that the statement is untrue** – A statement of fact that is simply mistaken is not fraudulent. To be fraudulent, a false statement must be made with intent to deceive the victim. This is perhaps the easiest element to prove, once falsity and materiality are proved, because most material false statements are designed to mislead;
- **Intent on the part of the defendant to deceive the alleged victim** – The false statement must be made with the intent to deprive the victim of some legal right;
- **Justifiable reliance by the alleged victim on the statement** – The victim's reliance on the false statement must be reasonable. Reliance on a patently absurd false statement generally will not give rise to fraud; however, people who are especially gullible, superstitious, or ignorant or who are illiterate may recover damages for fraud if the defendant knew and took advantage of their condition; and
- **Injury to the alleged victim as a result of fraudulent activity** – The false statement must cause the victim some injury that leaves her or him in a worse position than she or he was in before the fraud.

Different legal systems, ethical environments and attitudes may therefore have different impacts on the interpretation of fraud and the action to be taken to observe and prevent fraudulent activities, indeed, it is possible for the definition of fraud and corruption to be adapted to reflect the perceptions of society.[15] For instance, when Prospect Magazine reported on the French party financing scandals, it defined corruption as 'usually a crime of the elite, those with access to money and power'.[16]

---

[15] Palfrey, T. (2000) 'Is fraud dishonest?' **64** *Journal of Criminal Law* 518.

[16] http://boren.nu/archives/2003/12/25/french-favours/ King, T. (2004) 'French Favours' *Prospect* January.

This was particularly said to be the case where ownership of key sections of the press was assumed by the industrial elite, who through their ownership of the main titles succeeded in turning the spotlight away from themselves.

The same could not be said, however, of the corrupt customs officer so often encountered by Peter Biddlecombe on his travels, who facilitates the customs clearance process in exchange for a crisp note. Increasingly too, the involvement of organised criminal gangs in money laundering and benefit fraud does not represent the social elite, but a gang of well-organised, technically elite and mobile individuals, often perceived as some sort of Mafiosi.

British politicians in the Victorian era would have also disagreed with the notion of the elite being corrupt. Many politicians were men of great material wealth themselves and, therefore, were of independent means. Their wealth gave them the ability to be perceived as being motivated not by money, but by the public good.

## 10.4   CRIME AND PUNISHMENT

Unless the risk of detection is high and the scale of the punishment is proportionate enough to deter fraudulent or criminal activity then there is no incentive for the perpetrator to desist. The Committee of Public Accounts reported for instance that the low number of prosecutions for fraudulent trading in oil did not offer a sufficient deterrent to counter a fraud which then cost the Exchequer some £850 million per year.[17]

In some of the countries rated by Transparency International[18] as being amongst the more corrupt; vulnerability to fraud, theft and corruption is made all the greater, as noted above, either by it being customary that contracts and commercial transactions are accompanied by bribes and payments, or because criminal activity dominates the economy to such an extent that it becomes self-sustaining, and pays the executive and the organs of the state to turn a blind eye to what is going on. Where fraud and corruption become part of local custom, then there is no guarantee that

---

[17] Committee of Public Accounts *Customs and Excise Standard Report 2003–2004* (HC 695 2005–2006).

[18] Transparency International is a global Civil Society Organisation intended to fight against corruption worldwide. To increase awareness of the organisation's work an annual Corruption Perceptions Index is published http//www.transparency.org.

crime will be met with punishment. Indeed, those seeking to challenge those committing criminal acts may find themselves facing punishment for challenging the hegemony of the status quo.

Nevertheless, some countries have put in place processes to tackle the problems they face, with varying degrees of success; these are outlined in the two examples below.

---

**Box 10.1:    Fraud in Mumbai and the Indian Anti Corruption Bureau (ACB)**

Fraud and corruption have been rife in many parts of India for a number of years now and in particular within the city of Mumbai. Corruption exists in various forms but is symptomatic of misgovernance. Tackling this has been further hampered by the mismanagement of the Anti Corruption Bureau (ACB) located in Mumbai.

To tackle social imbalance and pervasive corruption, successive governments have responded with legal steps to address these issues. The complexity of the laws and systems in place to try and combat this have caused a number of problems which rather than tackling corruption, have allowed it to thrive:

- Appointments to the ACB are ad hoc, and because of the poor reputation of the ACB, a posting to the bureau is considered as a punishment rather than a reward. The bureau is under strength with very few computers, vehicles or other resources such as communication facilities.
- The fight against corruption needs a dedicated centre of personnel with specialist skills in particular to deal with white collar corruption which is believed to be increasing day by day.
- The track record of the anti corruption bureau is very poor. The conviction rate is below 10 per cent of the cases filed. Only 400 to 500 cases are filed annually with many going unreported.
- Action has never been taken against corrupt ACB officials themselves who have hampered prosecution and investigation cases, worsening the ACB's poor performance record.
- Patronage means permission is needed before prosecuting any higher official from the state government which is rarely forthcoming.

*Source:* Global Integrity http//www.globalintegrity.org.

**Box 10.2:     Growing Success of China's Anti-Corruption Policy**

Corruption in China has been a major cause of concern for the government for many years. Some commentators claim that it is to be expected when a country is transforming its economy through rapid economic growth and adoption of open market principles. However when President Hu Jintao took office in late 2002 he vowed to change things and has since attempted to implement strict policies to rectify the problem in the hope of guaranteeing social stability and the development of the market economy in the future.

The approach by President Hu has been to attack from the top, demonstrating that senior officials are not protected from investigation and prosecution. He has urged that the anti-corruption work should continue to focus on leading officials who have gained interests by misusing their power and has vowed to punish any officials involved in corruption cases. He is aware that there is no quick-fix solution and that the fight against corruption is a long-term project that will require dedication and cooperation from those around him.

At the beginning of last year the Central Committee of the Communist Party of China (CPC) issued an outline of an anti-corruption scheme that serves to punish and prevent corrupt activities by CPC members. According to the schedule, a basic framework for the mechanism should be installed by 2010 and a 'long-term education system, power-operation supervision system and a mechanism-based anti-corruption system will be completed later.' The outline says that the construction of the mechanism should be 'scientific, systematic, feasible and practicable'.

The Chinese Government has also tried to increase its participation on the international front, particularly since China's top legislature ratified the United Nations Convention against Corruption in a unanimous vote. The Government clearly felt that this unanimous vote demonstrates the Chinese determination to stamp out corruption in collaboration with the international community. According to Wu Dawei, vice minister of foreign affairs:

The convention is consistent with China's anti-corruption strategy of putting equal emphasis on the punishment and prevention of such crimes and does not contradict Chinese domestic laws. In the past, China has given the most severe punishment to those who receive bribes and sometimes ignored those who offered them. China is speeding up legislation and law enforcement in this field.

*Source:* Asia Times (2005) 'On the occasion of the ratification of the United Nations Convention against Corruption by the National People's Congress.'

If countries are to secure overseas investment and credit from both commercial sources and international organisations like the World Bank, as well as from donor governments, they must now show that they are making determined efforts to tackle economic crime.

## 10.5   PROBLEMS FACED BY THE UK: DIAGNOSIS AND CURE

The work of the NAO has identified three types of fraud, theft and corruption risks in recent years. These can be broadly split into the following categories:

- *Macro weaknesses*, such as those within the UK benefits system, whereby the complexity of the system leaves them vulnerable to fraud;
- *Micro weaknesses*, where individuals have abused a position of trust, or there has been a lack of proper checking or segregation of duties; and
- *A failure to test and pilot properly schemes*, as happened with Individual Learning Accounts,[19] creating a system where fraud was rampant and the scheme had to be abandoned.

## 10.6   MACRO WEAKNESSES: SOCIAL SECURITY BENEFITS AND TAX CREDITS

Complexity in schemes designed to handle and distribute public funds increase the risk of fraud taking place. In the UK where means testing is a pre-requisite for benefit claims, the quantity of information required,

---

[19] Comptroller and Auditor General *Individual Learning Accounts* (HC 1235, Session 2001–2002).

as well as the opportunity for applicants to mask their true financial situation has, along with increased rates of official error, resulted in fraud levels which has led to a qualified audit opinion on the accounts of the Department for Work and Pensions for many years.

The complexity of Housing Benefit, in particular, which results in processing difficulties in the local authorities who have to check claims and make the payments, is a particular area of weakness. This was reported on by the NAO in 'Tackling Benefit Fraud'.[20] My later report 'Dealing with the Complexity of the Benefits System', discussed in Section 8.1.1 – drew attention to the possible effects of poor design of benefit systems and the effect that this has on claimants and potential fraudsters:[21]

> Complex regulations may also make the system vulnerable to deliberate action by customers to falsify their circumstances or deliberately fail to report changes accurately or on time. In these cases, the Department categorises the customers' intent as fraud. In 2004-05, the Department estimated that this amounted to around £ 900 million.[22]

The department's strategy has been to tackle these risks through improved, clearer communication, and by making the public perception of fraud a negative one. This delivers benefits and responds to the desire of members of the public to be perceived as respectable.

The design of the tax credit system has also provided fraudsters with another, complex system which relies on interim assessments made on the basis of inaccurate data, subject to frequent change and manipulation. Unlike the American system which provides additional income to claimants through the provision of a deductible tax credit, reducing the end of year tax bill, the UK system uses the taxation system to make payments to claimants and, therefore, the immediate link between benefit and tax is lost.

In an effort to promote greater take up of the credit system, HM Revenue and Customs (HMRC) allowed on-line applications, which were manipulated by organised criminal gangs on a major and systematic

---

[20] Comptroller and Auditor General *Tackling Benefit Fraud* (HC 393, Session 2002–2003).

[21] Comptroller and Auditor General *Dealing with the Complexity in the Benefits System* (HC 592, Session 2005–2006).

[22] Comptroller and Auditor General *Dealing with the Complexity in the Benefits System* (HC 592, Session 2005–2006).

basis. The 2005–06 Standard Report of the Comptroller and Auditor General on HM Revenue and Customs stated that:[23]

HMRC estimated that in 2003–04 claimant error and fraud resulted in tax credits of between £ 1.06 billion and £ 1.28 billion (8.8 to 10.6 per cent by value) being paid to claimants to which they were not entitled... These are the first full results for the scheme since it was introduced in April 2003. These levels are unacceptably high and there is currently no evidence to justify a lower estimate for 2005–06. HMRC tries to maintain a balance between accessibility of the tax credits scheme to claimants and maintaining safeguards against the risk of error and fraud. It aims to achieve this by investigating claims which it judges present the highest risk and it checks these before or after claims are paid. In 2005–06, HMRC completed compliance checks and other actions against 195,000 claims, identifying incorrect payments made of £ 250 million and preventing incorrect payments of £ 447 million. In 2005 there was a serious attack on the tax credits system by organised criminals submitting false claims using stolen identities. HMRC identified incorrect payments of around £ 131 million in 2005–06. Its Organised Fraud Strategy Board is overseeing investigations into 41 separate organised tax credit fraud cases, most of which involve multiple claims using stolen identities. HMRC cannot yet give a precise figure for the overall sums involved, but its initial indications are that the total losses on these cases were £ 26 million.... HMRC closed the tax credits e-portal on 2 December 2005 as a consequence of these attacks and it accepts that additional controls need to be built into the e-portal before it can be re-opened.

The joint NAO and UK Treasury document *Tackling External Fraud* highlighted steps taken by the Department for Work and Pensions to tackle fraud through analysing the main features of different types of fraud – see **Box 10.3**.[24] The concept behind this approach is that prevention is better then cure, and if benefits can be correctly set up in the first place, they are easier to monitor and control, and scarce resources can then be effectively targeted to dealing with those cases where perceived fraud risk is highest.

---

[23] Comptroller and Auditor General *Standard Report on HM Revenue and Customs 2005–2006* (HC 1159, Session 2005–2006).

[24] Comptroller and Auditor General & HM Treasury (2004) *Tackling External Fraud* HMSO.

---

**Box 10.3:   Collection of Information by UK Department for Work and Pensions**

The Department for Work and Pensions collect information about the types of fraud, the characteristics of the customers and the way the fraud and customer errors are detected. These help the Department target resources to detect and prevent fraud. For example, the Department estimate that the average sum lost on a fraudulent Income Support claim is around £ 73 a week. Many detected frauds on Income Support are found to have lasted a year or more (indicating an average loss due to Income Support fraud of £ 3,800 a year).

For Income Support, the Department generate separate estimates of fraud and error for each of their three main client groups – lone parents, pensioners and disabled people. The measurement reviews also provide estimates of the main causes of fraud and error and the proportion of benefits overpaid due to each cause. For example, this enabled them to estimate that in 2001–02, 1 in 13 lone parent Income Support claims were fraudulent and that the failure to disclose they were living together with a partner was the cause of 40 per cent of the Income Support overpaid in fraud and error.[25]

*Source:* Department for Work and Pensions and National Audit Office.

---

## 10.7   MICRO WEAKNESSES: ABUSE OF TRUST

A failure to maintain proper internal controls can give rise for individuals to exploit known weaknesses to commit fraud. The NAO has reported, in recent years, on two cases which were widely reported in the press.

In *The Case of Joseph Bowden*, a farmer was sentenced to 30 months' imprisonment in October 2001 for nine charges relating to false accounting and deception in respect of some £ 131,000 of public money and private insurance claims of some £ 26,000.[26] Most of the charges were in respect of duplicate claims in 1994 to 1997 under the Arable Area Payments Scheme, administered by the Ministry of Agriculture, Fisheries

---

[25] Comptroller and Auditor General & HM Treasury (2004) *Tackling External Fraud* HMSO.

[26] Comptroller and Auditor General *Agriculture Fraud: The Case of Joseph Bowden* (HC 615, Session 2001–2002).

and Food (now the Department for Environment, Food and Rural Affairs) and the Fibre Flax Subsidy Scheme, administered by the Intervention Board Executive Agency (now the Rural Payments Agency). Checking carried out by the Ministry and the Board at that time did not identify problems with the claims.

---

**Box 10.4:     The Case of Joseph Bowden – False accounting and deception**

In October 2000, a farmer, Joseph Bowden, was sentenced at Exeter Crown Court to 30 months' imprisonment. He had pleaded guilty to nine criminal charges involving deception, attempted deception and false account.

**The Offences**

1. Most of the charges were in respect of claims between 1994 and 1996 under the Arable Area Payments Scheme, administered by the Ministry of Agriculture, Fisheries and Food (the Ministry); or the Fibre Flax Subsidy Scheme, administered by the Intervention Board Executive Agency (The Board). Joseph Bowden submitted claims or declarations under both schemes for harvested crops, which in part covered the same areas of land. In respect of fibre flax, he made declarations through different contractors covering areas of land that in part were the same. According to the grid references he included in his documentation, some of the areas claimed for were in the sea!

2. The Arable Area Payments scheme is the largest of the Common Agricultural Policy schemes operating in the United Kingdom. The total amount paid to around 40,000 farmers under the scheme in 2000–2001 was some £860 million. In any one year, the amount falsely claimed under the scheme by Mr Bowden amounted to some £40,000.

3. In addition the North Devon Swede Group, of which Joseph Bowden was the leading partner, submitted an ineligible claim for grant under a European Union structural funds programme scheme, for encouraging business in rural areas. The claim involved a grant for building new premises, which Joseph Bowden had already re-built using the proceeds of an insurance claim following the destruction of a barn by fire.

**How the offences were identified and what action was taken**

1. Joseph Bowden's activities started to come to light in May 1996 after a tip-off. Whilst the tip-off was inaccurate, the inspector sent to check the arable area claim was the same officer who the previous year had visited in connection with a fibre flax claim. He identified that Joseph Bowden might have been claiming for different crops on the same area of land and full investigations were begun. The frauds and attempted frauds were not identified earlier by routine checking because at that time:

- Prior to 1996, no cross checks by the Ministry and the Board were carried out between Arable Area Payments and Fibre Flax Subsidy Schemes to identify if claims had been submitted for the same area of land. In 1996 manual cross-checks were introduced to detect possible duplicate claims on the same file. These checks used unique field identifiers from Ordnance Survey Maps.

- Under the Arable Area Payments Scheme, map references identifying fields were required and these were all checked. Under the Fibre Flax Subsidy Scheme only 20 per cent of field identifiers were checked and unique filed references were not required. Fields could be referred to by name, for example, top meadow or bottom pasture. So a grower could supply contracted processors with different names for the same field.

*Source:* Comptroller and Auditor General Agriculture Fraud: The Case of Joseph Bowden (HC 615, 2001–2002).

The earlier case involved a member of staff within the Metropolitan Police, Anthony Williams who, on 19 May 1995, was found guilty of the theft of over £5 million from one of the Service's bank accounts.[27] At the core of the fraud were failures by the Metropolitan Police Service to observe the requirements of good financial practice such as dual signatures for payment and cheque authorisation, segregation of responsibilities and supervisory checking by management. This failure occurred because Anthony Williams dealt with high security operations, and there was a managerial desire to ensure only a few people knew about his work. The weaknesses apparent in the account over which Anthony Williams had control were not present in other accounts. But the

---

[27] Comptroller and Auditor General *A review of the Financial Controls over Indirectly Funded Operations of the Metropolitan Police* (HC 462, Session 1994–1995).

reductions that were consequently made in oversight procedures went too far, paving the way for this substantial fraud.

However, in recent years there has been much greater awareness of the risks posed by individuals abusing control systems, and a much stronger drive towards detecting and preventing similar criminal activity in future. An excellent example of such a programme is the National Fraud Initiative, run by the Audit Commission every two years since 1998, which is designed to detect fraudulent and erroneous payments charged to the public purse – see **Box 10.5**.[28] The initiative regularly updates those frauds it wishes to target as it is able to handle more and more, better quality data, covering a wider range of payments made by public sector bodies.

---

**Box 10.5:     National Fraud Initiative**

The Audit Commission's National Fraud Initiative (NFI) has run every two years since 1998 and is firmly established as the United Kingdom's premier public sector fraud detection exercise. It uses advanced data matching techniques to tackle a broad range of fraud risks faced by the public sector such as council tenants with a council property in each of two authorities or a public sector employee on long-term sickness leave from one organisation while working for another. Matches are provided as referrals to participating bodies in a user friendly application to allow prioritisation of matches and dissemination to investigators without compromising data privacy requirements. The value of fraud and overpayments detected by almost 1,300 public bodies taking part in the National Fraud Initiative (NFI) 2004/05 exceeded £ 111 million.[29]

*Source: National Fraud Initiative 2004–2005: public sector summary.*

---

In 2004–05 the initiative identified examples of the following frauds:

• The number of cases of occupational pensions continuing to be paid after the death of the pensioner rose from 2,076 to 2,497, an increase

---

[28] http://www.audit-commission.gov.uk/nfi/.
[29] Audit Commission (2006) *National Fraud Initiative 2004–2005: Public Sector Summary.*

of 20.3 per cent. Associated overpayments rose by 15.8 per cent to £6.6 million; and

- Pilot exercises, which were restricted to a small number of authorities, led to: the detection and recovery of just under £1 million of duplicate payments to trade creditors; the identification and ongoing recovery of £450,000 of overpayments to private care homes, relating to the invoicing for care of residents after the date of their death; and the cancellation of more than 5,000 disabled parking badges, many of which were in active use after the death of the badge holder.[30]

## 10.8    A FAILURE TO PILOT: FRAUD AND ABANDONMENT

If fraud and corruption are to be avoided, or at least their risk minimised, then the importance of rigorously testing systems and procedures before they 'go live' cannot be understated. The earlier reference to organised criminal gangs using stolen identities fraudulently to claim tax credits was due, in part, to HM Revenue and Customs using a web portal which did not fully comply with the required security standards.

One of the most significant cases reported by the NAO concerned the large scale fraud which resulted in the abolition of the Government's Individual Learning Accounts – see Section 2.5 of Chapter Two and **Box 10.6**.[31] The scheme aimed at widening participation in learning and helping to overcome financial barriers faced by learners, particularly amongst those who lack skills and qualifications. The scheme, which subsidised the costs of appropriate courses, was implemented too quickly and inadequately planned, with the result that many false claims were made for training that had not been provided.

---

**Box 10.6:    Individual Learning Accounts**

The National Audit Office found that the Department for Education and Skills was unaware of the number of accounts opened and incentives claimed without the knowledge of the theoretical account holders. The Department investigated 133 training providers, who had been paid a total of about £67 million, with 98 of the 133 being

---

[30] Audit Commission (2006) *National Fraud Initiative 2004–2005: Public Sector Summary*.

[31] Comptroller and Auditor General *Individual Learning Accounts* (HC 1235, Session 2001–2002).

referred to the police. The scheme, introduced in September 2000, attracted much more interest than the Department expected, with some 2.6 million accounts being opened and expenditure amounting to some £ 273 million (against a budget of £ 199 million).

The scheme was also not monitored properly, and it was later discovered that over a quarter of the learners who had registered as having started training had, in fact, not done any. There was no requirement to make spot checks on the eligibility of learning or to carry out basic validity checks to ensure the bona fides of account holders. Because there was no exception reporting, the Department was unaware that some 13 providers had registered over 10,000 accounts and 20 claimed payments of more than £ 1.5 million.[32]

*Source:* National Audit Office.

In the case of these Individual Learning Accounts, the failure properly to test the system resulted in fraud on such a scale that they were withdrawn. However, where systems are properly tested prior to their introduction, this can significantly reduce – if not always eliminate – fraud or error risk.

### 10.9   THE CHANGING NATURE OF FRAUD: IDENTITY THEFT, INFORMATION TECHNOLOGY AND ORGANISED CRIME

Typically the traditional view of fraud and corruption focuses on the provision of incorrect or misleading information, and the reliance on backhanders, commissions and bribes to grease the wheels of commerce. However, the nature of the threats faced by governments and businesses alike has changed quickly to reflect new technologies and new ways of raising funds through criminal means.

In the UK, the Fraud Advisory Panel acts as a forum to raise concerns about changes to fraud risks and raise public, business and government awareness. Of particular concern has been the growth in identity fraud, which has been discussed in the Panel's report 'Identity Theft: Do You Know the Signs?'[33] The increasing use of technology as a means of

---

[32] Comptroller and Auditor General *Individual Learning Accounts* (HC 1235, Session 2001–2002).

[33] The Fraud Advisory Panel (2003) *Identity Theft: Do you know the signs?*

doing business has meant that criminal elements are able to intercept and exploit information that would have previously been held securely as hard copy only. The ability to carry out money laundering through electronic funds transfers and wire transfers also means that it is possible for frauds to be committed across borders.

The use of information technology for fraud and money laundering purposes demonstrates the need for governments to ensure that legislation permits them to act against such criminal acts. Between 1996 and 1998, an employee of the United Nations Mission in Bosnia, Charles Kim defrauded the organisation of up to $ 500,000 by approving invoices for payment that he knew to be false,[34] a fraud later reperformed by a staff member at the British Embassy in Tel Aviv and reported on by the NAO.[35] Kim was prosecuted under US legislation covering wire fraud, because the payments he authorised to be made were made from a US bank account by wire transfer. However, in many jurisdictions, such a conviction would have been overturned because the criminal act had been carried out in another country.

My reports on the impact of organised criminal gangs on frauds against the tax credit system and against VAT and excise duties demonstrate the effect on the public purse of groups which, rather than relying on small scale opportunistic fraud, seek systematically to defraud the Exchequer of revenue. In Northern Ireland, organised crime was for many years responsible for the laundering of rebated diesel and its resale through fuel outlets, costing the Exchequer £230 million in 2003 alone.[36]

Equally moves against corruption can soon become mired in difficulties as vested interests seek to preserve the status quo. What started as a well resourced and politically supported Kenyan Anti Corruption movement, headed by the anti-fraud tsar, John Githongo soon ceased to make progress when those in power did not like the messages that were issued.[37] Consequently the favourable reports issued by the World Bank and Transparency International have now ceased,[38] and corruption in

---

[34] http://laws.lp.findlaw.com/2nd/001364.html.

[35] Comptroller and Auditor General *Foreign and Commonwealth Office Resource Accounts 2004–2005: Fraud at the British Embassy Tel Aviv* (HC 776, Session 2005–2006).

[36] HM Revenue and Customs *Annual Report and Autumn Performance Report 2004–2005* (CM 6691, 2005–2006).

[37] Africa Focus, Kenya (2006) *Githongo Report*; Freedom House (2006) *Freedom in the World – Kenya*.

[38] Transparency International (2004, 2005, 2006) *National Integrity Studies, Kenya (various); Global Integrity, Public Integrity Index; Global Corruption Reports*.

Kenya allegedly remains endemic, with arguments between political parties and others over who is responsible for it.[39]

## 10.10  CONCLUSIONS

Anderson and Gray's 2006 report for the World Bank highlights a number of factors in their concluding thoughts:[40]

> Anti-corruption efforts succeed when rules and regulations are simplified, interactions between firms and public officials are limited, and burdens on the private sector are reduced. As countries open up, corruption tends to decline, but even advanced countries need to be alert to the problem. Finally, although the policies themselves must be sound, there must also be tireless political advocates who will push them through.

In the UK, although there is much to be positive about because we bring together many of those factors which lead to low rates of corruption, the complexity of our tax and benefit systems leave the public purse seriously exposed to the risks of fraud.

There is nevertheless an increasing awareness of, and commitment to, tackling fraud. The National Fraud Initiative is a welcome development in this respect, using technology to identify greater numbers and values of frauds, then using the lessons learned to address risks. This leads to a greater deterrent effect because there is a perception that perpetrators will be found and prosecuted. Perhaps the success of anti-fraud and anti-corruption efforts in China lie with the realisation that the penalty will be swift and more effective than either an administrative penalty or a threat to withhold future benefits and reclaim those already paid from someone who has, by that stage, already relocated to another country or secured a new identity.

What is needed to ensure the auditor's effectiveness? The following are important:

- To look for signs of weakness and vulnerability in the way schemes are designed and implemented;

---

[39] Africa Focus, Kenya (2005) *Corruption Fight Stalling.*

[40] Anderson, J. and Gray, C. (2006) *Anti-Corruption in Transition: Who is succeeding and why?* World Bank.

- To be aware of the many basic and traditional ways dishonesty is carried out **(Box 10.7)**;
- To know whether the staff concerned with an activity have received advice and warnings about the propensity to fraud;
- To be aware of the scope for specialised assistance from forensic accountants **(Box 10.8)**; and,
- To be able to suggest incentives for the avoidance of dishonest behaviour **(Box 10.9)**

---

**Box 10.7:   Forty Commons Forms of Fraud**[41]

1. Pilfering stamps.
2. Stealing merchandise, tools, supplies, and other items of equipment.
3. Removing small amounts from cash funds and registers.
4. Failing to record sales of merchandise and pocketing the cash.
5. Creating overages in cash funds and registers by underrecording.
6. Overloading expense accounts or diverting advances to personal use.
7. Lapping collections on customers' accounts.
8. Pocketing payments on customers' accounts, issuing receipts on scraps of paper or in self-designed receipt books.
9. Collecting an account, pocketing the money, and charging it off: collecting charged-off accounts and not reporting.
10. Charging customers' accounts with stolen cash.
11. Issuing credit for false customer claims and returns.
12. Failing to make bank deposits daily or depositing only part of the money.
13. Altering dates on deposit slips to cover stealing.
14. Making round sum deposits – attempting to catch up by the end of the month.
15. Carrying fictitious extra help on payrolls or increasing rates or hours.
16. Carrying employees on payroll beyond actual severance dates.
17. Falsifying additions on payrolls and withholding unclaimed wages.

18. Destroying, altering, or voiding cash sales tickets and pocketing the cash.
19. Withholding cash sales receipts by using false charge accounts.
20. Recording unwarranted cash discounts.
21. Increasing amounts of petty-cash vouchers and/or totals in accounting for disbursements.
22. Using personal expenditure receipts to support false paid-out items.
23. Using copies of previously processed original vouchers or using a properly approved voucher of the prior year by changing date.
24. Paying false invoices either self-prepared or obtained through collusion with suppliers.
25. Increasing amounts of suppliers' invoices through collusion.
26. Charging personal purchases through company misuse of purchasing orders.
27. Billing stolen merchandise to fictitious accounts.
28. Shipping stolen merchandise to an employee's or relatives home.
29. Falsifying inventories to cover theft or delinquencies.
30. Seizing checks payable to the company or to the suppliers.
31. Raising cancelled bank checks to agree with fictitious entries.
32. Inserting fictitious ledger sheets.
33. Causing erroneous footing of cash receipts and disbursement books.
34. Deliberately confusing postings to control and detail accounts.
35. Selling waste and scrap materials and pocketing proceeds.
36. 'Selling' door keys or the combinations to safes or vaults.
37. Creating credit balances on ledgers and converting to cash.
38. Falsifying bills of lading and splitting with carrier.
39. Obtaining Blank checks (unprotected) and forging the signature.
40. Permitting special prices or privileges to customers or granting business to favoured suppliers for kickbacks.

*Source:* Coe, C.K. *Public Financial Management Prentice Hall.*

---

[41] Coe, C.K. (1989) *Public Financial Management* Prentice Hall.

**Box 10.8:    Forensic Services**

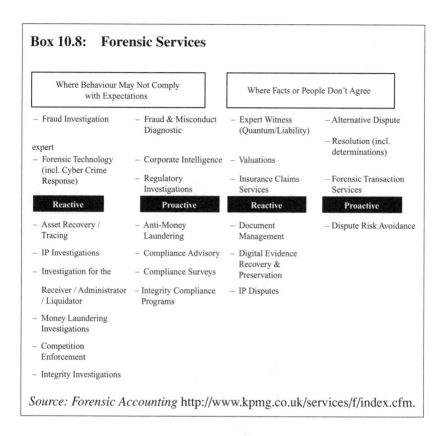

| Where Behaviour May Not Comply with Expectations | | Where Facts or People Don't Agree | |
|---|---|---|---|
| – Fraud Investigation | – Fraud & Misconduct Diagnostic | – Expert Witness (Quantum/Liability) | – Alternative Dispute |
| expert | | | – Resolution (incl. determinations) |
| – Forensic Technology (incl. Cyber Crime Response) | – Corporate Intelligence | – Valuations | |
| | – Regulatory Investigations | – Insurance Claims Services | – Forensic Transaction Services |
| **Reactive** | **Proactive** | **Reactive** | **Proactive** |
| – Asset Recovery / Tracing | – Anti-Money Laundering | – Document Management | – Dispute Risk Avoidance |
| – IP Investigations | – Compliance Advisory | – Digital Evidence Recovery & Preservation | |
| – Investigation for the Receiver / Administrator / Liquidator | – Compliance Surveys | | |
| | – Integrity Compliance Programs | – IP Disputes | |
| – Money Laundering Investigations | | | |
| – Competition Enforcement | | | |
| – Integrity Investigations | | | |

*Source: Forensic Accounting* http://www.kpmg.co.uk/services/f/index.cfm.

## 10.11   SUMMARY

Fraud, theft and corruption are widespread in all societies, though the forms they take are different and they change over time. The rational arrangements of bureaucracy are designed to make dishonesty more difficult, which they do to a degree. But the arrangements they introduce also provide many of the means for dishonesty, thus signatures for approving payments are both a safeguard against fraud but a means by which forgers can carry out fraud.

Fraud, theft and corruption can be analysed in terms of:

- *Macro weaknesses* – as in systems of taxation where complexity makes them vulnerable;
- *Micro weaknesses* – as in a failure to segregate duties; and

## Box 10.9:   If the price is right

Theft and corruption can be thwarted, it's just a matter of appropriate incentives

If you want to be rich, richer, less corrupt economy, he will live up to the new system. William Lewis, founding director of the McKinsey Global Institute, points out that illiterate Mexican workers on building sites in Houston are as productive as any construction worker. The Mexicans are perfectly capable of living up to the potential of the American system.

An alternative view, popular among the common-sense crowd, is that corruption is a problem in Indonesia because Indonesians are crooks by nature; poor countries are poor because they are full of people who are lazy or stupid or dishonest. I disagree out of faith, rather than because the evidence is

If you want to be rich, you can try to set up a brilliantly successful company. Or you can steal money. Transparency International, the corruption watchdog, has estimated that Mohamed Suharto embezzled up to $35bn when he was Indonesia's president, a figure that is in the same league as the entrepreneurial fortunes of Bill Gates and Warren Buffett. On a humbler scale, we all face the same choice. We can try to earn money by doing something useful, or we can try to steal or extort it from other people. A society where most people are doing something useful has a good chance of being rich; a society full of corruption will be poor.

That is a glib enough explanation of wealth and poverty, but what causes corruption? Many economists believe that corruption is a response to perverse incentives. For example, in Indonesia it takes an average of 151 days to legally establish a small business, according to the World Bank's "Doing Business" database. This is a large incentive to pay bribes or keep a business unregistered. It is not surprising that there is a strong correlation between red tape and corruption. In general, the harder it is to make money legally the more tempting it will be to do so illegally, and if people are not punished for stealing they will be more likely to steal.

The view that incentives are paramount suggests that if you take a person from a poor, corrupt economy and move him to a

compelling. But then, what evidence could there be? You would need to take people from every culture, put them somewhere where they could ignore the law with impunity, and see who cheated and who was honest.

That sounds like a tall order for any research strategy, but the economists Ray Fisman and Edward Miguel have realised that diplomats in New York city were, in fact, the perfect guinea pigs. Diplomatic immunity meant that parking tickets issued to diplomats could not be enforced, and so parking legally was essentially a matter of personal ethics.

Fisman and Miguel found support for the common-sense view. Countries with corrupt systems, as measured by Transparency International, also sent diplomats who parked illegally. From 1997-2005, the Scandinavians committed only 12 unpaid parking violations, and most of them were by a single criminal mastermind from Finland. Chad and Bangladesh, regularly at the top of corruption tables, produced more than 2,500 violations between them. Perhaps poor countries are poor because they are full of corrupt people, after all.

It's a very clever piece of work, but I will not be abandoning my faith in economic incentives just yet. In 2002, New York city was given much greater power to punish deadbeat diplomats: cars were towed, permits suspended, and fines collected from the relevant foreign aid budget. Unpaid violations immediately fell 90 per cent. When it comes to parking violations, personal morality matters, but incentives matter more.

*Source:* Financial Times Magazine, *July 2006.*

- *A failure properly to test and pilot schemes*, as happened with Individual Learning Accounts, creating a system where fraud was rampant and the scheme had to be abandoned.

The auditor needs to:

- look for weakness and vulnerability in the way schemes are designed and implemented;
- be aware of the many ways that dishonest activity is carried out;

- promote training in and sensitivity to the scope for fraud, theft and corruption;
- understand the range of specialised anti-fraud services that are available; and,
- be able to suggest incentives for the avoidance of dishonest behaviour.

The importance of strong social norms to reinforce a culture where fraud is unacceptable emphasise the need for the auditor to look further than her traditional skill set. The auditor needs to be aware of the extent to which a society's values and attitudes, social norms and conventions, reinforce or undermine the formal legal and other arrangements for dealing with fraud, theft and corruption.

# 11

# Programme and Project Management – Bureaucracies' Weakest Link?

Bureaucracy is a system that manages through the hierarchy – tasks are delegated to and divided between a succession of increasingly detailed lower layers of authority to secure the benefits of specialisation and division of labour, and then co-ordinated upwards through responsibility to each successive layer of higher authority. This can work well for settled tasks, when tomorrow is like today, and the external environment is static.

But experience showed that it did not work well when new projects and programmes had to be devised and managed.[1] Theoretical collaborators, required to work across the hierarchies, too often did so with reservations, with closer attention to the concerns and prejudices of their hierarchical superiors than to achieving a successful outcome by working closely with colleagues across the departmental hierarchies. And as public authorities in many countries, from the Second World War onwards, were increasingly concerned with major projects, as in defence and construction, but also with devising and running complex schemes of social welfare and support – all of them projects, though not always recognised as such – the inability of traditional bureaucracy to cope with this range of work became increasingly apparent.

---

[1] Programme and Project are often used interchangeably. But some differences may be distinguished, as in the following note:

'because projects and programmes are temporary management structures, organisations can use whatever terms they feel appropriate to describe them. However, it is normal practice to distinguish between the two. In particular, it is now generally recognised that projects should focus on creating specified deliverables, whilst programmes should focus on defining the what deliverables are required, on achieving the creation of new capabilities, and on ensuring that these capabilities are used effectively so as to realise business benefits. In ProgM we believe that recognising these differences results in clearer roles and responsibilities, enabling Project Managers to focus on "on-time" and "on-cost" delivery, whilst Programme Managers focus on co-ordinating projects to deliver the required new capabilities'.

Paul Rayner, Chairman ProgM, in correspondence with the author, dated 11 January 2007.

## 11.1   BUREAUCRACIES' FAILURES

The failures of bureaucracy were well catalogued from the 1940's, and the main ones will be listed in this section of this chapter.
  Relevant difficulties include:

* divided managerial control;
* a concentration on lowest price rather than best outcome;
* changes in specification and inadequate specifications;
* insufficient testing and piloting.

### 11.1.1   Divided Managerial Control

A project run by a bureaucracy too often has too many managers. This can be illustrated in hypothetical simplified form in **Box 11.1**. The team

---

**Box 11.1:   Hierachies versus Projects – A hypothetical example Ministry of Military Aircraft Supply**

The Minister

The Chief Official

| Department A | Department B | Department C | Department D | Department E | Department F | Department G |
| Airframes | Engines | Avionics | Weapons | Contracts | Finance | Staff |

To build an aircraft requires collaboration across all these hierarchies and at many levels. But here the main focus of staff attention is up and down the hierarchy, not across the hierarchies.

To overcome these problems, project or matrix managerial structures were introduced; taking officials from relevant hierarchies and forming them into a team with specific time, cost and quality targets. The leader might come from any appropriate hierarchy, and the members owed loyalty to the team as well as to hierarchical superiors.

| Project Manger for Aircraft A | | | | | | | |
|---|---|---|---|---|---|---|---|
| Functions Team Member | Airframe | Engine | Avionics | Weapons | Control | Finance | Staff |
| Dept A | ✔✔✔ | | | | | | |
| B | | ✔✔✔ | | | | | |
| C | | | ✔✔✔ | | | | |
| D | | | | ✔✔✔ | | | |
| E | | | | | ✔✔ | | |
| F | | | | | | ✔✔ | |
| G | | | | | | | ✔ |

Full Time Members ✔✔✔
Part Time Members ✔
Available for Consultation ✔

*Source:* National Audit Office.

arrangement can be varied over time. If there are special problems with the engine more members can be added; if the contract is difficult, the relevant expert can be full time.

This arrangement works better than a hierarchy, but it does not always overcome all the problems of achieving all the project's objectives, since dual loyalties still obtain. Sometimes project teams are formed quite separately from the bureaucratic hierarchy of the organisation of which they are part. Their staff have exclusive loyalty to the project. This can work; but it is usually necessary for the team to have links with some other parts of their organisation, especially finance and public relations. So a 'pure' project, floating free within an organisation is rarely possible. And another difficulty is that there are often more teams in a public authority than the available finances, skills and other resources can cope with. It is easy to set up a team, and announcing its existence often seems a valuable public relations move but if it lacks resources it will struggle.

### 11.1.2    A Concentration on Lowest Price Rather than Best Outcome

All public authorities should naturally be concerned with value for money. But one of the difficulties that bureaucracies have is that the money for projects has often to be drawn from several budget holders, each of them anxious to keep down costs, especially on projects for which they have a shared rather than total responsibility. Lord James of Blackheath put this well when giving evidence to the Select Committee of Public Accounts on the Millennium Dome project, erected in London to celebrate the year 2000, and whose cost rose from an estimate of £399 million to £628 million. Lord James said that the British government was 'always going for the cheapest option when dealing with project management...We have an obsession with getting the cheapest option than having to pay more to correct things'.[2]

### 11.1.3    Changes in Specification and Inadequate Specifications

In project management, the best is often the enemy of the good – changing threats and improving technology provide the incentive to change the specifications of weapons systems; and changing ministers and other

---

[2] Committee of Public Accounts Fourteenth Report 2001–2002 *The Millennium Dome* (HC 516, Session 2001–2002).

elected members often want to adjust projects to meet the immediate political needs of the moment. Such adjustments nearly always mean delay, extra costs and diminished performance – often to the point that any extra gain is outweighed by the negative implication of securing it.

Even when the desired outcome of a project is well defined, my reports have often highlighted failures in defining detailed requirements and specifications which can make it difficult for suppliers to deliver solutions and for public sector bodies to know whether the expected outputs are being delivered. My report on *The Provision of Out-of-Hours Care in England* (**Box 11.2**) provides a good example of the high levels of operational, and in this case legal, risk which authorities must bear where specifications are inadequately defined.

---

**Box 11.2:   The Provision of Out-of-Hours Care in England**[3]

Out-of-hours care is the term currently used to describe primary medical care during the period from 6:30 pm until 8:00 am on weekdays, and all weekends, bank holidays and public holidays. A new General Medical Services contract came into force in 2004, which allowed General Practitioners to opt out of the responsibility of organising out-of-hours care from 1 April 2004. Where General Practitioners opted out, they gave up an average of £6,000 per annum and passed on responsibility to their Primary Care Trust (PCT).

Prior to 2005, many PCTs had not managed or delivered out-of-hours services. They lacked time, experience and reliable management data, for example on demand, activity and cost. This shortfall in information made it very difficult for PCTs to write accurate service specifications and commission effectively. There was also confusion as to whether the out-of-hours service should be restricted to urgent care.

Many contracts were signed late or not at all, with significant legal implications. This was due to poor service specifications, disagreements between commissioners and providers over risk-sharing, and the inability to reconcile PCTs' limited budgets with providers' estimated costs.

---

[3] Comptroller and Auditor General *The Provision of Out-of-Hours Care in England* (HC 1041, Session 2005–2006).

> Where external providers delivered services, final arrangement
> with signed contracts were in place in only nine per cent of cases
> by the time the service began.
>
> *Source:* Comptroller and Auditor General – The Provision of Out-of-
> Hours care in England (HC 1041, Session 2005–2006).

## 11.1.4   Insufficient Testing and Piloting

Many citizens believe that public authorities are the slowest of all
organisations to decide upon new initiative and actions. However, a
recurring feature of political life is that many projects and programmes
are launched with inadequate testing and piloting – possibly because
political decisions having been taken, there is a desire to secure tangible
results quickly.

This can lead to disappointment and regret. Piloting solutions is
important to clarify that the project outcomes can meet users' needs.
The net result of a trial may be negative, in that the solution may not be
fit for purpose. To many in the public sector such a result is seen as a
failure when in fact it should be seen as a success in that the reasons for
failure can be explored and the project re-engineered to deliver a better
outcome. The alternative to piloting solutions is that schemes may be
introduced which do not achieve the desired outcomes and which must
then be rectified in the wake of adverse public comment. Such a process is inevitably more time-consuming and difficult than to ensure the
project is right before it 'goes live'. My report on the introduction of
the Countryside Rights of Way Act 2000 **(Box 11.3)** provides a good
example of the type of problems which may occur.

---

**Box 11.3:    The Right of Access to Open Countryside**[4]

The introduction of the Countryside Rights of Way Act 2000 provided
for the public to walk across large areas of countryside without being
restricted to footpaths. This was seen as an important extension of
civil liberties and the opportunity for city dwellers to learn more of
the countryside. Farmers, on the other hand, feared damage to crops.
So right of access had to be balanced between competing interests.

---

[4] Comptroller and Auditor General *Department for Environment, Food and Rural Affairs and the
Countryside Agency – The right of access to the open countryside* (HC 1046, Session 2005–2006).

The new right of public access, often referred to as the 'right to roam', applies to 6.5 per cent of land in England and covers mountains, moors, heaths, downs and registered common land. The Countryside Agency, in conjunction with the Department for Environment, Food and Rural Affairs, introduced open access on an area by area basis between September 2004 and October 2005.

The Agency did not pilot test implementation as they believed this would lead to them being unable to complete the project by 2005, although they did not adequately assess the risks of foregoing pilot testing. As a result, the Agency underestimated the work involved in determining what qualified as access land and how to map it, which lay at the heart of securing a balance between public access and farmer's rights.

While the right to roam was introduced nearly two months ahead of target, the Agency spent £ 52.6 million implementing the open access programme, compared to an estimate of £ 28 million. Once all other costs are included, total central government expenditure amounted to some £ 69 million, much of which could have been avoided by pilot testing and learning lessons there from.

*Source:* Comptroller and Auditor General Department for Environment, Food and Rural Affairs and the Countryside Agency – *The right of Access to the Open Countryside* (HC 1046, Session 2005–2006).

## 11.2   TRANSCENDING FAILURE

As noted in the previous section of this chapter, the problems of trying to plan and manage projects and programmes through bureaucratic hierarchies are well known and constantly repeated. Divided managerial control; lowest price rather than value for money; changing specifications and insufficient testing are prevalent today as they have been for many years.

Thus the recognition of these difficulties has not been enough to change behaviour. The auditor is likely to meet many examples of these difficulties, and the purpose of this section of the chapter is to suggest how he/she may make recommendations to overcome or, better still, to avoid them. The areas examined are:

- the promotion of trust and open communication;
- contracting;

- skills set for programme and project management;
- the pace of change;
- clear leadership;
- managing risk;
- understanding the needs and expectations of end users.

### 11.2.1   Trust and Open Communication

The fundamental problem of bureaucracy is suspicion. Within public authorities, for example, engineers, doctors, soldiers, sailors, airmen and educationalists suspect financiers and contract staff and 'human resources' departments. Financiers may see operational staff as 'wild' men and women with their heads full of unworkable ideas; and operational staff may see financiers as narrow minded 'Scrooges', who care more for money and rules than for public services. The lines of control and constraints encourage separation more than co-operation across the whole range of an organisation's work.

These difficulties are often magnified when a project or programme requires co-operation between public and private sectors, as with traditional contracting for goods and services; with modern outsourcing of facilities management and service provision either directly or through schemes for private finance and partnership as we have discussed in Chapter 6.

Traditionally, many public servants have seen private sector contractors, suppliers, managers and consultants as clever and unscrupulous people who are interested only in making money by pulling the wool over the eyes of naïve public servants. Similarly, many private sector people have seen public servants as pedantic bureaucrats who do not live in the real world, who see a problem in every solution and wish to ensnare the private sector with over complicated arrangements from which no economic return can be secured.

What is clear above all else, is that if these attitudes prevail, programmes and projects will fail – they will cost more than planned; be late; and be deficient in quality. My 2001 Report on *Managing Relationships to Secure a Successful Partnership*[5] highlighted that a successful project depends on three things: partnerships, communication and commitment. These success factors and the main barriers to achieving

---

[5] Comptroller and Auditor General *Managing the Relationship to Secure a Successful Partnership in PFI Projects* (HC 375, Session 2001–2002).

them – usually cultural – are equally applicable whatever the form of government/supplier relationship.

Unfortunately, the overwhelming evidence from my reports shows that the public sector and its suppliers still have some way to go to fully develop open and honest relationships where both parties trust each other. The National Physical Laboratory, – see Box 11.4 and – discussed in Section 6.3 above as a PFI scheme, suffered from a lack of communication and trust. Conversely, it is pleasing to be able to report periodically on more successful outcomes where the principles espoused in our reports have been followed. The extension of the PRIME contract **(Box 11.5)** provides a good example of the benefits of jointly analysing risks and opportunities, and sharing knowledge.

---

**Box 11.4:    National Physical Laboratory**[6]

The National Physical Laboratory (NPL) is one of the world's leading laboratories working on the measurement of physical properties such as time, length and mass. It sits at the pinnacle of the UK's National Measurement System for which the Department of Trade and Industry (the Department) is responsible.

On 31 July 1998, the Department and Laser, a special purpose company jointly owned by Serco Group plc and John Laing plc, signed a 25-year long PFI contract to build and manage new facilities for the NPL.

The project suffered considerable construction delays and difficulties in achieving the specification for some parts of the building. In December 2004, the Department and Laser agreed to terminate the PFI contract; this was the first termination of a major PFI contract involving serious non-performance.

The fundamental reason behind the termination was that the original private sector design of the new buildings was deficient. During the procurement, the Department did not insist on Laser demonstrating that its design could work. Following the award of the contract, the Department did not seek to resolve its concerns by discussions because the Department wished to ensure that responsibility for delivering satisfactory performance remained unambiguously with the private

---

[6] Comptroller and Auditor General *The Termination of the PFI Contract for the National Physical Laboratory* (HC 1044, Session 2005–2006).

sector. The Department expected Laser and its contractors to recognise that their best interests were served by resolving concerns about the design, and would be able to act accordingly.

*Source:* Comptroller and Auditor General *The Termination of the PFI Contract for the National Physical Laboratory* (HC 1044, Session 2005–2006).

---

**Box 11.5:    The PRIME contract[7]**

In 1998, the then Department of Social Security transferred the ownership and management of its estate to a private sector company, Trillium, now Land Securities Trillium (LST) in a PFI deal, the Private Sector Resource Initiative for the Management of the Estate, known as PRIME.

The creation of the Department for Work and Pensions (DWP) in June 2001 brought together the PRIME estate (private sector) and the former Employment Services estate (the public sector). In December 2003, DWP transferred the former Employment Service estate to LST through an expansion of the PRIME contract that had been agreed by negotiation rather than through a competitive process.

To achieve and demonstrate value for money the Department obtained a high degree of transparency and openness from LST. In the absence of true competition DWP simulated competitive tension by defining a 'should cost' model distinct from the public sector comparator as the primary financial test, and a separate credible, commercial alternative to the expansion. In implementing the 'should cost' model, DWP applied NAO recommendations from other examinations of PFI deals to pool resources with the contractor so as to obtain relevant common information through jointly commissioned surveys where commercial conflicts of interest were not an issue.

*Source:* Committee of Public Accounts Forty First Report 1998–1999 *The PRIME Project: The Transfer of the Department of Social Security Estate to the Private Sector* (HC 548, Session 1998–1999).

---

[7] Committee of Public Accounts Forty First Report 1998–1999 *The PRIME Project: The Transfer of the Department of Social Security Estate to the Private Sector* (HC 548, Session 1998–1999).

## 11.2.2    Effective Contracting Frameworks

In the spirit of trust and communication, the answer to successful contracting – whether formal contracts between organisations or commitments between departments of the same organisation – does not lie in 'tight' contracts, with every eventuality tied down clause by clause, and a belief that adversarial argument, with the threat of the law when appropriate, will lead to success.

First of all, success depends upon knowledge by all relevant parties of the strengths and weaknesses of their potential partners. Too often, insufficient time is spent by public authorities in testing the capabilities of bidders in terms of their finance; their track record; their subcontractors and the management of their supply chain. Most public authorities have rules enjoining these actions. But too often they are neglected because the degree of trust and communication between the parties rules it out. Again, private sector contractors too seldom investigate whether their public sector partner has the agreed finance and trained staff to fulfil their share in the transaction. Cynics say that collaborators in a project want one of the partners to fail so that, out of the resulting chaos, advantage may be secured – more profit for the private sector; compensation for the public sector and, perhaps, an easy exit from difficult circumstances. Yet from the view point of the public interest, such events are failures and proper contracting on the basis of partnership and trust should enable them to be avoided.

In the spirit of the contract providing the framework for collaboration based on trust and communication, the auditor can usefully look to see if the following elements contain:

- a clear specification, but not one that is so detailed that all scope for improvements in price, timescale and quality are necessarily ruled out from the start;
- a decision on whether the contract should be let by competition or negotiation and the need to observe the rules for public sector contracting required by the European Commission;
- arrangements for vetting the financial standing and quality of work of bidders;
- a fixed price or variable price contract. This is important if a contract is for the supply of goods and services over a considerable period of time. If a variable price contract is decided upon, the choice of indices of price changes is very significant;

- agreed arrangements for the assessment of the quality of the goods and services supplied;
- arrangement for payment. These should preferably be against milestones of performance rather than on the basis of weekly or monthly payments;
- a pre-agreed strategy for exit management if this should become necessary because, for example, of a change in policy or organisation. The strategy should deal with such matters as the buy back of assets or their transfer to another service provider, software licensing, third party consents and the position of staff; and,
- arrangements for settling disputes. It will be important to have agreed arrangements and not be forced to take expensive legal actions to settle difficulties.

The auditor should also be able to advise, where appropriate, upon such innovations as establishing project bank accounts, into which payments for work and services done are made and from which relevant payments are made. The account can be set up as a trust and its operation viewed online. It can provide an extra guarantee of payment and promote trust between all parties, thus contributing to the necessary team spirit of successful programme and project management.

### 11.2.3   Having the right Programme and Project Management Skills

Programme and Project management skills are needed to set up and manage arrangements which are based on the trust and communication within a clear contractual framework that is necessary to achieve the desired outcomes. The programme and project management capability successful to deliver change across the full range of government activity is a core skill, not just for the public sector but also for its private sector partners who are usually integral to delivering and sustaining the desired outcomes over a period of many years. These capabilities are very different from those of functional management and, in the past, both the range of activity to which they should be applied and their crucial importance to affecting beneficial change have been neglected in the public sector. Developing the programme and project delivery capacity of public bodies has therefore become an increasingly important priority but is not something with which many public servants feel intrinsically comfortable.

Whilst some of the specialist skills necessary to deliver programmes and projects have been available, others are in short supply. In British central government, for example, the civil service tradition of the 'all rounder' remains widespread, though the government seeks to develop managerial capabilities. The establishment of a Programme and Project Management Specialism to provide help, advice and support for programme and project management experts to develop their skills and careers within the Civil Service is particularly relevant. But until the actions of the public sector can be seen to match the aspirations, programme and project management is unlikely to take the central role it deserves – it is rare indeed for the head of a major department of state to be appointed on the basis of his/her track record in project delivery.

Nor will the necessary expertise become available overnight. There is bound to be a timelag in growing a suitably experienced and skilled cadre of specialists. More fundamentally, it is unlikely ever to be economic, efficient or effective for the public sector to retain all of the necessary skills in-house. Whether as service providers or to supplement the skills available in the public sector through consultants and other professional advisers, the private sector is therefore likely to continue to play a central role in providing the diverse range of skills and expertise required to deliver public services. It has not always been clear what public authorities want and consultants have not always delivered what was expected. Public authorities' behaviours have also varied. There have been timid approaches, where misplaced trust of outside consultants has been seen as at least creating an alibi for failure. And there have been others where relationships have been characterised by a highly suspicious customer who rejects partnership with consultants and has sought to manage them solely through the contract. As in any form of programme management, neither approach has tended to lead to a successful conclusion for either the authorities or the consultant.

Our report on Purchasing Professional Services (**Box 11.6**) highlighted some excellent examples of innovative practice but concluded that departments could achieve gains of at least 10 per cent by improving the way they purchased professional services. These gains could be used to deliver the same service and provide resources for departments to spend on other priorities or obtain a higher quality of service from suppliers. Recognising the potential benefits of the gains, it has been important that auditors should help departments to achieve these. Adopting the principles highlighted can not only result in significant value for money improvements but, by the encouragement to working more closely to a common agenda, should mean both government and suppliers of management consultancy services can enjoy a higher level of service delivery.

---

**Box 11.6:     Purchasing Professional Services**[8]

The NAO reviewed how departments can get better value for money from the £ 600 million spent annually on professional services from a wide range of suppliers providing specialist expertise, advice and assistance.

The report found that much could be done to improve government purchasing and management of professional services. Departments made too much use of single-source and informal tendering. Opportunities were being missed, both within and between departments, to pool advice to prevent purchasing duplicate work. Departments did not routinely collect and use management information on what they spend to assess value for money, to compare prices and fees paid, evaluate suppliers performance or assess the amount of business suppliers are receiving from departments collectively. This latter point is particularly important given that the top 25 suppliers account for more than a third of all expenditure on professional services.

Our report concluded that government and consultancy providers should enhance their working relationships to deliver the service that departments needed and expected, with a clearer understanding of respective roles and responsibilities. Our recommendations focussed on two aspects. First, developing more effective working relationships with key suppliers to ensure both clients and suppliers get maximum value from assignments by identifying opportunities to reduce cost and adopt innovative approaches. Second, departments should act as intelligent customers by discussing with suppliers all the elements of the contract including price, level of service, timescale, skill mix of a supplier's team and how costs such as travel and subsistence are to be remunerated.

Consistent with the recommendations in the report, in 2002 the Office of Government Commerce, in conjunction with the NAO, the Management Consultancies Association and the Institute of Management Consultancy, published 'Delivering world-class

---

[8] Comptroller and Auditor General *Purchasing Professional Services* (HC 400, Session 2000–2001).

consultancy service to the public sector – A Statement of Best Practice'. The Statement offers guidelines to both departments and consultancies on how to deliver better, more effective consultancy service to government. It is based around proven 'must do' principles for both public sector buyers and private sector suppliers including having clear written statements, the central role of risk assessment and performance measurement, approval of innovation, knowledge transfer and holding joint project reviews. The Statement covers the entire procurement cycle from initial negotiations through to project completion.

*Source:* Comptroller and Auditor General *Purchasing Professional Services* (HC 400, Session 2000–2001).

### 11.2.4   Recognising the Pace of Change and the Ability of Organisations to Adapt

Bureaucracies work best in a world which does not change. Such a world has seldom existed, and the pace of policy change and the diversity of potential methods to deliver desired outcomes mean that most of the public sector is going through a period of huge organisational, cultural and process change. The growth of public-private partnerships and commercialisation, the drive for electronic service delivery, the introduction of resource accounting, the commitment to more joined-up forms of service delivery and other fundamental reforms to the way public services are delivered are requiring the public sector to consider new ways of carrying out its business. Too often there is a disconnection between the rapid evolution of policy and the slower moving pace of organisational adaptation to deliver them. The challenges faced by the Postal Service **(Box 11.7)** are typical.

---

**Box 11.7:    Postal Services Efficiency**[9]

All public sector organisations rely to varying degrees on postal services in their communication with citizens, other public sector bodies, and internally. Since the Postal Services Act 2000, the mail market

---

[9] Comptroller and Auditor General *Improving the Efficiency of Postal Services Procurement in the Public Sector* (HC 946, Session 2005–2006).

has been increasingly opened to other suppliers. In effect no part of the postal market is now reserved for Royal Mail alone.

The NAO found that public sector management structures for postal services are often too fragmented. The fact that responsibility for post is often dispersed across public sector organisations makes it very difficult to implement efficiency measures such as aggregating mail to achieve volume discounts. Local managers are rarely held accountable for reducing postal costs, and information on postal spend can be better collated and analysed to enable organisations to take full advantage of the contracts they have negotiated.

Consequently post is not always considered as part of an integrated communication strategy, and opportunities to reduce the demand for post and therefore cost are missed. The scale of these opportunities is well evidenced by the work of the Pension Service of the Department for Work and Pensions which, through a switch to greater use of the telephone to meet its customers' preferences, estimates that it will reduce the volume of in-bound mail by 60 per cent.

*Source:* Comptroller and Auditor General *Improving the Efficiency of Postal Services Procurement in the Public Sector* (HC 946, Session 2005–2006).

### 11.2.5   Having Clear Leadership and Responsibility for Delivery

One crucial factor affecting the delivery of programmes and projects which is repeatedly highlighted by my work is the absence of an individual with sufficient authority and personal responsibility for ensuring that a project or programme meets its objectives and delivers the projected benefits. Too often in the public sector the absence of such individuals has had negative results. The importance of clear leadership and authority becomes even more important where there are several stakeholders involved in a project or programme. The typical public sector approach to regularly moving staff means that those setting up projects are rarely in post to deliver the outcomes, hence further diluting the sense of personal accountability and responsibility.

Of course, many projects are of such a scale and/or complexity that for one person to be in charge of everything is impossible. But the arrangements that are made must make it clear that all responsibilities are assigned so that there is clarity within the team and outside it. This point is brought out by the UK Office of Government Commerce in its

'Achieving Excellence in Construction' which sets out by appointments and responsibilities as in **Box 11.8.**

---

**Box 11.8:    Achieving Excellence in Construction**[10]

The Office of Government Commerce recommends a number of key appointments:

- **Investment Decision Maker** (IDM), who should be from the client organisation and who takes investment decisions based on affordability and cost justification.
- **Senior Responsible Officer** (SRO), who should be from the client organisation and who is personally accountable for the success of the project and should have the status and authority to provide the necessary leadership on the project.
- **Project Sponsor**, who can be from the client organisation or an external appointee, who provides the interface between ownership and delivery, provides ongoing management to ensure that the desired project objectives are met, must have adequate knowledge about the business and the project and be able to make informed decisions.
- **Project Manager,** who is likely to be an external appointment and who leads, manages and co-ordinates the external project delivery team on a day to day basis.

These appointees may work with others in a Project Steering Board. Yet their responsibilities should be manifest and clear, subject to review as the project proceeds, and with the duty to surface significant problems early, for co-operative consideration and resolution, with subsequent return of responsibility to the appointee concerned.

*Source:* Office of Government Commerce (2007) *Achieving Excellence in Construction.*

---

### 11.2.6   Managing Risk

The management of risk is dealt with in Chapter 9 which articulated the need for the parties concerned with a programme to understand the risks that a project may present, and assess and manage them through

---

[10] Office of Government Commerce (2007) *Achieving Excellence in Construction.*

information exchange and co-operation rather than mandated decisions of responsibility that encourage attempts to erode it.

This approach is illustrated in our audit report on the risks that will have to be assessed and managed if the Olympic Games of 2012 are to be a success. This is an example of how the auditor can look forward and, on the basis of past experience, itemise factors requiring special attention. The risks which have been distinguished in this project are set out in **Box 11.9**, and our intention is to produce a series of reports over the period to the Games showing how well these risks are being managed by the parties working together; and we intend to incorporate relevant lessons from the 2008 Olympics at Beijing into the analysis.

---

**Box 11.9: Preparations for the London 2012 Olympic and Paralympic Games – main areas of risk that need to be managed for successful delivery of the Games**[11]

1. Delivering the Games against an immovable deadline.
2. The need for strong governance and delivery structure given the multiplicity of organisations and groups in the Games.
3. The requirement for the budget to be clearly determined and effectively managed.
4. Applying effective procurement practices.
5. Planning for a lasting legacy.
6. The installation of effective progress monitoring and risk management arrangements.

---

### 11.2.7   Understanding the Needs and Expectations of End Users

Ultimately a project or programme will only be successful if it meets the needs of end users. The diagram in **Box 11.10** illustrates the relationship between capturing users needs and delivering successful outcomes. It emphasises the overlapping nature of the design, execution and delivery processes and of the verification and validation of the outcomes. In basic terms, 'verification' is about doing the project right and 'validation' is about delivering the right project and making sure it meets users' needs.

---

[11] Comptroller and Auditor General *Preparation for the London 2012 Olympic and Paralympic Games – Risk Assessment and Management* (HC 252, Session 2006–2007).

**Box 11.10: The hierarchy of capturing users needs and delivering successful outcomes**

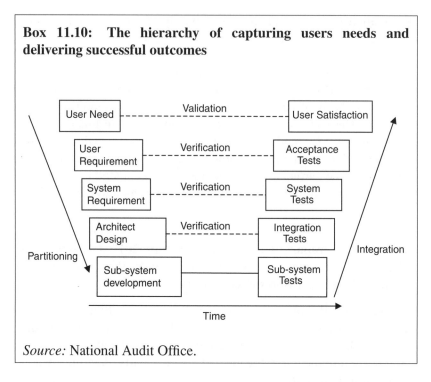

*Source:* National Audit Office.

One of the most common causes of project failure highlighted by our reports is where the needs of end users have not been understood and their expectations managed – the 'validation' part of the diagram in **Box 11.10**. Where this is not the case, too often the end result is disappointment and perceived failure. My report on Queue Relocation in Dunstable **(Box 11.11)** provides a good example of the problems of inadequately defining user needs, not testing modifications to proposals and the failure to communicate adequately with stake-holders.

**Box 11.11: Queue Relocation in Dunstable[12]**

Dunstable town centre suffers severe traffic congestion due to limited road capacity and high volumes of heavy goods vehicles. The Dunstable A5 queue relocation scheme was designed to provide a

---

[12] Comptroller and Auditor General *A5 Queue Relocation in Dunstable* (HC 1043, Session 2005–2006).

coordinated traffic management control system with the objectives of: improving the flow of traffic; reducing queues; improving safety and accessibility for pedestrians; improving the accident safety record at Caddington Turn junction and lessening noise and pollution.

After initial public consultation, the Highways Agency modified the specification for the scheme, but this resulted in even busier roads and longer waits at pedestrian crossings. These modifications were not communicated effectively to local residents and local councils who still expected the completed scheme to meet the original objectives.

The scheme was budgeted to cost £ 1.4 million and the final outturn was £ 2 million. Rather than relieving traffic congestion the scheme resulted in busier roads and longer waiting times at pedestrian crossing. Some key principles of sound project design and management were not followed such as:

- the scheme was not subject to sufficiently rigorous modelling to identify its likely impact;
- proposed costs were not benchmarked to test their realism;
- when the specification was revised, cost estimates were not re-evaluated; and
- user expectations of the schemes were not taken sufficient account of or managed.

Nevertheless, too high a price may be paid to try to provide some accommodation for a plethora of interests, and projects may collapse under the weight of appearing to offer 'something to everyone'. So the auditor should be able to warn that outcomes must be clear if projects are to succeed.

As my report on Smarter Food Procurement **(Box 11.12)** illustrates, the effect of not having a joined-up approach can lead not just to inefficiency but also to poorer outcomes for end users of such services.

**Box 11.12:    Smarter food procurement**[13]

The public sector in England spends around £ 2 billion per year on providing food and drink to service users, staff, the general

---

[13] Comptroller and Auditor General *Smarter Food Procurement in the Public Sector* (HC 963, Session 2005–2006).

public, clients and visitors. There is an increasing recognition of the linkages and potential trade-offs between the different Government policy agendas involved in food procurement. For example, an increasing number of studies point to the wider benefits to be gained by increasing the nutritional quality of public sector food, be that of pupils in school, or the longer term impacts on obesity and heart disease. Reconciling these agendas is not impossible, but to successfully combine them places considerable demands on the skills and capacity of those responsible for actually delivering food procurement.

There are a multitude of stakeholders involved in public food procurement. Departments, notably the Department for Environment, Food and Rural Affairs; the Office of Government Commerce; the Department of Health; and the Food Standards Agency, are therefore working with a range of bodies and stakeholders throughout often complex delivery chains.

The NAO concluded that there is significant scope for increasing efficiency simply through raising the professionalism of public sector food procurement, and by the public sector pursuing a more joined up approach. Such measures need have no negative effect on the quality of food served.

Indeed, increasing efficiency can have a positive impact on sustainability and nutrition by enabling organisations to use cost savings in some areas to help to finance improvements in others; for example, savings resulting from better checks on goods delivered could be used to improve the quality of ingredients purchased, or improved nutritional quality could lead to reduced hospital stays and so improve the overall efficiency of NHS Trusts.

*Source:* Comptroller and Auditor General *Smarter Food Procurement in the Public Sector* (HC 963, Session 2005–2006).

## 11.3   EXAMINING BROADER DELIVERY ISSUES

The auditor will usually be concerned with analysing programmes and projects which have discrete areas of activity. But public authorities are often concerned to try to link programmes together over time or across organisations. An example of the auditor's work here is the series of linked reports which we have produced on Hospital Acquired Infection **(Box 11.13)** and further examples are in **Box 11.14**. These reports provide a good example of the insight which producing such linked reports can have and the impact which we can add as auditors by taking an impartial, long-term perspective.

---

**Box 11.13:     Hospital Acquired Infection**[14]

My report on *The Management and Control of Hospital Acquired Infection (HAI)* in February 2000 was the first time that this subject had been comprehensively examined at the local and national level. Media interest focussed on the quantitative estimates: the 5,000 deaths, the £1 billion costs and the potential to save between £150 million to £300 million by better application of existing knowledge and good practice. Since then interest in these issues has grown, particularly in relation to concerns over significant increases in the 'Superbug' – Methicillin resistant *staphylococcus aureus* (MRSA).

The report commended the professionalism and dedication of NHS hospital infection control teams and identified many examples of good practice from which others could learn, but also that infection control was a 'Cinderella' service of the NHS. It identified the need to improve the strategic management of hospital acquired infection; the lack of information about the extent, cost and impact of HAI and the need for better information if it was to be given a higher priority. It also noted that there was considerable scope to improve the quality and safety of patient care by improving infection prevention, detection and containment measures. The report concluded that there was a growing mismatch between what was expected of infection control teams and the staffing and other resources allocated to them but that investing in better prevention and more effective responses would save lives and NHS resources.

In 2004, we carried out a follow-up investigation to determine progress but found that it was patchy. Following publication of our follow-up report England's Chief Nursing Officer was charged with responsibility for delivering improvements in this area, including ensuring that hospitals reduce MRSA by 50 per cent by 2008. Two particular initiatives, the 2005 'Saving Lives' campaign and the 2006

---

[14] Comptroller and Auditor General *The Management and Control of Hospital Acquired Infection in Acute NHS Trusts in England* (HC 230, Session 1999–2000).

'Going further faster' initiative have been important milestones in this fight against hospital acquired infections.

However one important issue does not appear to have progressed as far as it should have done is the belief that '*Infection Control is Everyone's Business.* The natural response by staff to an infection is still to expect the infection control team to deal with it. My 2005 report '*A Safer Place or Patients: Learning to improve patient safety*' considered the extent to which the NHS has been successful in improving the patient safety culture and encouraging reporting and learning from patient safety incidents. The report concluded that there was rarely any attempt at root cause analysis or any similar co-ordinated attempts to understand and address the problem and that the next important step in improving the quality and safety of healthcare is that where a patient does acquire an infection this should be recorded and lessons identified and learned from so as to reduce the extent of future infections.

*Source:* Comptroller and Auditor General *The Management and Control of Hospital Acquired Infection in Acute NHS Trusts in England* (HC 230, Session 1999–2000).

---

**Box 11.14:    Collegiate working with colleagues from other SAIs**[15]

Increased interest in cross-sector partnerships as a means of building new infrastructure and delivering public services prompted Audit New Zealand to investigate further the dynamics of this approach and, in so doing, inform leaders and decision-makers of the key issues to consider when working in partnership. Mindful of the proliferation of partnership-working across the world, Audit New Zealand researched the phenomenon in consultation with the United Kingdom National Audit Office and the Australian National Audit Office. Incorporating practical examples from home and abroad, Audit New Zealand published a report that addressed government's role in delivering and commissioning public services; posed questions to ask when deciding for or against a partnering approach; and offered guidance on how to manage contracts.

---

[15] Comptroller and Auditor General of New Zealand *Achieving Public Sector Outcomes with Private Sector Partners* (February 2006).

In assessing the role of government, Audit New Zealand noted that some of the foreign governments consulted felt that certain public services may not be suitable for delivery through a partnership approach. Assuming governments were enthusiastic about partnering, clear policy and direction from government was deemed highly important.

When deciding whether or not partnering would be a suitable approach to a given project, public bodies were urged to develop a high level of expertise and a sound business case to support their decision. The report stated that a business case should clearly show how the chosen partnering arrangement fits with, and helps to achieve, the vision and policy objectives of the public entity, as well as showing how a partnership approach would result in better value for money than other procurement options.

Effective contract management was seen to rest on clear contract documentation that defined the responsibilities of both parties, including the responsibilities for managing relationships, risks, assets and performance. The documentation would also need to define accountability requirements clearly.

Audit New Zealand reached these conclusions following visits to the Australian National Audit Office, relevant Australian State Audit Offices, and public and private organisations in Australia that have experience of partnering. In addition, Audit New Zealand communicated with public sector auditing bodies in the United Kingdom, and drew from some of my reports on this topic. The report included appendices describing in detail Australia and the United Kingdom's experience of partnering. By investigating examples of partnership working in countries where markets for partnering were already large – in the case of this report, Australia and the United Kingdom – Audit New Zealand was able to appreciate the key issues and prepare for the possibility of more partnership working in the future.

*Source:* Comptroller and Auditor General of New Zealand *Achieving Public Sector Outcomes with Private Sector Partners* (February 2006).

## 11.3.1   The Wider Picture

Attention to the factors examined in the foregoing section may well enable the auditor to advise his client on how to make a success of programme and project management. But the overcoming of defective performance may well require a reconsideration of wider factors; here too the auditor has a contribution to make by way of pointing out the constraints, challenges and opportunities they offer. The factors are:

- the environment within which the programme is provided;
- the organisation responsible for its conception and implementation; and
- the desired outcome.

### 11.3.2   The Environment

The social, economic and political and physical environment within which a programme is provided may well condition its chance of success. Auditors cannot change environments. But examples of where they can point to significant issues include the experience of some early programmes for assisting less well developed countries, where irrigation programmes installed by first class engineering silted up or became choked by weeds because the recipient lacked the skills to maintain them. And it is unrealistic to ignore the problems of truancy and anti-social behaviour in areas of social deprivation and to imagine that educational policies that work in areas of higher incomes will necessarily work in these poorer areas too.

### 11.3.3   The Organisation

The emphasis of this book's argument is upon the problems of bureaucratic organisations and the mind set so often associated with them. But other aspects of a body's organisational philosophy also impact upon the chance of project and programme success. The auditor needs to be alive to the attitudes to such features as:

- delegation of power and authority;
- decentralisation;
- outsourcing and reliance on the market; and
- engagement with and trust of voters, citizens, customers, suppliers, community groups and the whole web of social structures within which the organisation operates.

**Box 11.15** illustrates this point from the perspectives of English local authorities.

---

**Box 11.15:    Organisational Structures and Processes**[16]

'There are three key elements to the government's modernisation agenda:

* Service improvement
* Community leadership
* Democratic renewal.

Although each of these elements will be of concern to all authorities, it is likely that different priorities will be attached to the three different elements in different authorities'.

'There are three distinctive pictures for "ideal types" of what the strategic agendas of authorities might look like when they have chosen their priorities in each area of reform. There are distinctive implications in following these different priorities for an authority's organisational culture and structure, its political leadership style and decision-making arrangements, and its attitudes to participation, partnerships, the private sector and e-government. This essay explores the distinctive implications of prioritising through three imaginary, but entirely plausible, local authorities: "Greenshire county council", "Castlemead metropolitan borough council" and the "London borough of Wythen".

Greenshire county council believes that its most important task is to continuously improve the quality of its services.'

'Castlemead believes that its most important task is to work with its partners to develop a series of co-ordinated responses to the medium – and long-term problems facing the area.'

'The London borough of Wythen believes that its most important task is to re-engage with the local population and give real meaning to the concept of local democracy.'

---

[16] Leach, S. and Lowndes, V. (2006) 'Fitness for purpose? How local authorities can dare to be different' in Solace Foundation Imprint, *The Re-thinking of Local Government: Fitness for Purpose in a Year for Living Dangerously,* London SFI.

And the essay shows how the different task emphases require different organisational structures and processes – it is not the case that 'one size fits all.'

*Source:* S. Leach and V. Lowndes 'How local authorities can Dare to be Different.'

### 11.3.4 The Outcomes

It may sometimes be necessary for the auditor to point out, before a programme or project begins, that it is too ambitious for the resources of time, staff, money and technology to be invested in it for it to be capable of success. Auditors must be careful here; it is not for them to usurp the role of policy makers and certainly not to appear as the pessimistic cassandras so often held to be the role they wish to discharge. But sometimes it is necessary to speak up right at the earliest stage of programme's conception, and urge the authors to adjust it to a more practicable scheme or not to do it at all.

After such a démarche, the auditor may well be asked, 'What would you do then?' and he/she must be prepared with a response that indicates possibilities without appearing to be claiming omniscience or usurping the politician or the management's role. This is by no means inconsistent with my premise that the auditor should seek to be mentor and coach. As financial auditor they should have a good grasp of the organisation's prior performance, its risk appetite and experience in managing risk, as well as its project management capability. Drawing on knowledge of other organisations and private sector experience the auditor should be well placed to focus in a constructive way on the inherent risks in the proposal without questioning the policy. How well this is received will depend on the strength of the relationship between auditor and auditee. In any event the relationship should be founded on the principle of 'trusted advisor' which maintains the traditional role of auditor but in a forward looking way.

### 11.4  CONCLUSION

The various factors to which the auditor can draw attention to promote successful project and programme management are summarised in our work to specify the 'gold standard' for effective project control. These are set out in **Box 11.16** and emphasise the need for trust and communication; for sharing bad news as well as good news; and, for having clear objectives that lead to outcomes that meet beneficiaries' needs. It is these 'softer factors' that provide the framework of trust within which the 'harder factors' of control arrangements, specifications, and testing can be effective.

---

## Box 11.16:   Gold Standard[17]

**2**   Our gold standard for effective project control

**Establishing and sustaining the right cultural environment**

| Good practice sub-criteria | Enablers |
|---|---|
| Open, trusting and honest relationships between client, prime contractor and supply chain | Explicit "no surprises/no blame" culture (defined as not penalising staff for bringing potential problems to light early) between all parties. |
| | Regular and timely discussion of all matters that affect the project with no no-go areas. |
| | Mutual benefits through shared ownership of end product or outcome between all parties. |
| | Clarity of purpose and common understanding at all levels throughout all organisations. |
| | Agreements between the parties to undertake a project as a partnership or alliance. |
| Measurement of client-contractor relationships | Regular independent assessments of client-contractor relationships as these develop during a project. |
| Supportive and open corporate environment | Explicit no surprises/no blame culture (defined as not penalising staff for bringing potential problems to light early) on the project and within the wider project organisation. |
| | Clear information requirements with clear purpose. |
| | Clear boundaries of authority and action. |
| | Clear link between corporate and project governance. |

**Creating clear structures and boundaries**

| Efficient organisational structures, responsibilities and lines of authority | Management boards, frequency and purpose of meetings, project controls and performance measures all agreed at the start. |
|---|---|
| | Clear delegated authorities and decision-making/escalation criteria. |
| | Flexible approach demonstrated by both client and contractors. |
| Project management, commercial, financial and technical skills available | Projects can select staff. |
| | Organisation has a career development and skills training structure in place that covers each area of expertise. |
| | Tenure in post for a large proportion of a phase and over key events. |
| Thorough review and understanding of project delivery plan, objectives, assumptions, risks and opportunities | Explicit review and agreement of work packages, costs, specification, risks and opportunities prior to contract signature and setting of performance, time and cost boundaries. |
| | All stakeholders clearly informed and engaged in establishing structural foundations and boundaries. |
| | Subject matter experts used in drawing up cost and risk models. |
| Set performance, time and cost boundaries when all risks are understood/formal investment approval gates | Performance, time and cost boundaries based on clear understanding of risks and grounded in realism. |
| | Performance, time and cost boundaries and delivery plan independently reviewed before submission to investment board. |
| | Clear information and evidence requirements for business case. |

**Creating clear structures and boundaries (continued)**

| Good practice sub-criteria | Enablers |
|---|---|
| Ability to make trade-offs/change management mechanism | Mechanisms in place (such as working groups) for making informed trade offs between time, performance and cost as project progresses and delegated authority to do so. |
| | All stakeholders clearly informed and in agreement. |
| | Mechanism to apply lessons learned as project progresses. |

---

[17] Comptroller and Auditor General *Driving the Successful Delivery of Major Defence Projects: Effective Project Control is a Key Factor in Successful Projects* (HC 30, Session 2005–2006).

| Measuring progress and making decisions focused on successful project delivery | |
|---|---|
| Analysis of credible, timely and relevant metrics monitoring progress against the performance, time and cost baseline | Forward-looking analysis of information from techniques (such as Earned Value Management, milestones, planning/scheduling or risk management) and metrics (such as costs or in-service availability measures). |
| | Verification/validation of data. |
| Arrangements for transparency and accuracy | Shared Data Environment or clear method for sharing documentation between all stakeholders. |
| | Co-location of client and contractor teams/staff. |
| | Arrangements for access to contractor/client's data. |
| | Use of IT where practical (common software, email connection). |
| Contract as key component of project control | Recognition of contract as control tool during negotiation. |
| | Commercial staff reside with project. |
| | Contract is realistic, mutually beneficial and reflects ownership of risk. |
| Project-to-project peer reviews and Learning From Experience | Formal and informal mechanisms for exchange of ideas, problem-solving and sharing experience between projects for benefit of project staff. |
| | Formal capture of lessons learned. |
| Reporting to enable strategic decisions | |
| Consistent reporting system for all projects feeding into analysis for senior management | Reporting system based on principle of "generate once, use many times". |
| | Clear purpose for reporting system (whether that is to track delivery, track against corporate targets or for forward planning). |
| | Analysis of reports by dedicated staff. |
| Formalised, regular system of senior management review to give assurance of delivery | Clear information requirement, format and purpose for regular reviews. |
| | Feedback mechanism. |
| Independent, non-advocate reviews | Clear purpose for independent input (advice for project staff or assurance for senior managers, or both). |
| | Avoidance of duplication and over-burdening project staff. |
| | Benefits are clear - not viewed as a hurdle to overcome. |
| Ongoing measurement of supplier performance to learn lessons | Collection of data and maintenance of historical database. |
| | Senior level contact with contractors. |
| | Analysis of trends and issues. |
| | Contractors are clear as to confidentiality and use of data on their performance. |

And it is success in developing some of the 'softer' factors of the gold standard that permit the development of new structures for project management such as 'alliancing' where a customer comes together with a range of contractors and suppliers to deliver a complicated set of outcomes that cannot easily be secured by a single purchaser/prime contractor relationship. Examples include the development of oil and gas fields; and another example of a similar kind of approach is in the construction of Terminal Five at Heathrow Airport in London. The terminal is designed to handle 30 million passengers a year and, as **Box 11.17** shows it encompasses an approach to risk that is possible only in a situation characterised by trust and shared belief and commitment.

---

**Box 11.17:     Sharing Risk in Terminal Five at London Heathrow**[18]

'At the Heart of the T5 agreement is the concept that while BAA retains the risk, suppliers work as part of an integrated team to mitigate potential risk and achieve the best results. Teams of people from different companies work co-operatively on the endless smaller projects that make up a massive scheme such as this.

Instead of handing over a set amount to each contractor for risk – which often ends up as profit – these project teams are allocated a small contingency fund which, if unspent, is then available for another team. Rather than simply handing over the work, BAA takes an active management role. These teams act as "virtual companies", responsible for the task and working to the project's overall milestones.

If there is a failure by a contractor – say a ceiling needs to be replaced – then the work is redone with no blame. Riley says: "If the ceiling has to be done a second time, then the team will pay the cost with no profit margin. If it had to be redone a third time, then the cost would be down to the particular contractor".

Essentially, it is a no-blame culture aimed at getting the best results through co-operation, rather than the conventional adversarial approach.

Assuming the risk does not mean that BAA just lets the contractors do what they want. Quite the opposite. Because BAA takes on the risk, it has to ensure that its suppliers and contractors provide services to the highest possible standard, says Riley. "The agreement is predicted on best practice. That's the minimum standard". However, he accepts it is not always easy to define what that is in reality.

There is also no main contractor, which is unheard of for a project of this size. It is a very open process, with the suppliers' books available to BAA: a very different relationship than in many public sector projects where firms hide behind "commercial confidentiality".

A further benefit of co-operation is that it gives suppliers opportunities to work together to reduce costs. Riley cites the example of electrical switchgear which would normally have cost about £ 22 million, but ended up at £ 15 million because there was one client, rather than several. The 41 first-tier suppliers have signed the agreement,

---

[18] Wolman, C. (2005) 'Terminal Five gets off to a flying start'. *Public Finance* May 6–12.

but BAA also expects second and lower-tier suppliers to work in a similar co-operative way.

The new approach to risk had an early test. Because of the wet winter in 2002/03, the ground preparation got badly behind schedule, which could have meant a two-year delay. With other suppliers waiting to go on site, the consequential claims would have been huge.

But the fact that BAA had assumed the risk, together with the co-operative approach, meant that over the next seven to eight months the delay was clawed back, and there have been no legal claims.'

*Source:* Christian Wolman, *'Terminal Five gets off to a flying start'*.

Finally, in assessing the performance of public authorities in delivering change, it is important to remember that public accountability means a much brighter spotlight is shone on public as opposed to private sector delivery. As discussed above, there are plenty of examples of failure for the media to report but, encouragingly, the approach outlined in this chapter provides programme and project management success stories in the public sector. **Box 11.18**, for example, gives an illustration of success reported in Australia. Unfortunately, very often these good news stories are not reported widely outside the specialist press. But this does not mean that we, as the auditors, should not recognise auditees' achievements. Government departments often feel that they do not get the credit they deserve. We have an important role to try and ensure that the good news stories are as widely reported as the bad news stories.

**Box 11.18:    Implementation of the Working Holiday Maker visa programme in Australia**[19]

Australia's Working Holiday Maker (WHM) visa scheme sees over 100,000 WHM visas granted to young people from 19 countries and regions. On 1 July 2002, the Department of Immigration and Multicultural Affairs implemented a system for applicants to apply for WHM visas electronically over the Internet (eVisa) to relieve pressure on DIMA's overseas posts, and enable the Department to cope with the increasing WHM application workload. Approximately 98 per cent of WHM visa applications are now made on-line.

---

[19] Auditor General of Australia *Department of Immigration and Multicultural Affairs, Visa Management: Working Holiday Makers* (Audit Report No. 7 2006–2007).

The Australian National Audit Office (ANAO) reviewed DIMA's implementation of the eVisa programme to deliver WHM visas, and considered whether it was consistent with sound practice. The ANAO found that DIMA developed a sound framework for the effective administration of the WHM visa programme in accordance with relevant laws and policies. The eWHM mechanism was viewed as providing a robust, effective mechanism for handling WHM visas in an environment where the number of applications continues to rise. ANAO concluded that the implementation of the eWHM project has been largely in accordance with sound administrative practice for Internet delivery.

Recognising success is important, but by itself will not be enough to the public sector to deliver better programme and project outcomes in future. As auditors, the breadth of our analysis gives us a unique insight which, if fully leveraged, means we can act as both a mentor and coach both to those in the public sector charged with delivering change and to their private sector partners.

Our work in developing a programme and project management 'Gold Standard', as discussed above, provides a good illustration of the importance of stepping beyond traditional reporting mechanisms to help to deliver beneficial change **(Box 11.16)**. The key characteristics of this work are that we have focussed on learning from successful defence projects in the UK and overseas and from commercial experience. Our approach has given us the opportunity to work closely with the Ministry of Defence and its industry partners and with other audit offices, notably in the USA and Australia to build on their analyses **(Box 11.19)** and to share the learning more widely.

---

**Box 11.19:    US Department of Defense (DOD)'s acquisition of weapon systems**[20]

The United States Government Accountability Office (GAO) has carried out a series of reviews of the US Department of Defense (DOD)'s acquisition of weapon systems. DOD relies on a cadre of military and civilian program managers to lead the development and delivery of

---

[20] Government Accountability Office *Defense Acquisitions Best Practices: Capturing Design and Manufacturing Knowledge early Improves Acquisition Outcomes* (GAO 02-701, 15 July 2002).

its weapon systems; however programmes to acquire weapon systems often take longer, cost more and deliver less than planned. The GAO reviewed the way in which DOD uses programme managers, and compared this to the way in which private sector companies managed their product development programmes to see if best commercial practice could be applied to weapon systems acquisition.

They found that the success of commercial organisations' programme management centred around two key enablers; top-down support; and a disciplined, knowledge-based process for implementing product development programmes. Senior management took a long term overview in decision making, considering the product mix versus organisational goals, and issues surrounding affordability and sustainability. Programme Managers were responsible for executing the business case, and were held accountable for delivering the product to time, cost and specification. In contrast, the GAO found that DOD programmes were allowed to start without a business case being in place, and that DOD competition for funding led to pressure on programme managers to produce overly optimistic time and cost estimates. Funding and capability requirements also changed over time, which led to difficulties in holding programme managers to account as many aspects of the programme were outside their control.

GAO recommended that an investment strategy was developed which prioritised key capabilities, and that business cases were signed up to by senior stakeholders. This would then allow a system of accountability for successful programme outcomes to be instilled.

## 11.5  SUMMARY

Programme and project management has traditionally been a neglected skill in public authorities. Time, cost and quality results are frequently disappointing; there is a failure to appreciate that projects are not simply features of defence procurement and civil engineering but that schemes of health provision, social security, crime prevention and other aspects of government work are all projects and need to be managed as such; and there is often insufficient attention to the recruitment, training and reward of professionally qualified staff.

Common causes of project and programme failure include:

- divided managerial control;
- a concentration on lowest price rather than best outcomes;

- inadequate budgeting;
- changes in specifications and inadequate specifications;
- insufficient testing and piloting; and
- a belief that a tight contract is the condition of success and that every eventuality should be tied down clause by clause.

And, above all, plans devised and presented to appeal to the conflicting requirements of a plethora of stakeholders rather than a concentration upon a potentially successful outcome.

The transcendence of failure requires, in addition to trained and motivated staff, the auditor to understand and advise on the need for and how to secure:

- trust and open communication;
- effective contracting frameworks;
- clear leadership and responsibility for delivery;
- managing risk rather than mandating its acceptance;
- understanding the needs and expectations of end users; and
- examining the broader delivery issues of interdependent programme and projects.

And beyond these factors, the auditor needs to understand:

- the social, economic, political and physical environment within which the programme or project is being implemented. For example, it is no good ignoring the problems of truancy and anti-social behaviour in schools in areas of social deprivation and imagining policies that work in other area will work in these areas too;
- the public organisation responsible for the project – hierarchy, matrix, network or market – centralised or decentralised – power concentrated or dispersed; and
- the product – if the programme is to train, for example, software engineers, but few are attracted to the relevant courses or complete them, then the question to be tackled is whether the right kind of training product is being offered.

# 12
# Performance Measurement – Clarity or Confusion?

It was already clear by the 1960s that the hopes invested in the state bureaucracies as the means of supplying many of the services necessary for the welfare of the society were being disappointed.

In the UK, the Fulton Report of 1968[1] catalogued many of the failures that, in their view, could be attributed to a civil service operating in bureaucratic style.

- low GDP growth;
- the failure of technological projects in which large sums had been invested by the government, such as the BlueStreak Rocket and the Comet Aircraft; and
- the failure to use to the full extent the skills of middle level and junior civil servants.

Bureaucracy was not the sole cause of all these failures – since countries like the USA had bureaucratic governments too – but they were certainly evidence that the traditional form of bureaucratic public administration was not working as well as intended.

## 12.1  MANAGEMENT BY OBJECTIVES AND PERFORMANCE MEASUREMENTS

One solution seemed to be the introduction of 'management by objectives'. Instead of believing the bureaucratic mantra that if the right staff were recruited, their duties specified and co-ordinated in successive hierarchical layers then results would automatically be achieved, it came to be argued that the right way forward would be to set specific objectives for organisations as a whole, disaggregated for the various lower levels of the organisation, and cascaded down to objectives for each member of staff to achieve in a specified period of time.

---

[1] 'The Civil Service' (1968) London, HMSO.

Peter Drucker had been significant in this movement, following his thoughts that 'objectives are needed in every area where performance and results directly and vitally affect the survival and prosperity of the business',[2] and much of the early consideration of the management of performance took place in a commercial setting.

There are now so many developments stemming from the original idea of setting objectives and measuring performance against them that the auditor needs to appreciate the general features of what might be called the menagerie of performance measurement and the main kinds of beasts within it.

## 12.2    PERFORMANCE MEASUREMENT METHODOLOGIES

The traditional form, with the hypothetical example of a strategy for 'Improving Higher Education' is set out in **Box 12.1** and glossary of terms is in **Box 12.2**.

Other purposes of performance measurement include:

- To clarify objectives – if their achievement is to be measured, objectives should at least be clear.
- As inputs to managerial incentives – pay and bonus systems may be linked to target achievement.
- To help consumers and citizens make informed choices – the performance of, say, different universities may be compared and students may decided upon their application with this information in mind.
- To indicate the effectiveness of service activities to different stakeholders – the performance of hospitals may be relevant to the concerns of many stakeholders, including patients, their relatives, the medical profession, health service officials and ministers.

There are other ideas for performance measurement which focus on different but associated factors. For example, the model of the European Foundation for Quality Management is concerned with enabling factors designed to produce specific results, as illustrated in **Box 12.3**.

Another approach is the '7s' model at **Box 12.4**, developed by McKinsey and Company, which seeks to demonstrate the linkages between so called 'hard factors' – strategy and structure – and 'soft factors' – style, system staff and skills, all of which interact to produce the shared values which are argued to be the casual factors of good performance.

---

[2] Drucker, P. (1954) *The Practice of Management* Harper Brothers, New York, p. 63.

**Box 12.1:    A Strategy and Performance Methodology for Higher Education**

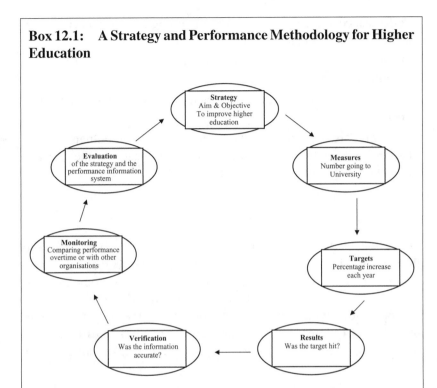

*Source:* Adapted from: HM Treasury, Cabinet Office, National Audit Office, Audit Commission, Office for National Statistics, '*Choosing the Right Fabric: a Framework for performance information*, p. 23.

---

**Box 12.2:    A glossary**

Measures can serve as dials – to indicate performance, as in a speedometer

Measures can serve as tin openers – to indicate a possible problem, as in a medical thermometer

Performance Measures = Direct Information

For example, the number of service calls made by Health and Safety Inspectors.

Performance Indicators = Proxies for measures

For example, if the objective of a programme is a reduction in alcoholism, its performance may be indicated by the proxy measure of the number of people going to Alcoholics Anonymous

Performance Targets – a level of measured performance to be achieved in a specified period of time.

Outputs, e.g. the number of operations a hospital performs in a specific period.

Outcomes, e.g. the number of patients restored to health by the operations

Outcomes are usually much harder to measure than outputs; in this case it has to define what 'restored to health' means for the patients of different ages and physical conditions.

*Source:* National Audit Office.

One difficulty that the auditor has in appraising the performance of these models is that their apparent simplicity and clarity dissolve when attempts are made to apply them. For example, how can comparisons of 'performance over time or with other organisations' in **Box 12.1** be put into operation without adding other criteria, as for example, to remove the effect of different levels of national economic prosperity and attitudes to higher education, if the comparisons are to be meaningful? And

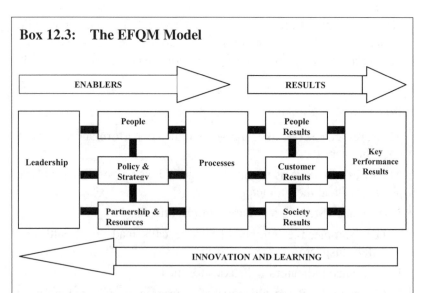

**Box 12.3:     The EFQM Model**

The 'Enabler' criteria determine what an organisation does; the 'Results' criteria determine what an organisation achieves. 'Results' are caused by 'Enablers' as illustrated above.

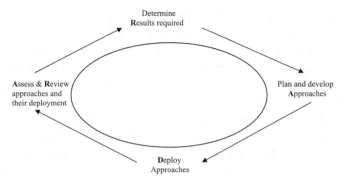

'Results will show positive trends and/or good performance, targets will be appropriate and met or exceeded, performance will compare well with others and will have been caused by the approaches'

*Source: The EFQM Excellence Model*: Brussels: European Foundation for Quality Management.

**Box 12.4:   McKinsey 7S Framework**

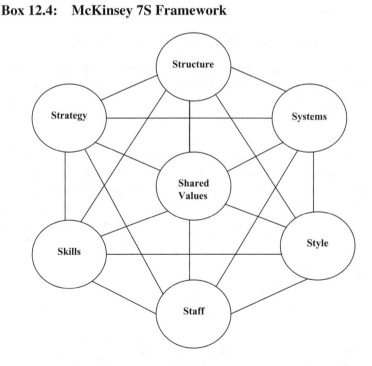

*Source:* T. J. Peters and R. H. Waterman Jr, (1982) *In Search of Excellence*. Harper and Row, New York.

while the attempts to set objectives and manage performance have certainly stimulated substantial improvements in the performance of many organisations, this seems often to have been the result of the excitement of emphasising a new approach or focus of attention rather than from the detailed application of one or other of these models. In short, it is not easy to separate any improvements from the application of the models themselves from those generated by the interest in the change itself and alterations in the social relationships of those involved. Thus the changes – which may be for good or ill in terms of performance improvement – could derive from a species of the 'Hawthorne Effect'[3] rather than the performance management system itself.

Another difficulty for the auditor's attempts to appraise performance measurement systems is that most of them consist of an eclectic mixture derived from several systems rather than the attempt to apply a single model, difficult enough as that is, as the foregoing analysis has sought to demonstrate. The following examples drawn from domestic and international experience illustrate the difficulties.

## 12.3   INTERNATIONAL EXPERIENCE

In the late 1980s, New Zealand was the country most widely quoted as leading change in the measurement of government. Responding to budget crises which forced changes in the levels and patterns of public expenditure, it implemented changes to the structure of public services which included an explicit focus on key performance measures. Under this system, Ministers were to set, and be accountable to Parliament for key outcomes. Heads of departments and agencies were accountable for delivering targeted outputs or projects, the associated indicators were explicitly linked with resources, and financial accounting was moved from a cash to accruals basis to make sure inputs and outputs were satisfactorily matched. Other changes included a programme of privatisation

---

[3] The Hawthorne studies were carried out in the 1920's in the Hawthorne Plant of the Western Electric organisation. They sought to test the relationship between physical conditions, such as good lighting, and productivity. The results surprisingly showed increasing productivity even when conditions were worsened. And the conclusion was reached that the improvements were due to the greater attention the management were paying to the workers and the increase in excitement and camaraderie associated at least in the short term with changes in what had been seen by many as boring jobs. For further information see C. Handy (1993) *Understanding Organisation* 4th edn., Penguin.

and commercialisation, creation of service–delivery agencies, and a degree of delegation to agencies of personnel management.

Reviews of these changes have usually noted significant improvements in efficiency, service delivery and accountability – especially from the first phase of activity. Others have noted high transaction costs, protracted negotiations, reduced flexibility and reduced trust and goodwill. And that later phases of commercialisation, such as that in health, have been far less successful. On measurement issues, the setting of clear political objectives and associated outcome reporting has not worked well. While hundreds of outcomes have been reported, few Ministers have been obliged to report and few outcome measures have been reported on a consistent or regular basis. Entity reporting of outputs has been more regular. But even here there have been problems in defining indicators which capture quality adequately, particularly of outputs such as policy advice. And there has been insufficient reporting of efficiency, productivity or unit costs. So while measurement was an important part of the changes, it has not been able to give a full assessment of performance even in the terms of the original design, let alone cope with different perspectives on what performance might mean.[4]

Surprisingly, given their history of management thinking, the USA has not been in the lead on public sector performance measurement. But in 1993 the Government Performance and Results Act (GPRA) made major changes to the performance planning and reporting requirements placed on federal agencies. It required agencies to develop strategic plans with long-term, outcome-orientated goals and objectives, annual goals linked to the long-term goals, and annual reports on the results achieved. Agencies were required to outline progress towards goals in annual performance plans, and report progress in annual programme performance reports. Initial compliance with these instructions was variable, with problems linking resources to performance goals, issues about data quality, and the identification of a series of management challenges. Later, the US GAO noted a widespread increase in the availability of the type of information required by GPRA over the first six years of its implementation. They also found, however, that the use of such information for decision-making had not increased over the period, and varied widely from agency to agency. On average, only around 60 per cent of

---

[4] Boston, J. (2000) The challenge of evaluating systemic change: the case of public management reform. Paper prepared for the IPMN Conference 'Learning form experiences with new public management', Macquarie Graduate School of Management, Sydney, 4–6 March.

managers used the information to a 'great or very great extent', and for some agencies that figure dropped to as low as 26 per cent.[5]

## 12.4   EXPERIENCE IN THE UNITED KINGDOM

Box 12.5 outlines some of the main measurement initiatives in the UK over the last 25 years.

---

**Box 12.5:   Performance Management Systems in the United Kingdom**

*Financial Management Initiative*

Launched in **1982** with the white paper *Efficiency and Effectiveness*; underpinned by the concept of *Management by Objectives* first outlined by Peter Drucker in 1954 in his book 'The Practice of Management'. The initiative was designed to promote *inter alia*:

(a)  A clear view of the objectives, and the means to assess performance against them; and
(b)  Well defined responsibility for making the best use of their resources.

*Next Steps Agencies UK*

Launched in **1988** by Sir Robin Ibbs – Director of the Prime Minister's Efficiency Unit. The idea was to separate the policy making work of government departments from the work of implementation, which was delegated to Departmental Agencies. Each agency set up with a Framework Document, agreed by the responsible Minister, setting out:

– Clear tasks
– Key Performance Indicators covering targets for volume, financial and quality of service.
– Annual performance reporting

*Private Finance Initiative*

This initiative was described in Chapter 6, and involves payment rewards and penalties according to performance against targets throughout the period of the contract.

---

[5] Government Accountability Office (2005) managing for results: enhancing agency use of performance information for management decision making. GAO-05-927, Washington.

*Public Service Agreement targets*

Introduced in **1998**, as part of the first Comprehensive Spending Review. Comprehensive Spending Reviews were designed to set out the resources each department would get over the next three years, and the targets that they would have to achieve with them. Public Service Agreement targets address the medium- to long-term priority outcomes of government policy. Each major government department agreed them with HM Treasury as part of each Spending Review.

*Best Value Performance Indicators (BVPIs)*

Introduced as part of the wider Best Value initiative under the Local Government Act **1999**. Under the initiative, each local authority had to establish a set of authority-wide objectives and performance indicators. New performance targets were to be brought together with other service targets in the authority's annual Best Value Performance Plan.

*Local Public Service Agreement targets*

The Government announced in the Spending Review 2000 that it would introduce local Public Service Agreements (LPSAs). LPSAs were piloted with 20 authorities starting in late 2000 and a rollout to all upper tier authorities began in September 2001. Individual authorities sign up to targets to deliver key national and local priorities in return for operational flexibilities and financial rewards for success.

*Comprehensive Performance Assessment*

Announced in the December 2001 White Paper, 'Strong Local Leadership – Quality Public Services', the first Comprehensive Performance Assessments were conducted in December 2002. Comprehensive Performance Assessment is a standardised assessment framework that generates a single rating for each local authority. The two key elements of a council's activities that CPA seeks to measure are its core service performance and its ability to improve.

*Performance Partnership Agreements*

Performance Partnership agreements are Agreements between the Head of the Civil Service and the head civil servant of each department. They summarise the programme of civil service reform within each department – what is to be done, why and how; and how the centre will help.

*Efficiency targets*

Following the review by Sir Peter Gershon of public sector efficiency, the Spending Review of 2004 announced the introduction of departmental efficiency targets to realise the Government's ambition of achieving efficiency gains across the public sector of £ 21.5 billion and reducing 80,000 civil service jobs by 2008.

*Local Area Agreements*

Local Area Agreements represent a new approach to improve co-ordination between central government and local authorities and their partners, such as Charities and non-governmental institutions, working through Local Strategic Partnerships. They focus on a range of agreed outcomes shared by all delivery partners locally.

*Departmental Capabilities Reviews*

Starting in October 2005, the Reviews are led by the Prime Minister's Delivery Unit and examine capacity within Departments to achieve their objectives. The reports are to include clear assessments of current departmental capability and key actions to be taken to improve.

---

What is striking from the experience summarised in **Box 12.5** is the extraordinary variety of measures and targets that have been introduced in the UK over the last quarter of a century. This indicates the difficulty of finding a generally satisfactory system that could be applied across public administration and endure over time. One of the results is that measurement in local and central government have developed in rather different directions.

In local government, a series of initiatives involving management practices and performance indicators evolved into a Comprehensive Performance Assessment (CPA). This framework added assessments of management capability, and the capacity to improve, to the existing set of quantitative performance indicators and inspection reports. The process involves self-assessment, peer review, inspection and indicator analyses, and is managed by the Audit Commission. Quantitative indicators and qualitative judgements are combined in informing an overall rating for each authority. High ratings attract lighter touch regulation form the centre, weak ratings raise the prospect of further management reviews.[6] Recently this approach has been revised to direct more performance scrutiny on areas of high risk and to take more assurance from consumer satisfaction. This is in keeping with a more general trend to have fewer but better defined performance which are much better defined.

Unsurprisingly, these developments have given rise to considerable comment about their effects and fairness. Within the local government community, there has been considerable support for the process – which professionals have seen as constructive and forward-looking, and valuable in creating a focus on performance issues. But they complained about the costs of CPA, and want it streamlined and more closely focused on outcomes, as opposed to internal processes.[7] And they have not always agreed with the ratings given. Academic work on CPA ratings has suggested that the ratings reflect external factors, such as deprivation, as much as performance.[8] In fact hard evidence on the contribution of CPA to better performance is scarce – perhaps an indicator of the difficulties of evaluating such contributions. And the leader of one high-performing authority has described CPA as a 'game' that 'risks becoming a meaningless process-driven exercise'.[9]

In central government, measurement initiatives have covered much of the same ground, but have not been brought together in an overarching model. Moreover, they have had less emphasis on comparison – perhaps understandable given the often unique status of central government bodies – and more emphasis on accountability, reflected in the extensive use of targets. Later sections illustrate some of the issues arising from this approach.

Within this complicated picture, some elements of continuity can nevertheless be detected: first, an increasing – though not complete – emphasis on outcomes rather than outputs; secondly, an attempt to bring the performance of voluntary bodies working with official agencies into

---

[6] Audit Commission (2006) *Briefing on the Audit Commission's Comprehensive Performance Assessment Frameworks*, Audit Commission, London.

[7] Local Government Association (2005), *Inspection – time well spent?* Local Government Association, London.

[8] For example, Andrews, R. (2004) Analysing deprivation and local authority performance: the implications for CPA *Public Money and Management*, January pp. 19–24; and Boyne G. and Enticott G. (2004) Are the poor different? An empirical analysis of the internal characteristics of local authorities in the five CPA groups. *Public Money and Management*, January, pp. 11–18.

[9] *The Economist* (2005) Made to measure – ranking public services 17 December.

the performance measurement regime; and thirdly, the way in which performance management regimes have been increasingly concerned with extending central control over government departments and agencies, and by departments and agencies over local authorities.

This survey of experiences and case studies demonstrates important features for the auditor to take into account when assessing the value for money of performance measurement systems. Beyond these general factors, the auditor must be aware of other difficulties concerning the specification and measurement of outcome measures.

They can be grouped under the headings of:

- difficulty in determining what interventions secure the desired outcome;
- the influence of external factors;
- links between the public, staff and delivery agents;
- specifications, incentives and accountabilities;
- accountability; and
- data quality and reporting.

## 12.5   THE DIFFICULTIES OF DETERMINING WHAT INTERVENTIONS SECURE THE DESIRED OUTCOMES

For any social outcome a Government might want to achieve – better educated school leavers, for example – there will often be many plausible interventions it could take to secure, or help secure, that outcome. In education, these could include: better trained teachers; relieving teachers of administrative work to concentrate on teaching; more teaching-related IT; better classrooms and physical infrastructure; smaller class sizes; different degrees of streaming by ability; and a more relevant school curriculum. Many of these interventions interact. And it may be that some need to be undertaken as a set if they are to deliver benefits. In the UK, the Treasury recognised this issue in its guidance for reviews of government spending, and suggested the use of 'models of causation' to clarify the relationships involved, and facilitate purposeful planning. It may be easy to list many of the factors that are relevant to the achievement of an objective. Yet it is by no means always easy to show which relationships are casual links. This is shown in the simplified examples in **Box 12.6.**

---

**Box 12.6:    Casual links between objectives and relevant factors**

**Case 1** – Objective – to win the Olympic 100 metre sprint

– Relevant factors include –
- Number of Olympic class sprinters in the country
- Training facilities
- Quality of coaching
- Incentives – present and prospective earnings and social status of athletes
– Causal links – impossible to demonstrate

**Case 2** – Objective – to maintain the water level in a reservoir

– Relevant factors include
- Rainfall
- Demand for water
- Leakage
- Evaporation rate
– Casual links can be demonstrated

*Source:* National Audit Office.

---

## 12.6    OUTCOME MEASURING – THE INFLUENCE OF EXTERNAL FACTORS

**Box 12.6** also illustrates another general issue concerning measures and targets – the significance of external factors on the outcome in question or, put another way, the extent to which any changes in outcome can be attributed to government action. For example, if there is a programme to reduce unemployment by retraining those who are out of work, how far is success due to the government policy for retraining and how far is it due to other economic factors, such as increasing investment and exports? Certainly, economic and statistical techniques may be used to disaggregate the effects of different factors, and while they cannot establish determinate casual factors, it is useful for the auditor to probe how far they have been employed and the reliability of the results.

The significance of external factors on outcomes may well be most significant in areas where government aims to stimulate change, or regulate existing activity, rather than deliver services. But issues of complexity affect all targeted outcomes, and raise questions over the choice of intervention, and their level of resourcing. Those choices in turn place a heavy burden on the research base, and the absence of evidence on effectiveness, and particularly cost-effectiveness, of different potential interventions remains a problem.

## 12.7   OUTCOME MEASURES: LINKS BETWEEN THE PUBLIC, STAFF AND DELIVERY AGENTS

One of the intentions of moving towards outcome targets was to use measures that had some relevance to the general public. But many of the output and efficiency measures used in British government have generated very little interest outside government: it is difficult to interest the man in the street with, to quote a real example, an 'Aggregated Cost Efficiency target', even when that is explained as a 'weighted index of average vehicle testing efficiency', to take an example featuring in one of our early reports into the work of an agency.[10] Reviews of the use of performance information confirmed this picture. One commentator observed 'Grand statements about the importance of performance information for democracy sit alongside extensive if patchy evidence that ministers, legislators and citizens rarely make use of the volumes of performance information now thrust upon them'.[11] And where public engagement with measurement has been greater, it changes the context in which measures are viewed from a managerial and professional context, to a lay, political context.

So missed targets have been taken in political and media discussion to represent political and managerial failure, regardless of any performance improvement that may have been achieved. Good performance usually goes unreported. And the whole business of setting targets has been criticised, seen variously as a device of central control, burdensome for front-line workers, or simply ludicrously ill-judged and ineffective as in **Box 12.7**.

---

**Box 12.7:   Target Distortion**

'Prescriptive targets from the centre are often devised with the best of intentions, but end up distorting local priorities and not delivering

---

[10] Comptroller and Auditor General *The Vehicle Inspectorate: progress with the first Executive Agency*. (HC 249, Session 1991–1992).
[11] Pollitt, C. (2006) 'Performance information for democracy' *Evaluation* **12**(1), 38–55.

what is best for residents. Take the example of Suffolk, where the local youth offending team wants to reduce the number of people entering the criminal justice system, but the Home Office has set a target for increasing the number of offenders brought to justice. Which should have priority – a local decision, taken by a local authority accountable to local people, or a Whitehall diktat?

Take another example from Barnsley. There the local priority is the prevention of antisocial behaviour, yet the police are subject to targets to reduce robbery, which is not a widespread problem in the town. There are countless other examples of councils being prevented from addressing the issues that matter most to local people because they are obliged by the central government to play the tick-box target game.

This has not only demoralised frontline staff but also wasted their ability to improve public services for people they serve.

*Source:* Sir Simon Milton 'D-day for Local Government' in *Public Finance* for 24–30 November 2006, p. 17.

## 12.8   OUTCOME MEASURES: SPECIFICATION, INCENTIVES AND ACCOUNTABILITIES

In the early rounds of target-setting, the targets sometimes addressed issues so difficult to define or measure that they came to be seen almost as jokes. An example would be in the target to 'Increase by 500,000 by 2004 the number of people experiencing the arts'.[12] These targets did more than provide fodder for those unsympathetic to the government or indeed to the use of targets in general. They also stripped all force from the underlying efforts to improve the relevant services because they failed to capture their essence. So, for example, whatever actually happened concerning visits to art galleries, theatres, libraries and similar activities all could be represented as 'people experiencing the arts' and it would not take much ingenuity to claim that an extra 500,000 people had been involved by 2004 – regardless of the quality or cultural value of the experience.

---

[12] HM Treasury (2000) *2000 Spending Review: Public Service Agreement Targets.* CM 4808, the Stationery Office, London.

Targets which are set out in a complicated and detailed manner are also defective as in the target for improving air quality which was underpinned by eight standards such as:

Carbon monoxide 11.6mg/m3: 8-hour mean by end 31/12/2003

Benzene: 16.25$\mu$g/m3: running annual mean by end 31/12/2003[13]

How can the public interpret this? Also, there is a risk of capture by specialists, as the only people who can understand the system.

Thus targets which are vague or complicated often have questionable value. Professor Colin Talbot has observed[14] that the main point of a target is to adjust behaviour. But if the target is so complicated that there is no simple interpretation of success, how likely is it to change behaviours? Similarly, targets have some value if they help identify the scale of resources that need to be committed, or help choose between interventions which act at different speeds, or with different relative risks and rewards. Directional or over-complicated targets do not facilitate such judgements. Yet in reviewing the range of targets set for British central government in 2004, the Statistics Commission found that the majority of targets set still had material shortcomings in the way they were specified. Examples are in **Box 12.8.**

---

**Box 12.8:     The Statistics Commission Review of Targets**

In 2006, the Statistics Commission reviewed all of the Spending Review 2004 targets, and associated descriptions of progress measures, from a statistical perspective. They found issues with most of the targets they reviewed, and concluded that 'In view of the importance of PSA targets, we recommend that more consideration should be given to the adequacy of the statistical infrastructure to support their future evolution'. They identified a number of common issues, including those of clarity, complexity, and the problems of 'aspirational' targets, as well as general issues about lack of precision, as illustrated below.

**The shared target of Department of Trade and Industry, Office of the Deputy Prime Minister and Her Majesty's Treasury was criticised for lack of clarity.**

---

[13] DETR (2000) *Air Quality Strategy*. Cm 4548, The Stationery Office, London, p. 37.

[14] In evidence to Select Committee on Treasury, 20 July 2000.

The target was to 'make sustainable improvements in the economic performance of all English regions by 2008; over the long term, reduce the persistent gap in growth rates between the regions; demonstrate progress [in making sustainable improvements in economic performance] by 2006'.

*Issues identified*. Use of measures depending on judgements about the economic cycle; lack of suitable regional productivity data; 'progress' element measured in ways partly judgemental and qualitative.

**The Office of the Deputy Prime Minister's target for the planning system was criticised for complexity.**

The target was 'the planning system to deliver sustainable development outcomes at national, regional and local levels through efficient and high quality planning and development management processes, including achievement of best value standards for planning by 2008'.

*Issues identified*: assessment of progress necessarily subjective; no specification of how individual indicators should be combined to assess overall progress; indicators of effectiveness and efficiency not properly specified.

**The Department of Health's target for reduced waiting for treatment was criticised as simply an aspiration.**

The target was 'by 2008 no one waits more than 18 weeks from GP referral to hospital treatment'.

*Issues identified*: data not in place to measure progress; requirement for 100 per cent achievement means target is aspirational rather than realistic.

*Source:* Statistics Commission (2006) Report No. 29 *PSA targets: the devil in the detail* Statistics Commission, London.

Another way that faulty specification of targets can hinder, rather than help, performance improvement is through focusing on outputs or other intermediate aspects of performance, rather than the desired outcome.

There have been examples of perverse incentives in the UK NHS. The most striking example of perverse behaviour was caused by the adoption of targets for reduced waiting time for treatment. The first mistake was to target initially the number of people on waiting lists. Since waiting lists can most easily be reduced by treating those with simple conditions first, 20 per cent of clinicians surveyed in our health audits said that they frequently treated patients in a different order to their clinical priority in order to reduce waiting lists. Moreover, the data systems used to monitor waiting lists were weak, using inconsistent definitions from site to site, and rarely subject to effective validation.[15] These circumstances, combined with pressure to hit targets, led to nine health trusts to manipulate waiting list data as shown in **Box 12.9**.

---

**Box 12.9:    Manipulation of targets**

The target set for the National Health Service was that no-one should wait for longer than 18 months for treatment. The report showed examples of manipulation by: deliberate alteration of records; misuse of legitimate procedures to suspend patients from lists; simple omissions of data; and ploys to start the clock running only at late stages of waiting. Examples included:

**Barts and the London Trust**

Patient records altered; inappropriate suspensions and patients deleted from, and other inappropriate adjustments to, waiting lists.

**Salford Royal Trust**

Patients waiting 18 months not reported; inappropriate suspensions from lists; outpatients not added to waiting lists until the month of appointment; inpatients not included on lists.

*Source:* Comptroller and Auditor General *Inappropriate Adjustments to NHS Waiting Lists* (HC 452, Session 2001–2002).

---

The Department of Health moved to a series of targets based on waiting times, rather than waiting lists. But here too problems emerged. Targets

---

[15] Comptroller and Auditor General *Inpatient and Outpatient Waiting in the NHS* (HC 221 2001–2002).

designed to enable patients to secure appointments with local doctors within two days backfired. Doctors were reluctant to accept appointments booked further ahead, even if that suited both parties, because that spoilt their statistics.[16] A report into ambulance response times showed that six of 31 ambulance services did not follow official guidance on recording response, and that the resulting misreporting made it easier to hit response time targets.[17]

Commentators on indicator systems have identified a number of unintended consequences from their use. They include:

- Tunnel vision: managers, faced with many different targets, choose the ones that are easiest to measure and ignore the rest.
- Sub-optimisation: managers choose to operate in ways that serve their partial interests but damage the performance of the system as a whole.
- Myopia: managers focus on short-term targets at the expense of longer-term objectives.
- Measure fixation: if proxies are used for difficult to measure outcomes, those proxy indicators become the focus rather than the desired outcome.
- Misrepresentation: data are distorted or misreported to create a good impression.
- Misinterpretation: statistical imprecision is ignored in interpreting results – most notably in league tables.
- Gaming: managers 'play the system' rather than service goals – for example, deliberately under-achieving by reference to current potential so as to make future performance gains easier, and/or have future targets at a lower level.
- Ossification: obsolete indicators remain in the set because no one can be bothered to revise or remove them.[18]

And commentators have identified another assumption: that, given known measurement problems, the parts which can be measured in priority areas may be taken to be representative of the whole. In the health area, their area of study, they conclude that neither assumption

---

[16] Bevan G. and Hood, C. (2006) 'What's measured is what matters: targets and gaming in the English public health care system' *Public Administration* **84**(3).

[17] Carvel, J. (2006) Ambulance times misreported 999 response times. *The Guardian,* 15 August.

[18] Pidd, M. (undated) Lancaster University Working Paper, summarising material from Smith, P. (1995) On the unintended consequences of publishing performance data in the public sector. *International Journal of Public Administration,* **18** (2 and 3) 277–310.

is justified. They are particularly critical of the lack of routine audit or validation of performance information.[19]

Many of these characteristics have been evident in the examples quoted so far in this chapter. But it is worth illustrating the issue of misrepresentation, since this distortion can arise even where no targets have been set, merely indicators defined. In the UK, one of the clearest cases of misinterpretation relates to the use of indicators to form school league tables. Schools are rated according to the proportion of their students who achieve good examination grades. One of our audit studies looked at the preparation and use of these league tables, and found that, if they were to be used to judge a school's performance, there were a number of flaws. First, the initial tables listed raw results, paying no attention to the quality of intake to the school, or other external factors. And even when measures of added value were trialled, published data paid no attention to the known statistical variations and uncertainties. My study showed that, far from producing a fair ranking for a set of local schools, most of the time the tables could only distinguish those at the top from those at the bottom. Any finer judgements were lost in statistical noise. Moreover, taking account of external factors dramatically reduced the range in performance between 'best' and 'worst' performing schools. Yet these issues were ignored in presenting the tables to the general public.[20]

## 12.9   OUTCOME MEASURES: ACCOUNTABILITY

In introducing targets and measures, one of the things governments often hope to achieve is accountability for the use of public money. In the case of UK Public Service Agreement (PSA) targets, Ministers were to be accountable to Parliament, and named officials accountable to Ministers. In fact, many of the factors we have already discussed hinder a full accountability. Lack of precision or clarity in targets means that many different interpretations of progress are possible. In considering widely different government and opposition claims for targets hit or missed, a select committee of the House of Commons observed that both claims could be correct: interpretation depended on a range of assumptions

---

[19] Bevan G. and Hood, C. (2006) 'What's measured is what matters: targets and gaming in the English public health care system' *Public Administration* **84**(3).

[20] Comptroller and Auditor General *Making a Difference: performance of maintained secondary schools in England* (HC 1332, Session 2002–2003).

about, for example, the extent to which all sub-clauses of a target had to be met, which had not been specified at the outset.[21] Similarly, the lack of understanding of changes in indicator values that are attributable to Government actions prevents any clear management accountability.

These issues of incentive and accountability highlight the lack of leverage that funders of services feel they have over the performance of delivery agents. In a recent survey of PSA target owners, only 60 per cent thought they had adequate leverage over key delivery agents such as local authorities and voluntary bodies. And strikingly, while nearly 90 per cent of target owners saw delivery chain performance as crucial to success, only half had good information on delivery chain efficiency, while just 10 per cent used indicators in personal or corporate performance contracts.[22]

In part, this reflects the continuing uncertainty over how to deal with particularly good or bad apparent performance. It is usually impossible to withdraw funding from poorly performing delivery units without penalising the citizens they serve. Similarly, few are attracted to paying high performing units more money. Recently, there have been elements in local services which give high performing units greater freedoms from inspection and regulation. And poor performing units risk having 'turnaround' management teams imposed on them. But continuing issues over what truly represents 'performance', and whether the measures are adequate, many limit the zeal with which these initiatives can be pursued.

### 12.10    OUTCOME MEASURES: DATA QUALITY AND REPORTING

Data quality is fundamental to making a performance measurement system work as intended. Any weaknesses in data affect not only monitoring of progress, but also the quality of planning, and the ability to set baselines. Yet we find that governments often push ahead with measurement initiatives, and revise and extend them, without ever securing an appropriate flow of information to support them.

---

[21] Public Administration Select Committee (2003) *On target? Government by Measurement.* HC 62-I, Fifth report 2002–2003. The Stationery Office, London.

[22] Comptroller and Auditor General 'PSA targets: performance information. Results of a survey of UK Government Departments' Finance Directors and target owners about information underpinning the pursuit of performance targets'. http://www.nao.org.uk/publications/other_publications.htm.

In the case of UK central government, data quality has not been an explicit part of the system design. For example, no arrangements for the external validation of performance information featured in the original designs in any of the Executive Agency, PSA or Efficiency Programme initiatives. There was no indication that government recognised the seriousness of data quality for the success of the initiatives, or the potential significance of gaming or manipulation.

Where we have validated the reported data, or the data systems, we have found widespread problems. Taking our work on the Executive Agencies in the round, around 20 per cent of information streams have suffered from failings in design, operation or reporting.

These disappointing results have a number of causes. First, targets have often been set without considering data availability or suitability. In part, this finding reflects the political nature of outcome targets – and a tendency to make targets longer and with more sub-elements, so placing increasing demands on monitoring and reporting systems.

Second, while there has been clear responsibility for achieving targets through designated 'target owners', there has been no similar obligation for someone to guarantee data reliability. And as a consequence, there has been little formal consideration of what quality of data was needed – in terms of degrees of bias, uncertainty, timeliness and cost that could be tolerated. In these circumstances, it is difficult to judge risks, or think of cost-effective control systems. In fact, we have found that many officials think of risk purely in terms of data manipulation, when most of the problems we observe with data systems are sourced in operational or reporting errors. As a result, departments initially gave little thought to the adequacy of data sourced externally, or to that from established statistical systems – despite the fact that these statistics were not produced with performance monitoring in mind.

Third, clear reporting standards were seldom set. While over time more quantitative performance reporting has emerged, judgements about what may be considered 'on track' are still opaque. And often Departments have failed to disclose unavoidable weaknesses in their data systems, which would help readers gain a fairer view of progress. Moreover, there is no established procedure for amending targets, and associated data systems, as circumstances change.[23]

The measurement of efficiency is little better. Here departments have struggled with the consequence of a lack of good information linking

---

[23] Comptroller and Auditor General *Second Validation Compendium Report* (HC 985, 2005–2006).

inputs with outputs – the classic measure of efficiency. Instead many efficiency measures are centred on inputs or processes, which leaves output and quality dimensions to be covered by other means – usually as a broad check on whether input changes can be taken to represent efficiency gains, rather than as part of an integrated measurement system. The results have not been persuasive. I concluded that Government claims of £4.7bn of efficiency gains as at September 2005 could only be viewed as 'provisional', and should be subject to further verification. It is not that we doubt that some gains have been made, but we cannot be sure that they have been fairly valued.[24]

Looking beyond UK central government, data quality has posed problems in other areas and administrations. In some performance regimes, data quality issues have been more clearly addressed at the design stage. In UK local government, assessment of the robustness of systems behind the production of Best Value indicators was built into the Code of Audit practice for local authority auditors. And in the USA, the Reports Consolidation Act of 2000 adds to the provisions of GPRA by requiring federal agencies to assess the completeness and reliability of their performance data. While reflecting the importance of reliable performance information, neither provision has yielded that outcome. The Audit Commission publish local authority indicators in a compendium, and drawing on their own analysis and the assessments of local auditors, attach a 'health warning' to indicators they judge as questionable. Their review of performance plans in 2000 showed that some councils' systems were not robust, even where the indicators in question had been produced for some years.[25] And in the United States, only five of 24 Agencies provided an assessment for fiscal year 2000, none of which identified any material inadequacies in performance information. Yet review of Inspectors' General reports revealed the identification of 'management challenges' in this area for 11 of the 24.[26]

## 12.11 CONCLUSIONS

The idea of securing improvements by setting targets and measuring performance against them has usefully focused attention on achieving

---

[24] Comptroller and Auditor General *Progress in Improving Government Efficiency* (HC 802-I, 2005–2006).

[25] Comptroller and Auditor General *Measuring the Performance of Government Departments.* (HC 301, 2000–2001) Appendix 4.

[26] General Accounting Office (2002) *Performance Reporting* GAO-02-372. Washington.

results in both public and private sectors. But as this chapter shows, the focus of attention can become directed to the targets themselves which can come to be seen as having, as it were, a life of their own, almost apart from what staff see as the realities of their work.

When this happens, the pursuit of the targets may cause changes in behaviour in a dysfunctional way. One example is the way in which targets for waiting lists for health treatment came to distort behaviour, as discussed earlier in this chapter; and the difficulties were well summarised by Robert Cole as follows: 'Although immensely popular and widely used, it may be wrong to use targets in any but the most gentle way. There are three difficulties. First, you might set the wrong target. Second, even if you set the right target people might ignore other important stuff in their attempts to meet the pre-agreed goals. Third, the ground may shift during the period that a target is in place, making it useless. This can happen even if you set targets with the best and most intelligent of intentions, and if you use a set of targets broad enough to ensure that all management considerations are taken into account.[27]

What is really needed is a 'performance culture' in which measurement has a part, but is not the exclusive focus of attention. And, indeed, this was the original intention of the performance frameworks described at the start of his chapter – management by objectives, the EFQM model and the McKinsey 7S framework. But as explained, the way in which such ideas were implemented often meant that most attention was paid to the most visible aspects of measurement – whether the target was being hit – and too little to the overall management capacity which measurement supports, and which should be directed towards the achievement of outcomes.

What should the role of the auditor be, particularly if she wants to promote the performance culture of the kind that I have just described? The following activities are relevant:

- Probing the real purposes of performance measurement frameworks, looking to highlight opportunities for a better match between context, framework and purpose. In this way auditors can take a critical stance on the use of performance measurement but take a constructive line in recommending improvements.
- Examining whether targets are simple, understandable and precise; challenging but measurable and achievable; relevant to outcomes; and

---

[27] Robert Cole Evening Standard, London May 2006.

sufficiently few in number to concentrate rather than dissipate energies and attention.

- Acting to promote better practices, drawing on their own experiences of measurement in a variety of public bodies and contexts, and on the wider literature. Auditors often have a broader view of practices than any individual body they audit. And in some cases, their 'corporate memory' of previous measurement initiatives and lessons learnt is longer and easier to access.
- Promoting the proper operation of the framework that has been set up in areas such as the validity of measures, incentives and sanctions, reporting and data quality, so that the frameworks both evolve and achieve their potential to improve performance.
- Looking to promote coherence of measurement through the delivery chain, and across similar bodies, to reduce measurement costs and increase the scope for productive comparison and benchmarking. Coherence in measurement also offers the prospect of clearer communication through the delivery chain, and also with external stakeholders. Auditors can often play a useful role by making plain the impact of measurement regimes on front line staff and service consumers.

To sum up; the lesson of this chapter is that what is needed to transform a measurement culture into a performance culture is:

- measures and targets that make sense to those who must achieve them;
- measures and targets that make sense to the public;
- measures and targets that provide clear direction and are unambiguous to measure.

If an organisation has the leadership qualities to do all this it may successfully:

- assess and manage risk;
- release staff potential;
- secure successful change in line with strategic objectives.

## 12.12  SUMMARY

Since the Second World War, many democratic governments have embarked on ambitious programmes for economic and social welfare. But the bureaucracies responsible for carrying them out have often faltered, and plans have not been achieved.

What could be done? One answer seemed to lie in the fashionable management prescription of 'management by objectives' put into operation by specifying performance measures and associated targets. And ever since the early eighties one system after another has been introduced in the UK and other countries.

But there have been problems with designating appropriate measures, targets, outputs and outcomes. There have too often been:

- too many targets to serve clarity of action and its evaluation;
- targets which are too vague and too general, so that whatever happened could be said to have achieved the target;
- too rigid targets, that undermined morale and led to 'gaming';
- targets that led to unintended consequences;
- difficulties in determining the actions that could be the causes of achieving outcomes;
- lack of clarity about who is responsible for achieving targets;
- data underlying measures and targets are unreliable.

And there are difficulties when:

- measures and targets change too quickly, making it difficult to track progress over time, even though it may be politically convenient to do so;
- the performance system does not generate auditable information necessary to appraise the results achieved, and special 'add on' measures are necessary to produce it.

But where leadership is provided whereby performance measures and targets generate a new enthusiasm and staff morale, that turns a performance measurement system into a performance culture, then real improvements in outputs and outcomes may be achieved.

# 13

## Organising the Audit

How should the external auditor organise his or her own affairs if they are to combat bureaucracy effectively; turn from critic and nark to coach and mentor; and make recommendations that may both conserve resources and effect improvements in the public services of auditees?

There are several pointers, though no one single organisational framework. The key points are:

- Auditors should work with colleagues, in teams where sensible, sharing ideas and thoughts with others and with auditees before making recommendations.
- Teams should consist of 'insiders' and 'outsiders' – health teams should contain medical experts with a professional authority and access to relevant networks; road transport studies should include consulting engineers. An audit assignment is a project, and should be managed as such.
- Some auditors will have their career in a public audit office. But they should not spend their whole working life there. In the NAO we send secondees to private sector firms (financial service firms, but also for example, Diageo, the John Lewis Partnership and Glaxo Smith Kline); to staff of parliamentary committees; to government departments; local authorities, the health service and to other audit offices in the UK and internationally, for example to Poland, France, Germany, Italy, Canada, Australia, and New Zealand. And we have inward secondments from a similarly wide range of countries and organisations.
- Audit assignments should be sought outside the main range of domestic business to give experience of other approaches. The NAO has had contracts to audit the United Nations; the World Health Organisation; the World Food Programme and many other international organisations. We have had contracts with the European Commission to work in Hungary, Lithuania, Slovenia, Latvia, Bulgaria, Romania, Ghana and other countries.
- The NAO has memoranda of understanding with many countries, including China, Russia, Azerbaijan, and Venezuela.

- The NAO has 'centres of excellence' with colleagues specialising and advising other colleagues on areas like performance measurement, project management, economic and statistical techniques.
- The NAO recruits university graduates of high quality and gives these young men and women the support to secure professional qualifications as accountants and auditors, but some in other subjects too. The NAO recruit people with the skills needed when they are in mid career. Typically these come from the City of London, or professional firms, or from health administration. The NAO has an external auditor appointed by Parliament from the private sector, who assesses annually whether value for money is delivered. NAO financial auditing standards are examined by the Institute of Chartered Accountants in England and Wales; over 25 per cent of our financial audit is done by private sector firms, though NAO retains responsibility for this work; and outside experts examine our performance audit reports as the NAO works on them. These experts come from University staffs, currently the London School of Economics and Political Science and Oxford University. They examine the logic and clarity of the embryonic report, its use of graphics, and the relevance of its evidence. The NAO agree the facts of the report with the auditee, and while we show them the conclusion and recommendations are drawn from the facts, the NAO take responsibility for them as professional auditors should.
- The NAO tries to produce reports which are accessible to different audiences – to Parliament; to auditees; to technical and academic experts; and to the media. It aims for short reports – ideally around 20 A4 pages – with supplementary volumes and material on the NAO website – http://www.nao.org.uk – where this is useful.
- The NAO takes part in professional associations – for example, the NAO is an active member of the UK, European and United States evaluation associations. Conferences are an important means by which we seek to achieve wider sustainable impacts. Examples include: a seminar involving senior civil servants and academics from the London School of Economics and Political Science and Harvard and Tilberg Universities to debate what more could be done to embed innovation in departments; annual conferences on latest developments in performance measurement, regulation and public private partnerships; and conferences arising from specific studies such as that organised jointly with the Royal College of Physicians, the Stroke Association and Connect – the communication disability network – on how to improve prevention and health care for the medical condition known as stroke.

To broaden out understanding of issues and the wider context influencing the delivery of value for money the NAO seeks to engage with a range of distinguished people. Examples include James Mirrlees, joint winner of the 1996 Nobel Prize in Economics for his work on the economic theory of incentives under asymmetric information (this is important in the context of designing services which meet people's expectations); leaders of industry such as the Director General of the Confederation of British Industry; key suppliers to government (such as Capita, TNT and British Aerospace); and informed commentators in the media on the delivery of public services.

Taken together, these approaches are intended to combine professional competence with an engagement in the worlds our auditees live and work in, and with a wider experience forged from experience in the private sector, the voluntary sector and internationally.

## 13.1   WHAT RESULTS DO WE ACHIEVE?

Do we succeed as coaches and mentors? Three examples can be given:

- **Financial savings arising from our work**. The NAO's mission is to help the nation spend wisely. One of the ways the NAO's success in fulfilling this mission is evidenced is through the financial impact of the savings and efficiency gains that departments and agencies achieve as a direct result of our recommendations. In order to underline the importance of this aspect of our work to all NAO staff, and to provide a clear headline message to Parliament and the taxpayer on the 'return on investment' that the NAO provides, I introduced a target in 1989 of identifying savings each year of at least seven times the cost of running the office. In 1998 the savings target was increased to eight times the cost of the Office and from 2007 is now nine times. We have consistently achieved our target for financial impacts over the years (**Box 13.1**) and have reported total savings of more than £5 billion since 1993.

The NAO achieve a financial impact when, as a result of its recommendations, departments either reduce the resources employed to achieve their objectives or increase revenue, for example by reducing fraudulent non-payment of taxes or duties. Sometimes financial impacts are direct cash savings. These often arise from studies where the NAO has identified scope for improved financial management. For example, by

**Box 13.1:**    **Financial savings from NAO work**

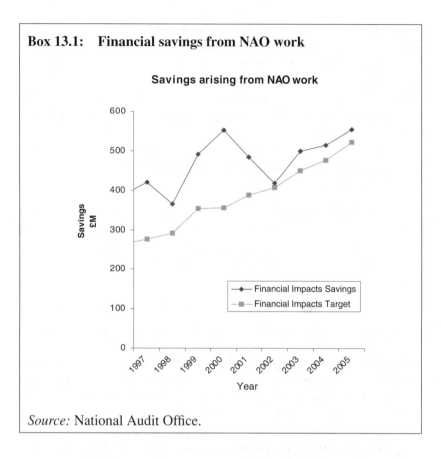

**Savings arising from NAO work**

*Source:* National Audit Office.

recommending changes in account management leading to better rates of interest for the New Opportunities Fund, a body which distributes National Lottery Funding, the NAO identified savings to the fund of £3 million a year. The financial impacts which the NAO claim are independently validated by our internal auditor and our external auditor. Further examples of how financial impact can arise from the auditor's work are illustrated in **Box 13.2.**

• **Improvements of a non financial nature.** Of course, it is not all about the money. Citizens and legislatures are as much interested in the quality of public services and what taxpayers' money delivers. An interesting example of this is the work of the NAO in examining the effectiveness of innovative building techniques. Certain parts of the UK suffer from housing shortages which have an impact on house prices and the high costs can mean that key public sector workers

**Box 13.2:** These are some areas/activities which are usually always a good source of financial impacts because of the inherent risks to value for money

| Theme | Likely impact types | NAO examples |
|---|---|---|
| **Procurement** | Reduction in costs through better contracting, bulk buying<br><br>Reduction in costs through economies in usage<br><br>Rationalisation of facilities<br><br>Benchmarking costs against those of other organisations or other internal business units | **Engineering and Physical Sciences Research Council (EPSRC): procurement of equipment from Research Grants**<br><br>The NAO report made a number of recommendations to improve the way scientific and related equipment, required for research proposals approved by the EPSRC, should be purchased. Consequently, these recommendations were adopted by all the Research Councils and by Higher Education Funding Council for England, saving £ 25 million over 4 years.<br><br>**Purchasing Professional Services**<br><br>By implementing recommendations by making better use of their collective buying power and extending the use of call-off contracts to purchase professional services, departments saved £ 60 million over 3 years. |
| **Transactional services** | Reduction in error and fraud in transactions between citizens and departments | **Payment of Social Security Benefits to Overseas Customers** |

| | Reduced response times | Following the implementation of recommendations arising from the report, the Inland Revenue introduced a strategy to confirm the eligibility and identity of state pension beneficiaries. This involved the issue and subsequent check of a letter sent to all customers living abroad. The strategy was designed to ensure all customers received a letter to confirm their continuing entitlement to State Pension (life certificate) within a five year maximum period. |
| | More effective deployment of front-line staff | |
| | More effective revenue collection | |
| | More effective debt reduction | This led to overall savings of £34.8 million over 7 years. |
| **Asset management** | Better control and management of assets, projects and resources | **Managing Reductions in Vacant Family Quarters** |
| | More effective stock and inventory control | Our report found that the Ministry of Defence (MoD) had 14 000 vacant houses costing £39 million a year in rent and maintenance. Our recommendations led to the MoD carrying out a significant disposal programme to reduce these vacancies, disposing of 2,365 properties. This saved £21 million over 3 years, arising from savings in maintenance costs. |
| | Raising revenue from disposal of assets | |

| | | |
|---|---|---|
| **Back office functions** | Reducing bureaucracy and the complexity of processes<br><br>Improved efficiency of processes | **The Medical Assessment of Incapacity and Disability Payments**<br><br>An NAO Report published in 2000 found delays in making decisions about payment of incapacity and disability benefits. Long decision times meant people were experiencing long waits to receive benefits and in some cases, there were overpayments.<br><br>Following the report, the Department for Work and Pensions introduced and met new performance targets for accurate and timely processing. These reduced the processing times for Incapacity Benefit, Disability Living Allowance and Attendance Allowance and reduced the backlog of Incapacity Benefit cases from around 368,000 in 2001 to under 40,000 in June 2003. This saved £110 million over 3 years in incorrectly paid benefits. |
| **Cinderella services** | Finding efficiency savings in areas not seen as priority service by departments | **Prison Catering**<br><br>By examining variation in catering costs between prisons, our report recommended how the costs of prison meals might be reduced in a number of ways with no detrimental impact on food quality, for instance by reducing the number of food contracts. Acting on these recommendations, the Prison Service saved £11 million over four years. |

| Savings to citizens | Improved utilities management leading to lower charges for consumers | **Office of Telecommunications (OFTEL): helping consumers benefit from competition in the telecommunications market**<br><br>Recommendations from the report resulted in OFTEL investigating the prices British Telecom charged customers to rent a handset and directed it to reduce the price by 25 per cent, saving consumers £45 million over 5 years. The report also resulted in a leaflet advising consumers of ways to save money in their telecommunications expenditure.<br><br>**New Electricity Trading Arrangements**<br><br>The report highlighted the disparity between the falling wholesale of electricity and the broadly static retail price which meant that domestic user of electricity were not benefiting. The resulting media coverage of the report lead to an upsurge in enquiries from members of the public looking to switch suppliers to get a better price, saving each consumer an average of £35, and £4 million overall. |

*Source*: National Audit Office.

cannot afford to live in areas of high demand for their skills. Working with professionals from a range of disciplines the NAO validated new methods of construction intended to build houses much more quickly and at a cheaper cost. This work helped developers and component manufactures understand and use the new construction methods. Through NAO work, improvements in efficiency and productivity to the value of £ 23 million are likely to be achieved, releasing funds to build 900 extra new homes a year. These benefits were realised for two reasons: risk premiums were reduced because of the greater reliance that could now be placed on building cost assumptions and the detailed process plans the NAO helped endorse, showed how to make best use of innovative methods of construction. Ultimately the NAO's contribution was in helping develop confidence in new fairly untried approaches. Other examples include work carried by NAO on how easy and effective it is for citizens to obtain redress where the quality of public services is poor. In this instance we highlighted a range of good practice which needed to be more widely adhered to. In a study of urban green spaces which are essential to the quality of life of people living in cities, we drew attention to the need to give greater priority to what had become a 'Cinderella service'. Key to achieving this was greater transparency of the costs of maintaining and preserving green spaces to appropriate quality standards and my report set out how this might be secured to minimise the risk of under investment in the future.

- Auditors also need to be alert to new emerging sectors where their input can add value. Increasingly in the UK and other countries the public sector is relying on voluntary organisations to develop and deliver services. Through its work the NAO has sought to promote and support this policy while also maintaining parliamentary scrutiny and interests. **Box 13.3** summaries the NAO's approach and experience.

---

**Box 13.3:   Working with the third sector**

In recent years, the role of the third sector (also referred to as the voluntary and community sector) in public service delivery has risen up the political agenda. The Office has developed a number of different ways to approach this area of public policy, to promote value for money and better public services.

- In June 2005, a report was published on how government departments had taken forward their aim to increase the sector's role and improve the way they fund third sector organisations. That report was the subject of an inquiry by a Parliamentary committee. In response to the NAO and the Committee's reports, the Government introduced new initiatives and has kept up the pace of reform.

But this initial report and Parliamentary interest did not mark the end of the NAO's interest or involvement with is area of policy:

- Working closely with the relevant parts of government, and with sector experts, the NAO developed and published a 'decision support tool' which provides a step-by-step guide to public funders of third sector organisations. This web-based tool brings together and reflects all the latest guidance from within government, and is suited to use as a foundation for more detailed guidance on departmental intranets and web sites, and is also available to third sector organisations.
- The 2005 report covered much ground, and so the NAO is also working on more detailed topics, especially where the 2005 research found practice to be most wanting. These projects will result in reports to funders and the sector.
- Finally, the transfer of responsibility for third sector matters within government brought this area of policy under the remit of another Parliamentary committee. The Office has provided that committee with extensive briefing about the main issues, to help the committee focus its interest and design future inquiries.

Finally, the real proof of the impact the NAO has as mentors and coaches are the words and direct experience of real auditors. Below five NAO colleagues recount their experience **(Box 13.4).**

Nevertheless, like everyone, the successes the NAO has had are not the end of the road. The objective of securing still greater value for money from public sector audit is therefore before us.

## 13.2   CONCLUSION AND SUMMARY

There is no single way successfully to organise successfully a public sector audit office, as the multiplicity of their forms across the world

**Box 13.4:**

Securing positive change through audit –
five auditors comment on examples of position change they have contibuted to

**Erica Nicholls**

When I picked up the audit for the Higher Education Funding Council for England the client relationship was poor. To improve things, we sat down with the client to listen to their concerns and develop a relationship plan which included measurable commitments from the NAO. We've now been able to report back to the client that we've met all of their expectations and as a result their trust has increased. We're about to host a large conference on Higher Education that the client helped coordinate (see page 9 for Laura Sinfield's review of the Conference) and there's no way that could have happened if we'd not had a good relationship.

**Paul Keane**

When I was the Director on Transport we examined the work the Highways Agency does to build slip roads from motorways to private developments. It's supposed to be self-financing but we found some projects were in deficit by up to £1 million. The Agency wasn't chasing up debt and there were poor information flows relating to these projects. However, as a result of our audit recommendations, internal processes improved and cost recovery picked up. It also helped that we focused on these projects as a key risk and returned to them year after year to make sure things had improved.

**Joy Beishon**

I agree that tailoring the product to the individual needs of the client is really important. My example is from when I worked for a lottery distributor. We found that we weren't getting grant applications from as many parts of the country as we wanted. So we held a series of regional events and tailored our delivery to each region and client base, and our recognition of how needs might differ by region was very well received.

**Simon Reason**

About three years ago the Regulation team arranged an independent regulators' conference. There are more than 200 regulators in the UK but beyond the largest five or six regulators that everyone's heard of, they don't talk much to each other. The conference enabled regulators to share information with each other and (because they already know us) delegates were actually more interested in talking to each other than to the NAO. Although the conference wasn't a standard VFM output it helped the regulators do their job better. Just because an impact might be partly intangible that's not a reason for not trying to pursue it. The conference was such a success that this November, we're holding our fourth one.

**Jess Hudson**

Our clients also need to understand our business so they understand what we're trying to achieve and can see there is a shared agenda. The way we deliver our message is also important. I once gave a presentation to a troubled agency at the Department for Trade and Industry and they really bought into the messages at the presentation. We need to make sure we do enough to support the implementation of our recommendations. We could do more to help clients develop action plans, and to follow up and review progress. If we just leave clients with recommendations it's like giving them a ladder with no rungs on it.

amply testifies. But key points in securing success include:

- the sharing of ideas and experience between colleagues in the audit office; with relevant outside interests; and with auditees – though in all these instances the auditor's independence must be maintained;
- working in teams where appropriate, with teams consisting of insiders and outsiders, and such audits managed as projects;
- audit staff drawn from a wide range of backgrounds and experiences, with secondments in and out of the office, from and to the public, private and voluntary sectors, and in international assignments.

Success has several dimensions, all stemming from recommendations that auditees see make sense in their practical worlds, rather than being visited upon them from 'on high':

- financial and other resource savings actually achieved through economies and efficiencies suggested and put into effect;
- improvements in the effectiveness of public services as experienced by those who receive them or otherwise benefit from them;
- reductions in theft, fraud, corruption and other crimes; and
- assurance to legislatures, executives and the public at large that public services are open to full inspection by independent external auditors and that the accountability of public servants can be demonstrated.

Public sector auditing is a bulwark of constitutional and democratic government. But organising it economically, efficiently and effectively is a continuous challenge in the light of changing social, economic and political circumstances. There is no final blueprint for success, since final success itself has different meanings in different and changing circumstances. Nevertheless, the ideas in this chapter have a general relevance for the promotion of organisational improvement.

# 14

## Concluding Thoughts

This book is about public sector auditing. It is not about the different legal and constitutional frameworks within which public sector auditing is conducted. The ideas and approaches that it sets out are relevant to unitary and to federal states; to states like the United Kingdom, with devolved administrations with their own audit arrangements; to regional governments; and to governments of local authorities and municipalities. This is not to say that jurisdictional features are irrelevant to the success of public sector auditing – if auditors are not independent of executive government; if they cannot write and speak freely; if their access rights are tightly circumscribed; if executive government unduly restricts the size and remuneration of the staff; then public sector audit will not produce work of good quality. But this general point apart, this is not a book about the legal framework within which public audit is discharged.

Secondly, whether it is reaching a view on whether the accounts of an organisation give a 'true and fair' view, or the determination of a performance audit, public sector auditing requires the exercise of judgement. Not every auditor examining the same phenomena will come to the same conclusions. Auditing is about the application of principles not the application of rules. There is a spectrum here – at one end, the auditor may find prima facie evidence that, according to the relevant law, fraud has been committed. And most fellow auditors would agree. But, at the other end of its spectrum, where complex social and economic programmes are being examined, different appreciations and interpretations become manifest. And there are further difficulties still, as **Box 14.1** brings out.

---

**Box 14.1:   The Problems of Audit**

'Inevitably, there are a number of difficulties with quantification of impacts. There are often *identification problems* even where it is agreed that auditors have had some kind of effect. What is it exactly that the audit work has achieved? There are *attribution problems* in identifying a chain of events between a specific piece of audit work and the actions taken by auditees. It can also often be difficult to disentangle the effect of audit from the work of other third parties or the organisation itself. There will almost certainly be *measurement problems* because of incomplete data or simply the complexity of the effects. Even harder is considering the counterfactual – what would have happened without the audit intervention. Attempting to measure impacts is thus difficult and at times, impossible. For it to be done thoroughly in every case would certainly be expensive and a poor use of public money.

In addition, not everyone believes that audit has a positive or indeed any effect. Some have questioned the validity of the claimed influence and at times have suggested audit reports have little or no impact (e.g. Morin 2001 on the basis of examining a number of Canadian reports). Others have suggested that they succeed given particular circumstances (van der Meer 1999 in a Dutch example). There is also a growing literature that argues that audit and other scrutiny work has detrimental or perverse effects. These include concerns about the scale of audit – an excess of 'checking rather than doing' (Power 1997, Gray and Jenkins 2007), the perceived effect of scrutiny activities on innovation and risk taking (Cabinet Office 1999), the tendency for audits to make auditees 'skilled at games of compliance but exhausted and cynical about them too' (Power 2003:199); the perceived tendency of auditors to pounce on minor errors (Behn 2001); what has been called the 'performance paradox' – the simultaneous proliferation of measures with their failure to stimulate improved performance (Leeuw 2000), the tendency of auditors to make everything they look at 'auditable' (Power 1997), and perverse 'game playing' effects such as the prioritisation of patients requiring minor procedures in order to reduce waiting lists (Perrin 1998, Bevan and Hood 2005)'.

*Source:* J. Lonsdale and M. Whitehouse (2006), UK National Audit Office '*Adding Value? Measuring the Impact of Performance Audit in the Education and Social Welfare Fields*' Paper given at the Conference of the American Evaluation Association held in Portland, Oregon, 2–4 November.

There is also the point that the auditor must have information. This is much more than the account books and ledgers of popular conception. Indeed, what these yield may be difficult to comprehend and appreciate for auditors and everyone else, as **Box 14.2** shows.

---

**Box 14.2:    Fundamental Flaws in Annual Accounts**

- They don't make easy reading
- They don't show how a business is doing compared with others in its sector
- They don't identify strengths and weaknesses

- They don't identify the scope for
- improvement

- They don't support decision making
- They don't show all the numbers that matter

- Too many of the numbers they do include are based on judgement
- Most of the numbers are seriously out of date by the time anyone sees them

*Source:* Steven Pipe *Accountancy Age* 5 October 2006.

---

But if financial auditing and performance auditing is to take place at all, auditees must have relevant records in files, accounts and now, overwhelmingly, in electronic records of resources received and expended, of goods and services purchased and sold, of programmes conceived and implemented, of corporate functions discharged. An auditor may have to create supplementary information, as recorded in this book. But he or she cannot create and keep the auditee's entire set of records without becoming part of executive management themselves, and ceasing to be the external auditor.

Indeed, this book is about external audit: those appointed from outside the organisation to audit its performance. It is right to recognise that many of the external auditor's techniques will be used by internal auditors; consultants appointed by the auditee; internal efficiency and delivery units and similar organisations. They can all do good work. But their responsibility lies to the Minister, the Board or the Chief Executive of the organisation concerned. They are not independent in the way that the external auditor is designed to be.

## 14.1    TRAPS

Auditing therefore requires the exercise of judgement. And the more widely the auditor shares the preparation of his or her judgements with colleagues and auditees the more likely they are to commend acceptance as soundly based, well thought out and relevant. One useful way to secure such results is to work in teams where the size of the task makes this worthwhile. But whether alone, or as a member of a team, it is for the auditor to reach his own judgement and to stand by it, whatever the pressures may be to change his or her mind. If the auditor departs from this, news of it will surely follow, since in today's world there are few secrets and confidentialities. And while resiling from his or her judgement may get the auditor round an awkward corner; win the immediate thanks of the auditee – though no long term gratitude; the price will be the loss of reputation among colleagues, superiors and, indeed, clients as well.

Another trap is to fall victim to fashionable prescription. Chapter 8, for example, drew attention to the benefits that might come from learning positive lessons from retail management. But as **Box 14.3** shows, the enthusiastic adoption of the mantra of 'Excellence, Quality and Customer Service' may come to be more a matter of appearance than reality and the auditor must be alive to this.

In a similar way, auditors must be alive to the dangers of relying thoughtlessly on partnerships, outsourcing and public private partnerships. These arrangements work well when, in the classical 'make or buy' decision of the economists' analysis of the optimum size of firms, an organisation 'buys in' what it truly cannot do more economically, efficiently and effectively itself.[1] But, appearance may disguise a disappointing reality.

Jobs directly touching customers are being continuously 'decontented', contracted out, and remotely located.

The widespread resort to part time and temporary workers is another manifestation of this trend. These expedients reduce the value employees can create and the degree to which consumer problems can be solved.[2]

And problems of partnerships were well brought out by James Strachan, the former Chair of the Audit Commission, in **Box 14.4**.

---

[1] Ronald Coase (1937) 'The Nature of the Firm' *Economica* **4** (386–405) gave the clearest demonstration of this point by showing that the boundary of a firm – and by extension other organisations – is set at the point where conducting an activity internally is marginally more expensive than buying in the necessary good or service.

[2] Quoted by Stefan Stern in 'In search of the suppliers' reflex reaction' in the Financial Times for 12 October 2005.

## Box 14.3:   Failure to deliver

### [ ON MANAGEMENT ]

# Same old mantra

Excellence, quality and customer service is the boast,
but why do so many companies fail to deliver?

BY Christopher Grey

**B**efore the fall of the Berlin Wall, the Soviet satellite states favoured peculiarly ironic names. Thus, the German Democratic Republic boldly declaimed that for which it was least obviously known: democracy. In the same way, we all know people whose boasts are loud in inverse relation to the truth. But are businesses any better? How many of us, as customers, experience the frustration of being held in a call centre queue with a disembodied voice telling us that we are 'valued customers'?

I have a rule of thumb. When I buy from an organisation that trumpets 'excellence', I expect to experience failure; when it speaks of 'quality', I expect incompetence; and when it takes pride in 'customer service', I know I will receive shoddy treatment. Excellence, quality and customer service are the Holy Trinity of mediocrity. If I come across a company declaring its commitment to all three, I run as fast as I can. How can we explain this? Is it that these businesses are dishonest? Sometimes. Are they incompetent? Yes, more often than they are dishonest – but still not normally so.

Rather, they have diligently followed the received wisdom of 30 years of management literature from Peters and Waterman, through the Total Quality Management prescriptions, to the Business Process Re-Engineering ideas, and beyond. They have zapped bureaucracy, downlayered, downsized, subcontracted, off-shored and performance-measured. But could it be that this is the problem?

Let me offer you a case study. My local train station has a stationmaster called Michael. He is paid to sell tickets. He also sweeps and cleans the station; decorates the waiting room at his own initiative; is always polite and friendly; knows his customers by name and delights in selling tickets to obscure destinations off the commuter line. If a train is delayed, he phones local customers to give up-to-the minute information and for those already there he walks down the platform, telling each passenger what has happened and why.

Michael wears the uniform and badge (declaring him to be a Customer Service Operative) of the train company he works for. One day a week he is required to work at a larger station and is replaced by someone from the pool of employees. These substitutes are invariably rude, uninterested, cannot sell non-standard tickets and never venture out of the ticket office. They too wear the uniform and badge. But Michael is part of the local community and he cares about his customers because he knows them, not because he has been on a customer service

course, and he cares about railways because – well, just because that is what lights his fire.

The irony is that Michael's attitude is exactly what customer service courses aim for. Yet they do so not by selecting for, recognising and rewarding real service, but by promoting phoney, ersatz service. A few years ago I did some work with a senior executive in a supermarket chain that was legendary for its successful customer care culture and was the subject of a widely used business school case-study. She wanted to discover whether shopfloor staff believed in the value of customer focus and did her study just after the apparently successful conclusion of an expensive training programme. I expected that the staff would not really believe in the customer focus value. I was wrong: 85% of them said they had not even heard of it. In the same way that the supermarket had redesigned its displays, so zones mimicked traditional high-street stores – greengrocers, fishmongers, butchers and so on – the entire edifice of customer service was a fake.

Why did this company believe it was doing things right when it was getting it so wrong? It relied on the reports of store managers, who all said that staff had signed up to the values when what they meant was that the staff had seen the video. And it believed customer surveys. What senior managers should have done was to go quietly and unannounced as customers to their own business, and experience the realities for themselves. The company has now been taken over, following a drastic profits slump. So does this mean that the lesson has been learnt? No – because it is still trumpeting the same old mantra of the customer, but with a reduced cost-base.

Which brings us back to Michael, for now there is talk that he will be sacked as part of a cost-saving plan – after all, other stations on the line are unmanned (including the one closest to my house, which I avoid because the ticket machines and car park are always vandalised – but that is a cost that doesn't show up in the accounts). I am sure that the managers of the train company are well-intentioned and I am sure that they are well aware of the latest management thinking. In fact, I checked its website and it is committed to excellence, quality and customer service. But I'd rather buy from a company that delivers these things, rather than one that boasts about them. ∎

Christopher Grey is professor of organisational theory at the Judge Business School, University of Cambridge

LUCINDA ROGERS / HEART

*Source: World Business* July/August 2006 p. 15.

## Box 14.4:    The problems of partnerships in British local government

Among the current forms of partnership encouraged by the government are: Local Strategic Partnership; Crime and Disorder Reduction Partnerships; children's trusts; Supporting People; Urban regeneration companies; Connexions; SureStart.

- Supporting People (SP) provides a good example of the challenges facing partnerships. The programme, which provides housing services to vulnerable people, controls annual expenditure of £ 1.72bn. Local administering authorities use joint commissioning bodies, bringing together local authorities, primary care trusts and local probation boards. But some commissioning body members are unclear about their roles and responsibilities and not all health and probation representatives attend regularly.
- Often the commissioning body does not, in practical terms, govern the programme and, where the role of the accountable officer is also weak, leadership falls to a council's SP lead officer – a middle management position. Reporting arrangements from that officer are often weak, or even non-existent. Councils might not recognise either formally or informally that they have any responsibility for the SP governance role.
- SP lead officers cannot ensure a strategic approach across all partners, or ensure that there is joint planning and complementary budgets from the various partner organisations. Blame for any service failures might be publicly laid at the door of just one of the partner bodies, as might the cost of inititating replacement services. Vulnerable users can lose valuable services, without knowing who to go to for redress.

*Source:* James Strachan 'The Ties that Bind' *Public Finance* October 28-3 Novemeber 2005.

A final trap is failing to recognise that a prescription that works well or is embraced at one point in time can well become outmoded or be replaced. Sir Michael Barber, the former Head of the Prime Minister's Delivery Unit argued that when Tony Blair became Prime Minister in 1997 it was thought that the best way of improving productivity in schools and other services was by 'command and control . . . often essential if a service is to improve from awful to adequate'. Then followed quasi markets as ways of improving on adequacy – devolving 'responsibility to schools, GP's and foundation hospitals; more choice for parents and patients and the introduction of alternative providers'. After this, a third model 'involves the combination of devolution and transparency . . . the government contracts with, or delegates to, service providers and holds them accountable ... as authors David Osborne and Ted Gaebler put it (in *Reinventing Government*, 1992 Penguin) it requires governments to 'steer rather than row'.[3] The public sector auditor must be alive to changes such as these, especially where they come from the policy prescriptions of government, as these changes in the United Kingdom have done.

## 14.2   THE FUTURE

We cannot tell now what form future changes may take. But on current trends it seems that most changes will turn around closer relationships between:

- different levels of the public sector – collaboration between central, regional, local and municipal authorities in the provision of services; and collaboration between the public sectors of different states whose citizens share common concerns;
- public sector institutions, private sector firms and voluntary institutions such as charities;
- public sector institutions and individual citizens, where attempts are made to provide services in line with the choices of individual citizens – and sometimes to influence the choices they make in their dealings with each other and with private sector firms as in attempts to alter lifestyles and behaviour; the promotion of 'healthy eating'; and 'concern for the environment' are two examples.

Examples of such developments have been given throughout this book, and the way that they develop further will be influenced by the impact of the mass media in a world of almost instant communications. People's preferences are increasingly discussed and analysed by the media and together with the impact of advances in technology, such as the internet, the citizen has become a much more demanding consumer of public services and much less patient with any government's claims for confidentiality and secrecy.

The consequence of this greater openness and flexibility may, paradoxically, operate in the reverse direction. Public servants may sometimes become fearful of being held up to obloquy, and attempts may be made to take refuge in more processes and procedures, thus turning back

---

[3] Sir Michael Barber (2006) 'Reform of public services is a test for managers' Financial Times, 27 September.

to the bureaucratic rule bound world that so many recent developments have sought to change; this is certainly a danger to guard against.

But whatever form future developments may take, the external auditors' role as coach and mentor – as well as the traditional concern with the audit of financial statements, and the legality and regularity of expenditure – will remain and will continue to be required. In the discharge of this role there is a final risk to be assessed and managed: it is this.

One of the difficulties faced by the traditional public sector auditor was that she became almost exclusively identified with the material on which she worked and the tools which she employed – the financial accounts and financial records of public authorities; the rules governing their compilation; and the auditing and other standards governing the auditor's determination of whether the accounts gave a 'true and fair' view and/or the financial records gave acceptable evidence of legal expenditure.

The auditor's role was often seen as having no significance beyond the documents and procedures with which he was concerned, valuable as it was if evidence was produced of broken rules, fraud, theft and corruption. And auditors themselves often – though not always – seemed to accept this formal and important but narrow role.

The thesis of this book is that the auditor can go beyond this role and contribute to beneficial improvement and change. But there is a risk that, in the present and future, as in the past, she may become identified with the formal presentation of the material she is examining and the methodologies which she employs; as if this was the whole of her contribution.

Marshall McLulan and Quentin Fiore saw this point when they argued that the form and technology of communication shapes the way that messages are formulated, conveyed and received.

---

**Box 14.5:    'The Medium is the Massage'**

'Societies have always been shaped more by the nature of the media by which men communicate than by the content of the communication. The alphabet, for instance, is a technology that is absorbed by the very young child in a completely unconscious manner, by osmosis so to speak. Words and the meaning of words predispose the child to think and act automatically in certain ways. The alphabet and print technology fostered and encouraged a fragmenting process, a process of specialism and of detachment. Electric technology fosters and encourages unification and involvement. It is impossible to understand social and cultural changes without a knowledge of the workings of media.'

*Source:* Marshall McLuhan and Quentin Fiore (1967) *The Medium is the Massage* Allen Lane The Penguin Press.

As the argument of Box 14.5 suggests, old methodologies may limit the scope of the auditor's work. This is the truth that the arrival of value for money or performance auditing revealed. But, in their turn, there is a danger that the new methodologies employed by auditees and examined by auditors – efficiency measures; cost/effectiveness; targets; governance arrangements, for example – may come to be seen as essentially what public programmes are about, the only things that politicians, public servants and auditors care about.

It will be a challenge for the auditor to carry out and to present his work in such a way as to ensure that neither his auditee nor the public at large – nor he himself – come to think of his work in this way. If they do, the auditor will once again be seen as discharging the role of the critic and nark, and not the role of coach and mentor which, in the argument of this book, the external auditor may discharge through a proper concern with the full outcomes of public programmes, rather than too great a concentration on the methodologies for measuring the outcomes – often described as the 'tick box' mentality. By resisting any such temptation, the auditor may truly serve and promote the welfare of all the providers and recipients of public services.

# Appendix

## Value for Money Methodology

The purpose of this appendix is to describe in broad terms how value for money studies may be conducted. It is based on the experience of the National Audit Office of the United Kingdom, but no claim is made that this methodology is the only possible approach to work of this kind. Indeed, the National Audit Office itself is continually refining and improving its methodology. **Box A.1** summarises the attributes of a competent value for money study and the remainder of this annex explores the attributes in four sections, covering:

- the choice of subject;
- the team to carry out the work;
- the study process and methodology, and;
- techniques.

### A.1 THE CHOICE OF SUBJECT

Under the law in the UK the formal decision on what subject to study must be made by the Comptroller and Auditor General. But ideas come from many sources – the teams in the office from their knowledge of the auditees' policies and programmes; suggestions from members of Parliament; from auditees themselves; from pressure groups; from trade associations; from academics; from the media; and from individual citizens. In choosing, it is important to:

- focus on the implementation, not the merits, of policy evaluation, which is outside our remit;
- to embark on studies which the Office has or can secure the facilities and skills to undertake; and
- to carry out studies which can 'make a difference', such as securing financial savings and/or proposing improvements in the management and delivery of public services.

In terms of making a difference and securing added value for the taxpayer, careful consideration needs to be given to the potential for recommendations to be understood, appreciated, and put into effect by the auditees without, for example, vast expense, for which they do not have the money; or changes in personnel and practice that would be extremely difficult to undertake, because, for example, changes in the law would be required. The exception to these considerations is for studies where changes need to be made to reduce the risk of theft, fraud and corruption. All studies have a budget and a timescale and are subject to quality review, as explained below.

---

**Box A.1:     Securing effective audit – the attributes of a good value for money study**

(i) **Defining a clear set of issues to be examined**

The auditor should typically identify two or three broad issues that the study might best address. These should be then analysed into a series of sub issues that need to be covered using some formal framework. For example, for several years the National Audit Office have used the issue analysis approach under which issues should be:

➤ Mutually exclusive – they don't overlap with each other; and
➤ Collectively exhaustive – between them, they cover every aspect of the topic

**A study of hospital operating theatres might consider one or more (but almost certainly not all) of the following:**

Design and suitability for purpose
Quality of construction and lifetime costs
Throughput of patients
Availability of appropriate surgical tools
Cleanliness
Utilisation rates
Arrangements for managing theatre lists
Frequency and causes of cancelled operations

Therefore, the challenge is to select the 'right' issues. These are likely to be the ones for which:

➤ information is available
➤ we are able to design an appropriate methodology
➤ there is some parliamentary or public interest
➤ there is the potential to bring about positive change

## (ii) Having appropriate methodologies

A 'methodology' is a technique for gathering or analysing data. Typical methodologies include reviewing departmental files, carrying out a survey, or running a series of focus. We often talk about our methodologies as being either 'quantitative' (that is to say, involving numerical data) or 'qualitative' (involving verbal or visual information). A good study will normally combine quantitative and qualitative data to provide rounded evidence in support of its conclusions and recommendations.

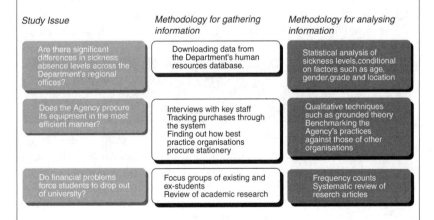

| Study Issue | Methodology for gathering information | Methodology for analysing information |
|---|---|---|
| Are there significant differences in sickness absence levels across the Department's regional offices? | Downloading data from the Department's human resources database. | Statistical analysis of sickness levels,conditional on factors such as age, gender,grade and location |
| Does the Agency procure its equipment in the most efficient manner? | Interviews with key staff Tracking purchases through the system Finding out how best practice organisations procure stationery | Qualitative techniques such as grounded theory Benchmarking the Agency's practices against those of other organisations |
| Do financial problems force students to drop out of university? | Focus groups of existing and ex-students Review of academic research | Frequency counts Systematic review of reserch articles |

A good VFM examination will probably include at least three or four different methodologies. Capturing a range of data and triangulating findings from different sources is an important way of building strength into the final report. The most appropriate methodologies will depend on the subject matter and the issues being addressed.

## (iii) **Obtaining sufficient, relevant and reliable evidence**

A good report is based on evidence that is sufficient, relevant and reliable. Whether the evidence meets these criteria will rest upon:

> how independent the sources of evidence are
> how well the data have been analysed
> how carefully the evidence was gathered
> the purpose of which the evidence will be used

As a broad principle, we should take evidence from people as well as documentary sources, since useful information is not always written down and written material can quickly become out of date. Evidence from external stakeholders – such as users of public services and third parties involved in service delivery – can be just as valuable as that obtained from departments.

Researchers and VFM auditors often talk about 'triangulation' of evidence. This means forming findings and conclusions that are supported by different strands of evidence from more than one source. Quite simply, such conclusions are likely to be more reliable than those based upon one source of evidence. An example is given below.

> Conclusion: Prisons offering over 20 hours per week of formal education and training tend to suffer for fewer disciplinary problems among inmates
> Sources of evidence: Prison Service statistics, a survey of 100 prison governors, and review of academic research, all of which led to the same conclusion.

*Source:* Value for money handbook: a guide for building quality into value for money examinations – NAO, http://www.nao.gov.uk.

### A.2   THE TEAM

The policy of the office is for the team undertaking a study to consist of 'insiders' and 'outsiders' – the leader and some members from the office, people with knowledge of the subject and/or expertise in the techniques that might be used. And people from outside the office, often from universities and from specialist firms, such as consulting engineers, when that is the necessary experience. 'Outsiders' might also come from overseas, when international comparisons are important.

The team will be supported by reference partners – some from inside the office, and others from outside. Some studies may be contracted to a team completely outside the NAO, in the way that the London School of Economics Public Policy Group produced *Achieving Innovation in Central Government Organisations* and RAND Europe produced *International Benchmarking of Fraud and Error in Social Security Systems*. But the Comptroller and Auditor General takes the responsibility for such studies as he is legally required to do.

### A.3    STUDY PROCESS AND METHODOLOGY

The following diagram sets out the study process and quality review arrangements.

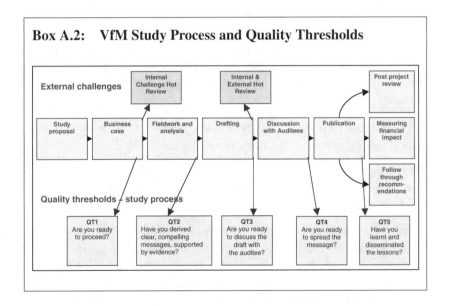

**Box A.2:    VfM Study Process and Quality Thresholds**

The idea of a study has to be translated into a business case, setting out the reasons for doing the study; the issues that would need consideration; how the evidence would be collected and analysed; the risks of the study failing to achieve its objectives; a budget and a timetable; and a plan for publication and communication to national, local and technical media as appropriate.

If the business case passes the Internal Challenge Hot Review, and the Comptroller and Auditor General agrees to go ahead, the study begins. The arrangements for quality assurance consist of quality thresholds; internal and external quality reviews; sharing best practice, high quality training, and robust project management processes, each of which are briefly discussed below.

**Quality Thresholds:** We have a *quality thresholds* (QT) system, of which there are five stages (QT1 to QT5) during the study cycle (**Box A.1**). Teams must assure themselves that they have done sufficient research and analysis to make key decisions at certain points in the life of the study to ensure a quality product. Quality thresholds ask VFM staff to focus on the really important questions – teams should be able to answer 'yes' to the questions posed at each threshold before moving on to the next phase of the work. Quality threshold 5 is particularly important because once the study is published the team responsible for it draws together assessments from different stakeholders, press, external reviews, audited body within a single quality folder and submits it to the Assistant Auditor General overseeing the study for review. All quality folders are delivered to a central VFM Development Team who review the contents and disseminate lessons across the office.

**Internal and External Quality Reviews:** These look at the extent to which the objectives of the study are being achieved:

- how sound the evidence is;
- whether the right techniques are being employed; and
- whether appropriate use is being made of graphics and statistics.

Hot reviews take place during a study, so results can be incorporated in it. Internal hot reviews are carried out by NAO staff independent of the study. External hot reviews are undertaken by academics from the London School of Economics and Political Science (LSE) and Oxford University and draw from natural and social science disciplines.

**Sharing Good Practice:** There is a lot of excellent work taking place around the office and we ensure lessons about how we might improve are shared across the VFM community. The external LSE and Oxford reviews, for example, contain lessons on how reports could be improved and made more rigorous and this information is disseminated throughout the office. Our *Peer Assist* initiative (see **Box A.3**) also provides a way in which staff can share insights into a study area and learn from others before carrying out their own work. It supplements the 'hard' knowledge and information already gathered by the team, with the inferred, unwritten knowledge and experience of others.

---

**Box A.3:    Peer Assist: Theory and Practice**

**Peer Assist in theory**

The Peer Assist approach most commonly takes the form of a workshop but teams have also chosen to capture views and experiences through web-based surveys and one-to-one sessions. Like many of the best ideas, it's based on common sense. Peer Assist simply aims to formalise ad hoc approaches to sharing knowledge by providing a forum (real or virtual) for seeking assistance from colleagues across the NAO.

**Peer Assist in practice**

For the study on *New Road Building and Road Widening* the study team held a Peer Assist session to consult with others in the Office who had experience in evaluating major construction projects. This brought together people who were able to inform the team on a number of related issues, including letting and managing contracts for the construction and management of major projects, and how major projects can be benchmarked against each other or against similar projects, to establish value for money.

---

**Training:** With courses in everything from project management and statistical reasoning to media training and audit interviewing, the NAO VFM Development Team work alongside organisations such as the National Centre for Social Research and the Said Oxford Business School in delivering courses which are interesting, directly relevant and of a high professional standard. We also ran a five-day research methods course, provided by Cardiff University, which successfully introduced further essential research methods to new staff. Our analytical rigour is now strengthened by a financial analysis course delivered by Oxford University. This allows us to meet our readers' expectation for VfM reports that have something original to say about costs while also equipping our staff with the skills to carry out cost apportionment analysis, cost benefit analysis and to build economic models to enhance the measurements of financial impacts. On the qualitative side, we have a training course provided by the National Centre for Social Research ensuring staff have access to the full repertoire of qualitative analysis skills. The training covers an understanding of human behaviour, how to structure and ask questions and how to interpret qualitative data as well as providing the practical skills required to use software such as NVivo and Atlas.ti for the qualitative analysis of large bodies of textual, graphical, audio and video data.

**Project Management Skills:** Each study needs to be well planned, resourced and executed. While it is important to produce a high quality output, teams also need to deliver on time and within budget. The key principles of good project management applied during each NAO project cover:

- breaking the work down into manageable parts;
- allocating resources;
- handling risks;
- motivating staff and dealing with challenges;
- reviewing progress and putting projects back on track;
- celebrating success and learning lessons; and
- using project management tools and templates, including a networked Microsoft Project system.

The importance of controlling and managing our VFM work is recognised throughout the office and all study teams systematically use the software Microsoft Project to produce and maintain a study plan which is published on a shared server allowing study progress to be centrally monitored by a programme management team.

**Value for Money Study Techniques:** We use a very broad range of techniques, some of which are discussed below. **Box A.4** illustrates some of the techniques we use, what each is designed to achieve and when it is best applied.

**Box A.4: Techniques and How They Can Help in VFM Examinations**

| Technique | What is it all about? | When is it best used? |
|---|---|---|
| **Meta Evaluation / Analysis** | Synthesis of the findings from many evaluations, studies, and pieces of research to construct an overall picture based on common and/or combined results and conclusions. | When there is a large amount of secondary evaluation available (e.g. health and social fields) where evaluation by study team may be prohibitive in terms of cost/time. Good for longitudinal analysis. |
| **Organisational Mapping** | Sets out in diagrammatic form the formal and informal relationships and links between and within organisations. Includes investigation of incentives and business processes to promote effective partnering. | To explain how organisations work together in pursuit of common goals (joined up government and service delivery). |
| **Web Based Data Collection Tools** | Using the web to identify and collect relevant material and to obtain stakeholder views on study questions.<br><br>For example e-mail questionnaire, web-based survey, one to one internet interviews and web based focus groups. | At feasibility / preliminary study to gather information on study area. During study to collect data and views. |

| Technique | What is it all about? | When is it best used? |
|---|---|---|
| **Logic Models** | Obtaining organisations opinions on the intended outcomes of programmes and services to map out the logical pathway from inputs through to outcomes and thus enable cause and effect to be better identified. | Where outcomes of activities may be uncertain and the factors which contribute to them unclear. Enables examiner to build up a good understanding of programme and expectations of customers and identify key performance points. |
| **Cost Benefit and Cost Effectiveness Analysis** | Estimating the costs (direct and indirect) and expected benefits (tangible and intangible) from the outcomes of an activity. | Assessment of the overall benefits of recommendations and used in the assessment of options, priorities and decisions. |
| **Risk Assessment** | Testing the quality of organisation's business risk management process to identify areas for examination, or evaluation of organisation's risk assessment. Good for identifying whether resources devoted to managing risk are consistent with level of risk to organisation and stakeholders. | At the problem formulation stage to identify key risks to achievement of organisation's objectives, risks to VFM and to outcomes. During study to consider quality of risk assessment for example for a major project, programme or public service. Will involve assessment of action is response to identified risk and contingency planning. |

| | | |
|---|---|---|
| **Cognitive Mapping** | A versatile technique that can for example enable those directly involved (stakeholders) in service delivery to map out all potential factors contributing to a real or perceived outcomes. | At the start of a study to identify key questions/issues.<br><br>Good for problem formulation. |
| **Multi-Criteria Decision Analysis** | Maps out in a decision tree the options at key stages leading to expected and unexpected outcomes. | At the problem formulation stage to identify the key issues/area the study could examine and the main stakeholders. |
| **Mystery Shopping** | Covertly playing the role of a service user in order to experience and assess the service first hand. | For quality of service examinations both during diagnosis and analysis. |
| **Multi-Variate Analysis** | Allows the examiner to test for the key driver impacting on an observed output / outcomes – by assessing the effect of a change in one independent variable on the dependent variable. | Multi-variate techniques provide a robust way to make specific predictions about potential savings associated with changes in practice. It puts the examiner in a strong position to make soundly-based practical recommendations. |

# Bibliography

Accenture (2003) 'eGovernment leadership: engaging the customer study'.

Africa Focus, Kenya (2005) *Corruption fight stalling.*

Africa Focus, Kenya (2006) *Githongo Report.*

Algemene Rekenkamer *Performance and Operation of Public Administration Strategy 2004–2009* (http://www.rekenkamer.nl).

Algemene Rekenkamer (2006) *Reducing the Administrative Burden for Businesses* (http://www.rekenkamer.nl).

Amber, T., Chitterder, F. and Obodovski, M. (2004) *How Much Regulation is Gold Plate?* British Chamber of Commerce, London.

Anderson, J. and Gray, C. (2006) *Anti-Corruption in Transition: Who is Succeeding and Why?* World Bank.

Andrews, R. (2004) 'Analysing deprivation and local authority performance: the implications for CPA' *Public Money and Management*, January 19–24.

Anselmi, T. (1982) *Commission Report*, Italian Chamber of Deputies.

*Asia Times* (2005) 'On the occasion of the ratification of the United Nations Convention against Corruption by the National People's Congress'.

Audit Commission (2006) *National Fraud Initiative 2004–05: Public Sector Summary.*

Audit Commission (2006) Briefing on the Audit Commission's Comprehensive Performance Assessment frameworks.

Auditor General of Australia Department of Immigration and Multicultural Affairs, *Visa Management: Working Holiday Makers* (Audit Report No. 7 2006–2007).

Augustine, N. (1997) *Augustine's Laws*, 6th edn, Viking.

Báger, G. (2004) *Conclusions of the Study of Privatisation in Hungary*, Hungarian State Audit Office. Research and Development Institute, Budapest.

Barber, Sir Michael (2006) 'Reform of public services is a test for managers' *Financial Times* 27 September, p. 17.

Barnett, C. (1986) *The Audit of War*, Macmillan.

Becker, G. (1968) 'Crime and punishment: an economic approach', *The Journal of Political Economy* **76**, 169–217.

Behn, R. (2001) *Rethinking Democratic Accountability*, Brookings, 2001.

Benn, T. (1989) *Against the Tide: Diaries 1973–1976*, Arrow.

Better Regulation Commission (2006) *Whose Risk is it Anyway?* October.

Bevan, G. and Hood, C. (2006) 'What's measured is what matters: targets and gaming in the English public health care system', *Public Administration* **84**(3).

Biddlecombe, P. (2002) *French Lessons in Africa, Travels with my Briefcase through French Africa*, Abacus.

Blair, T. (speech) June – http://www.number10.gov.uk.

Boston, J. (2000) 'The challenge of evaluating systemic change: the case of public management reform' Paper prepared for the IPMN Conference 'Learning form experiences with new public management', Macquarie Graduate School of Management, Sydney, 4–6 March.

Bourn, J. (2003) *Press Notice: The Operational Performance of PFI Prisons*, HC 700, Session 2002–2003.

Bovens, M., 'tHart, P. and P.B. Guy (eds) (2001) *Success and Failure in Public Governance: a comparative analysis*, Edward Elgar.

Bower, T. (1992) *Maxwell: The Outsider*, Viking.

Boyne, G. (2003) 'What is public service improvement?', *Public Administration* **81**(2), 211–227.

Boyne, G. and Enticott G. (2004) 'Are the poor different? An empirical analysis of the internal characteristics of local authorities in the five CPA groups', *Public Money and Management*, January 11–18.

Braithwaite, J. and Ayres, I. (1992) *Responsive Regulation: Transcending the deregulation debate*, Oxford University Press, New York.

Butler, P.D., Adonis, A. and Travers, T. (1994) *The Politics of the Poll Tax*, Oxford University Press.

Cabinet Office (2000) *Professional Policy Making For the Twenty First Century*.

Carvel, J. (2006) 'Ambulance times misreported 999 response times', *The Guardian*, 15 August.

Chapman, L. (1979) *Your Disobedient Servant: the continuing story of Whitehall's overspending*, Penguin.

Coase, R. (1937) 'The nature of the firm', *Economica* **4**, 386–405.

Coe, C.K. *Public Financial Management*.

Cole, R. *Evening Standard*.

Columbia Accident Investigation Board (2003) *Space Shuttle Columbia and Her Crew*, Houston NASA.

Committee of Public Accounts (4th Report HC 273, 1902) Votes 6, 14.

Committee of Public Accounts (2nd Report 1963–1964).

Committee of Public Accounts (4th Report HC 277, 1982) Clan III Vote 15.

Committee of Public Accounts *Sale of the Water Authorities in England and Wales* (7th Report, HC 140, Session 1992–1993, Her Majesty's Stationery Office, London).

Committee of Public Accounts, British Rail Maintenance Limited: The Sale of Maintenance Depots (22nd Report, HC 168, Session 1996–1997).

Committee of Public Accounts *The Sale of AEA Technology* (60th Report, HC 749, Session 1997–1998), Conclusion xv.

Committee of Public Accounts *The PRIME Project: The transfer of the Department of Social Security estate to the private sector* (41$^{st}$ Report, HC 548, Session 1998–1999).

Committee of Public Accounts *Improving the Delivery of Government IT projects* (1$^{st}$ Report, HC 65, Session 1999–2000).

Committee of Public Accounts *The PFI Contract for the New Dartford and Gravesham Hospital* (12$^{th}$ Report, HC 131, Session 1999–2000), conclusion x, The Stationery Office, London.

Committee of Public Accounts *The Millennium Dome* (14$^{th}$ Report, HC 516, Session 2001–2002).

Committee of Public Accounts Summary and Conclusions, *New IT System for Magistrates' Courts: The Libra Project* (44$^{th}$ Report, HC 434, Session 2002–2003) The Stationery Office, London.

Committee of Public Accounts *The PFI Contract for the redevelopment of West Middlesex University Hospital* (19$^{th}$ Report, HC 155, Session 2002–2003) The Stationery Office, London.

Committee of Public Accounts *Inland Revenue: Tax Credits* (14$^{th}$ Report HC 89, Session 2003–2004).

Committee of Public Accounts *Customs and Excise Standard Report 2003–04* (HC 695, Session 2005–2006).

Committee of Public Accounts *Achieving value for money in delivering public services* (17$^{th}$ Report, HC 742, Session 2005–2006).

Committee of Public Accounts *The Refinancing of the Norfolk and Norwich PFI Hospital* (35$^{th}$ Report, HC 694, Session 2005–2006).

Committee of Public Accounts *The BBC's White City 2 development* (24$^{th}$ Report, HC 652, Session 2005–2006) The Stationery Office, London.

Committee of Public Accounts *Tax Credits and Deleted Tax Cases* (5th Report, Session 2005–2006).

Comptroller and Auditor General *Sale of Shareholding in British Telecommunications plc* (HC 495, Session 1984–1985).

Comptroller and Auditor General *Achieving Innovation in central government organisations.* (HC 1447, Session 2005–2006).

Comptroller and Auditor General & HM Treasury *Tackling External Fraud.* (2004).

Comptroller and Auditor General *Inland Revenue Standard Report 2004–2005.*

Comptroller and Auditor General *Public Service Agreements.* (HC 476, Session 2004–2005).

Comptroller and Auditor General *Evaluation of Regulatory Impact Assessments.* (2005).

Comptroller and Auditor General *A Framework for evaluating the implementation of Private Finance Initiative projects: Volumes 1 and 2.*

Comptroller and Auditor General *The Efficiency Programme: A Second Review of Progress* (HC, Session 2006–2007).

Comptroller and Auditor General *PSA targets: performance information. Results of a survey of UK Government Departments' Finance Directors and Target Owners about Information Underpinning the Pursuit of Performance Targets* http://www.nao.org.uk/publications/other_publications.htm.

Comptroller and Auditor General *The Vehicle Inspectorate: progress with the first Executive Agency* (HC 249, Session 1991–1992).

Comptroller and Auditor General *The Sale of National Power and PowerGen* (HC 46, Session 1992–1993).

Comptroller and Auditor General *The Sale of the Twelve Regional Electricity Companies* (HC 10, Session 1992–1993).

Comptroller and Auditor General *Severance Payments to Senior Staff in the Publicly Funded Education Sector* (HC 2002, Session 1994–1995).

Comptroller and Auditor General *A Review of the Financial Controls over Indirectly Funded Operations of the Metropolitan Police* (HC 462, Session 1994–1995).

Comptroller and Auditor General *British Rail Maintenance Limited: Sale of Maintenance Depots* (HC 583, Session 1995–1996).

Comptroller and Auditor General *Sales of the Royal Dockyards* (HC 748, Session 1997–1998).

Comptroller and Auditor General *The Sale of the Stationery Office* (HC 522, Session 1997–1998).

Comptroller and Auditor General *Department of the Environment, Transport and the Regions: The Private Finance Initiative: The first Four Design, Build and Operate Roads Contracts* (HC 476, Session 1997–1998).

Comptroller and Auditor General *Privatisation of the Rolling Stock Leasing Companies* (HC 576, Session 1997–1998).

Comptroller and Auditor General *Examining the value for money of deals under the Private Finance Initiative* (HC 739, Session 1998–1999).

Comptroller and Auditor General *The PFI Contract for the new Dartford & Gravesham Hospital* (HC 423, Session 1998–1999).

Comptroller and Auditor General *The Flotation of Railtrack* (HC 25, Session 1998–1999).

Comptroller and Auditor General *Kosovo: The financial management of military operations* (HC 530, Session 1999–2000).

Comptroller and Auditor General *The Millennium Dome* (HC 936, Session 1999–2000).

Comptroller and Auditor General *The Management and Control of Hospital Acquired Infection in Acute NHS Trusts in England* (HC 230, Session 1999–2000).

Comptroller and Auditor General *The Sale of Part of the UK Gold Reserves* (HC 86, Session 2000–2001).

Comptroller and Auditor General *Measuring the Performance of Government Departments* (HC 301, Session 2000–2001).

Comptroller and Auditor General *Purchasing Professional Services* (HC 400, Session 2000–2001).

Comptroller and Auditor General *The Implementation of the National Probation Service Information Systems Strategy* (HC 401, Session 2000–2001).

Comptroller and Auditor General *Inpatient and Outpatient waiting in the NHS* (HC 221, Session 2001–2002).

Comptroller and Auditor General *NIRS2: Contract extension* (HC 335, Session 2001–2002).

Comptroller and Auditor General *Managing the relationship to secure a successful partnership in PFI projects* (HC 375, Session 2001–2002).

Comptroller and Auditor General *Inappropriate Adjustments to NHS Waiting Lists* (HC 452, Session 2001–2002).

Comptroller and Auditor General *Agriculture Fraud: The case of Joseph Bowden* (HC 615, Session 2001–2002).

Comptroller and Auditor General *Individual Learning Accounts* (HC 1235, Session 2001–2002).

Comptroller and Auditor General *Redevelopment of MOD Main Building* (HC 748, Session 2001–2002).

Comptroller and Auditor General *Tackling Pensioner Poverty: encouraging take-up of entitlements* (HC 37, Session 2002–2003).

Comptroller and Auditor General *The PFI Contract for the Redevelopment of West Middlesex University Hospital* (HC 49, Session 2002–2003).

Comptroller and Auditor General *Using Call Centres to Deliver Public Services* (HC 134, Session 2002–2003).

Comptroller and Auditor General *Innovation in the National Health Service – The acquisition of the Heart Hospital* (HC 157, Session 2002–2003).

Comptroller and Auditor General *New IT systems for Magistrates' Courts: the Libra project* (HC 327, Session 2002–2003).

Comptroller and Auditor General *Ensuring the Effective Discharge of Older Patients from NHS Acute Hospitals* (HC 392, Session 2002–2003).

Comptroller and Auditor General *Tackling Benefit Fraud* (HC 393, 2002–2003).

Comptroller and Auditor General *Progress in Making E-services Accessible to All: Encouraging use by older people* (HC 428, Session 2002–2003).

Comptroller and Auditor General *Difficult Forms: How government agencies interact with citizens* (HC 1145, Session 2002–2003).

Comptroller and Auditor General *Citizen Redress: What citizens can do if things go wrong with public services* (HC 21, Session 2003–2004).

Comptroller and Auditor General *Difficult Forms: How government departments interact with citizens* (HC 255, Session 2003–2004).

Comptroller and Auditor General *Criminal Records Bureau Delivering Safer Recruitment?* (HC 266, Session 2003–2004).

Comptroller and Auditor General *English Regions: An early progress report on the New Deal for Communities Programme* (HC 309, Session 2003–2004).

Comptroller and Auditor General *Evaluation of Regulatory Impact Assessments Compendium Report* (HC 358, Session 2003–2004).

Comptroller and Auditor General *PFI: The STEPS Deal* (HC 530, Session 2003–2004).

Comptroller and Auditor General English Regions *Getting Citizens Involved: Community Participation in Neighbourhood Renewal* (HC 1070, Session 2003–2004).

Comptroller and Auditor General *Managing Risks to Improve Public Services* (HC 1078, Session 2003–2004).

Comptroller and Auditor General *Standard Report on the Accounts of the Inland Revenue 2003–04* (HC 1082, Session 2003–2004).

Comptroller and Auditor General *Delivering Public Services to a Diverse Society* (HC 19, Session 2004–2005).

Comptroller and Auditor General *Regeneration of the Millennium Dome and Associated Land* (HC 178, Session 2004–2005).

Comptroller and Auditor General *Evaluation of Regulatory Impact Assessments Compendium Report* (HC 341, Session 2004–2005).

Comptroller and Auditor General *Department of Health Innovation in the NHS: Local improvement finance trusts* (HC 28, Session 2005–2006).

Comptroller and Auditor General *Driving the Successful Delivery of Major Defence Projects: Effective project control is a key factor in successful projects* (HC 30, Session 2005–2006).

Comptroller and Auditor General *Filing of Income Tax Self Assessment Returns* (HC 74, Session 2005–2006).

Comptroller and Auditor General *Progress on the Channel Tunnel Rail Link* (HC 77, Session 2005–2006).

Comptroller and Auditor General *Maintaining and improving Britain's Railway Stations* (HC 132, Session 2005–2006).

Comptroller and Auditor General *Department for Work and Pensions Resource Account* (HC 447, Session 2005–2006).

Comptroller and Auditor General *Reducing Brain Damage: Faster access to better stroke care* (HC 452, Session 2005–2006).

Comptroller and Auditor General *Gaining and Retaining a Job: the Department for Work and Pensions' support for disabled people* (HC 455, Session 2005–2006).

Comptroller and Auditor General *Extending Access to Learning through Technology: Ufi and the learndirect service* (HC 460, Session 2005–2006).

Comptroller and Auditor General *Dealing with the Complexity of the Benefits System* (HC 592, Session 2005–2006).

Comptroller and Auditor General *Improving Poorly Performing Schools in England* (HC 679, Session 2005–2006).

Comptroller and Auditor General *Foreign and Commonwealth Office Resource Accounts 2004–2005: Fraud at the British Embassy Tel Aviv* (HC 776, Session 2005–2006).

Comptroller and Auditor General *Department for Work and Pensions: Using Leaflets to Communicate with the Public about Services and Entitlements* (HC 797, Session 2005–2006).

Comptroller and Auditor General *Tackling Child Obesity – First steps* (HC 801, Session 2005–2006).

Comptroller and Auditor General *Progress in Improving Government Efficiency* (HC 802-I, Session 2005–2006).

Comptroller and Auditor General *Developing Effective Services through Contact Centres* (HC 941, Session 2005–2006).

Comptroller and Auditor General *Improving the Efficiency of Postal Services Procurement in the Public Sector* (HC 946, Session 2005–2006).

Comptroller and Auditor General *Smarter Food Procurement in the Public Sector* (HC 963, Session 2005–2006).

Comptroller and Auditor General *Second Validation Compendium Report* (HC 985, Session 2005–2006).

Comptroller and Auditor General *The Provision of Out-of-Hours Care in England* (HC 1041, Session 2005–2006).

Comptroller and Auditor General *A5 Queue Relocation in Dunstable* (HC 1043, Session 2005–2006).

Comptroller and Auditor General *The Termination of the PFI Contract for the National Physical Laboratory* (HC 1044, Session 2005–2006).

Comptroller and Auditor General *The Paddington Health Campus Scheme* (HC 1045, Session 2005–2006).

Comptroller and Auditor General *Department for Environment, Food and Rural Affairs and the Countryside Agency – The right of access to the open countryside* (HC 1046, Session 2005–2006).

Comptroller and Auditor General *A Foot on the Ladder: Low cost home ownership assistance* (HC 1048, Session 2005–2006).

Comptroller and Auditor General *Standard Report on HM Revenue and Customs 2005–2006* (HC 1159, Session 2005–2006).

Comptroller and Auditor General *Child Support Agency – Implementation of the child support reforms* (HC 1174, Session 2005–2006).

Comptroller and Auditor General *Progress in Tackling Pensioner Poverty: encouraging take-up of entitlements* (HC 1178, Session 2005–2006).

Comptroller and Auditor General *Evaluation of Regulatory Impact Assessments 2005–2006* (HC 1305, Session 2005–2006).

Comptroller and Auditor General *Achieving Innovation in central government organisations: Detailed research findings* (HC 1447-II, Session 2005–2006).

Comptroller and Auditor General *Department for Environment, Food and Rural Affairs, and Rural Payments Agency: the delays in administering the 2005 Single Payment Scheme in England* (HC 1631, Session 2005–2006).

Comptroller and Auditor General *Sure Start Children's Centres* (HC 104, Session 2006–2007).

Comptroller and Auditor General *Preparation for the London 2012 Olympic and Paralympic Games – Risk assessment and management* (HC 252, Session 2006–2007).

Comptroller and Auditor General of New Zealand (1999) *Events surrounding the Chartering of Aircraft by The Department of Work and Income* October http://www.oag.govt.nz.

Comptroller and Auditor General of New Zealand (2006) *Achieving Public Sector Outcomes with Private Sector Partners* (February).

Cornforth, C. and Paton, R. (2004) 'Editorial', *Public Money & Management*, **24**, 197–199.

Department of Health, *National Standards, Local Action, Health and Social Care Standards and Planning Framework 2005–2006–2007–08*.

DETR (2000) *Air Quality Strategy* Cm 4548 The Stationery Office, London.

Disability Alliance (2004) *Race Equality in the Benefits System*.

Drucker, P. (1954) *The Practice of Management*, Harper Brothers, New York.

Dunleavy, P. (1981) *The Politics of Mass Housing in Britain, 1945–1975: a study of corporate power and professional influence in the welfare state*, Oxford University Press.

"Dunnhumby" (2006) *Financial Times Magazine*, 11 November, 18–22.

EBRD (2005), *Annual Report 2005: Annual Review and Financial Report.*

Easterbrook, G. (2003) *The Progress Paradox*, Random House, 2003.

Edinburgh Institute of Chartered Accountants of Scotland (2006) *Principles not Rules: a question of judgement.*

European Foundation for Quality Management: 'The EFQM Excellence Model': Brussels.

Evaluation: Special Issue: Dialogue in Evaluation **7**(2), April 2001.

Flin, R. and Crichton, M. *Risk Based Decision-Making: Mitigating threat – maximising opportunity* in Comptroller and Auditor General *Managing Risks to Improve Public Services* (HC 1078, 2003–2004).

Fraud Advisory Panel (2003) *Identity Theft: Do you know the signs?*

Freedom House (2006) *Freedom in the World – Kenya.*

Fulton Report (1968) *The Civil Service'*, London, HMSO.

Gordon, A. (1996) *The Rules of the Game*, John Murray.

Government Accountability Office (1996) *Performance Reports* (GGO-96-66R) (February).

Government Accountability Office (2002) *Performance Reporting* (GAO-02-372).

Government Accountability Office (2002) *Defense Acquisitions Best Practices: Capturing design and manufacturing knowledge early improves acquisition outcomes* (GAO 02-701).

Government Accountability Office (2002) *Medicare: Communications with physicians can be improved* (GAO-02-249).

Government Accountability Office (2005) *Managing for Results: Enhancing agency use of performance information for management decision making* (GAO-05-927).

Government Accountability Office (2005) *Hurricane Katrina: Providing oversight of the nation's preparedness, response, and recovery activities* (GAO-05-1053T).

Government Accountability Office (2006) *Credit Card: Increased complexity in rates and fees heightens need for more effective disclosures to consumers* (GAO-06-929, September).

Government Accountability Office (2006) *Contract Management: DOD vulnerabilities to contracting fraud, waste, and abuse.* (GAO-06-838R)

Government Accountability Office (2006) *Observations on the Oil for Food Programme.*

Government's Annual Report 1997–1998 (Cm 3969).

Government's Annual Report 1998–1999 (Cm 4401).

Gray, A. and Jenkins, B. (2002) 'Policy and program evaluation in the United Kingdom: a reflective state?' in Furubo, J. (ed.) *International Atlas of Evaluation, Transaction.*

Gray, A. and Jenkins, B. (2007) 'Checking out? Accountability and evaluation in the British regularity state' in Bemelmans-Videc, M.-L., Lonsdale, J. and Perrin, B. (eds) *Making Accountability Work: Dilemmas for Evaluation and for Audit, Transaction.*

Gray, P. (1998) 'Policy disasters in Europe: an introduction' in Gray, P. (ed.) *Public Policy Disasters in Western Europe*, Routledge.

Greer, A. 'Policy co-ordination and the British Administrative System: evidence from the BSE Inquiry', *Parliamentary Affairs* **52**(4), 589–615.

Grey, C. (2006) *World Business* July/August p. 15.

Grout, P.A. (2005) *Value for Money Measurement in Public-Private Partnerships*, European Investment Bank Papers, **10**(2), 32–57.

Haltiwanger, J. and Singh, M. (1999) 'Cross-country evidence on public sector retrenchment' *The World Bank Economic Review*, **13**(1), 23–66.

Handy, C. (1993) *Understanding Organisation* 4th edn. London, Penguin Books.

Hansard (2000) Government Resources and Accounts Bill Standing Committee 18 January.

Harford, T. (2006) 'If the price is right', *Financial Times Magazine*, July.

Hart, P. and Bovens, M. (1996) *Understanding Policy Fiascos*, 145–146.

Haythornthwaite, R. (2006) 'Britain's secret shame: we just love red tape' Financial Times, 9 February.

Hennessy, P. (1989) *Whitehall*, Fontana Press.

Heywood, P. (1997) *Political Corruption*, Political Studies Number 3.

Hilton, A. (2006) 'Depressing truth behind rush for Thames Water', *Evening Standard*, 7 August, 25.

HM Revenue and Customs *Annual Report and Autumn Performance Report 2004–2005* (CM 6691, 2005–2006).

HM Treasury (1998) *Treasury Minute on the Sixtieth Report from the Committee of Public Accounts*, CM 4069.

HM Treasury (2000) *2000 Spending Review: Public service agreement targets* CM 4808, the Stationery Office, London.

HM Treasury (2002) *Refinancing of early PFI transactions Code of Conduct.*

HM Treasury (2003) *PFI: Meeting the investment challenge*, Section 7, London.

HM Treasury (2003) *The Green Book: appraisal and evaluation in central government*, The Stationery Office, London.

HM Treasury (2005) *Corporate Governance in Central Government Departments: Code of Good Practice* July.

HM Treasury (2005) *The Hampton Review of Inspection and Enforcement.*

Hood, C. (1991) 'A public management for all seasons?' *Public Administration*, **69** (Spring).

Hood, C., Scott, C., James, O., Jones, G. and Travers, T. (1999) *Regulation Inside Government: Waste-watchers, quality police and sleaze-busters*, Oxford University Press.

Hood, C. Baldwin, R. and Rothstein, H. (2000) *Assessing the Dangerous Dogs Act: When does regulatory law fail?* P.L. Summer, Sweet and Maxwell.

Hopwood, A.G. (1996) 'Looking across rather than up and down: on the need to explore the lateral processing of information', *Accounting, Organisations and Society*, **21**(6).

Horton, S. (2006) 'The public service ethos in the British Civil Service: an historical institutional analysis', *Public Policy and Administration*, **21**(1), 36–46.

International Monetary Fund (2000) *Transition Economies: An IMF perspective on progress and prospect*, Issues Brief, 2000/08.

INTOSAI *Guidelines on Best Practice for the Audit of Economic Regulation* http://www.nao.org.uk/intosai/wgap/ecregguidelines.htm.

INTOSAI Working Group on the Audit of Privatisation (1998) *Guidelines on the Best Practice for the Audit of Economic Regulation.*

INTOSAI Working Group on the Audit of Privatisation (2004) *Guidelines on Best Practice for the Audit of Risk in Public/Private Partnership.*

INTOSAI *Auditing Standards and practical experience* (http://www.intosai .org).

James, S., Murphy, K. and Reinhart, M. (2005) 'The Citizen's Charter: how such initiatives might be more effective', *Public Policy and Administration* **20**(2), Summer 10.

King, T. (2004) *Prospect Magazine.*

Krkoska, L. and Robeck, K. (2006) *The Impact of Crime on the Enterprise Sector: Transition versus non-transition countries* European Bank for Reconstruction and Development July.

Laughlin R., Broadbent J. and Gill J. (2003) 'Evaluating the private finance initiative in the National Health Service in the UK' *Journal of Accounting, Audit and Accountability*, **16**(3).

Leach, S. and Lowndes, V. (2006) 'Fitness for purpose? How local authorities can dare to be different' in Solace Foundation Imprint, *The Re-thinking of Local Government: Fitness for Purpose in a Year for Living Dangerously*, London SFI.

Lindblom, C. (1959) 'Science of Muddling Through Public', *Administration*, **19**.

Ling, T. (1997) *The British State Since 1945*, Polity Press.

Local Government Association (2005) 'Inspection – time well spent?'

Lonsdale, J. (2000) *Advancing Beyond Regularity: developments in value for money methods at the National Audit Office*, unpublished PhD thesis.

Lonsdale, J. and Whitehouse, M. (2006) UK National Audit Office 'Adding Value? Measuring the Impact of Performance Audit in the Education and Social Welfare Fields' Paper given at the Conference of the American Evaluation Association held in Portland, Oregon, 2–4 November.

Marsh, D. and Stoker, G. (1995) *Theory and Methods in Political Science*, 119.

Martin, S. (2005) 'Evaluation, inspection and the improvement agenda: Contrasting fortunes in an era of evidence-based policy-making', *Evaluation*, **11**(4), 496–504.

McLuhan, M. and Fiore, Q. (1967) *The Medium is the Massage*, Allen Lane The Penguin Press.

Milton, Sir Simon (2006) 'D-day for local government' *Public Finance*, 24–30 November.

Morris, M. (1995) *Creating Public Value*, Harvard University Press.

Mueller, D.C. (2003) *Public Choice III, Chapter 16*, Cambridge University Press.

Mulgan, G. (2006) *Good and Bad Power*, Penguin 229.

National Audit Office – *Value for Money Handbook – a guide for building quality into VFM examinations* – http://www.nao.org.uk/.

National Audit Office *Choice Memorandum Presented to the Select Committee on Public Administration.*

National Audit Office *State Audit in the European Union.*

Newman, J. (2001) *Modernising Governance*, Sage.

Newman, J. (2004) 'Constructing accountability: network government and management agency', *Public Policy and Administration*, **19**(4), (Winter) 29.

*New Scientist* (1989), article: 'Treasury must wait 21 years for key to door of plant research institute', Issue 1691, 18 November 1989.

Niskanen Jr, W.A. (1973) *Bureaucracy: Servant or Master?* Institute of Economic Affairs London.

Normaton, E.L. (1966) *The Accountability and Audit of Government*, Manchester University Press.

Office of Government Commerce (2006) *Regulatory Impact Assessment – Public Contracts Regulations 2006.*

Office of Government Commerce (2007) *Achieving Excellence in Construction.*

Office of National Statistics (2002) *Review of ONS Pension Contributions Statistics: Report of the Review Panel.*

Osborne, D. and Gaebler, T. (1992) *Reinventing Government*, Penguin.

Palfrey, T. (2000) 'Is fraud dishonest?' *Journal of Criminal Law.*

Parker, D. (2004) *The UK's Privatisation Experiment: The Passage of Time Permits a Sober Assessment*, CESIFO Working Paper, February, No. 1126.

Payne, P. (2006) 'Trouble at mill' *Whitehall and Westminster Review* (21 November).

Peters, T.J. and Waterman, R.H. Jr, (1982) *In Search of Excellence*, Harper and Row, New York.

Pickett, S.K.H. and Pickett, J.M. (2005) *Auditing for Managers: the ultimate risk management tool*, John Wiley & Sons, Ltd.

Pidd, M. (undated) Lancaster University Working Paper, summarising material from Smith, P. (1995) 'On the unintended consequences of publishing performance data in the public sector', *International Journal of Public Administration*, **18**(2 and 3), 277–310.

Pipe, S. (2006) *Accountancy Age*, 5 October.

Pollitt, C., Girre, X., Lonsdale, J., Mul, R., Summa, H. and Waerness, M. (1999) *Performance or Compliance? Performance Audit and Public Management in Five Countries*, Oxford University Press.

Pollitt, C. and Bouckaert, G. (2000) *Public Management Reform*, Oxford University Press.

Pollitt, C. (2003) *The Essential Public Manager*, 81.

Pollitt, C. (2006) 'Performance information for democracy', *Evaluation*, **12**(1), 38–55.

Ponting, C. (1986) *Whitehall: Tragedy and Farce*, Sphere Books.

Power, M. (2004) *The Risk Management of Everything*, Demos.

Prime Minister's Strategy Unit (2002) *Risk: Improving government's capability to handle risk and uncertainty* (November).

Public Administration Select Committee (2003) *On target? Government by measurement* HC 62-I, Fifth Report 2002-2003. The Stationery Office, London.

Radin, B. (2006) *Challenging the Performance Movement: Accountability, Complexity and Democratic Values*, Georgetown University Press.

Risk (2002) *Improving Government's Capability to handle Risk and Uncertainty*, Strategy Unit, November.

Schumpeter, J. *Economic Theory and Entrepreneurial History 1949, Change and the Entrepreneur.*

Seligman, M.E.P., and Cxikszentmihalyi, M. (2000) 'Positive psychology: an introduction', *American Psychologist*, **55**, 5–14.

Seligman M.E.P., Steen, T.A., Park, N, and Peterson C. (2005) 'Positive psychology progress: an empirical validation of interventions', *American Psychologist*, **60**, 410–421.

Sennett, R. (2006) *The Culture of the New Capitalism*, Yale University Press, 35–36.

Short, P. (1999) *Mao: A Life*, Hodder and Stoughton.

Smith, A. (1776) *The Wealth of Nations*, Book I, Chapter X.

State Research Institute of Systems Analysis, Audit Chamber of the Russian Federation (2005), *State Property Privatisation in the Russian Federation 1993–2003*, Moscow.

Statistics Commission (2006) Report No. 29 *PSA targets: the devil in the detail*.

Stern, S. (2005) 'In search of the supplier's reflex reaction', *Financial Times*, 12 October.

Stewart, J. and Ranson, S. (1988) 'Management in the public domain', *Public Money and Management* (Spring/Summer) 15.

Strachan, J. (2005) 'The ties that bind', *Public Finance*, 28 October–3 November 3.

Tett, G. (2005) 'Office Culture', *Financial Times Magazine* (21 May) 22.

*The Economist* (2005) 'Made to measure – ranking public services', 17 December.

Transparency International (2004, 2005, 2006) *National Integrity Studies, Kenya (various); Global Integrity, Public Integrity Index; Global Corruption Reports*.

UK Government's Approach to Public Service Reform June 2006 – http://www.strategy.gov.uk/publications.

United Kingdom Passport Agency: *The Passport Delays of Summer 1999*, Report by the Comptroller and Auditor General (HC 812 Session 1998–1999).

USA Social Security Administration *Social Security Programmes Throughout the World*.

Volcker, P.A., Goldstone, R. and Peith, M. (2005) *Report on the Manipulation of the Oil for Food Programme*.

Von Hayek, F. (1994) *The Road to Serfdom*, University of Chicago Press.

Voszka, E. (1999) 'Privatization in Hungary: results and open issues', *Economic Reform Today*, Issue No. 2.

Wolman, C. (2005) 'Terminal Five gets off to a flying start'. *Public Finance* May 6–12 2005.

World Bank (2004) *Economies in Transition: An Operations Evaluation Department evaluation of World Bank assistance*, Washington.

Yeung, K. (2005) *Securing Compliance*, Hart Publishing.

# Index

*Index compiled by Terry Halliday*